THE END OF HIDDEN IRELAND

To Dena and Terence

Acknowledgments

In the years between the conception and the completion of this book many debts piled up: debts to family and lifelong friends and colleagues for love and patience, debts to other researchers, writers, and interpreters for knowledge and understanding, and a debt of gratitude to institutions that encouraged and supported the project along the way. How much of that indebtedness has been paid will be judged only by whatever merit the following work contains.

The first steps in my research were made possible by New York University and the National Endowment for the Humanities, who allowed me the two years I needed to follow the track from London to Liverpool, Dublin, and eventually to Strokestown where I discovered the existence of the townland of Ballykilcline in County Roscommon. For their expert help and patience, I thank the staffs of the National Library of Ireland (in particular Phil McCann for his advice in selecting photographs from the Lawrence Collection), the National Archives of Ireland, the British Library, and the British Public Record Office at Kew Gardens. I am especially fortunate to have met Luke Dodd, the curator of the newly opened National Famine Museum at Strokestown, County Roscommon, whose knowledge and hospitality were not only essential in pursuing my research but made it the most agreeable phase of my work. He introduced me to Patsy Duignan of Strokestown, whom I thank most affectionately for her companionship and for her bringing me to meet John Reynolds of Ballykilcline; it was through his extraordinary memory that I first thought I had heard the original voice of Ballykilcline. My thanks are also due to Stephen Campbell for his invaluable summary of the events of 1847 around Strokestown.

I have already expressed my gratitude to the many friends and colleagues who read the manuscript at various stages of its preparation. I would like to thank them collectively for their wisdom and generosity. But I am especially eager to acknowledge a few whose advice and encouragement went well beyond the call of duty. Of these, I thank first the memory of the late Dennis Clark, who knew best how to mix learning and kindness. Kevin Whelan of the Royal Irish Academy not only revealed to me some of the intricacies of the Irish land system but also the meaning of genuine fraternity among scholars. Kerby Miller, whose monumental work on Irish emigration rarely left my side as I wrote, repeatedly lent time he could barely spare in reading and critiquing drafts of this manuscript with rare impartiality and candor. Among the others who made important differences in the final shape of this work, I express my gratitude to my editors Nancy Lane and Paul Schlotthauer of Oxford University Press, and to Denis Donoghue, Peter Linebaugh, and Michael Herity.

More personal debts of gratitude mounted during the years of travel, absences from home, preoccupations, and presuming on friendship that were spent in the process of writing this work. For indulging me with their companionship, encouragement, and patience during this prolonged immersion I am forever grateful to my dear friends Bill Fleming, John Gillis, Richie Fox, Michele Stoddard, William Fishman and Carl Prince.

My immigrant parents, Anne and Patrick, and my brother, Jack, none of them now alive to accept my gratitude, and my sisters, Eileen and Nancy, have always been the true source of my love for Ireland. To the degree that this book has honored them, it is a small repayment of their lifelong faith in me. Finally, the dedication of this book to my wife and son is a paltry recognition of the sacrifices they made as my fellow travellers in London, Manchester, Birmingham, and Liverpool. At a particularly low point in our sojourns, nearly penniless and broken down in an old Morris Traveller on the road from Manchester to the Liverpool ferry, they showed that the emigrants' grit has not been entirely lost.

Contents

I

Introduction

Of all the changes experienced by European peoples in the nineteenth century, none was more profound or more widely felt than migration. Whether it was merely a few miles from village to town or a journey across great oceans, its effects were usually irreversible, distancing minds as well as bodies from the past. In the century before 1914 alone, some forty million individuals crossed the Atlantic, the greatest movement of peoples since the dawn of civilization and an event comparable in its human effects to any of the great wars or revolutions of the modern era. While Irish emigrants did not make up the largest part of this movement, no other country lost a larger part of its population to it or was altered more profoundly by the loss. Nearly a million had already left Ireland before 1845 and in the terrible decade that followed the country sent out a quarter of those remaining, more than two million emigrants. Added to those who died of the hunger and its companion diseases, the slightly more than eight million people of old Ireland were reduced by almost half. Thereafter, tens of thousands followed every year, until the ritual of mourning the departed in the "American wake" became as familiar a part of life as burying the dead.

The narrative that follows describes a minute part of this historic movement. It is based mainly on the experience of the townland of Ballykilcline, a community of small farmers and laborers living on an obscure estate in the Irish midlands near the provincial market town of Strokestown, County Roscommon. Such a community as Ballykilcline was known as a *baile* in the Irish language and so it was called by its people, becoming the common prefix "bally" in English maps and surveys. But by the nineteenth century the general usage in English, both for the community and the surveyed unit of land in which it lived, was the "townland." Hence, this Roscommon community was known as the townland of Ballykilcline.

3

Ballykilcline consisted of about one hundred families, most of whom had been on the land or in the vicinity for an unknown number of generations, some of them apparently since before the conquest. Like thousands of other townlands, Ballykilcline was emptied by death and emigration in the winter and spring of 1847–1848, the blackest year of the great hunger. Within a few years after its emigrants arrived in the New World the townland's name disappears from the local estate surveys and the ordnance maps, leaving only a few traces of its existence in the overgrown stone foundations and patterns of its roads and paths, its history remaining precariously in the memory of a few of the oldest residents, with whom the living part of the townland's history will most likely die. Many peasant communities in Ireland and elsewhere have left such attenuated images of their existence, receding like microscopic images in the wrong end of the telescope, making it more difficult to see who they were and how they may have understood what was happening to them.

Although Ballykilcline left clearer traces than most prefamine townlands, our view of its internal life is still impeded by the nature of the record that does survive. Because it was kept by outsiders whose main purpose was either to collect the rents or to enforce the law, the townland did not expose its mind to the record-keepers willingly. As a part of "the hidden Ireland" that Daniel Corkery celebrated some seventy years ago, it was an axiom of survival to evade that surveillance by all means possible.[1] Fortunately, the residents' evasions were not entirely successful; because they lived on lands belonging to the Crown and refused to pay their rents, an account was created that offers glimpses into their mental and material life that do not exist for many of these otherwise nearly invisible communities. For the most part, it offers a downward-looking view from various strata of the pyramid of "deputies" that stood between the townland and its landlord, ending in this case with a permanent committee of the House of Lords, sitting in London. It is primarily the record kept by its deputy in Dublin, Her Majesty's Clerk of the Quit Rents, that allows us to see how the tenants began to decipher their place in the world and to envision the prospect of entering it as strangers, something none of them had been before. What came to be known as the "Ballykilcline rebellion" was largely a response to that vision, of removing themselves three thousand miles across an ocean they had never seen from the townland's narrowly circumscribed landscape of life and labor, perhaps a radius of fifteen miles, containing for most of them their entire experience and expectations along with the memory and bones of their ancestors.[2]

The only moment in the townland's history that left traces enough to enlarge our view was a period of fourteen years between 1834 and the residents' emigration. There is no sign that the townland's life was in any way eventful before that time and after the evictions its occupants scattered to the winds of New York and probably far beyond. Although many of them were literate, none left a memoir of this time. The only indications that the townland became conscious of "making history" were that neighbors for miles around gave the name "rebellion" to the tenants' struggle and that they received an extraordinary degree of attention from the authorities. For those who wish to see their experience from within, this window into their history contained several distinct but dusty panes, one of false victory and three of misery. A lease that had been held for the previous forty-one years by the local landlord, the Lords Hartland of Strokestown, lapsed in 1834. In effect, Ballykilcline was left waiting to be "rediscovered" by the Crown's distant ministers, "Their Lords, His Majesty's Commissioners of Woods and Forests," who managed the far-flung lands and revenues of the Crown from Westminster. This took about two years, a time of illusions of great luck in which the tenants paid no rent and lived among their neighbors as those rarest of creatures in rural Ireland, triumphant rebels. The commissioners eventually made themselves known when they issued writs of eviction on the tenants in 1836, offering to let them back into their homes if the two years of arrears were paid. The "rebellion" of Ballykilcline, consisting of ten more years of rents withheld and sporadic confrontations with bailiffs and police, began with these eviction notices, which they ignored.

The last episodes in their microrebellion began with the failure of a lawsuit they brought against the Crown, coinciding with the onset of the hunger in the spring of 1846. Both were fatal blows to their hope of staying in their homes. The interval between this point and their departure eighteen months later was the "time of petitions." Resistance broken by the law and the blight, most of them were reduced from demanding to begging the right to remain, besieging every level of the Crown bureaucracy with "Memorials" of hunger, suffering, and "good will." The Crown offered free passage to the New World if they willingly surrendered their cabins and holdings. The last trace of them was as famine emigrants, entries on estate and ship-brokers' accounts and finally on passenger arrival lists in New York.

Even for its own sake, the record of their piecemeal "discovery" of the New World seemed worth pursuing as an artifact of the European peasant's Atlantic migration, a piece of the history of those who were about to undergo what some have called "the great transformation" of the modern era. One part of this process was in breaking the peasant's hold on the land and stimulating an outward flow of wage-laborers. In most of western Europe this process took generations. Overseas emigration into wage labor in North America might be described for most of the famine emigrants as an accelerated version of the general experience, a transition from village to urban slum in a matter of months or even weeks. But for those who migrated in this era as well as those who remained, the first stages of this transition had begun much earlier, reaching them in small, imperceptible increments, disguising the fates that awaited them.

One might say that in Ireland that process becomes noticeable with the seventeenth-century settlements, in which the bulk of the land eventually changed hands and came under the Anglo-Irish pyramid of grandees, squires, and their numerous deputies, while the land's former masters and their descendants nursed hopeless schemes in exile or in squalor. In the colony it envisioned, the Anglo-Irish ideal was not unlike the *hidalgos'* dreams of Mexico or the dreamed-of *lebensraum* of Prussian warlords: a hereditary elite of unassailable landlords living in picturesque comfort amid a sea of cowed but still merry tillers of the soil. And in Ireland, the defeated were already Christians, superstitious but morally disciplined against murder and theft by centuries of eloquent, scolding priests who were now largely cut off from their source of power.

But the pastoral idyll of the Irish landed elite was adamantly static, self-indulgent, and consequently porous to all manner of intrusions from the outside. The commercial and demographic dynamism of England leached through the Irish countryside, demanding its food, the Englishman's bread, beef, and cheese, for the cash, goods, and protection of the metropolis. Filling this need through a system of subdivision that maximized rents and reduced the peasantry to poverty and the potato was the source of the landlords' comfort but also the groundwork of ultimate ruin for squire and tenant alike. Before the blight fell, the foundations of the land system were already being undermined by debt and arrears accumulated not only by its inherent wastefulness and injustice but by its dependence on outside forces over which no power in the country had control. The main conduit of these forces on the eve of the famine was the network centering on Liverpool, through which the bulk of the land's produce and eventually its surplus population was extracted. Ireland was Liverpool's hinterland much more than it was Dublin's, Belfast's, or Cork's. The Lancashire port was not only Ireland's marketplace but its mediator with England and its gateway to the outside world.

For the majority of emigrants, Liverpool was also their first sight of the world outside of Ireland. Liverpool in 1848 was the most turbulent and exotic Atlantic city of the age. Next to London only, it was also the commercial capital of the British Empire on the eve of the Pax Britannica, the disreputable junior partner in the great enterprise. Because of the immense shadow that London cast over all other cities of the British Isles as the center of empire and the wellspring of Victorian culture, Liverpool's extraordinary character and importance is often obscured. Above all, Liverpool's place in the great European migration of the nineteenth century was unrivaled. It had established its primacy in the previous century as the carrier and countinghouse of the slave trade and left its imprint through that callous business on the future of three continents, linking them for two centuries in an Atlantic economy of labor, manufacture, and commerce that bestrode the world. When that migration began to shift in the first half of the nineteenth century from one of Africans in chains to one primarily of distressed European peasants, the Liverpool maritime dynamo had already shouldered its Old World rivals aside and again carried the lion's share of the traffic across the Atlantic. If its ships are seen as movable parts of the city itself, it might be said that more people entered the nineteenth century via Liverpool than through any other city—more than London, more than New York, immeasurably more than Paris or Vienna.

The thought of witnessing the passage of a peasant community from its thresholds through the great emigration port and into the Atlantic seemed to offer an opportunity to observe an instance of the migration in an unusually high focus, possibly enough to see some of the human outlines of the transformation that is generally supposed to accompany the movement from peasant to industrial life. It seemed especially promising when that community left an articulate record of its thoughts in its own words. The events that began to expose Ballykilcline to the outside world and to a progression of insights that revealed its residents' place in that world were particular to that community. But similar encroachments from outside, economic, informational, and aesthetic, were part of the experience of virtually every Irish household before one or all of its members emigrated. All emigrants needed cash and information. They had to make calculations about the past and the future that few had ever made before, especially about the need to sever themselves from a social milieu that had previously governed all aspects of their daily lives, defining their place and fixing their identity within it.

The great majority of the peasantry in the 1840s was still outside that world of calculation. This was especially true of the townlands, first because many there were insulated to a startling degree for Europeans from up-to-date knowledge of the outside world, and second, because in varying degrees their internal economies were too marginal to respond "rationally" to distant market forces. But perhaps most decisively, "voluntary" emigration from the townlands before the famine was restrained by a culture and worldview consonant with this seclusion, deeply suspicious of outsiders, secretive in its dealings with them, and scornful of those who strove to become like them, whether in regard to property, social station, or personal ambition.

A particularly passionate edge was given to the conflict between the traditional and modern value systems in rural Ireland because the latter was regarded as alien by the common people and associated with their oppressors. A resentful consciousness of subjection colored nearly all communication between the townland peasants and the nearest outposts of the intruder. In the case of Ballykilcline, this conflict was played out in its relations with the nearby market town of Strokestown. There could be found the houses of their landlord, his agents, the constabulary, the court, the gaol, and the Church of Ireland, no longer an army of occupation but supported at a distance by Dublin Castle and the power of a great empire. That confrontation between native communities and the outposts of the empire was often attended by coercion on one side and resistance on the other. From time to time the conflict was dramatic and revolutionary, but more often it was shadowed in the mundane and unrecorded events of daily life, blank interstices of history in which life on the land became more and more intolerable, more exposed to observation, more despised, and more vulnerable to the "liberating" information and material enticements from the industrial and commercially dynamic cores.

The suffering of the famine and the accompanying migration was the same experience compressed into a sudden calamity. This left an especially bitter memory in the minds of the survivors. But the destruction of the "old Ireland" left behind essentially the same myth as all other peasant cultures of the old regime, in which the peasantry suffered the loss of real and imagined old liberties and of a morally superior civilization. But in English eyes, the men and women of Ireland were a paradigm of the barbarian: an easily conquered race, apparently cheerful and satisfied in conditions of the most revolting poverty, and lacking in any ambition to exert themselves out of it. Forgetting the history of violence and coercion that had brought them to it, this colonial imagery drew the Irish peasant as a brute creature whose food was that of the domestic animals, especially the pigs, of civilized Europe. He was an eater of the lowly potato, a crop that, like corn, required the minimum of human intelligence and discipline to maintain an indolent life. In the early years of the conquest, when western Europe was enslaving widening concentric rings of the Atlantic world, these features marked the Irish peasantry more than any other European peoples of the time as born slaves.

In quiet times, when he was not pictured as "the wild Irish" rebel or rapparee, the Irish peasant was invariably the fool or the grotesque. Writing just after the famine, William Carleton thought that depiction was based on the peasants' speech in English, "unjustly heaped upon those who are found to use a language which they do not properly understand." With ridicule came contempt, as he said, "for it is incontrovertibly true, that the man whom you laugh at, you will soon despise."[3]

An array of pseudoscientific glosses was added soon after, but this was the imagery of racial colonialism at the time of Victoria's accession, dividing humanity into a ragtag taxonomy of species and subspecies in which "Paddy" stood beside the Fedayeen or Aborigene, just above the apes on the "monkey chart." Its logic of the classification of species was as indecipherable to the townland emigrants as their thinking was to the landlords who sent them across the Atlantic. The economic and political consequences for England's first true colony are notoriously melancholy, a culture torn within itself, riven with ancient hatreds and grievances impervious to reason, its creative future still hemorrhaging in generation after generation of escaping youth. The young men and women who can now be seen making their way out of Ireland, more European than they have ever been but still laden with the mark of illegality in almost every city of North America, carry the colonial history of their ancestors with them. Until the recent past, the heaviest part of that burden was often that part of their identity lost in leaving, including the memory of those left behind, carried like a penance in their baggage.

1

The Townland

All the houses in line to my right and my left were made of sun-dried
mud and built with walls the height of a man. The roofs of these
dwellings were made of thatch so old that the grass which covered it
could be confused with the meadows on the neighbouring hills. In
more than one place I saw that the flimsy timbers supporting these
fragile roofs had yielded to the effects of time, giving the whole thing
the look of a molehill on which a passer-by has trod.[1]

Alexis de Tocqueville,
Journeys to England and Ireland

Tocqueville called this half-hidden settlement, which he visited in Galway
in 1835, "Village X." It was almost certainly a part of an Irish "townland,"
one of the thousands that contained the bulk of the population before the
famine. It undoubtedly had a name. Tocqueville had seen many like it in
his tour of the Irish countryside but never asked for nor gave a name to
these communities. Compared to the settled French and English villages
he knew well or the neat, thriving country towns he had seen in America
a few years before, "Village X" showed little sign of permanence or civil
order. He saw no sign of work or commerce, no track for wheeled vehicles,
no center or perimeter to identify it. With one exception, the structures
that made it up were of one low story; many were "semi-underground"
dwellings hardly distinguishable from their surrounding landscape.

Detailed descriptions of the more than sixty-two thousand townlands that
contained the peasantry of prefamine Ireland are too rare to draw a uniform picture of their physical characteristics. Regional differences in their
size, their wealth, and building styles undoubtedly existed and distinguished
the poorest from the more prosperous and from those that had been more
or less transformed by the intrusion of commerce and goods radiating from

the metropolis. Virtually all had felt the effects of these influences to some degree before the famine, especially those within the immediate orbit of the port and market towns. But even in these the persistence of traditional habits in material and mental life remained quite stubborn until hunger and emigration transformed them forever.

The townlands and the smaller settlements within them (the *bailia*) were the most dominant, if invisible, feature of the Irish cultural landscape and had been since well before the conquest.[2] These settlements were not villages as most Europeans of the age would think of them, not units that could be easily counted and taxed, not always entities that had standing in law, often not even possessing the geometrical silhouettes that Europeans had long associated with civilization; nevertheless, the townland settlements were the nuclei of peasant society in Ireland before the famine. The occupants of such a settlement as "Village X" knew its name even when the law and the landlord did not. They knew who belonged to it and who did not. They knew its history, its kindredship, and reputation among the townlands that surrounded it, and, as the distant voice of the townland of Ballykilcine attests, they knew that it contained powers of collective force that might for a while protect its strongest as well as its weakest parts from the incursion of destructive forces from the outside.

The community Tocqueville visited a decade before the famine was within walking distance of the ancient town of Tuam, on the lands of the Marquis of Sligo. It was located in a "ravine" shut in by hills covered with treeless pasture, its only road the bed of a stream, dry in the summer months. The houses on either side leaned into the banks of the ravine. Few had either windows or chimney, the daylight entering and smoke escaping by the door and through holes in the thatch, giving the whole the appearance, he thought, of a lime kiln. In most, Tocqueville saw only bare walls, a rickety stool, and a small peat fire burning slowly and dimly between four flat stones. The occupants, young and old, pressed to the doorways and cast surprised looks at him as his feet kicked up the stones of the stream. "The pig in the house. The dunghill. The bare heads and feet. Describe and paint that . . . ," he noted in his diary.[3]

The seasoned and observant French traveler at first supposed that he had discovered a settlement of beggars but soon learned that he was in a community of small tenant farmers, some of them holding from twenty to thirty acres and most likely "landlords" themselves, with their own subtenants on tiny parcels of subdivided lands. With its nearly invisible population of a few families, no church, and only two structures above a man's height, it contained a priest referred to as "your honour." Its children were expected to attend school daily in its seatless, mud-walled schoolhouse. Unless Tocqueville's depiction is wholly imaginary, the obscure townland was clearly a community conscious of itself and its name. Viewing it through a strong Gallic sympathy, Tocqueville found a stunningly vigorous and civil social cohesion amid the mud and rags of what he conceived to be a "village."[4]

The startling bareness of material life in the townlands struck all observers. Most also noted the relative idleness of their occupants, strong young men lying about on fine days and others huddled in smoky cabins as the sun shone. But a few, including Tocqueville, were more deeply impressed by the unexpected vitality and civility they contained. Of the buildings of "Village X," only two could be distinguished from the rest. One, a small stone structure of two stories and four windows, housed the priest, a sunburnt young man who dressed and wore his hair like a layman. The second was the schoolhouse, larger but almost as "wretched" as the other buildings and graced by a number of windows, "or rather holes in the mud walls into which the remains of window-panes had been put." In its one room were thirty children: "The space was too crowded to sit down, and in any case there was only one seat in the school. At one end stood the teacher, a middle-aged, barefoot man teaching children in rags." Here still were the two native vocations that had vied for the minds of the peasantry in the underground years of the Penal Laws, the *ecclesia et mundus* of the old world surviving like weeds in this stoney ravine. That this bleak village supported both a respected priest and a thriving school strongly suggests that even the most materially bereft of the rural poor had also managed to maintain a degree of mental contact with the European world from which the country had been sequestered for more than a century.[5]

Lying in boggy and rocky Galway, "Village X" was probably somewhat poorer than many others and the types and shapes of their dwellings differed greatly from some other parts of the country. But virtually all contained its characteristic features. Maria Edgeworth's "Nugentstown" in Longford consisted of "one row of miserable huts, sunk beneath the side of the road, the mud walls crooked in every directon, some of them opening in wide cracks or zig-zag fissures, from top to bottom, as if there had just been an earthquake. . . ." Brian Merriman described in Gaelic the "dripping soot from above and oozings from below" and the "brown rain falling heavily" through the soot-soaked thatch. The cabins of "hidden Ireland" were not only "the custodians of its mind," as Daniel Corkery said, but marked the bodies of its occupants and set them apart when they walked in broad daylight.[6]

Many of the townlands contained ancient settlements but lacked a distinct physical presence in the countryside. Like "Village X," many were barely visible from a distance, their low, thatch or turf-covered structures merging with the surrounding earth and flora. Their simple, ungeometric construction and disposition and their sparse, mostly portable possessions suggested an impermanence that was in sharp contrast to the inhabitants' clear sense of identity, as though their homes could be moved to other places without disturbing the consciousness of their occupants. But enduring, often mythical affinities with their immediate landscape, with lakes and mountains, rivers and rocks, were preserved everywhere in local folklore and rituals; movement among neighboring townlands due to marriage, fostering, or landlessness was commonplace, but involuntary displacement outside that sphere of experience was felt to be a form of exile. These settlements sustained a consciousness supported by communal memories that identified the townland as the historic place of birth and belonging in the minds of their inhabitants but presented only elusive, half-hidden flanks of their identity to outsiders. It was an extremely fragile form of social organization and especially vulnerable to forcible intrusions from the outside, such as those threatening Ballykilcline during the 1830s. Yet, as their persistence up to the famine suggests, the townland's settlements represented a degree of mental collectivity and tradition based on family history and kinship sufficient to present a stubborn resistance to the forces of dissolution. Together with the long months of idleness that their marginal economies dictated, the insubstantial structures and surreptitious culture of the Irish townlands was also a setting in which conspiracy and evasion thrived. These traits certainly made rural Ireland an easy place to overrun but a difficult countryside to rule.

The Hidden Townland

The village was not a native form of settlement in Ireland. Its absence from Irish life set the country apart from England and most of western Europe until very recent times and probably accounts for a good deal of the vivaciously untidy character of the countryside and for many of its miseries. Before the famine the bulk of the agrarian population of Ireland lived in units of land division called townlands in surveys and estate records. But, before the Ordnance Survey of the 1830s, the word *baile* or *baile fearann* (meaning the settlement and the landholding together) described not only the townland as a division of the land but the human communities dwelling within it, creating one of the many incongruities between native and official perceptions of the land and the rights attached to it. This marriage of meanings, one material and the other mental, persists into the twentieth century, when most of the people still identify themselves to one another by their townland's name, referring to the community it contains and its memory rather than its mere location and dimensions.

The early origins of the townland settlement are lost primarily because, unlike the ancient stone villages of Tuscany or Lanquedoc, it left behind no artifactual trace; "from the silence of the archaeological evidence," its principal geographer warned, "it might be concluded . . . that the Irish medieval landscape was empty of human habitation." Although its form and measurement differed from one part of the country to another, it had been used everywhere as a unit of taxation in Gaelic times and it remained so beneath the tax system imposed after the Williamite conquest. Under this system, *townland* was merely an English loanword grafted upon the old usage to establish the administrative division of the land for the purpose of measuring the impositions due from it. Its inhabitants were taxed in either case, but much else had been lost in the translation, including, as the poet Seamus Heaney expressed it, "the fume of affection and recognition that came off the word." Like so much else in prefamine Ireland, the official ordering of the land in its surveys and divisions no longer coincided with the perceptions and consciousness of the population.[7]

"Rundale," an indigenous practice of distributing plots of land among townland families, added still greater confusion and frustration for those who hoped to impose an orderly geometry on the countryside. The leading scholar of rundale and the rundale "clachan" [or village], E. Estyn Evans, describes the practice as follows:

> Rundale was much simpler and more flexible than the three field system, requiring less equipment and less organisation. It was egalitarian, and could operate without the benefit of a landlord, but it was complicated by the subdivision among co-heirs and in former times by the periodic reallocation of the holdings, which were scattered in many small plots so that all shared land of varying quality. The word used to describe the confusion of innumerable scattered plots and tortuous access ways in the infield was 'throughother', a word which has often been applied to other aspects of Irish life.[8]

These rundale villages remained the home of perhaps three-quarters of the population just before the great famine.[9] In one count, there were some 62,205 townlands covering the country, some of them consisting of one or two dwellings on one acre of land. The average townland comprised something over three hundred acres and supported from fifteen to thirty households, often of related families with just a few family names predominating.[10] At any given moment in the different regions of the country many variations could be found in the internal features of the townlands. Many persisted to the famine nearly unchanged, especially in the West, sustained by an equally old system of values, traditions, and associations. The famine would deliver the coup de grace to most of the rundale townlands and would be especially hard on those least touched by change, since these were likely to be the poorest, the least English-speaking, and the most dependent on the potato for survival. But the townland's place at the core of the peasantry's culture and economy was already doomed when the famine struck; it had been eroding for generations under more and more penetrating intrusions from the outside world, together with "defections" by its own more ambitious sons and, already, from among its restless daughters.

The conquests and confiscations of the seventeenth century were traumas on a grand scale and mortally disrupted the upper levels of Catholic and "Old-Irish"[11] society. Peeling away structures that had been created by still earlier conquests, the Williamite settlement replaced them with a predominantly Protestant, landed gentry that mimicked its English counterpart but lay like a crust over the native culture, absorbing much of the remnant of the earlier elites but failing to penetrate very deeply into the common Gaelic culture. The effects of the Penal Laws were also largely restricted to the same strata of social and landed elites, leaving most of the native institutions and practices that governed the uses and distribution of land largely undisturbed, especially in the remoter districts. Unlike the open-field vil-

lage of England, the *bailia* had no standing in the law either as a measure
of property or as a jurisdictional or political unit, and certainly not as a claim
to rights or civil identity on the part of their occupants.[12] The "moral
economy" governing rights to the land bore some resemblance to the common rights of villagers in England in that they could not usually be alien-
ated, at least in the eyes of the inhabitants, but the townland itself lacked
even the contested standing of the English village in the eyes of the law.

So far as their nearly worthless structures had marketable value, townlands
could be counted as property, as villages were in England, but to be born
in one conferred no legal identity whatever. Some English villages also
became mere repositories of seasonal labor, rural tenements maintained by
sporadic wages and the poor rates. But unlike the denizens of the urban
slums for which many of their inhabitants were bound, most of the Irish
identified themselves by their townland's name and history. Adults might
know the names of literally hundreds of other townlands, complete with
bits of their history, the prominent families and individuals in them, their
histories as combative or pliant tenants or sometimes as rivals in brawls and
faction fights. Yet even populous settlements of five hundred or more lacked
the main street, the marketplace, church steeple, public house, or common
that gave a tangible existence and a legal identity to the villages of England
and western Europe. In this sense, the difference between such villages and
the *bailia* was precisely the difference between citizen and colonial subject.[13]

Most landlords and their agents knew the townlands that dotted their property and usually recognized their existence in rent books and surveys even
though these often gave a very imperfect, almost guesswork picture of the
real patterns of settlement. Almost invariably, such near outsiders viewed
the townland and their settlements as merely another obstinate obstacle to
any rational management of the land and the people, an occult device that
muddled responsibilities between master and tenant, perpetuated the old
listless ways, and bred conspiracy. As we shall see, the people of Ballykilcline
would not necessarily disagree—for those in the townland who helped to
interpret the outside world for the rest, the townland's only defense against
the landlord and the law was to act as an obstruction to rationalizing the
land system. Its very incoherence was their protection; it had left room for
their half-hidden coexistence for centuries. And with that system, ruinous
as it was, also went all the essentials of their way of life. Their means of
resistance—conspiracy, pretense, foot-dragging, and obfuscation—were the
only ones ordinarily available to them, "weapons of the weak" like those
employed by defeated and colonized peoples everywhere.[14] The destruction of the townland community, whether by improvement, eviction, or
emigration, inevitably threatened the survival of their language, their family and community systems, and the authority of tradition, including the
distinct form of Christianity peculiar to rural Ireland before the famine.[15]
The tenacity with which the peasantry held onto all this and the catastrophic

force of events eventually needed to pry them loose attest to the value they placed on the life the townlands contained.

Conflict between landlord and tenant could arise from any number of issues, but in the end it was almost always about land. For the landlords, the rather languid sort of life they had cultivated depended on rents; for the tenants, life depended on access to land. Both were notoriously uncertain in Ireland. Taken for granted by most of the rural population, the annual round of uncertainty and dispute over the land was one of the most characteristic features of the Irish land system and constantly deplored by the improvers and parliamentary commissions. There was a growing minority of "rationalizing" commercial landlords, both large and small. But nearly every level of rural society had accustomed itself in different ways to the vague future such a system dictated, and the picaresque stigma of waste and recklessness fell on the Irish landlord and peasant almost equally—many a gentleman's "encumbered estate" was merely "Paddy's" indebted subdivision on a larger scale, both the product of feckless inertia and a culture that thought that prosperity was more the result of good luck than of good management.

Though there probably was a good deal that the squire, the "upstart" native farmers, and the peasant shared in this stereotype, the cultural gap between the owners and the tillers of the land still remained broad enough to cause much conflict and incomprehension, tangibly expressed in their profoundly differing perceptions of the land, the rights to it, its division, and its uses. However much the landed classes had been beguiled by the cultural landscape and delegated their ultimate power through layers of native intermediaries, they remained the heirs and upholders of a still alien overlay in matters of the law and property. Although the land had been brought under principles of ownership and tenure based on Norman and English law by the eighteenth century, practices deriving from the Gaelic past, in particular the *brehon* law, which vested ownership not in individuals but in the *derbfine*,[16] remained a part of the intuitive values the peasantry applied to the arrangement of land among themselves. The townland was the main surviving instrument of these traditions: while various individuals in a community were tenants in law, recorded by name in the rent or tax books and on surveys in some kind of geometric pattern, an almost liquid substructure of unwritten arrangements governing access to land persisted among individuals and kinship groups within the townland. The result often had the look of subterfuge and defiance in the eyes of landlords and their agents. Families or individuals evicted for nonpayment or as troublemakers would turn up repeatedly as "unofficial" subtenants of those in good standing, frequently their relatives. Parcels of land leased to an individual would often default in rent because its use had been relet or divided among any number of others in a system of underground obligations (which in Ballykilcline were called "fines"), creating unfathomable disputes about who owed what to whom. It was not even unusual for a tenant to demand "compensation" from a baffled landlord for obligations of this origin that were a complete mystery to him. Just as often, the landlord would never have heard the complainant's name before.

In effect, this subculture was a method of defiance, an effort to force the landlord to deal with the townland as a collective entity rather than as the pathetically vulnerable individuals each tenant or subtenant was by himself. Some among the resident landed classes, especially those who saw themselves as "improvers," knew a good deal more than others about the workings of the silent economy of the townlands, but as we shall see, even these could live amidst the townlands on their estates for years, passing through them daily, and remain unable to make a sure count of their occupants or of who and how many belonged in their rent books. Although virtually all condemned this subculture, many tolerated its eccentricities or merely surrendered to them in frustration. One of the perennial sources of frustration concerned differences and disputations over the true measure of tenants' holdings, an endless cause of contention not only between landlord and peasant but, just as bitterly, sometimes murderously, among the tenants themselves. Divergent mental geographies, one graphic and the other oral, governed the use of land simultaneously. One, embodied in the landowner's survey, was upheld by the law and the other by deeply embedded custom, a moral economy that was inextricable from peasant family and kinship systems but had no legal standing. In consequence, nearly any form of resistance to summary evictions, distraints on property, or arbitrary rises in rents might be construed as a criminal offense.

The common law in England, abused as it had been in the past century, offered some protection to the rights of tenants and villagers—or when it failed at least lent legitimacy to their protests. Its absence was the essence of colonialism in Ireland, distinguishing the rundale settlements absolutely from even the poorest of English hamlets. As in England, a tolerant or complacent landlord, not an unusual figure in the countryside, might find life more agreeable in overlooking the unofficial practices of the tenants if the rents were passably well met. But in any dispute about the measurement of land, and therefore the rights of all parties to it, the survey was the law of the land, the very foundation of the colonial system and all but unchallengeable by the small tenants and laborers who inhabited the townlands. It represented a system that had been implanted by the conquest, and behind it stood ultimately the authority of the Crown and irresistible force.[17]

Conflicting Measurement

European conquests since the seventeenth century were invariably followed by a meticulous measurement of the land and the imposition of a legal code that redefined the rights to it. From the time of William Petty, the great surveyor of Ireland in the post-Cromwellian era whom Marx called the father of political economy,[18] the appearance of the level and transom among the rear guard of the conquering armies presaged hard times for the inhabitants, much as the appearance of the railroad surveyor did for the plains Indians. For after the surveyor invariably trailed the court, the lawyer, the land agent, the deed clerk, the assessor, and the collector of rents, the latter known unaffectionately in the Irish countryside as the "driver." He was also the evictor, in Ballykilcline a man from the townland of no particular distinction except that he had the threat of the law, bailiffs, constables, sheriffs, magistrates, and courts behind him—and in the last resort troops of the regular army, widely known as "redcoats" due to their tunics. When the law of the land was violated, as by the nonpayment of rents, the driver pointed out the offender to the constables, nailed the notice of eviction on the doorpost, and gang-bossed the casual laborers who pulled down the flimsy house.

The Cromwellian and Williamite surveys of Ireland were undertaken to insure that there would be a minimum of bickering and litigating in slicing up the fruits of the conquest and were naturally rendered in English "Statute" measure of acres, roods, and perches. The older measure originating with the Tudors, the "Plantation" acre, had come to be generally known as the "Irish" acre since over nearly two centuries it had become customary in the country and was at least understood by most of the common tenant population in their dealings with the landlord and the figuring of rents. Beneath these reassuring geometries, however, were still older and even more fluid measurements of entitlement, obligation, and possession that E. Estyn Evans described as the "throughother" culture of the townland.[19]

By the nineteenth century, there were thus two ways of measuring the land officially employed and both were usually cited in transactions with the intention of avoiding discord and litigation, something never fully achieved. Still another source of dispute over land rights and boundaries existed in the widespread survival among the townland tenants of contracting land agreements among themselves in "sums" or "collops," a measurement of land use (usufruct) rather than of area, such as "a cow's grass," the roughly two acres needed to graze a milk cow or to fatten two yearling calves or to support six to eight sheep. And just as in the Statute and Irish measures, these "sums" could be divided into fractional measures, the "foot" (a quarter cow's grass) or the "cleet" (half a "foot"), which conformed to the often minutely subdivided fields and pastures of the townland tenants.[20] In some localities that were described as "extreme" examples of this contretemps of cultures (that is, in western townlands that drew startled attention from English observers and European travelers), even long-resident and well-informed aficionados of enlightened agriculture found the microcosmic internal arrangements of townlands an imponderable mystery, as in one well-known "exposé":

> In some instances, a tenant having any part of a townland (no matter how small), had his proportion in thirty or forty different places, and without fences between them, it being utterly impossible to have any, as the proportions were so very numerous, and frequently so small, that not more than half a stone [8 pounds] of oats was required to sow one of such division. Thus every

tenant considers himself entitled to a portion of each various quality of land in his townland; and the man who had some good land at one extremity, was sure to have some bad at the other, and a bit of middling in the centre, and bits of other quality in odd corners, each bounded by his neighbour's property, and without any fence or ditch between them. Under such circumstances as these, could any one wonder at the desperation of a poor man, who having his inheritance in thirty-two different places, abandoned them in utter despair of ever being able to make them out.[21]

Common understanding was further muddled after the Act of Union by replacing the old Irish currency, in which the tenant's rent had previously been assessed, with a British currency of 8 percent to 9 percent greater value—all payments had then to be converted upward through each level of measurement and tenancy. This perplexing system was obviously subject to much abuse from above, especially by the various strata of middlemen, land agents, and collectors. Both land measure and currency had also to be translated into the assessments of tithes and cesses (land taxes) to which the tenantry was subject, greatly exacerbating bitter issues in which there was simply no common ground.

Beneath this reigning superstructure of law, measurement, and currency was a still-tenacious subculture whose internal economy had been penetrated but not yet governed by cash or paper transactions, whose concepts of rights in property, inheritance, and land tenure bore small resemblance to the established law, and whose measurements of the land in dealings among themselves were nearly indecipherable to the Crown surveyors. When lands of the ruling Gaelic and Anglo-Norman families were forfeited and partitioned by the seventeenth-century surveyors and later sold, subdivided, sublet, consolidated, or cleared by succeeding generations of landlords and their surveyors, the resulting charts of estates and holdings, like layer upon layer of cracked paint, rarely matched the existing boundaries or the actual disposal of the population on the land. What order the system contained could be seen only from above, as though a geometric transparency had been laid upon an undulating landscape of oral agreements and movable boundary stones, invisible filaments that bound the people to the land by tradition, affection and self-defense.

The Townland of Ballykilcline

The obscure settlement of the Irish midlands was given as full a regalia of address as Joyce's "Citizen Cusack" in all official documents: the townland of Ballykilcline, in the Barony of Ballintobber, parish of Kilglass, in the electoral district of North Roscommon, County Roscommon, which was its full address in Crown Estate files, comprised 602 "Statute Acres," or 371 acres, 2 roods, 30 perches in "Plantation" or "Irish" acres. It was the lifetime residence of a population that varied from 526 men, women, and children in the best years to about 470 when conditions were bad and mortality, tramping, and itinerant begging high. This at least was the location and description of the townland as it appears in the Ordnance Survey, the census, the landlords' surveys and rent books. It was always the designation the townland received in the chain of records leading from the local Crown Agent, through His Majesty's Quit Rent Office in Dublin all the way to London and the Commissioners of His Majesty's Woods, Forests, Land Revenues, Works, and Buildings, who managed the estate for the Crown. In the minds of the "occupants," as official documents always called them, their place on the earth is much harder to fix. They obviously knew "where" they were, since they had always been there, with the exception of a few who had married into the lands from short distances away, mostly from within the so-called marriage field of about fifteen miles, within which most of the townland matches were made. Those not native to the townland were almost invariably drawn in from this small circle, near and familiar townlands whose internal society was much the same and whose people also had not traveled much beyond the geography of kinship and mutual experience.

The people of Ballykilcline lived about three miles from the provincial market town of Strokestown, whose name would have been known only to a relatively few Irishmen from elsewhere interested in agricultural commerce, to some dealers and haulers in primary and rough-manufactured rural goods, to the clerks of the fledgling postal services, and to the overwhelmed bureaucracies of Dublin Castle and the collectors of Irish rents. With a population of only about fifteen hundred souls, it was no larger than thousands of the villages of England and the western continent. Viewed from Dublin, about ninety miles east, Strokestown was one of the smaller market towns along the Longford-Mullingar road, distant enough to be considered in the "west" and therefore near the outer edges of the "Pale," a fading but still living idea in the metropolis. Apart from some of the great families who held large estates and maintained country residences in the area and sojourned regularly in Dublin, London, and on the continent, the local nabobs—the gentry, the magistrates, the clergy, and officials of Strokestown—lived in provincial obscurity. From the perspective of cosmopolitan London, even these largely anglicized, literate, newspaper-reading, mostly Protestant, property-owning, or professional folk were ordinarily portrayed as incorrigible rustics.

Of the townland of Ballykilcline and its occupants, the outside world was almost completely oblivious. Those like James Burke, the Officer of the Quit Rents in Dublin, and the London Commissioners knew it only as one troublesome file among many and always relied upon a tendril of deputies for all their information regarding it. The depth of its obscurity may be gauged from the fact that even the local notables of the town and its environs, themselves on the very frontier of cosmopolitan Europe, were with few exceptions in a state of ignorance, fear, and estrangement from the townland people, though they were next-door neighbors. When arrests were to be made by the local sheriff or notices to be served by the excise officers, local "intermediaries," regarded as informers by the tenants for revealing their identities, had to be employed because local authorities seldom could distinguish one face from another of the townland people when they made an appearance at the local fairs and markets.

So much of these middling and upper strata of Irish rural society had been in place for so long that it would be inaccurate to describe them any longer as an alien or conquering elite; quite naturally, they had come to regard themselves in their own minds as the cornerstone of Irish civilization, or at least its provincial upholders. The separation between them and the townland tenants was frequently bridged by individuals both in the neighborhood of Strokestown and in like situations all over the country, but that divide was the central fact of life governing the social relationships of the Irish countryside, as it was in other colonial settings throughout the European empires. It was in this regard more than in parliamentary legislation that Ireland's true colonial status persisted. Although the armed blockhouses of the plantation era were now gone, the mentalities of the frontier were still much more than vestiges.

Needless to say, this frontier was crossed in both directions. In sheer numbers, the native Irish who were "anglicized" in their language and "commercialized" in their values either wholly or superficially over the years were far greater than the reverse. The Penal Laws as well as the Relief Acts opening careers to native Roman Catholics, the erosion of the Irish language along with the spread of English in the population, the imposition of English law together with the increase of native landownership—all helped to speed the process of cultivating a native-born elite and intermediate classes before the famine. By the time of the famine, a large "middle" class of Roman Catholic farmers, graziers, tradesmen, and the beginnings of a native professional class had emerged in the vicinities of the market towns. But probably most decisive and lasting of all, the inexorable intrusion of English capital into the Irish countryside through hundreds of such market towns as Strokestown had already proceeded very far in the transformation of traditional Irish society. In general, changes experienced through this agency had proceeded furthest around those zones in the country where capital was most concentrated, near the cities of the East and Northeast and to a lesser extent in the South. Except for the port cities, the West and the midlands were to be affected later, as in the case of Strokestown, primarily through the penetration of the turnpike and canal systems that made the provincial market towns viable.[22]

The long-standing barriers of language, economies, social conventions, values, and even of religion were being eroded with increasing speed in the generation before the famine, although it was that cataclysm that did more than anything else to bring the "old regime" of the Irish peasantry to an end. In this sense at least, Ballykilcline is emblematic of the history of the thousands of rural townlands whose transformation or, in many cases, disintegration entered the final stage in the famine years. The incidence of famine mortality and emigration on the peasantry have been examined very closely, and their effect on changing traditional practices in inheritance, marriage, cultivation, and even religion is reasonably well understood, at least on the most general scale. But these catastrophic events were merely the climactic phase of a cumulative process of change in the countryside that had begun with military conquest but was ultimately determined by the relentless, routine extraction of the produce of the land and the labor of its people. To the degree that this prolonged process may be described as "modernization" it must be seen as a form disfigured by colonialism, bearing the contradictory traits that mark so much else in Irish history, proceeding in fits and starts, with much backsliding and attended by armed force and violence.

When the first eviction notice was served on the tenants of Ballykilcline in 1836, the authorities who wrote it were still struggling to identify the territory to be vacated in language that the inhabitants might understand to refer to themselves and their homes. The notice ordered them to quit possession of "The Crown lands called or known by the name of Ballykilcline, otherwise Killtullyvarry, Bungariffe, and Aghamore or by whatsoever other name or names the same or any subdenomination thereof maybe called or known. . . ."[23] The tenants themselves knew their home by all these names, and a few more. In fact, the holding referred to in the Crown documents as Ballykilcline contained at least three settlements in the minds of the inhabitants. Almost any grouping of cabins and their surrounding fields was regarded by the occupants as an entity and given a name. Maria Edgeworth was not exaggerating much when she said that a mere two or three cabins gathered together were sufficient to constitute a "town," at least in the minds of their inhabitants.[24] The settlement visited by Alexis de Tocqueville appears to have been of this sort, a settlement of perhaps fifteen or twenty dwellings, strung out beside the "road" apparently at random.

According to the records and rent books of the 1830s, there were twenty-seven townlands on the Roscommon estate of Lord Hartland, the master of Strokestown House. The surveyors of the Hartland estate noted the names of these small clusters, apparently transposing them from older existing surveys. Although the clusters had no meaning in law, the surveyors and the estate's agents applied their names to maps and accounts as convenient units for evaluations and the collection of rents. Ballykilcline was one among these, until this time indistinguishable from the rest. But at least as far back as the 1790s, the leases referred to the whole six-hundred-acre property as the "townland of Ballykilcline," designating one townland name to represent all the rundale villages within it. The submerged settlements within its official boundaries, especially Aughamore and Kiltullyvarry with their noticeable concentrations of family names, overlapped the surveyors' fixed borders in their pattern of family ties, spilling into townlands on the neighboring estates of the Marquess of Westmeath (into Lecarrue and Carriganban) and other lands belonging to Lord Hartland (Barrawalla).

Although Ballykilcline did not differ noticeably from the neighboring townlands of the estate, its occupants were about to enter a process of discovery that set them apart from the rest in at least one crucial respect. Having paid their rents for more than forty years to none other than the lords of Strokestown House and their local middlemen, the occupants of Bally- kilcline did not yet know that they had been tenants of the Crown all along, nor did they know that the lax and tolerant Maurice Mahon, the third Baron Hartland, was merely the Crown's lessee. His lease expired in 1834 and, unless it were renewed, their fate would be in the hands of the Crown bu- reaucracy. This fact and the layer upon layer of the superstructure above was revealed to them only by degrees after the expiration of the lease, when the last Lord Hartland, declared incompetent by reason of insanity, vacated the place his family had occupied for forty-one years as surrogates of the Crown. The peasants' place in relation to that outside world and the pos- sibility that they might soon have to travel in it was also unveiled to them in the same process, one layer at a time.

2

The Land System

A paralytic body where one half of it is dead or just dragged about by the other.[1]

Daniel Corkery, *The Hidden Ireland*

By May of 1848 the last of the tenants of the Crown Estate of Ballykilcline were packing up whatever they would be able to carry on their backs for the long journey by foot and ferry to Liverpool. Their sacks contained mostly pots and clothing of such a ragged simplicity that even for Europe's barest peasant fashion belonged to a bygone age. What other domestic possessions remained in the cabins when the date of departure had been proclaimed the previous August would have been sold since in the neighborhood, in what later came to be called an "emigrant auction," or traded for food or given or thrown away as having absolutely no negotiable value. By the spring, as the local Crown Agent put it, the troublesome lands were to be "perfectly untenanted."

Although most of the 602 acres of hilly land were not among the richest in the neighborhood for commercial tillage, they were suitable for subsistence farming and grazing and shaped in agreeable contours overlooking beautiful Kilglass Lake. Emptied of its nearly five hundred inhabitants, the property immediately began to attract the attention of potential buyers from the district and, a little later, from more distant parts of Ireland and England. Following the clearance, one of the first inquiries to be received by Her Majesty's Commissioners came from John Kelly of Essex Town in Roscommon, a county surveyor who had advised the Crown to sell at a minimal price: "From the disturbed state of the District," Kelly contended, "many would hesitate to purchase those lands but as I am well known in that part of the County and have always treated the people with kindness I do not apprehend any annoyance from them." With his own "professional exertions" and some expenditure of capital in drainage, Kelly thought "it might be made a tolerable reserve for the decline of life."[2]

The sequence of events that brought this gloomy end to Ballykilcline can be traced to at least 1688 in surviving documents and more murkily in legend before that time. The lands in which the townland was situated were forfeited to the Crown in the rebellion of that year, becoming one of the far-flung Crown estates in Ireland administered by His Majesty's Commissioners of Woods and Forests. The townland was carved out of much larger forfeited properties to the east and west that were also divided into appropriate parcels and disposed of by the Crown to local lessees and servitors, eventually being incorporated in 1794 into the estate of Maurice Mahon, the first Baron Hartland, whose seat was at Strokestown House. Before that time its history is mingled with that of the feuding chieftains of the O'Conors of Roscommon. The barony of Balintobber, including Strokestown and Ballykilcline, comprised the territories of the O'Conor Don (the "brown") and the lands further west of the O'Conor Ruadh (the "red"). They had been rival chieftains, but both had been compelled to submit to the queen in the Elizabethan conquest, when their lands were divided into baronies by Sir John Perrot. Thereafter, they were to surrender their Brehon titles, accepting a knighthood in compensation. They executed indentures of submission and accepted the lands in regrant to them and their heirs.

The O'Conor Don maintained a seat at Ballintobber, where the ruins of the castle were still visible in the 1830s. As told at that time by the brother of the O'Conor Don, the M.P. for North Roscommon, Hugh O'Conor died in 1762 without a male heir and the castle and estate passed into the hands of the Burkes of Galway through the female line. Some years later, Alexander O'Conor of Cloonalis was said to have uncovered a will made by the late Hugh among the papers of Lord Athenree, "devising" his estate to the O'Conors of Cloonalis. In 1784, Alexander was said to have "collected a mob of 400 or 500 of the retainers of his family . . . and seized upon the castle and estate of Balintobber by open violence." The incident created a sensation at the time and was looked upon as "the commencement of an insurrection of the natives to regain their former possessions." Cavalry and artillery were sent from Athlone to dispossess "the disorderly mob" from the ruins of the castle at Ballintobber, at which point they quickly dispersed and, according to Alexander's heirs, "their insane leader took refuge in the bogs." Title to the former O'Conor lands was sold and resold in the succeeding ten years, eventually to be included in the large surrounding estate of the first Lord Hartland.[3]

What the people of Ballykilcline knew or thought of this oral history of the land is not known. It is also unclear in the O'Conor Don's account how or why the marginal six-hundred-acre property of Ballykilcline was retained by the Crown, to become a deeply dormant file in London for decades. There was enough confusion in the title to encourage the tenants, with the M.P.'s help, to challenge it in law when something of a pretender "of the name of Conor" made an appearance in the 1840s. Not surprisingly, there were numerous "Conors" and "O'Conors" in the district and a large family of "Connors" in Aghamore. But who the pretender "Conor" was and what was his claim on the land was a mystery to the Crown's commissioners then and will probably remain so forever.

In 1794, the townland was leased by Letters Patent from the Crown to "Charles, Viscount Dillon of Costelloe," to hold from the 1793 for forty-one years at a rent of £216 in the Irish currency then employed (£199 in the new currency). Almost immediately, Dillon assigned his interest in the lands to Maurice Mahon, the first Baron Hartland, who was one of the many rewarded with a title for supporting the Act of Union in the Dublin parliament.[4] With nearly thirty thousand acres of land in north-central Roscommon, the Mahons were one of the great landed families of the county. As one of the improving landlords of the midlands, the first Lord Hartland also laid out the market for the town of Strokestown and encouraged local manufacture, including a brewery. But he apparently had little taste for managing the lands directly, since he subsequently let out most of his holdings to middlemen of the district, local big farmers and graziers who were expected thereafter to produce the flow of rents, maintain order, and oversee the deferential hierarchy of the neighborhood.[5] In the obscurity of the Irish countryside, something fairly close to this idyll was sustained through most of the century of the Penal Laws, with intense but futile disruptions from time to time. The territory of north-central Roscommon in which Ballykilcine lay had been altogether ordinary in this respect, neither the most nor the least disturbed of districts during the preceding century.

When the forty-one-year lease to Ballykilcline expired on 1 May 1834, negotiations were opened by the Commissioners of Woods and Forests with Lord Hartland for the outright sale of the lands for the sum of £8,738 (a conventional valuation of Irish leases at twenty-two times the annual rents). James Weale, a prominent surveyor of the firm of Brassington and Gale, which frequently represented the Crown's estates in Ireland, was sent to make an evaluation for the sale at this time and estimated that the lands could produce "at least £9500" if sold at auction in one lot, but "all things considered" he advised the sale to Hartland at the lower price. He agreed with his fellow surveyor, John Kelly, that there were some liabilities in the property that might lessen its appeal to buyers: "It is subdivided into very minute holdings, occupied generally by cottier Labourers; and consequently the population settled in it is excessively numerous, their dwellings of a miserable description, and the Lands more or less worn out by continued burning of the soil for tillage. . . ." The latter was a practice often decried by visitors to the country, along with such alleged habits as tying the plow to the horse's tail, as sure signs of a barbarous culture.[6]

Weale made it clear in his reports to the commissioners that Crown revenues were not the only factor he was considering in recommending the sale to Lord Hartland. Until recent years, the value of the fee simple for Crown lands in Ireland had been established at twenty years' rents. But since 1830 Weale himself had evaluated Crown lands in Galway and Cork at from

twenty-two to twenty-five years' rents; the higher price was attainable in
two recent sales in Galway because in one case there was resident "barely a
sufficient number of labourers for its cultivation" and in the other because
the property formed part of the buyer's demesne lands[7] "without a single
cabin on it." In similar circumstances, Weale thought that the twenty-five-
year valuation (that is, more than £9,800) would be appropriate for the
Roscommon land, but he added, "I would not advise a stranger to purchase it at that price." The surveyors instead advised the Crown to take the
loss of more than one thousand pounds (at a time when furious questions
arose in Her Majesty's Quit Rent Office over minute fractions of this
amount) not only because heavily tenanted land brought a lower price in
Ireland than vacant land but because of less specific reasons, reasons even
more imperative than the royal purse. Weale assured the commissioners that
he had set the price "without deviating from the official principle—that the
price be assessed only on due consideration of the respective interests of
the Land Revenue, of the occupying tenantry, and of the Public Peace."
The obstacle on the Roscommon estate was the tenantry and the peace, as
he made clear enough in his report of April 1834:

> Circumstanced as the Roscommon property is, it is most desirable not to break
> up *suddenly* the existing relations between the Crown lessee, his middleman,
> and the actual occupiers. . . . But a sale to a stranger would have that effect,
> and before such a sale could be made it would be a matter of serious consid-
> eration, *in the present state of the country, how the cottier tenantry should be
> treated or provided for. This* cause of embarrassment prevents me from advis-
> ing an immediate sale of Trust Estate in Galway *although* the revenue is cer-
> tainly prejudiced by the postponement.[8]

Weale was delicate but direct: Crown land could not simply be sold off in
Ireland to the highest bidder, who might then immediately begin the infamous and peace-disturbing process of large-scale eviction and clearance.
The public peace and the benevolent image of the Crown, not to mention
the interests of the occupying tenantry, should take precedence in this case
over the royal revenue. Weale was a meticulous professional and apparently
no more audacious than others of his trade in making such a recommendation; even at a time of relative quiet in the district, he merely considered these priorities as the established policy of His Majesty's Commissioners
with regard to Crown lands in Ireland.

   The commissioners accepted the surveyor's advice without hesitation and
offered the sale to Lord Hartland at the lower price. At first sight, the case
of Ballykilcline (and that of other Crown lands in Galway and Cork that
the Crown's surveyors handled)[9] may seem to have been an incident in which
the Crown behaved differently from most private estate holders in Ireland.
But with some notable exceptions, most of the largest landholders only rarely
set profit alone as the sole criterion in the management of estates, particularly when it came to mass evictions. Like the Crown, the great landlords
often had to consider public opinion both in Ireland and in England in

making clearances, even when they might be defended as "improvements." Both reputation and tranquility were easily shattered by too-close attention to the rent book. For that reason especially, many landlords preferred to place middlemen as a screen between themselves and public embarrassment or worse. Thus, Lord Hartland had placed local gentlemen and strong farmers as subtenants between himself and the townlands, and when his lease to Ballykilcline terminated in 1834 the Crown much preferred to keep its distance as well by renewing the lease and retaining its middleman or, failing that, to rid itself of the property even at a loss. In this decision Weale's well-informed advice was wise, as subsequent events proved.

This system, in which the tillers of the soil rarely confronted any but the "deputies of deputies of deputies" of their landlord, had been the cornerstone of the Irish land system for generations and was widely thought (at least by many Irish landowners and their agents) to work reasonably well. For the absentee landlord wishing only the steady flow of rents, the middlemen, stewards or subtenants, were inescapable. Except for relatively few of the larger Irish landlords who sometimes exerted great efforts in managing and "improving" their estates, placing substantial middlemen between themselves and their tenants offered the heirs to great estates, who were frequently scattered through distant parts of the country, an almost irresistible relief from the onerous intricacies of rent books, arrears, rates, and, especially, collections. Some of the advantages of this method, as well as some of the root causes of conflicts between landlord and tenants, can be seen in the arrangement created by Hartland before 1834.

Under the terms of the 1793 leasehold, purchased by the first Baron Hartland from Dillon, the Crown's tenant paid just under £200 a year in the new currency. This amount was not subject to change for forty-one years. Subsequently, Hartland had installed middlemen who held long leases under him for approximately three-fourths of the lands of Ballykilcline. Hartland continued to receive rents from the tenants of the remaining quarter of the lands directly as well as from his subtenants. When all the leases expired on 1 May 1834, the total annual rents being paid by the occupying tenants (who were in fact the subtenants of the subtenants of Lord Hartland's middleman) amounted to £412, of which £106 was paid to Hartland directly and £306 to his lessees.[10] After paying the quit rent of £199 to the Crown, the Hartland estate may have profited some £50 to £60 in years when all rents from both occupants and middlemen were fully paid—a feat accomplished only in the best of years. The nearly £200 received punctually each year by the Crown, percolating up from the underground spring of peasant rents, was almost entirely net profit, reduced only by the cost of managing the arcane Ballykilcline account—a mite-like entry in the annual report of His Majesty's Commissioners of Woods and Forests to Parliament. As the Crown's bookkeepers and agents learned after 1834, this arrangement in which the tenants of its tenants were made responsible for the local extraction of rents from the peasantry was the only method through which the monarchy could both produce its revenue and maintain order in Ireland. When the Crown was forced to manage its Irish estates directly, there was neither profit nor peace.

The Base of the Land System

As peasant emigrants from all over Europe were to learn when they entered the transatlantic shipping network through the great emigration ports, their fate was largely determined by the arrangements and necessities of an international commercial system hitherto beyond their sight or comprehension. There is no evidence that the rent payers of Ballykilcline had as yet any clear understanding of the economic structure of which their hard-won shillings of rent were the foundation. For the 602 acres of the townland the occupying tenants were paying nearly 14s. an acre; on top of this were the tithes and cesses that also supported institutions like the parsonage and the Poor Law Guardians, which were beyond their control and largely beyond their interests. The middlemen of Lord Hartland, gentlemen and commercial farmers of the neighborhood, paid an average of 10s. an acre, and the Crown tenant himself about 6s. 13d, which was the Crown revenue. This arrangement was modestly profitable to the Crown, which had paid for the conquest and continued to pay the cost of keeping the peace, only so long as its tenant bore the burden of managing the estate and collecting the rents. Though less than £200 a year percolated to the top, the scheme also helped to support at least two levels of loyal elites and demi-elites below, a miniature of the Ascendancy pyramid that weighed on the rents and labor of the peasantry. Had they paid only the Crown's rents, the appearance of the townlands would certainly have been far less dismal than it always seemed to outsiders.

Although the occupying tenants paid twice the rate paid by Lord Hartland for each acre and 40 percent above that of his middlemen, Ballykilcline was by no means among the most rack-rented estates in Ireland; nor by most accounts could Lord Hartland be described as a rapacious landlord. Seventy-four tenant households paid an average of less than £6 a year for the use of fewer than eight acres apiece, less than 17s. a head each year, of which about 8s. went circuitously to the heirs of the land's conquerors. There is no indication that the tenants were aware of their shillings' ultimate destination until some time after the Crown's agents replaced those of Lord Hartland in collecting their rents in 1834, when the first signs of their resistance also appeared.

When the Crown resumed possession, His Majesty's Commissioners found that the rents had been "tolerably punctually paid" in the years before, and there was no mention of recalcitrance or disturbances in the district. Nevertheless, Weale had been quite right in describing the tenantry as living in congested destitution and apparently had been in much the same state for as long as anyone could remember. They had survived the previous forty years, both good and bad, without leaving a record either of starvation or defiance. But what is clear in the record of Ballykilcline is that after paying even these modest rents, tithes, and cesses, no surplus of cash or goods remained among the occupants to be expended on anything else that might improve their material life nor even to bring them within the range of the "goods explosion" of mid-nineteenth-century Europe. With apparently scant exception, the evidence of their material possessions before the famine did not include glass windows, manufactured shoes, eyeglasses, steel tools other than the spade and sickle, mirrors or combs, steel needles or scissors, patent medicines, or manufactured soaps.[11] Paper, writing implements, and steel weapons were in very short supply, although many in the townland knew well how to use them. As everywhere among the Irish peasantry, however, there was a steady and relished consumption of the products of the century before, tea, sugar, and tobacco, imported and all addictive and therefore regarded now as "necessities" by most of the population. Of the same generation of manufacture, imported woollens and cotton cloth, in the form of secondhand clothes, hats, ribbons, and women's "fancies" (cotton undergarments and "kerchiefs" of many colors) had intruded on peasant life to the degree in which they were employed as symbols of "microstatus" within the townlands, separating the haves and the have nots in their economy of minimum consumption. The decline of native production and investment that followed the wars and the Act of Union was at least partly responsible for the scarcity of these manufactured goods among the peasantry, as was the scarcity of the skills to produce, process, and distribute them without the town middlemen. Ironically, of the remaining native skills, the chemistry of distillation and the elementary metallurgy that went with it was methodically and brutally suppppressed.[12]

It is possible to place the material life of the population of Ballykilcline in approximate relation to that of the rest of the Irish peasantry of the 1830s. For more than a century, the small farmers of Roscommon had been under pressure from graziers to vacate or contract their holdings through enclosure, reducing many of them to cottiers or landless laborers, depending on wages and marginal tillage for subsistence. This was the most common condition of the people of Ballykilcline and the neighboring townlands. Measured only by the available evidence of its diet, housing, and clothing; its wealth in cash, crops, animals, and access to land; and by what can be inferred of its private domestic possessions, the townland must be seen as somewhere near the middle of the scale between the least prosperous artisans and small "farmers" who enjoyed some fixity of tenure in their land and the most bereft "rundale" peasants of the west coast, such as those in the Donegal parish of Gweedore. Within this range, everything suggests that they were closer to the latter than to the former in their access to material possessions.

No such inventory of possessions exists for Ballykilcline as that compiled by the National School teacher for the district of Gweedore, on the harsh northwesterly coast of the island. That parish was made famous by the pamphlet *Facts from Gweedore,* which was published by its landlord, Lord George Hill, to prescribe and defend his methods of eradicating the "rundale sys-

..n" of settlement and land use, which he saw as the main obstacle to rational improvement in western Ireland.[13] Although Gweedore may be taken to be, as E. Estyn Evans put it, "a model of a region of difficulty and survival" and an index of an extreme scarcity of goods and tools, most evidence suggests that the bulk of the townland populations were a good deal closer to its level of material life than to that of the fifty-acre farmers referred to as "Class II" in the 1841 census: those occupying well-maintained houses of more than one story, mostly English-speaking or bilingual, already half-wedded to the prudish values and polite pretensions of Victorian Ireland, consuming a diet ruled more by meat and dairy goods than by the potato, accustomed to firearms, and politically active. This class was a rough, fledgling version of the respectable yeomanry of Kent or Lincolnshire. These farmers and their households were an emerging model of the crafty, devout, and conservative countryman that dominates most of our images of old Ireland. In his "memorial" of 1837, the National School teacher made an inventory of possessions he found among the four thousand inhabitants of his parish: the material wealth of the community consisted of 1 cart, no coach or any other vehicle, 1 plough, 20 shovels, 32 rakes, 7 table forks, 93 chairs, 243 stools, 2 feather beds, 8 chaff beds, 3 turkeys, 27 geese, no bonnet, no clock, 3 watches, no looking glass above 3d. in price, and no more than 10 square feet of glass.[14]

There is no reason to doubt the accuracy of the Donegal teacher's account, bearing in mind that he was admittedly describing a starving population—as he put it, "looking at their children likely to expire in the jaws of starvation." He claims to have traveled very widely in Ireland, England, and Scotland, as well as in Canada and seven of the United States and "never witnessed the tenth part of such hunger, hardships, and nakedness." What seems to be wanting in his compassionate account is a perspective that might have led him to ask if such amenities as mirrors and feather beds had *ever* been present in Gweedore. The absence of such things as clocks, watches, coaches, bonnets, boots, or looking glasses, at least, could not have been remarkable to a seasoned Irish traveler, almost none of whom failed to note the shocking scarcity of those manufactured goods that had become commonplace even in the poorest villages and slum tenements of western Europe.

Though its population was much more numerous, Gweedore's inventory of goods does not differ sharply from what the inhabitants of Pobble O'Keefe or Irvillaughter, on Crown estates in Cork and Galway, counted among their possessions. As in Ballykilcline, the dwellings were described as miserable huts, the holdings minute, and the lands burned out. In the scale employed by the Irish census of 1841 in classifying the rural population, *all* of the people of Ballykilcline would have fallen into "Class III," which included laborers, smallholders, and "other persons without capital, in either money, land, or acquired knowledge" (presumably meaning education). They were a part of the 68 percent of the rural population in this category in 1841. Their wealth in land could not be measured by their possession of it, since they owned none in law. In this regard, they were among the 81 percent (94 percent in Connaught) of the entire agricultural population occupying holdings of fewer than fifteen acres. With average household holdings of just under eight acres (barely over one acre for each person), Ballykilcline belonged to that majority of the farming population in the country as a whole (55 percent) that held fewer than ten acres.[15] Land was, of course, the principal measure of wealth and welfare in the country, as in any peasant society. But for the townland peasantry it was measured not by posssession of land but by access to it, since virtually none owned their small parcels and few even held long leases to them. All the inhabitants of Ballykilcline were "Tenants from Year to Year, or at Will," as the Crown commissioners described them.

Without either the reserve capital that tenant right represented or the security of tenure that even short leases assured, the people of Ballykilcline can be described only as landless agrarian laborers. As the events of the 1840s were to show, the once all-important distinctions between those "holding" twelve or fifteen acres as tenants-at-will, the "farmers," and those to whom they might let an acre or two from year to year to sow potatoes were becoming something of a cherished illusion. Everyone knew very well who the "important" farmers were; they were dependent upon them for access to the land and often as their defenders and mediators with the law and the landed elite. It is also evident that members of this townland "elite" were themselves highly conscious and sensitive about their standing. Because their holdings might be lost at almost any time, this status did not depend on land alone but on a variety of personal, mental, and traditional factors like courage, intelligence, or the possession of a "good name," with the weight of generations behind it. It was such intangible qualities as these that accounted for the leading role played by the strong family of Connors in the townland. For the most part, it was through these leading figures that the townland's relations with the outside were conducted—with the landlord's agents, the tax and tithe collectors, and, at critical moments, with the police authorities.

In Ballykilcline these figures became known as the "Defendants," a word too close to the "Defenders" of 1798 to have no meaning in this part of the country. As events were to show, to the local Ascendancy and its deputies this term meant little more than the list of tenants who defied notices of eviction and illegally reoccupied their homes. Apart from that act and the appearance of their names in the rent ledger, no other form of identity could be assigned to them from outside the townland. This was their best defense against official surveillance and turned out to be a real threat to law and order in the neighborhood. There is also convincing evidence that this microelite took a kind of authority unto itself, enforcing compliance to its decisions and "disciplining" individuals who tried to make private accommodations with the outside. In the case of Ballykilcline, it was a largely inadvertent threat to this social arrangement—the routine notices of eviction of the tenants of record for nonpayment—that precipitated the townland's defiance and set into motion the events that ended in its destruction. It becomes clear once the rent strike takes on the reputation of a "rebellion" in the neighborhood that a few of the unrecorded tenants also carried some clout in the community, but the Crown's agents and informers were essentially right in thinking that by thus provoking the larger tenants they had bestirred a collective panic and a will to resist in all but a few cabins.

Without the paraphernalia of petty possessions to display rank in the form of adornments of dress or dwellings, the social distinctions of the townland remained almost invisible to the outside and even to many quite nearby. Shoes and hats were present in the townland, but they were rare—none for women and children and not more than a dozen or two worn by adult men. Almost certainly, the hats were signs of status in the townland, as they became among many "pacified" native Americans or Polynesians. The manufactured brimmed or high-crowned hats of felt, battered shapeless, sweat-stained, and drooping from rain, that clearly marked the "Paddy" in caricature and in the earliest photographs, had not been long in rural Ireland. This haberdashery had never been manufactured locally; a generation out of fashion elsewhere, most had adorned more genteel heads years before and had finally been picked up for pennies near the end of their half-life from the itinerant peddlers of second-hand goods who plied the market-day crowds in country towns like Strokestown. They were part of the flotsam and jetsam of the rag trade flowing from east to west circuitously seeking its lowest market, where the final drops of profit could be wrung out. Like leaves in the wind, there is no telling how far they had blown or what path they had followed before settling on the heads of Connor and McDermott, the commanding figures of Ballykilcline. Shoes traveled the same silent routes, along with sundry other manufactured and processed items from within the industrial core of western Europe, and some, like cotton cloth, tea, or tobacco, from distances beyond the cognizance of the townlanders. This was one of the markets of last resort in Europe, where commodities of the lowest and most exhausted quality found their last buyer.

Comforting as they were in wet and stony Ireland, such personal adornments as shoes and hats were no more a necessity at this time than ladies' ribbons or mirrors, since most of the population went without them entirely. They were small luxuries whose value was mainly symbolic and whose use was controlled by social norms within the townland. The dress of the men, women, and children, whether homespun, secondhand, or merely ragged, was close to uniform and easily recognized by friend or outsider as a badge of townland poverty. Excessive display of such accessories as shoes, hats, or colored ribbons, or their misuse as "vanities," stood out conspicuously and could become the object of community disapproval or ridicule— as such foibles often were also in Victorian caricature of the Irish.

Chastising strictures operated over a wide range of behavior in the townland. Some, like the penalties imposed on one who took up the holding of an evicted neighbor, were often very violent because such an act was seen as an open challenge to fundamental social and familial bonds. Such punitive assaults tended to become more severe as the threat to those bonds increased, not only the tangible outside threats from collectors and constables but the inevitable defections that weakened the protective shell of conformity. Strong farmers and graziers who rejected customary reciprocities and obligations could be slandered or derided as "Englishman" or "Sassenach," implying not so much political disloyalty as a lack of generosity. Disgruntled sons might invoke communal custom against fathers refusing to subdivide farms. In return, parents often cursed sons and daughters for abandonment if they sought to escape the soul-killing tyrannies of their communal poverty through emigration.[16]

Scarcity was also the determinant of townland economies. It was the premise upon which many of its communal values rested—the goods of the earth were finite and an unequal share could be had by one individual only at the expense of another. Unlike some other peasant communities of Europe, Irish townlands never became explicitly egalitarian in dealing with land or property, but they did develop a "moral economy" that generally condemned private initiative and accumulation as something alien and inimical to the community. Before the nineteenth century, when there was little prospect of a surplus of wealth in the countryside as far as the native peasantry was concerned, this outlook was also a strategy of survival: any added "layers" of middlemen in the land system would simply tighten the noose of subsistence a bit further. What surpluses arose with the rising food prices of the Napoleonic war years widened the gap between them and the "strong" farmers who had the disposition and resources, especially in leases to land, to take advantage of changes in the market. It was that disposition that came between the two native classes, since it was composed of values that were in conflict with those of townland poverty.

The depression following the wartime boom after 1815 both enlarged the economic gap and magnified the cultural differences already present between these rural classes, separating them along a fault line of social and personal choices from their fashion of dress and dwelling to the emotional basis of marriage and kinship, one preferring to marry late and keep their holdings intact and the other marrying young and subdividing in the face of certain hardship. The well-clad, neatly housed, and pragmatic farmer, mocked as the upstart "jackeen" in the laborer's cabin, scorned contact and rejected identification with the ragged denizens of the townlands. Social equality had never reigned in Ireland, but the development of this agrarian middle class in the nineteenth century added yet another layer of "alien" culture in the eyes of poor. Sectarian passions were also mixed into these relations by the persistent view, originating in the Penal Laws era, that conversions from the native faith were nothing more than sheer venality. When added to competing interests on the land, as in disputes over the rents and rights of subtenants and laborers, the breach between these native classes could also express itself violently. This tendency was clearly on the rise in the countryside in the decades before the famine, fueled by the increasing land hunger in general as well as by the "defection" of individuals and families from the communalities of the past, and the half-hated, half-cherished poverty that went with them.[17]

The conflict within the peasantry was above all about food, and therefore about land. But it was also at the center of an internal moral and social crisis that townlands like Ballykilcline were experiencing in the 1830s and 1840s. There is too little evidence to tell how the increasing scarcity of the forties and the intensification of conflict that went with it permeated private life, especially family life, in the townland. But all general indications of the period suggest that the conflicts being played out because of scarcity between classes and competing neighbors did penetrate relations between fathers and sons, in which access to land defined both paternal authority and youth's expectations of marriage and status in the community. Although there is characteristically little mention of women in the townland records, it is also to be expected that similar conflicts radiated into relations between man and wife as well, especially where the traditional roles of paternal power were being conspicuously overwhelmed by circumstances.[18]

Another aspect of the culture of scarcity is faintly visible in some oddly ascetic values associated with the consumption of goods. Just as acquisitiveness or hoarding were still generally held by subsistence tenants as violations of traditional moral proprieties, private immodesty in dress, discordant pretensions of manner or speech or personal vanities in man or woman could bring sharp rebuke or ridicule down on individuals or entire families. The townland strove to maintain its covert economy with an internal moral and even aesthetic code that was equally at odds with that emerging all around it.

The profusion of goods coming within the reach even of the remote countryside in the decades before the famine, however trifling in value and quality, posed another challenge to the community. The brightly colored ribbons and kerchiefs, the mirrors, combs, razors, scissors, scents, cosmetics, cotton goods, toys, and weapons—sometimes "illustrated" in labels and catalogues—represented a more insinuating side of that challenge than evictions or greedy farmers. These trinkets were the alluring tokens of progress and of the sheer potency of the civilization above them that in the end could not be resisted by either force or guile. They had not been utterly unknown in most of the country, but previously they had belonged for the most part to an alien elite, safely beyond the means or desires of the poor. But their widening proliferation across that onetime barrier, first among the households of townsmen and commercial farmers and (as the Gweedore inventory suggests) more slowly down to the peasant populations, was a mortal threat to the intuitive bonds of the community. They contained glimmerings of knowledge of the outside world—very often fantasies of it—that loosened loyalties to a withering culture, especially among the young. Indeed, it may have been that the fantasies were even more corrosive of old bonds even than concrete knowledge, for in the process of trying to survive in isolation, townland society employed both a moral stigma and a willful ignorance of the outside world as part of its strategy—its intermediaries filtered information and distorted realities that were felt to threaten its moral foundation. In its struggle against a contending ethic of commerce and individualism, this set of intuitions was the identifying core of the townland community. The townland did not wish its poverty on itself, but unable to escape it, made it work for a while as a unifying banner of resistance.

Beneath the emotional and moral responses it produced, scarcity was the main objective reality to be faced by the townland mentality. Its characteristic features—its fatalism, its hatred of vanity, its faith in luck, its furtiveness and combustibility—were natural responses to the demands that scarcity imposed on both communities and individuals. All its traits had cultural roots in the deep past, but seldom before had the pressures on the peasants' resources to assure food and shelter been more intense than in the generation before the famine. Overpopulation, subdivision, falling prices, lean years, debt, and rising evictions—ruinous poverty varying from place to place but witnessed by all—could not but have heightened the emotional uncertainty at the center of their experience. In their letters and "petitions," as well as in their more violent efforts to keep hold of the land, their panic and rage is clear—the ultimate shame of beggary, which a great many of them were in fact soon to experience, approached more closely each year. So, it is not unexpected to find in that generation a rising incidence of violence, rural "outrages," and conspiracies against those felt to be outside its moral boundaries, including many of their own class and kin.[19]

Traditional forms of cooperation among neighbors in labor and landholding, like *meitheall* or "cooring," joint holdings in both land and animals, and "booleying"[20] were also adaptable to the struggle with scarcity and, perhaps equally as important, they could help to restrain the annual panics and the inevitable internal squabbling and "defections" that came with them. As the threat mounted, communal discipline and solidarity became all the more necessary, and in enforcing them the townland employed a variety of devices, both coercive and persuasive. They were aided inadvertently in this by the general hostility and fear of the classes above them, which reinforced their social segregation and obstructed communication between the townland and the outside. That gap had been present for centuries but had widened as the acceptable standards of material life and civility had risen among the people of property even in rural Ireland. Especially, perceptions of poverty had changed on their part, making it more than ever a moral stigma, an inherent failure of character and intelligence, and something increasingly associated with the general stigma of race. The absence of the material goods to articulate social distinctions and pretensions also tended to confirm impressions that had taken root long before both in Ireland and Britain: that the rural poor of Ireland were a more or less uniform mass whose individuality was hardly discernible, except perhaps by gender or age. In a sense, the poverty of the townland population became its identity both in their own eyes and in those of all others, hostile or benevolent, who came into contact with them.

3

Land and Society around Strokestown

Q. *Is it true that the Irish landlords squeeze their tenants as much*
as posssible?

A. *Yes. But they are in great trouble themselves.*

> Alexis de Tocqueville and Mr.
> West, Member of Parliament for
> Galway, 1835[1]

Peasants and landlords of the nineteenth century lived in an economy of
arrears. Nearly everywhere in the Old World debt was as intrinsic a part of
the tenant-farmer's life as the smell of manure or the fickle weather. But
debt, being man-made, was often the source of great bitterness and conflict. In the peasant nostalgia of Ireland, the weight of debt was always
thought to have been lighter on all previous generations and the penalties
for default far more devastating than they used to be. Arrears of all kinds,
outstanding pledges and "fines," promises of labor, crop shares, or grazing rights between neighbors and kin were not only expected and tolerated
as an unavoidable necessity of life but formed an important bond within
the townland community: a concrete expression of belonging and of adherence to traditional codes of conduct. But money debts in the cash-poor
countryside divided both classes and cultures.

The network of owing that was so characteristic of the subsistence sector of Irish agriculture was unmistakably sanctioned by the cottiers' moral
economy and was essential to their survival in conditions of more or less
permanent scarcity. The way in which debt was regulated among equals in
the townlands by the 1830s still bore many traces of the distant past: labor,
land, and cattle were the only large denominations of currency or credit
among them; reciprocity, joint ownership, and the inalienability of land still
ordained the moral canons of transaction; the oral tradition as interpreted

36

by memory, not statute, defined the law. Resort to the police, the sheriff, or the courts in settling their disputes was a clear betrayal of these principles, though the perennial factiousness of these communities together with the slow erosion of their solidarity made the intervention of outside authorities a common occurrence. Dominant families and individuals are detectable in the townlands on close examination, but ascriptive status or privileges were minimal—both the individual's and the family's reputation and honor had to be constantly negotiated but depended always on their adherence to these community norms and even more so on intangible virtues of character, talent, and intellect, as these qualities were gauged in a culture with few outward signs of one's worth.

In practice, there had always been notorious sources of conflict as well; perpetual, almost ritual disputation, family feuds, and occasional violence were the accustomed ways of settling differences over the fine points of the moral code. Up to a point, even these disputes could be a constructive form of social intercourse or occasions for the community to voice its collective will. This was the milieu in which the leading figures of Ballykilcline—the "Defendants"—flourished. In the microcosm of the townland they could be distinguished from their neighbors; some raised cattle and grains for the market and some collected rents from subtenants. They were "farmers" in the eyes of the townland, but they were also small tenants and laborers who might be seen toiling for wages beside their neighbors in the fields of the demesne and those of the big farmers. Their authority still sprang more from family history or personal qualities of intelligence and memory than from any substantial advantage in land or material wealth. Among these relative equals at the lowest end of the rural economy, this "throughother"[2] process of settling obligations produced a surprising degree of social harmony, despite the apparent chaos; at the least, it put limits to the conflict over land, since among the weak the punishment for debt could not be very harsh and the ultimate penalty, eviction from the land, was beyond the power even of the strongest.

But such methods did not necessarily apply to dealings between the townland and the lords of the land and their agents. Increasingly, they also failed to apply to those layers of the agricultural population that had begun to adopt a more commercial ethic in which profit rather than equity in the access to land was uppermost and calling in the bailiff was considered nothing more than doing business. Thus, the intensifying bitterness between the cottier-laborers and the commercial farmers became the main source of violence as the century progressed; this was as much a conflict of basic cultural values as of economic interests—an oppressive Catholic farmer was seen not only as an oppressor but as a betrayer, in a category akin to the accursed informer or convert. What can be seen of the relations between the cottiers and farmers around Strokestown also tends to bear these feelings out: in the crises of the forties, the Catholic farmers always distanced themselves from the tenants and, even in some sectarian conflicts, they succumbed to pressures to ingratiate themselves with the Ascendancy, on whom most of them were dependent. Among the farmers, graziers, and squireens in the area of Strokestown, that dependency also rested on reciprocities, including the exchange of allegiance and social deference for access to land.

Among the larger landlords, the most familiar practice in managing the land was to sublet to resident middlemen of the area in substantial blocks; most of these, in turn, were accustomed to lease smaller portions on shorter leases, creating several layers of intermediaries between the lords of the land and the peasantry who worked it. Many of the larger and middling landlords in this pyramid had long since begun to adhere to the same commercial ethic, some ruthlessly and others halfheartedly, before the "upstart" native farmer had become a familiar phenomenon in the three decades before the famine. It is safe to say that nearly all were resented to some degree by those who shouldered the pyramid of rents. To some extent, this was because the accustomed lords of the Ascendancy, especially those like Lord Hartland who remained resident, were still under some constraint from the long tradition of paternalism, a central part of which was the toleration of debt among the tenants as something that the nature of the country made inescapable. That toleration also had a sibling in the subculture of clientage among the indebted Protestant squirearchy that cemented loyalties within the provincial gentry, loyalties seen by many as essential to their survival amid a sea of bitterness and conspiracy. Conspicuous abuses of either custom, like the blatant rack-renting of cottiers or the "ruining" of gentlemen tenants, could still do damage to a family's good name among its peers. In that sense at least, the cottiers and the gentry on the land colluded in upholding an old regime of economic values that was about to bring ruin to a large part of both under the weight of nearly universal debt.

In the crisis that gripped the Barony of Ballintobber in Roscommon on the eve of the famine, the violence from below and the resort to force from above was ignited primarily by the calling in of those debts, dissolving an archaic social contract that had never produced real harmony or prosperity but had evaded the general desperation that now spread through all classes.

The Mahon Murder

In the eyes of the outside world, nothing had ever happened in or around Strokestown of greater consequence than the murder of Denis Mahon, a Major in the famed 9th Lancers and heir to the Hartland estate, on the evening of 2 November 1847. Six other landlords were killed and one badly wounded that winter, as well as at least ten middlemen. Horrified attention was given to the "outrages" throughout the press in Ireland and England. New emergency police powers were voted by Parliament in the "Crime and Outrage Bill" at the insistence of Lord Clarendon, the Lord Lieutenant, including a "black act" that imposed condign penalties on men moving about at night in disguise or blackened faces. Culprits and suspects of these or other crimes were rounded up in each district, many were tried and some convicted—and a few, some of them probably guilty, hanged in public. But no case riveted public attention in Ireland and abroad as did the shooting of Major Mahon of Strokestown, by some accounts a fair landlord and a philanthropic man. And no other event, other than the famine itself, did more to undermine relations between the classes of the district, as well as those between the town and the townlands around it. Objectively, the two events were unrelated; Mahon's murder resulted from a policy of clearances he had set in motion years before the blight. But in the minds of the tenantry, not unnaturally, their desperate suffering and the heartlessness of eviction were inseparable links in a causal chain.

Mahon had become the heir to the extensive Hartland lands in Roscommon two years before and was a leader in organizing relief schemes for the area in the second year of the famine. On the evening of his death he was returning by carriage in the company of a friend, Dr. Terence Shanley, and his coachman, William Flanagan, from a meeting of the Board of Guardians in Roscommon town. Dusk was falling as they approached a bridge at Fourmilehouse near Doorty, one of the twenty-eight townlands on his own lands. According to Shanley, the Major held the reins of the phaeton himself and having just looked at his watch said to his friend, "Ten minutes before six. We should be home about half past six." Two blasts of "duck shot" were then fired from behind the coping of Doorty bridge, one wounding Shanley and a second hitting Mahon squarely in the chest. He was said to have cried "O, God," before falling dead.[3]

It was an immediate sensation in the Irish and English press, both of which gave detailed coverage of the murder and the subsequent investigation. Furious speeches were made in Parliament on homicidal conspiracies in Ireland and the iniquity of the people—and in retort by Henry Grattan, Jr., on the iniquities of the land system and landlord callousness, especially mass evictions and forced emigration in the midst of famine. The latter referred to the assisted emigration of some nine hundred tenants from Mahon's townlands in the spring of the same year. It had been rumored among the remaining tenants that hundreds of their kin and neighbors had perished by shipwreck owing to Mahon's miserly arrangements for the voyage. The rumor of shipwreck was false, although the real fate of the emigrants on their arrival in Canada at the infamous Grosse Isle quarantine would have proved at least as infuriating in the townlands: of the nearly 500 emigrants aboard the *Virginius* out of Liverpool, 158 had died at sea and the rest were described by the Canadian medical officer as "ghastly, yellow-looking spectres" as they emerged from the holds. No more than 6 or 8 were reported well enough to disembark on their own. Together with the ships chartered by Lord Palmerston to send out his Sligo tenants in the same year, the *Virginius* became the emblematic image of the "coffin ship" as it took shape in the first years of the famine.[4]

Bonfires were reported burning for miles around Strokestown on the night of the murder. Most of the public, the press, and the M.P.'s naturally assumed that the shooting was an act of revenge carried out by conspiracy.

The first findings of the local police inspectors, reported in the *Times*, confirmed and expanded speculation on the existence of a widespread plot: "From the conduct of all the parties in the vicinity brought before us, and their uniform denial of all circumstances which must have been within their knowledge, we can have no doubt but that an extensive and deep-laid conspiracy existed against the gentleman's life." The police also claimed to have reason to believe that "a general resistance against rents and the legal exercise of the rights of property is in existence and likely to extend."[5]

The supposed plot was ideally suited to be enshrined in either the Ascendancy or the nationalist parable of famine "outrages" just then being born. Mahon was either a paragon of landlord paternalism, forgiving arrears, tirelessly organizing relief for the starving, and rescuing thousands at great personal expense by sending them to a land of plenty. Or he was the personification of landlord rapacity—as he himself paraphrased a local critic—"amusing" himself in "burning houses and turning out the people to starve."[6] While neither version throws much light on the assassins' motives, which have remained murky to this day, the murder catalyzed feelings at all levels of local society that throw an uncommon shaft of light into the obscurity that otherwise conceals most of provincial life and relations during these years.

Sides had to be chosen in Parliament, in the country houses and market towns, and even in the townlands; dormant sources of conflict were exposed along lines of property, sect, and race and within each; and the grisly conjunction of murder and starvation released a nearly universal denunciation of the foundering land system. In the formerly torpid locale of the murder, now swarming with police and dragoons and buzzing with dire rumors, the incident produced a near-panicked sense of urgency on all sides and at all levels of society. As much as any other single event, the murder exposed the "great fear" of 1847 in Ireland. Local men of property armed themselves against imagined threats and ambush, demanding troops to "put the land to rights" and crush defiance by the harshest measures. From the already starving townlands came oaths of obedience and peaceful intentions in the hopes of escaping retribution and surviving on the land.

The prevailing emotion in the townlands was fear, mixed with but more than anger. It is clear that Ballykilcline's open conflict with the Crown and its agents, filling nearly ten years of local history beginning with first evictions in 1836, was well known and closely followed by their neighbors and kin. Indeed, it was given the honorific title of the "Ballykilcline rebellion" by its neighbors. The other townlands are otherwise silent, but their lives were intertwined by both history and biology to such a degree that to know something of one is to know something of them all.

The People of Ballintobber, Roscommon, in the 1840s

Official surveys tell little about the thinking of the common people, but they clearly highlight some of the stark contrasts in the material life of the rich and the poor. According to the 1841 Census of Ireland, County Roscommon contained 253,591 men, women, and children dwelling in slightly more than 45,000 houses scattered across the county's 585,408 acres. The east-central section of the county, in which the town of Strokestown and the townland of Ballykilcline were located, is designated in the census as the Barony of Ballintobber North, an area of about sixty square miles containing a population of 19,370, about 323 people per square mile.[7]

A number of contrasts might be made between this part of Roscommon and other regions of the country. It was well within the network of good roads and canals that had sprawled from Dublin eastward in the half century before the famine and was therefore less removed than most of Connaught from metropolitan commerce and culture. This position was reflected in the local economy, whose priorities responded to fluctuations in the international market more promptly than those farther west. The big farmers and landlords of the neighborhood, who were mostly resident, shifted from grains to grazing and back again as prices in the English market rose and fell after the Napoleonic Wars. Market towns like Strokestown, with their provincial amenities, petty middle classes, police barracks, schools, and shops, were fairly numerous and not widely separated. Commercial travelers, magistrates, factors, and peddlers ate and drank their bread and beer and conversed in English with the local notables and farmers in the licensed houses on fair days. Any European would have recognized it as at least an outlying part of Europe's own civilization, hierarchical, commercial, and geometrically laid out.

At the same time, visible among the market crowds, in the back lanes of the main streets or within strolling distance of the town was a world at least half-apart—ragged, shoeless, and uncombed, speaking an exotic tongue, believing in miracles and charms, and surviving on a diet most thought fit only for beasts. Situated very near the geographical center of the country, the Barony of Balintobber North was a mixture of rural Ireland's contradictions. The classification of the houses of the barony in the 1841 census gives a clear picture of the spectrum of wealth and status it contained, although the classification's accuracy becomes more doubtful at the lower end of the scale. The census takers used four classes in their survey of dwellings: the first class included all structures from the mansions of the great down to substantial houses averaging somewhere near £200 in the cost of their construction; the second included the good farmhouses of the countryside and respectable townhouses. The third and fourth classes, descending to mud-built cabins of one room, are more difficult to distinguish by the familiar evaluations of stories, glass windows, and outbuildings, since their construction did not differ radically in these features, nearly all being without them. One estimate of the lower order of dwelling occupied by the majority of the rural population puts the cost of construction of the better sort (that is, third class) at £6–£10 and the lowest at £3–£5. It is probable that a still lower order of habitation, the troglodyte dwellings described by Tocqueville and some recent scholars, was frequently missed by the census walkers.[8] Of the 3,414 houses of Ballintobber North, the census counted 6 in the first class, 241 in the second, 1,622 in the third and 1,498 in the lowest (with 43 uninhabited and 4 "under construction").[9]

At first sight, the scarcity of first-class houses in the barony is the most striking of these numbers. Many more houses of £200 value would be found in eastern districts of this size and the number approached zero in many parts of the far West. But it is not atypical of the mixed settlement of resident landowners in the midlands, whose numbers tended to thin out with remoteness. Even though such numbers alone do not tell us very much about the routine of life among the landed elite in Roscommon, they do suggest the limited social attractions and relative isolation from others of their class that many landed families found in rural Ireland—that was one of the main inducements of landlord absenteeism. Added to the wide cultural gap between them and the general population, that isolation probably helps to explain as well their addiction to rumor, their constant suspicion of conspiracy, and the occasional trigger-happiness of the local gentry when the townlands showed signs of open defiance.

The Landowners

There was a "striking slatternliness as common to the rich as to the poor" in rural Ireland. Many a mansion was "as untidy in its half-cut woods, its trampled avenues, its moss-grown parks, its fallen piers, its shattered chimney stacks, as the cabin with its dung-pit steaming at the door, its few sorry beasts gathered within doors for the night, its swarm of scarce-clad children running wild on the earthen floor. The slatternliness of the Big House was barbaric: there was wealth without refinement and power without responsibility." All witnesses since the previous century seem to agree about the general dishevelment and neglect of the countryside. "Anti-Christ governed the Catholic poor, not without difficulty," Daniel Corkery said, "but the Lord of Misrule governed everything: and did so with merely a reckless and daring gesture: at his behest it was that everyone lived well beyond his means."[10] Here Corkery was describing the houses of the old Gaelic families of Munster, but it was a taste the country seems to have imposed on the provincial gentry of any confession.

Far from calming the relations between rich and poor, this fraternal slovenliness merely undermined the security that the landed classes might have enjoyed if they had been able to keep their houses in order. Most lords and squires were inclined to see their conflicts with the tenantry as ipso facto conflicts between the common people and the state. By and large, the landlords expected and received almost unquestioned support from the police, the magistracy, and the military apparatus in their disputes with tenants who combined against them, with or without violence. But the tide had slowly begun to turn against the Irish landlord by the beginning of Queen Victoria's reign. The constant demand from the Irish landlords for armed force against refractory tenants, on the one hand, and the increasing tendency of the parliamentary and Crown authorities to view the Irish landlord as a crude and wastrel cousin, undermined public sympathy for them in England, especially in progressive and humanitarian circles. Lord John Russell voiced the growing rift in a debate over Irish landlord demands for yet another expansion of police powers: "It is quite true that landlords in England would not like to be shot like hares and partridges . . . but neither does any landlord in England turn out fifty persons at once and burn their houses over their heads, giving no provision for the future."[11] While some sentiments for the Irish peasantry may have been touched, the metropolitan image of "Paddy" did not improve in this process.

As conditions worsened and the costs of relieving the distress of the defunct land system were debated, both Parliament and Dublin Castle tended increasingly to damn both lord and peasant as equally outside the pale, leaving many of the Irish gentry feeling marooned on the smaller island. Partly because of the tainted odor of their deeds in the country, the mere possession of Irish land or title never conferred the status or honor of comparable holdings in the tamed English countryside or even in the backwood glens of Scotland. All the more in the softened patrician values of early-Victorian England, the Irish landlords bore a stigma of callousness and improvidence among those whom they would like to regard as their equals in the mother country. Absentee landlords, if anything, were regarded with even greater distaste. Even before the shameful disclosures of the parliamentary inquiries of the thirties and forties and the worldwide opprobrium accompanying the famine, public opinion in the capital had been primed to impose some discipline on the profligate Irish landlord, which it did in the Encumbered Estates Act of 1849. Although fraternal rather than punitive, like scolding a younger sibling, the act clearly proclaimed English disapproval of the way the Irish landlord had abused the privilege of his property.

From a very different quarter, Marx and Engels, always drawn but puzzled by the peculiarities and contradictions of the Irish land system (which neither had observed firsthand), offered a much-quoted caricature of the Irish landlord. The landowners, who everywhere else have become "bourgeoisified," are here reduced to comic penury.

> Their country-seats are surrounded by enormous, amazingly beautiful parks, but all around is waste land. . . . These fellows are droll enough to make your sides burst with laughing. Of mixed blood, mostly tall, strong handsome chaps, they all wear enormous moustaches under colossal Roman noses, give themselves the false military airs of retired colonels, travel around the country after all sorts of pleasures, and if one makes an inquiry, they haven't a penny, are laden with debts, and live in dread of the Encumbered Estates Court.[12]

Of the Anglo-Irish gentry, the most prominent member regularly resident in the immediate vicinity of Ballykilcline was the Reverend Maurice Mahon, the third Lord Hartland, who was Ballykilcline's landlord until

1834. The Marquess of Westmeath, whose lands surrounded Ballykilcline on three sides, was rarely in the country. The Mahon family had dominated the history of the area, in fact, since the Williamite conquest. Thirty thousand acres of what had once been the ancestral lands of the O'Connors had been confiscated in the Cromwellian conquest and were finally endowed by Letters Patent upon Maurice Mahon in 1695 in recognition of his service in subjugating the country. The Mahons remained a powerful but untitled family until 1800, when Maurice Mahon was created a Peer of Ireland as the first Baron Hartland in recognition of his role in dissolving the Irish Parliament, of which he had been a member.[13]

Although the Mahons would eventually come to resemble Engels's caricature of the insolvent Irish gentry, throughout their early history they enjoyed wealth, prosperity, and high station, eventually marrying into the family of the Earls of Longford and thereby becoming close in-laws of the great Duke of Wellington. Even before achieving this high station, the Mahons had gained prominence among the Roscommon gentry; in the early eighteenth century they had begun construction of a stylish Palladian mansion in the Italianate fashion of the time, surrounded by profligate acres of deer and park land, gardens employing some fifteen gardeners, oak and beech walks, and the various "follies" and whimsies in vogue on the country estates of Georgian England and Ireland.

In his tour of Ireland in 1770s, Arthur Young described the parks of Strokestown House as the finest he observed in the country. The first Baron Hartland also planned and reconstructed the town of Strokestown, which sat on his lands, along lines that he thought suitable to the rising stature of the family and, as many others expected at the turn of the century, the rising prospects for commerce in Ireland. The main street of this obscure market town he wished to be on a scale with the widest market street in Europe, with the ornate gothic gates of his demesne closing one end and the gray-stone and spired Church of Ireland parish facing it at the other. He endowed a free school, a textile dying and finishing manufactory, and a brewery in the town, which for a time succeeded in furnishing wage labor to the people of the surrounding townlands. The enlightened efforts of the first Baron Hartland to bring his part of the Irish midlands into the metropolitan world could not be called a total success—Strokestown remained a provincial market town of secondary importance, even locally. But, as we shall see, the town generated enough vigor before the famine to open a crack in the curtain between town and country that let some light in and some peasants out. Some of these settled as a rudimentary working and serving class in town and supplied one of the principal lines of communication for the townland with the outside. A few, like Johnny Cox, one of the local "drivers" of townland families, served as a reverse conduit, transmitting and "filtering" information to the land and legal system represented by the town.

The history of the town and estate under Lord Hartland's heirs mirrored the general torpor that settled on the Irish economy after 1815. The Reverend Maurice Mahon, the third and last Baron Hartland, was complacent or incompetent in managing the estate, leaving it deeply in debt arrears when he went mad, according to a commission "de lunatico inquirendo," on 15 February 1836.[14] The last of the Barons Hartland were clearly not up to the standard of their father. The second Baron had also run up debts to his own tenants and the last, "poor Maurice . . . the best natured soul that ever graced a pulpit," as a family friend described him, was distracted from the things of this world.

The sad end to the short-lived Mahon line seems to have been brought about by a series of calamities in the summer of 1830. The second Baron, Thomas, was laid low by an accident in that year, leaving land and title to Maurice. By a sad coincidence of misfortunes for both the family and its tenants, the heir apparent had recently been committed to private care after a mental collapse. He had apparently been likeably feebleminded for some years, able occasionally to deliver his Sunday sermons but otherwise confined to the house, where he was cared for within the family with the help of Mick Black, who had been his personal servant and protector since his youth. The immediate cause of his final collapse is unclear, but a report from his guardian to Lady Hartland suggests that it had been brought on by the departure that summer of his wife, the former Miss Hume of Wicklow, together with her daughter of a previous marriage.[15] "Poor Maurice is wonderfully better," the guardian wrote describing a visit with the baron, "he was quite collected & quiet and did not say one word we could have wished different. . . . [A]s to the servant, we are quite sure that in a few days he will be quite reconciled, but at first he thought it was somebody to controul [*sic*] him—and he said he was used to Mick Black, and he did not like a stranger." A separate allowance had been arranged for the departed Mrs. Mahon and her daughter, Lady Hartland was told, but "he will not bear her name, or Miss Hume's—we shall make it a rule never to speak of them—and do all we can to divert and comfort him, poor fellow." The second Baron Hartland died of his injuries later the same year. All the evidence from the time, as well as the local memory of the Hartlands' years as the lords of Strokestown, suggests that the family were thought to be equally charitable and good-natured to their domestics and the tenantry as they had been to "poor Maurice" in his illness.[16]

Major Denis Mahon pressed his case to the Lunacy Commission to have Maurice declared incompetent and laid his claim to the Mahon legacy as the closest surviving heir. He did not take possession until 1845, after nine years of litigation with another cousin in Galway, but was appointed executor of the Hartland estate, including the town, Strokestown House and its demesne, and most of the populous townlands surrounding it, as well as several thousand acres not far away in Carrick-on-Shannon. Until then a Hartland tenant of two small holdings in Farnbeg (and £7 in arrears),[17] he was now in more or less complete control of the lives of some twenty-nine townlands containing a native population of no less than six thousand men, women, and children, few of whom had ever heard his name.[18]

The Major was also eager to come into his fortune, including at least £13,000 in unpaid rents. In his nine years as executor and expectant heir, Major Mahon did all he could to bring the Hartland estate to order, laying out large sums to rescue Strokestown House and its demesne from neglect and employing experienced local agents to reduce the massive arrears owed by the tenantry.[19] By the time he finally inherited in 1845, he had had little success in this and was finally persuaded to retain one of the "professional" firms of land agents "to bring the tenants to obedience," as the current jargon of that trade put it. Mahon was no different in this than hundreds of other perplexed landlords in the 1840s; it was an era of boom for these estate-management firms, since it was an era of distress for many landlords. In the thinking of the time, the dilemma of the Irish land system required a detached and "expert" perspective, whatever the short-term expense to the heir or the permanent hardship of his tenants.

The Locale and the Murder

Disturbances often arose from similar circumstances throughout the country. In situations like Mahon's, the withdrawal of a landlord from the management of an indebted esatate left the tenants and the hired land agents to confront each other in circumstances loaded with violent potential. The atmosphere in the Strokestown area had also been heated prior to the Mahon murder by the turmoil in the townland of Ballykilcline, a few miles north of Strokestown House. This townland was no longer part of the estate, since Hartland's lease of the Crown lands had been allowed to lapse in the confusion following Maurice's collapse. Since that time, its tenants had refused to pay their rents and openly defied the local Crown Agent and his bailiffs. Just six months before the murder and within three weeks of the departure of the *Virginius* emigrants, the Crown had evicted the leaders of the "Ballykilcline rebellion" along with the townland's nearly five hundred occupants. Although no evidence was ever presented to link them directly with the crime, it is indicative of their reputation in the neighborhood that they were among the first to come under suspicion during the preliminary police investigation.

Though the murder permanently attached a dangerous character to the area, Strokestown did not have a particularly violent or eventful record before that time, despite the celebrated fracas of the O'Conors over Balintobber nearly a century earlier. A few of the local grandees became targets of disturbances in the forties, though less tragically than Major Mahon. Besides the Marquess, later the Duke, of Westmeath, the patrician class was represented by Lord de Freyne of Frenchpark, a day's journey away, and Lord Crofton of Moate Park. After the blight of 1846, when it became plain that a deep famine winter was ahead, Lord de Freyne was hanged in effigy opposite his main gate in Frenchpark and dragoons were called in to disperse a starving crowd of three hundred at the gates of Crofton's Moate Park. Such crowds were not always dangerous or even threatening when they assembled at the landlords' gates. The site was inherently ceremonial, conspicuously marking the line between the master of the land and his "subjects." On other occasions, the gates of the demesne might equally be used to announce the birth of an heir or to distribute charity to the poor, opened to admit the privileged and favored and bar all others as they had done in Picardy or Somerset for centuries. But like so much else in this ancient colony, such mimicries of patrician England had an archaic and implausible air.

The ubiquitous "parks" dotting the Irish landscape had become a de rigueur hallmark of patrician status, signifying dominance and privilege in Ireland and proof of refinement to their often snickering English peers. Like Strokestown Park House, the Irish park's architecture was basically formulaic: a prodigal expense of the best land in a display of wealth-to-burn; continental, especially Italianate, structural designs that loudly stated their enduring kinship with Europe and, for the eyes of the neighborhood, majestic and unapproachable stone walls and wrought-iron gates. The exotic and inedible flora and fauna from distant reaches of the empire, the walled gardens and walks, and the spendthrift manipulation of nature for the sake of beauty rather than nourishment proclaimed the patrician park's divorce from the surrounding civilization more unequivocally than the blockhouses and castles of a previous age had done. Their wonders were hidden from the outside only formally, since local laborers, gardeners, tradesmen, and servants moved constantly through their walls. That the local population understood the message they conveyed is clear: displays of fealty or affection were expressed there, but when they gathered in times of trouble to express their anger or entreaty, the gates of the parklands were also the chosen site.

The grandees played a crucial political role in the country districts as well, often controlling the appointment of magistrates, justices of the peace, sheriffs, and parliamentary nominations. This system did not differ greatly from that prevailing in the English countryside before the reforms of the thirties. But patrician solidarity was far more imperative in Ireland. In September of 1843, an attempt was made on the life of Richard Irwin, a magistrate and a brother of Edward Irwin, Esquire of Knockhall (which adjoined Ballykilcline). Immediately following, Major Mahon convened a meeting of county justices presided over by Lord Lorton for the purpose of demanding action of the lord lieutenant against such outrages. Its resolution, written by Mahon himself, argued the extreme urgency of the threat to the landed classes: "that until decisive Steps are taken by Government to put a Stop to the seditious publications scattered through the Land, as well as the mob exciting and to all intents and purposes treasonable speeches that are constantly being made at Assemblages of the People, it may be expected that frequent murderous attacks, similar to the one which has brought us together this day, will be made, and which can be considered in no other light than Massacre in detail."[20]

The most conspicuous member of the local aristocracy, the elusive Marquess of Westmeath, was absent from this meeting and throughout the ensuing conflict. The proprietor of most of the beautiful lakeland to the northeast of the townland, the Marquess makes an appearance in the record only after the Mahon lands were quiet and Ballykilcline was empty. Like a number of other local gentlemen, he made a proposal for the once-troubled acres bordering Lake Kilglass, which he thought "would benefit from consolidation." Apparently following the advice of his own land agents, he proposed to "exchange" a parcel of his estate located in Culleenaghmore, four "English miles" distant, for Ballykilcline. He promised the commissioners he would carry on "extensive works" there, "as much for the civilization of the country as for your benefit." He admitted he knew no benefit his proposal would be to the Crown: "I cannot certainly point out any . . . ," he wrote. But he assured them he desired "no advantage whatever" on his own behalf. It was in his mind, however, that the commissioners might wish to set an example "in a country that up to recent events was completely sunk in barbarism & in which I am endeavouring to set on foot an improved system of agriculture without which the country will not only remain a waste but have a population of lawless creatures without a hope of their reclamation."[21]

Gentlemen and Squireens

Between the gates of the great house and the cabin door there were few certainties about class in prefamine Balintobber. Each intermediate layer depended on its peculiar relationship to the state, the law, the church, or especially to the land as the source of its status and influence. Police or military barracks, commanded by an officer corps recruited mainly from Irish or Anglo-Irish Protestant families, were never more than a day's notice from the site of any disturbance. The male sons of this Irish-Protestant gentry were the *hidalgos* of the British empire, a military caste that was already playing a disproportionate role in the imperial armies.[22] In troubled Ireland the Anglo-Irish "captains" and "majors" were thick on the ground, as regulars in garrison towns, in the militia and constabulary, or retired and holding honorary commissions in the yeomanry. They were as familiar a figure in respectable Protestant society as the priest was in its Catholic equivalent and were similarly a bond and reassurance in their communities. Four generations of Mahons had held commissions from captain through general, and a later generation of the family would do the same service in Flanders, still loyal sons both of the British Empire and British rule in Ireland.[23]

The Resident Magistrate and a few locally prominent attorneys, including some Catholic lawyers like Hugh O'Ferrall, were generally within the hierarchy of polite country society at some level and were often one of its key connections to the big landlords who offered the best employment for them. But there were only one dozen resident lawyers among the quarter million people of Roscommon in the 1840s, a shamefully small number for a place aspiring to English civilization. The small number probably reflected the relative sluggishness of local commerce and the scarcity of fee-paying clients in the general population more than any lack of dispute. In this part of the country most quarrels had to do with the land, and these were more often handled by the land surveyors, of whom there were more than one hundred in the county. They occupied a similar position as professional dependents of the landed classes and almost invariably their deeds and surveys represented authority in any dispute between lord and tenant.[24] Apart from the Church of Ireland bishops and a few well-born vicars, the parish clergy generally lived modestly, supported by tiny congregations, many of them barely surviving at a respectable level from year to year. Most accounts of their social life agree that within this fringe of Anglo-Irish provincial society life was an easy but benighted routine of boredom and petty comforts.

Seen through the prism of native grievances, these local representatives of the law and the established church were easily cast as symbols of oppression when passions were high. The attempt on the life of Richard Irwin in 1843 may have been a herald of things to come, following poor harvests, evictions, and growing desperation among the cottiers. Described by a local diarist as "Dick Irwin . . . that phlegmatic opulent grazier," with a pauper tenantry, no motive was uncovered for the assault made on him, though as both a magistrate and grazier many were possible. Five years later, the Reverend John Lloyd, also a member of a prominent Roscommon family (including the penurious Reverend William Lloyd of Ballykilcline), was murdered near Elphin. A culprit by the name of Owen Beirne was tried and hanged for the latter offense, but again no motive was ever uncovered. Magistrates could not avoid becoming involved in obscure disputes between landlords and tenants, and, however benevolent, the parish clergy could not be disassociated from the hated tithe. As in all parts of the country, many members of both professions were also private landlords and middlemen or, as Irwin and Lloyd, were unluckily associated with powerful local families against whom any sort of vendetta may have festered.

Overlapping family ties and patronage were as central to professional favor in the Ascendancy as they were in the townlands. But the management of land produced more local livings than all other institutions, employing functionaries and dependents at every level of this middling society, from gentlemen farmers and powerful land agents to the "drivers" and constables who dealt directly with the population. The complexities of the land system also made the surveyor a familiar and respected figure in most regions of the country. Private disputes could and did arise among members of this class, but in the agitated atmosphere of Roscommon in the 1840s they displayed a high degree of solidarity in all their dealings with the tenantry.

Before coming into his inheritance on the death of Lord Hartland in 1845, Major Denis Mahon was one of this class, Protestant, well born, well married, and well connected, though just as desperately short of income as most of the rest. As executor of Hartland's estate and later as master of Strokestown House, he not only hobnobbed with the local aristocracy but took the lead in mobilizing the landed interests of the neighborhood. His high local status was undoubtedly due in part to his being heir apparent, but the firm public stand taken by him and his agent, John Ross Mahon, against his own tenants and other troublemakers in the neighborhood (including the local monsignor) also placed him visibly at the forefront of the militant gentry, to his great misfortune.

Some of the other local gentlemen who pressed Denis Mahon to make an example of troublesome tenants were themselves middlemen of the Hartland estate. It was a standard practice for local squires and strong farmers to lease parcels of a few hundred acres from the great landlords, subletting it in turn to undertenants. Most of the latter were small "farmers" of the townlands, holding lots that were rarely greater than twenty acres as "tenants-at-will." Like the much-deplored subdivision among the peasantry, this practice both mirrored the social pecking order among the gentry and reinforced bonds of mutual interest. But in hard times it was as vulnerable as that in the townlands. When it was put to the test in the famine years, it also became a cause of bitter conflict and division: some of the gentlemen tenants abandoned their leases as it became plain that the subtenants were unable to pay the rents, leaving Mahon and his agent to deal with their eviction, to pay the additional poor rates, or to assist their emigration. Some others, who were in arrears of rent themselves, were less squeamish than the major about turning poor families out on the road and made wholesale evictions in his name, intensifying the popular animosity against him. Even his agent, who was drawing the handsome fee of £500 a year to protect Mahon's interests, adopted a similar method of deflecting local passions away from himself.[25] Just months before his assassination in November of 1847, Mahon seems to have become bitterly aware of the limits his gentleman tenants placed on their loyalties as they scrambled to detach themselves from the embattled estate: "I am sure you will agree with me," he wrote to his agent in Strokestown, "that this is not a time to saddle a landlord with additional difficulties when no rents are paying. It strikes me that it is not fair for those who have had their profits for years to turn short on the landlord when they find the times get bad."[26]

It is probably not surprising that many of the rusticated gentlemen of the district were a good deal more pugnacious than either Lord Hartland or his heir in their views about local law and order in the townlands. While they invariably addressed Mahon and their other social superiors with the utmost deference, it seems to have been their consensus that both he and the Crown agents were dangerously indulgent of the tenantry and that leniency posed a far greater risk to them, exposed in their unwalled country houses, unable to sponsor emigration plans or to retreat abroad, than to the occupants of Strokestown House.

The predicament of tenant-landlords was based on two nearly unalterable realities: a reliance on the big landlords for access to the land and leases that made the difference between solvency and penury for most of them, and the necessity that they remain on or near their holdings and contend with their subtenants on a near face-to-face basis, without the luxury of middlemen other than their "driver" or other petty go-betweens. These arrangements naturally tended to focus grievances on the "landlord" closest at hand, the squireen or big farmer, who out of sheer necessity might well be more predatory than the patricians. Virtually all of them were avid for leases to increase their rents but were fearful of the tenantry in this relatively exposed position. Thus the squires, graziers, and big tenant farmers of the neighborhood were usually the most eager to call for the troops and drastic measures when there was trouble. The large-scale clearances and emigration schemes of the first year of the famine offered them the irresistible prospect of markdown leases from hard-pressed landlords and a subtenantry reduced both in numbers and combativeness.

One of the prominent tenants of the Hartland estate was Thomas Conry, who held the townlands of Killdologue and Cloonahee when Major Mahon inherited. Although he was apparently of a Roman Catholic family in the neighborhood, Conry's association with the demesne went back at least to the early 1820s, when he was Hartland's steward, a substantial tenant, and keeper of accounts for the second baron. His association with Strokestown House may have been more complex, since the old baron's personal books were paying out £300 a year to Conry on a "Bond Debt" of £2,000 contracted in 1826 (for the time, a usurious 15 percent interest).[27] Conry may have been one of the reasons for the insolvency of the estate when Mahon inherited. But in this relationship, he was also something of a buffer between the Hartlands and the native population, advising the second baron on such things as repairs to Strokestown House, and tradesmen and artisans who could be trusted in their work, and interpreting the erratic tempers of the population. Having the baron's ear in such matters must have given Conry substantial leverage in his circle as well as opportunities to influence commercial and agricultural arrangements on the local level.[28] He remained an active and important figure in the district and one of the chief middlemen, although it seems that his entré at Strokestown House ceased after Maurice's collapse.

Conry remained a tenant under Major Mahon and worked with him on the local Board of Works in the first two years of the famine. But he was also one of the middlemen who saw an opportunity in Mahon's emigration scheme to dispose of his tenants at his landlord's expense. Somewhat naive at first in his dealings with the squires, Mahon was becoming increasingly exasperated with their obvious venality during the crisis. When Conry requested that his own tenants be given the emigrant bounty, Mahon instructed the agent to make certain "whether they have, in the first instance, got rid of their under tenants, as I consider it hard on me to send out people who not only owe me rent but also leave me a parcel of pauper undertenants."[29] He clearly regarded this as a breach of the gentleman's agreement between the landlord and his larger tenants but apparently did not realize that "getting rid" of the undertenants would now expose him, rather than the middlemen squires, to the wrath of those evicted.

Another of Mahon's middlemen, Patrick Browne, held the townland of Clonfad as co-lessee with his aged, and apparently senile, father. Like Conry, he too saw the estate's crisis as an opportunity to rid himself of pauper tenants while the estate's agent, John Ross Mahon, was on the lands in the company of the sheriff and constables. He succeeded in evicting some of the poorest of them amid the confusion but was found out trying to charge the small fees for serving evictions (the "haberes") to Mahon and had to repay it. Browne's case was complicated by the fact that he was the brother of the Bishop of Elphin, the leading Catholic clergyman in the county, a factor that made Browne's behavior in the crisis of 1847 more conspicuous than it might otherwise have been. There were also a number of Protestant families in residence for generations, most also dependent on the great landlords: Godfrey Hogg, Alexander Reynolds Sandys, and Mr. Morton of Strokestown were modest lessees who had apparently constituted, with families like the Conrys and Brownes, the core of a placid provincial gentility for years before.

The Catholic and Protestant squires and big farmers do not seem to have behaved differently in their intercourse with each other or in their treatment of subtenants before the famine. Nor had sectarian divisions noticeably affected relations with Strokestown House until a furious local dispute arose a few months before Mahon's murder between the major and Father Michael McDermott, the "Venerable Archdeacon of Elphin" (as his parishioners called him), who resided and preached in Strokestown. In sharply conflicting versions of the quarrel's beginning, a few things are clear. Denis Mahon attended a meeting of the Strokestown Relief Committee in August of 1847 on his return from England, three months after the first of the Mahon emigrants had left Strokestown, with rumors of disaster already circulating. When he questioned the minutes of the committee regarding the lists of those eligible for relief, McDermott immediately took offense, according to Mahon, rising "in a violent passion and asked how I dared to come there and tyrannise over him?" In Mahon's account, read after his death in the House of Lords, McDermott's abuse continued unbridled: "I was a stupid ass . . . [said McDermott]. Such an ass, that if I had had any schooling then it was quite thrown away on me. . . . that I had spent my winter in London to amuse myself, and had left my people to starve in the streets and die."[30]

The Reverend McDermott's rendering of the quarrel was quite different. In his version, attested to by three whom he described as "practical Catholics" present at the meeting, Major Mahon imperiously demanded the cash book on entering and proceeded for the next two hours to interrogate the board on the accounts, casting suspicions on the reverend chairman, whom he insisted on addressing as "Mr. McDermott" (which he also does in his private correspondence).[31] Both accounts of the quarrel may have been substantially true. Mahon was laboring under the mounting debts of the estate and gloomy financial reports from his agent when he returned to Ireland to take charge in person and might well have lost patience when presented with yet more irksome bookkeeping from the board of local worthies. And it is obvious from the Strokestown priest's language on this and later occasions that he was incensed by the clearances and regarded himself as the defender of his suffering parishioners.

In the tiny room of the Strokestown sessions house where the altercation took place, in the presence of half-a-dozen nearly mute witnesses, the two men acted out a part of the moral drama of the famine—the rights and obligations of property at a moment when they seemed besieged and discredited set against the moral leadership of the native church in its first major test since emancipation. Denis Mahon clearly thought himself to be a humane and enlightened landlord, doing all that was possible for his stricken tenantry. But the issue at stake in the conflict with the priest, as he put it, was "that whatever I did with regard to my property I conceived rested with myself, and that I would not allow him or any man to interfere with me in that respect. . . ."[32]

McDermott confessed that Mahon's charges of fraud slandered himself and his calling, adding not too convincingly in a letter to the Major that "my calling does not allow me to resent the insults I receive. . . ." But the depths of feeling the incident had touched in him, and perhaps something of the incendiary tone of his sermon oratory, were not revealed until a month after the murder, when he published a stridently unrepentant letter defending himself in the *Evening Freeman*:

> The infamous and inhuman cruelties which were wantonly and unnecessarily exercised against a tenantry, whose feelings were already wound up to woeful and vengeful exasperation by the loss of their exiled relatives, as well as by hunger and pestilence, which swept so many victims to an untimely grave—in my opinion may be assigned as the sole exciting cause of the disasterous event which has occured. I saw no necessity for the idle display of such a large force of military and police, carrying outside so many rounds of ball cartridge, and inside some substantial rounds of whiskey, bacon and baker's bread, surrounding the poor man's cabin, setting fire to the roof while the half-starved, half-naked children were hastening away from the flames with yells of despair, while the mother lay prostrate on the threshold writhing in agony, and the heartbroken father remained supplicating on his knees. I saw no need for this demonstration of physical force, nor did I see any need for brutal triumph and exultation when returning after these feats were nobly performed. Nor can I conceive that the feelings of humanity should permit any man to send his bailiffs to revisit these scenes of horror and conflagration, with an order, if they found a hut built or a fire lighted in the murky ruins, to demolish the one and extinguish the other, thus leaving the wretched outcasts no alternative but to perish in a ditch.[33]

Three weeks before his death, Mahon had also been informed that the priest repeated his denunciation from the altar in Strokestown, which McDermott denied. This charge, coming so soon before the shooting, raised all the old demons of papist plots throughout the country and even in Parliament after the deed was done. It is not known what effect McDermott's hot eloquence might have had in the already disturbed townlands. But what sectarian harmony had existed in the neighborhood previously was clearly shattered by the charges and countercharges of the dispute. The Bishop of Elphin, farmer Browne's brother, joined in the melee of published letters about the role of the Catholic clergy in fomenting acts of violence, in language even less restrained than his archdeacon:

> If for an instant we could even by connivance sanction the wild systems of revenge, we should justly deserve the execration of all honest men; but if it be a crime in exhorting our poor afflicted flocks to patience and resignation to the will of Heaven, to sympathise with them in their sorrows, and remind their oppressors of their sacred obligations, I for one plead guilty to the charge.[34]

If the bishop's eloquence was inflammatory, equally strong passions were not far from the surface among the local Protestant minority. Mr. Morton of Castlenode complained to Mahon's agent for ignoring his proposal to "colonise" Strokestown with Protestants, as in the plantation days. He repeated a rumor circulating among the other Protestant tenant-landlords that the rebellious tenants would refuse their rents indefinitely and had taken up the notion that the land was now theirs, having been "deserted" by its lawful owners, and would now consider any concession as a sign of weakness. Such fears evoked the archaic conflict between Protestant and Catholic notions of their claim to the land, one based on the rights of conquest and loyalty to the Crown and the other on the immemorial rights of nativity.[35] Morton expressed the prevailing mood of the Protestant squirearchy, which often expressed the illusory wish for an industrious and obedient Protestant tenantry, such as they imagined peopled the English countryside. Such sentiments could hardly have gone unnoticed in the townlands, where just such a "substitution" of tenants was seen as the ultimate calamity of total dispossession, remembered from Penal times and known to have occurred elsewhere in the country more recently. John Ross Mahon also espoused these views privately to the major's successor, Henry Sandford Pakenham Mahon: "I quite agree with you," he wrote to his new employer, "that it would be a great object to get some Protestant tenants—& I hope we shall succeed in doing so."[36] While there is no evidence of violent conflict between the Protestant militants like Morton and their Catholic counterparts, all the recent assaults in the area had been directed against Protestant landlords and middlemen: Mahon and the Reverend John Lloyd had been murdered; Richard Irwin, the magistrate-grazier, had barely escaped an attempt on his life; many had been threatened anonymously; some had fled; and the land agents, mostly Protestants, traveled under guard and never ceased calling for the dragoons.

The big Catholic farmers like Patrick Browne were caught in the polemical crossfire. In this provincial setting their social identity was ambiguous. Apart from a handful of native Catholic gentry, those with leases as middlemen were mostly graziers or commercial producers, "upstarts" in the eyes of many, who had jettisoned much that was sacrosanct but inefficient in traditional culture. Whether they had emerged from the townlands themselves or from older Catholic landed families, their material interests were often in conflict with the townland people and they conducted business much as any other landlord, maximizing rents, serving evictions, buying cheap, and selling dear. Many like Browne, at the marginal edge of the landed class, were especially callous in their dealings with tenants and laborers, squeezing rents and wages and "taking on airs" that were even more detested in them than in the Protestant squireens.[37] If the peasantry had always hated the exactions and pretensions of petty landlords, there was a special bitterness reserved for ambitious native farmers, who were felt to have betrayed their own. For their part, by the time of the famine there was not much separating them from the Protestant squirearchy in their views of the peasantry, whom both generally regarded as ignorant as well as dangerous.[38]

In the heated atmosphere of 1847, the Catholic proprietors could have found little comfort among local Protestants, despite their mutual interests. With most of the local gentry incensed over the stance of the Catholic clergy, the respectable Catholic tenants generally went out of their way to display their disapproval of and distance from the pauper masses. Many complained of receiving anonymous threats, suffering damages to property, ostracism, and other abuses. One, Owen Cox, a strong farmer, claimed to have spent £300 in building a police barracks on his property. In what written record survives, the ingratiating tone assumed by members of this class stands out. In letters made public after the murder, one declared: "I always use my utmost exertions to promote peace among the people, and, above all, respect and punctuality to their landlords and the proprietors of the soil." A month after the shooting, not long after he had ejected his own tenants, Patrick Browne submitted another such testimonial, which was read by Lord Farnham in the House of Lords. Mahon's tenants were neither harassed nor ejected, he claimed, and those who owed rents were treated leniently:

> The state of this part of the country is indeed melancholy. Life is not worth a days purchase. It is even dangerous to speak of Major Mahon's kindness to his tenants in this district. An intimate friend of mine received a threatening letter denouncing him for so doing, and with his large family, he feels miserable, and anxious, if possible, to leave the country.[39]

"Squireens": The Little Squires

Sprinkled around the landscape within an hour's walk of the town were well-windowed stone houses, veneered in gray stucco, usually of two stories, and roofed with Welsh slate. They stood out conspicuously in size and shape from the native dwellings of all kinds. These buildings, some walled with cast-iron gates, were unmistakably the homes of a transplanted, nostalgic culture, gaunt mimicries of the country houses that had come into favor among the provincial bourgeoisie of Ulster, Wales, and the north of England a generation earlier. In the 1841 census of houses, the majority of these houses fell into the group costing from £200 to £500 to construct at the low Irish rates for manual labor and the high rates for skilled workers in glass, masonry, and iron. Many still survive throughout the country in slight variations. Some show a taste in their architectural detail, landscape, and furnishings that is in tune with the regency and neoclassical styles common in Britain: square, symmetrical elevations, central entrances with self-conscious pillared porticos and leaded fan glass. Their internal spaces—obligatory dining and sitting rooms (or drawing room–cum–library in more pretentious examples), segregated kitchens and bedrooms, and discreet niches for servants—asserted the propriety and order in the private lives of the occupants. A few of their essential contents may be safely supposed: china and silverware; curtains and drapery; floor coverings; wall hangings and mirrors; clothes, linen, and food cupboards; laundered cottons; desks and writing materials; a family bible; an almanac; English catalogues and random books; keys, locks, and doorbells; glass lamps and candlesticks; soap; polishes; pictures; heirlooms; and memorabilia of travel abroad. As in Lucknow or Kingston, virtually none of these were manufactured locally.

Pet dogs were a man's fashion, mostly retrievers, border collies, and useful mixed breeds that fit a need or pretension. Hunters, both dogs and horses, would have been expected on the grounds of Strokestown House or Frenchpark, but ridiculed in two languages if they were kept by Conry or Browne. Even the local squires like Sandys or Hogg would have sunk fatally in debt if they had tried to maintain old pretensions in these things. Then as now, racing and wagering on horses was a craze that cut across class and sect. It was often ruinous for high and low, but was a high point of rural life, expressing the universal love of horses and belief in luck. The keeping and knowledge of firearms, mostly shotguns and boxed pistols, were taken for granted among the many captains and yeomen of the class. All kept servants, most from two to five. Spinets seem not to have been uncommon, along with petit point and flower gardens, although the daily lives of mistresses among the lower gentry was infamously dull and lonely.

The disaffinity of these households with the domestic customs and architecture of the countryside was unmistakable to any passerby. But the milieu had also subverted many of their pretenses, as it did the speech of nearly all who dwelt in it for long. The smell of burnt turf and tow, the sources of heat and light that they shared with the natives, filled and sooted all indoors and, together with the neglected grayness of their facades, betrayed their whereabouts in the world. Shabbiness and disrepair were pervasive and widely overlooked in broken plaster, uncaulked or cracked glass, unkempt gardens, outdated dress, and unmended walls. Even if the domestic budget allowed for better, the skills of manufacture and repair were scarce in Roscommon, where there were no gas fitters, no spectacle or clock makers, no delft or china dealers, no stationers or papermakers, no instrument or toy makers, and only three plumbers, fifty-six "painter-glaziers," and one bricklayer. Indoors, solitary addictions to spirits and dangerous patent medicines may also have contributed to the high rates of commitment for mental disease, as it did in all classes of the country.[40]

Godfrey Hogg of Churchview in Strokestown, Alexander Reynolds Sandys of Carracrim, and the Reverend William Lloyd of Ballykilcline, all middling subtenants of the Hartland estate at one time or another, occupied houses of this kind. Like their Catholic counterparts, Conry, Browne, and Owen Cox, they were in and out of arrears themselves during the lean years of the forties. Lloyd barely maintained appearances on a paltry share of a tithe and the eleven acres attached to the Glebe House on the fringes of Ballykilcline. Hogg and Sandys, who compare most closely to Marx's caricature of the Irish squire—haughty, idle, and in debt—were among those who demanded stern measures against "outrages" and were also anxious to seize an advantage out of the distress of the Hartland estate. Hogg had made an unsuccessful offer of £400 a year for the Ballykilcline property, parts of which two other members of his family had held as sublessees under Hartland.[41] He made the most common argument in the circumstances, that it was better to have one "respectable tenant" to a "numerous pauper Tenantry . . . to deal with, who have been so long (I might say) triumphant over all law." He promised not to treat the present tenants "horably . . . or turn them out, unless it be their wish, and not without first purchasing them out. . . ." Any references for "Character, Solvency, and Humanity," he said, could be made "to some of the most respectable Gentlemen in the County who will likewise be my Security."

The eagerness of the three men for these disturbed and indebted lands was sustained by the hope of new income. For example, Sandys also made a meager offer of £225 for the six hundred acres, hoping that "the disturbed state of the district," as Weale had put it, would have reduced its appeal to outsiders. Had he been granted the lease at that figure, he would have realized £186 a year of new income, on paper, if the tenants paid the rents. Compared to the £20 to £50 that the smaller tenancies yielded, he could at least have imagined a style of life free of debt and worthy of a gentleman, a condition that was becoming increasingly elusive for these "squireens." A number of offers of a similar kind were tendered at bargain prices from similar sources who claimed to know the ways of the tenantry and how to manage them without scandal. Wisely, the Crown's commissioners declined them all.[42]

All such proposals condemned the violence and ignorance of the peasantry but do not necessarily reveal the local sympathies of the applicants. Sandys was a bellicose backwoodsman, but it may be that Hogg's good intentions were quite genuine. A few years before, he had pleaded compassionately for one of the older and poorer tenants, Thomas Fallon, who was faced with eviction: the old man, he assured the agents, was "industriously inclined . . . a Tenant I never found a better pay or more punctual. . . . He would be well able to pay now but he has met a family affliction, in the loss of his son who went to America taking away a good part of what was due out of his holding."[43]

Sandys was of the Anglo-Irish military caste in family history and in mentality. He put in his bargain bid for the Ballykilcline lease at the same time as Hogg. His proposal reveals yet another dimension of the forces of order in the area that emerged from the backwoods during the crises of the forties. Dated 23 February 1842 and possibly dictated, it is written in a skilled, embellished script but employs outmoded spellings, grammar, and style:

To The Right, Hon/*ble*, The Earl, of Lincoln, First Commissioner, of Her Magestys, Woods, and Forrests—

               &   &   &

My Lord

     With Sentaments of the most profound respect, I beg leave to lay befour your Lordships these' few lines—by way of *Proposal* for part of her Magestys Woods, and Forrests in this Country Ireland And as the Great Grand Son— of the Brave Captain Sandys, at the Head of his Grenadiers, crossed the River Shannon Athlone—in spite of all the Enemies Fire Could do—and took the Town and Garrison—some time in or about the Year 1691 as Recorded in English History—As Luck—and being one of his off spring—I hope your Lordship will consider I deserve a preference. . . .

     I Propose—and Promise to Pay—Her Most Gracious, Magesty—Queen Victoria—Her Heirs—and successors= the Sum of Twelve Shillings Sterling per acre—old Plantation measure, for all the Arable, and Pasture—in the Town and Lands, of Ballykilcline, in the Parish of Kilglass—Barony of Boyle, and County of Roscommon by my geting to Lease as Soon as convenient— as without a Lease—I dare not Stand on the Lands—were they to Know—I Proposed for it—as they are all an Out Lawed—refractory—Set of poor Tenants—Some of them eight in family living on half *acre* of Said Lands of Ballykilclian they think and are Vain Sure—that they will have it as an Estate—not paying any Rent for a lenth of time= even the Quit Rent—some of them told me so last week—some time past two Gentlemen *seemingly*= came from Dublin taking the name of Kilelian & thought to useurp a right to Said Lands—but they were Beat off= I Know from the respectable Persons, who would take part with me—that I would get little or no trouble in geting the Quite, and Peaceable Possession of Said *Lands* Your *Lordships answer* I shal atend to on Recp/*te*

        And I beg leave to subscribe myself—
           Your Lordship—most obedient,
           and Very Humble Servant, at Command—

                         Alex/*dr* Reynolds Sandys
                         Carracrim February 25th 1842
                         Post Town Roscommon[44]

The repeated references to support from respectable persons in the district against refractory tenants, as well as the apparent willingness of the referees to stand "security" for one another, suggest that some spirit of mutual aid existed among the squires, at least among the Anglo-Irish squires; indeed, to deny a fellow gentleman even grudging support against mob violence seems to have been almost unthinkable. Like antebellum American planters or Boer farmers, gentlemen of Sandys's class regarded a threat against one, even the most disreputable one, as a challenge to all and would quickly close ranks against it.

Middlemen, Agents, and Poor Gentlemen

Like many other landlords with disordered estates, Major Mahon turned to a land agent. Determined to restore his legacy, he employed John Ross Mahon of the Dublin firm of Guinness and Mahon. The measures used by the agents were often harsher and more provocative than custom dictated, since one of the principal functions of the professional agencies was to disconnect the proprietors from the restraints that generations of conventional practice, especially subdivision and perennial arrears, had ingrained. The mass emigration of the Mahon tenants that had ignited murderous passions in Strokestown was just such an innovation in estate management, a policy with high initial costs that promised a conclusive solution to the problem of congested, pauperized estates in the long term. It had been urged on the major by Guinness and Mahon and arranged along the lines of similar projects recently launched by other large city land agencies, like Stewart and Kincaid, on other estates. All of the land agencies operating in the district used the same limited number of ship agents, charterers, and provisioners, whose networks and fare schedules integrated them into the Atlantic emigration business through Liverpool and New York.[45]

Denis Mahon had repeatedly expressed a patrician reluctance to take the extreme measures recommended by the agent, even after receiving the most dire projections from him about the future solvency of the estate. But agents now exerted a greater authority than they had in the past. The hard times and disturbances of the forties, the loss of rents, and rising poor rates brought many big landlords to their door, many thinking them a last resort to bankruptcy or a sale of land at great loss, a fate that awaited many of the distinguished landholding families who were in debt. The famine and the Encumbered Estates Act of 1849 brought a booming business in distressed landlords and the brokerage of land sales. Skimming £500 a year from the estate, John Ross Mahon took an almost pedantic tone in his dealings with his cousin, reversing and radicalizing his instructions and threatening to resign unless given sweeping authority in dealing with the refractory tenants. He would not take responsibility for the estate, he said, "until the land is cleared of at least two-thirds of its population. . . . If you do not there is no prospect in my mind of your getting any rent for years, if ever again, for the land in their possession. . . ."[46]

What Edward Gibbon Wakefield had proposed for decades and Lord Monteagle, a commissioner of woods and forests and an Irish landlord himself, still urged in Parliament was now the private specialty of the big land agencies: large-scale assisted emigration. The cost and commissions startled the new heir to Strokestown. Summarizing the Mahon case to his partner in Dublin, Ross Mahon concluded that he could not carry on the major's business "with satisfaction to him or credit to ourselves" unless £24,000 were spent on clearances and emigration. "There are 1600 families, average size of holding 3 acres. Two thirds should go to make the farms 9 acres and no less will do now I think—no rents paying that I hear of among the lower classes of tenants."[47]

Major Mahon was eventually browbeaten by the logic of the agent's arguments, namely, that the most eminent and enlightened Irish landlords, Lord Palmerston, the Fitzgeralds, Lord Clonbrock, and Sir Robert Gore-Booth, all clients of Guinness and Mahon, had adopted the policy of mass assisted emigration. At least nine acres per family (as compared to the three acres prevailing on the estate) was the minimum estimated by the agency to replace the potato with oats as a staple, and the cost of emigration would be half the cost of maintaining paupers on outdoor relief or in the Roscommon Poor House for years to come. Their melancholy bookkeeping was unanswerable.[48]

The aura of authority carried by the specialized land agencies derived from their dubious claim to a "science" of land management and accounting, associated in Ross Mahon's mind with the then-fashionable precepts of political economy. In this respect, the new land agents pretended to a legitimacy well above that of the inglorious local agents who had harvested the Irish rents for generations and were still the most despised figures in the land system. Some of the new agencies, including Guinness and Mahon, went on to become influential bankers, but their grand schemes of assisted emigration during the famine were badly tarnished by the international scandals that resulted. Shortly after the assassination, John Ross Mahon retired to his Dublin offices, convinced that "well-known bad characters" in the neighborhood had subscribed a fund to hire an assassin to destroy him.[49]

Such haven from the local unpleasantness was less easily available to the humbler functionaries of the land system. John Ross Mahon had been a cousin of the Mahons of Strokestown, with a family seat at Castlegar, Galway, in addition to his partnership with the wildly prosperous Guinnesses in Dublin. His successor as the estate's agent was John Kelly (the same who had earlier promised to make Ballykilcline "perfectly untenanted"), also a distant cousin of the Mahons but the sort of man on the spot who not only had the necessary experience to represent an absentee employer but the informants, henchmen, and temperament to defy angry tenants in person. He was of a second generation of land agents in Roscommon who had served the Mahons and other local landlords over the previous three decades and now filled this role for Denis Mahon's successor, under the orders of Guinness and Mahon. Another second-generation deputy, George Knox of Strokestown, did the same for the sequestered townland of Ballykilcline under the direction of Her Majesty's Quit Rent Office in Dublin. At a straitening stipend of £50 a year (one-tenth the fee demanded by Ross Mahon), Knox was still unable to free himself from debt and also lacked Kelly's mettle in facing down peasant threats. Kelly and Knox both

held modest tenancies near Strokestown and, a generation before, both families had enjoyed a certain reflected glory as spokesmen and confidants of
the gentry. But the Kellys and Knoxes of Strokestown were now at the lower
end of the spectrum of respectability, dependent on the patronage of those
above them, who were now strangers, and tainted by their close contact
with the dismal tasks of eviction and pulling down cabins, which even their
peers looked upon with distaste. By the thirties their fortunes were sliding
because of the increasing disorder of the rent system and the intrusion of
the Dublin agencies. It was Kelly's advice to Mahon "to forget for five years
at least that you have such a thing as property in Roscommon, to leave it
totally in the hands of your agent."[50] Conry, Browne, Hogg, and Sandys
were middlemen-tenants, often in arrears, with subtenants of their own who
also subdivided their holdings.

These lesser proprietors existed in almost every locality as a landed elite
more directly engaged in the management of the land and its inhabitants
than most of the great proprietors.[51] The class was itself stratified into differing levels of wealth and status, from the nobility to marginal, debt-ridden
squireens perilously close to the masses. Below them in size and income of
holdings were a variety of lessees and sublessees, both Protestant and Catholic, who sublet tenanted parcels in the range of thirty to one hundred acres
and who also regarded themselves as safely within the margin of the respectable classes.[52] It was within this modest range that most of the Catholic
tenant-landlords in the vicinity of Strokstown were found.

In such troubled times, it was those near this margin who seem to have
emerged as the shrillest of sectarian voices. Morton, Sandys, and Denis Kelly,
a devotee of "Papist plots," did most to inflame the conflict surrounding
Father McDermott, circulating rumors of "Molly Maguires" and "murder
funds," and accusing prominent Catholics of complicity, as Kelly did even
of the attorney general.[53] Self-interest and inveterate prejudices corresponded very closely in their case. On their part, the Catholic squireens and
farmers like Patrick Browne were forced either into a mute or ingratiating
stand in the local debacle. Whatever their private thoughts about the public denunciation of their clergy (in Browne's case of his brother the bishop)
for their role in stirring up popular emotions, any open sympathy or association with agitators in the townlands would be the end of any social pretensions they aspired to among the squirearchy—however indebted and
shabby, this was still a predominantly Protestant caste.

At the lower margin of local Catholic society was a layer of what might
be called peasant entrepreneurs, who also filled various intermediary roles.
Each townland harbored what the authorities usually called "ringleaders"
when there was trouble, most of them indistinguishable from the general
peasantry but possessing some personal force or advantage in the size of
their holdings or the strength of their family that gave them influence in
their communities. These distinctions were often invisible or murky to outsiders, including landlord and police, who tended to perceive such individuals as intrinsically criminal, too low and barbarous to be motivated even

by thoughts of profit. Also regarded as criminals in the eyes of the townlands were many of the local bailiffs, "drivers," and gang-bosses—the indispensable scouts and sergeants who were recruited from the same class and knew each subtenant by name and character and who brought the land system's chain of command to the cottier's door. Most of these, too, had private interests in the land as tenants of record and petty landlords in the silent microcosm of the townlands. Between the two were acted out most of the daily routines of dominance and resistance in the Irish countryside, and enmities between them were frequently personal and fierce. It was to violent elements of this class that Ross Mahon referred when describing the plots on his life: "I am confidently informed that a considerable sum of money has been subscribed among the people in the neighbourhood, for the purpose of rewarding a person hired to assassinate me, and that this plot has been got up by persons in comfortable circumstances but who owe several years rent, and who also are well-known bad characters."[54]

The agent did not identify his informant or the "well-known bad characters." But he took these rumors from the townlands seriously and left for Dublin not long after. That Major Mahon's well-paid agent fled the troubled neighborhood to conduct his business from Dublin is probably not surprising. Together with the defaults and scattering of his other middlemen, it was a final peeling away of the insulating layers that protected the landlord from the sight and anger of the townlands.

4

Ballykilcline: Deputies and Defendants

The landlord might have been in London or some other place. And he lived in this house, up on the top of the hill.

And there was agents *appointed then for to collect the rents. And there was another . . . the bailia. There was a man that would be in every district that used to watch the tenants, do ye see, and not let them be abusin the land or doin any harm.*

The bailia—or bailif—they weren't liked at all. They were hated; they were hated.

He was under the agent. The agent was under the landlord, and the bailia was under the agent.

Hugh Nolan of Ballymenone[1]

The name of the townland of Ballykilcline appeared on the Ordnance Survey Map of Ireland of 1841 and again in 1886. In between, although it continued intact in the memory and usage of the few people who still lived there, its official existence was uncertain, present in some surveys but overlooked in others. That was because the names of townlands identified not places as much as their occupants and were liable to lose their meaning when their occupants departed. Their physical presence, the uncut stone or turf and thatch dwellings, the "semi-underground" dwellings described by Tocqueville, and the foot-worn paths connecting them, quickly disappeared into the landscape when unoccupied. Seen in that light, the "clearance" and "leveling" of townlands, whether by emigration or eviction, was intended by land managers like Guinness and Mahon to remove all evidence of their existence, creating a *tabula rasa* on which a more orderly plan could be drawn.

63

Most layouts of "improved" and "consolidated" estates were envisioned on a model that had been imposed all over England in an earlier century through enclosure and commercial agriculture. The desired effect was of hedged meadows, solitary stone and windowed houses, village markets, and neat fields of grain. One can see this intention entering the awareness of the tenants of Ballykilcline in their "Memorials" and "Petitions," along with a consciousness of the hopeless imbalance of land and people in which they lived. Conceived by a progressive landlord and his agents as the only rational solution to perpetual poverty and turmoil, to the tenants the prospect of their expulsion en masse was a vision of oblivion. Ultimately, these irreconcilable notions defined the townland's relations with the Crown and its local deputies.

Conflicting views survive about the origins of the conflict between the Crown and its tenants in Ballykilcline. There is no doubt that the lapse in the Hartland lease created some confusion. As "poor Maurice's" executor, Denis Mahon had let the lease expire either by neglect or a lack of funds to renew it. There followed a delay of some two years, till 1836, before the Crown Commissioners addressed themselves to the obscure file. In the meantime, no rents had been demanded of the tenants. The Commissioners' first inclination was merely to offer them new leases, but only on condition that all arrears were paid. The first notices of eviction were issued when the leading tenants failed to meet this offer, almost certainly because they lacked the cash. What later became known as the "Ballykilcline rebellion" began when the fourteen evicted tenants ignored the notices and re-occupied their holdings.

From the Commissioners' point of view, colored at all times by their local informants, the case was simple: the tenants were habitual recalcitrants and were conspiring to evade their rents. How the townland saw their situation is much less clear. Seeing themselves alone among their neighbors for two years as the only townland to be "released" from their accustomed rents, they either discovered or concocted reasons to prolong their new freedom— or, as some in the area thought, to lay a permanent claim on the lands based on their native rights and thereby threaten the entire land system.

Deputies

What survives of the history of the "Ballykilcline rebellion" is contained mostly in the deceptively tidy accounts of the Crown's deputies in Ireland, especially of George Knox of Strokestown, the local agent whose duty it was to report on the affairs of the tiny Crown Estate to John Burke of Her Majesty's Quit Rent Office in Dublin. From Burke, Knox's information was passed on to the Crown Commissioners in Westminster. Apart from his ledgers of rents and arrears due and the lists of legal tenants, the information passed by Knox through this pipeline, upon which the perceptions of Parliament rested almost entirely, must be taken guardedly. His view of the people and events of the townland record a good deal more about the fears and prejudices of a marginal Anglo-Irish gentleman of a provincial market town than it does about the mind of a community that began and ended as a mystery to him although he had lived his whole life nearly within view of it.

Most of the land agents were restrained by a rough professional ethic. Even at the marginal level of Knox or Kelly, outright embezzlement from the estate books was unusual, if not unknown, and there were often more prudent opportunities for an ambitious agent to enrich himself in the tangle of patronage, transactions, and services of mismanaged estates. But compared to the urbane and expensive agent of Denis Mahon, Knox was much less successful in enriching himself in the business. There were poorer Protestants than Knox who appear in the Strokestown records of these years, at least one schoolteacher, several storekeepers and clerks, the Reverend William Lloyd, Thomas Roberts, also an agent, and John Saul, the Hartland's steward. Until he was appointed as the Crown Agent for Ballykilcline (at a stipend of £50 a year, about 25 percent of the rents), Knox would not have been above the company of these middling local figures, all apparently literate and in the same Church of Ireland congregation. But Knox was sensitive of the diminished position of his family in local society and retained airs of squirely pretension. He held short leases from time to time but was in arrears to Denis Mahon at the time of the shooting and in need of his stipend. Like the Conrys, Knox's father, Maurice, had claim to some prominence as an agent in some of the affairs of the second Lord Hartland during the teens and twenties. But the chaos following the last lord's illness had meant a waning in the Knoxes' fortunes. By the time of his death in the winter of 1847, George Knox was trying desperately to provide for his own future and that of his son, Thomas (who succeeded him briefly as the Crown Agent after his death), appealing forlornly to the Quit Rent Office and to local patronage after he had, as he thought, cleared Ballykilcline of its occupants.

His was not an ideal perspective from which to observe the workings of a disturbed townland, much less to defend the Crown's interests in it. Living safely in Strokestown but still easily alarmed by rumors, he regarded the tenants as a dangerous tribe of savages. Even before the sensational events of 1847, only on rare occasions and under orders from Dublin would he enter the twisting paths of Ballykilcline: "They are the most lawless and violent set of people in the County Roscommon," he complained to Burke, "and whenever it was necessary that I should go to the lands to have any service effected on behalf of the Crown the Stipendiary Magistrate never would venture among them unless accompanied by dragoons, infantry and police, and even with this force they invariably insulted the bailiff in the execution of his duty, and did everything in their power to resist the laws."[2]

Although he soon after applied, unsuccessfully, for the position of stipendiary magistrate, as far as his records show he made this daring excursion not more than twice during his tenure as agent, the last when he thought the townland to be empty. The earlier assaults on local gentlemen no doubt had had an effect on his sense of security. But the reaction to the Mahon clearances, the same policy he advocated for the miscreants of Ballykilcline, threw his mind into a state of siege and kept him behind locked doors in Strokestown. Apart from his two nervous forays into the low hills a few miles north of the town, he was dependent for his knowledge about the temper and conditions in the townland on John Cox, whom he described as his bailiff.

Except through his contact with the Reverend Lloyd, who lived on the near edge of Ballykilcline, and Cox the driver, the agent was effectively isolated from the inhabitants of the townland. The houses of the local grandees were no more open to him than to other small tenants and the town tradesmen. And Strokestown, a turnpike town of some sixteen hundred people, many of them drawn from families of the surrounding townlands, offered little in the way of society or sympathy for a Protestant gentleman and rent collector whose presence in any local crowd inspired silence in them and fear in himself. His natural fellowship would have been with the squireens, like Hogg and Sandys, though perhaps on sufferance since the years of the Knoxes' decline. But for the most part his daily life seems to have been quite secluded.

With the "wily and obsequious Cox" (as Cox's neighbors called him) as his only eyes and ears among the tenants, Knox could report little more than rumor to his superiors in Dublin and London. He was nearly as distant from the life of the place as were the Commissioners or Burke, who knew for certain only that the tenants had paid no rent for a decade. His reports, which had all along recommended the wholesale ejectments that the Crown originally wished to avoid, became increasingly alarmist as the hunger worsened in 1846, increasingly obsessed with military protection and the building of police barracks on the estate. Burke as well as the Attorney General in Dublin seem to have detected an excess of anxiety in his reports when they rejected his pleas and in June of 1846 recommended to the Commissioners that the tenants be offered new leases. The orders that Knox received from London soon after could not have been reassuring. He was to accept "proposals" from the occupiers for leases at the old rate, as of 1 May. In the case of the fourteen "ringleaders," two years' arrears would be required and they were also to find "some respectable and solvent party from an adjoining townland, to be approved by you, to join them in security in each lease" (it was to meet this condition that Godfrey Hogg had vouched for one of the poorer tenants). At this time, no other arrears were to be demanded, but this policy was shortly altered (on Knox's advice) to require the previous year's rents from all. What George Knox's relations with the local townland populations were in the years before can only be surmised from the fact that his immediate recommendation on becoming the Crown Agent had been to ignore any promises or proposals they might make and remove them all.[3]

Little can be said about Knox's private or family life because, unlike the peasantry, he was not counted and scrutinized for the rent books. He lived at Clonfree House with his wife, the former Jane Mahon (apparently unrelated to the Mahons of Strokestown) of Fruithill in Derry, who was said to be an "ardent Covenanter." A son, Thomas, appears briefly as his successor in keeping accounts for the estate during the emigration proceedings in 1847. What became of him, or would have become of the father once the land was vacant, is not recorded. The slovenly rolls and accountings submitted by Thomas when his father fell mortally ill in that year suggest either that the turmoil of the evacuation had put him under some strain or that the tidiness of the father had diminished in the son.

The elder Knox had been well aware that the clearance and reorganization of the estate was likely to make his position redundant and he made several proposals to the Clerk of the Quit Rents that he hoped would relieve him of his arrears and provide for the future. He suggested to Burke in April of 1846 that one of the better houses in the townland be repaired for him to occupy "in Order the more eventually to bring the Tenants to Rights, for some time." It is a surprising proposal coming from Knox, who shortly before had begged from Strokestown for "Protection at my Residence, as my life is not safe one moment at the present." He claimed to have received repeated "Threatening Notices" and had dared not venture out in the past six months "without being armed, and expecting to be attacked at my House every night." He enclosed for the Commissioners a clipping from *Sanders Newsletter* describing his land being "turned up" and himself threatened. His assumption was that the assailants were from among the Defendants of Ballykilcline, yet at no point was he able to name or bring charges against any, never claiming even to have seen them. It is not likely, however, that all the alleged assaults against him were imaginary.[4]

Once the clearance was completed, he declared that he was prepared to return as Commissioner of the Peace and High Constable of Roscommon (at £100 a year) to "look after the management of the property"—a slightly shady proposition even in the broad-minded network of patronage that governed these arrangements. He also informed Burke, who had been indulgent thus far, that he had recently been "Strongly Recommended to the Lord Lieutenant, by the Noblemen and Magistrates of our County as a Person duly qualified from time of life and Intelligence to hold the Situation of a Stipendiary Magistrate."[5] As Cox the driver was soon to do, he also made proposals for leasing some of the better holdings; since he was no farmer, this was presumably to produce income from subletting, the very habit that the clearances were designed to end. Neither proposal was acted on before his death. But when Thomas Knox, after a few months of dubious service, requested a cadetship in the "Irish or English Police Force," he was curtly refused.[6]

The other gentleman of Knox's approximate station whose life was linked to the townland was the Reverend Lloyd. His relation to the Reverend John Lloyd, who had been murdered nearby, is uncertain, but both had some connection to the large family of Lloyds who were prominent in this part of Roscommon. Lloyd was the Church of Ireland Rector of the parish of Kilglass, living in the Glebe House on the near border of Ballykilcline. He had been married at twenty-eight and by the time he was forty-two his wife Eleanor, seven years younger, had borne him seven children, three sons and four daughters. Also in the household were five adult servants: one older and two younger men for outdoor work, one older woman, Anne Stuart (50) and Maria Gill (20). There is no mention of the servants' living in, but at least three may not have boarded in the Lloyd household since they bore names (Stuart, Fox, and Winne) of tenant families nearby.

The Lloyds occupied a little more than eleven acres of garden, pasture, lawn, and arable field at the crossroad of Aughamore, the center of the old "clachan" settlement in the area still dominated by the two stone structures of the Glebe House and the Round Fort. In contrast to Knox, there is no indication of fear or suspicion between Lloyd and the tenants; a few even cited him in petitions as their witness of good conduct and loyalty to the Crown. Amid the rising sectarian strife in Strokestown and bitter complaints from the local Catholic priests about the loss of their parishioners, Lloyd remained unscathed and apparently neutral.

Lloyd too was dependent for his income on the Clerk of the Quit Rents, whom he beseeched regularly about his bare-bones tithe of £14 10s. 9d. per annum, which did not always arrive promptly enough for him to meet his debts. The tithe was due to him from Charles Armstrong of Galway town, who was described as the "Lessee of the Improprietor of the Tithes of Kilglass." Two ladies of Dublin, Mesdames Moorhead and Gray, inherited the Kilglass tithe in 1834 when Armstrong died and also besieged Burke with demands for their £30 10s. per annum, out of which Lloyd was to be paid. These arrangements were irksome enough at one point for Lloyd to hire a "Tithe Collector" of Carrick-on-Shannon to dun the Dublin ladies and Burke. Since even fewer tithes than rents were forthcoming from the townland after that time, the Quit Rent Office felt compelled to pay both claims, after long delays, until the lands were sold. With Lloyd also paying the Quit Rent Office £10 10s. a year in rent, the parson sometimes found it necessary to withhold the rent himself until the tithes were received from Dublin.[7] Lloyd and his large family took no rents from the townland and depended primarily on his small Strokestown congregation and the cultivation of his eleven acres for support.

Despite the anomalous position of most Protestant parsons in Ireland's rural districts, Lloyd was far better assimilated into the neighborhood than was Knox, not only in the size, youth, and location of his family but also in their apparent serenity among neighbors like Patrick Connor and the Stewarts, whom the agent regarded as outlaws. Unlike the murdered John Lloyd, the parson living in Ballykilcline had no subtenants. The near poverty of his household must have been clearly visible to the townland, with three of its people attached to it as servants; this may also have helped to bridge the gap that usually separated the Anglican clergy from the peasantry. Whatever Lloyd's sympathies may have been with regard to the striking tenants, he kept them to himself. But it does not seem likely that they coincided exactly with Knox's. Yet he could hardly have defied the combined prejudices of the local squires, like Hogg, Sandys, and Morton, on whose goodwill and largesse he also depended as parson. His was another form of dependency, on the very periphery of the land system that caused most of the conflict between the local classes. Lloyd seems to have trod that line with delicacy, offending neither his patrons nor his servants. Perhaps one indication of the parson's character survives in an incident still remembered with some affection in the neighborhood, in which he and Patrick Maguire, a "cart man" and tenant of Ballykilcline, were seen careening wildly through the countryside in the wee hours atop an elegant carriage "commandeered" to carry the parson home from a merry night at the Lloyds of Rockville, a far more prosperous line of the family with extensive lands near Rush Hill, some ten miles away across Kilglass Lake.[8] Such escapades might well have offended his respectable relatives and parishioners but improved his standing greatly in the townland.

Even Lloyd's straitened circumstances would not have reduced him to the level of society that contained the likes of "Johnny" Cox, whom Knox called bailiff and all others called driver. A native of the townland, with a younger brother among the cottiers, Cox was not necessarily as isolated from human company as his employer. While he was hated and cursed by most of the townland, his position as Knox's driver still made him a man of importance among them, someone who in ordinary times should not be offended lightly. Cox more than the reclusive agent was the usual object of the abuse that Knox constantly complained of: according to Knox, he was insulted and "defied" when he made his rounds for the unpaid rents, all of which were absolutely fruitless for a period of more than ten years, and had sometimes had "waters" thrown on him while "servicing papers." It should be noted that Cox was capable of embellishing his reports to the agent when his personal interests required and such incidents were based on his word alone.[9]

It seems likely that Cox was able to bolster his credibility with his employers during the decade-long drought of rents by such reports of harassment. His was a dangerous profession in the Irish countryside and many of his colleagues lost life or limb in a bad year. It was also in his interest to keep the agent from closely inspecting the business of the estate in person. To begin with, he apparently maintained one of the three shebeens along the road between Strokestown and Ballykilcline, an activity that would have not only put him in contact with the local network of illicit distillers and the underground trade in grain and sugar but provided a customary site for gathering news and recruiting informers.[10] He had also had half his year's pay, £5, withheld in 1847 for "misconduct and trespass": permitting a friend, a lathmaker, to remove bog deal and oak from the lands; carting off manure and stone himself; and grazing a large herd of cattle on fields that had just been cleared of tenants. Undaunted, he proposed to lease various vacated parcels at £1 per acre and to relet them for grazing "free of taxes &

Rates" but was refused. Cox then requested, in view of his faithful service, to be appointed as constable in the barracks that Knox had persuaded the Commissioners to build on the lands of Owen Cox, the driver's brother, when the tenants were removed, in order to prevent their reoccupation. If the Crown had kept the estate, these efforts could have set Cox up as a substantial tenant farmer in the district thereafter, holding as much land as sixty to eighty individuals had previously subsisted on. Knowing the trouble the Crown was having in selling the estate, both the agent and his driver then made application to rent some of the better arable land, this time for 13s. per acre, and were again refused by Burke because "the rents specified therein being much below the value of the land."

By the time the last of the emigrants had departed in 1848, Cox was in a position to make proposals for these substantial tracts of land, knowing at that time that the Crown was seeking to relet them in plots of thirty acres or more, because of the capital he had realized from his fees as bailiff and for escorting the emigrants from Strokestown to Dublin. These services had produced at least £110 for Cox in the seven months before April 1848, out of his charges to the Treasury for conveying the emigrants to Dublin, the rental of his carts and the Bianconi cars from his brother, and the individual fees paid to him by Knox for leveling the empty cabins as each batch of occupants departed. He also received his regular salary as bailiff and, when the Commissioners ordered clothing and provisions for emigrants at the last moment, it was Cox again who made the arrangements. A compensation of £3 was also granted to him by the Commissioners for injuries he said he suffered while demolishing cabins. Some complaints were later received from departed tenants that further "impositions" had been made on them by the driver en route to the Dublin ferries.[11]

There were many others like Cox in the townlands of the Hartland estate, familiar faces in the town and in the countryside and sometimes objects of suspicion in both. A few make an appearance in the investigation after Mahon's murder, both as potential sources of police information and as suspects in the plot, men who appeared to know most of the reputed "bad characters," who moved about freely, and who had some knowledge of firearms. Most were men from local families who had become drivers and "cartmen" by performing assorted services for local landlords, agents, farmers, and merchants, including carrying goods by cart and, for some, delivering the dreaded warnings and notices to the cabin doors. This labor entailed the ever-present risk of violence. The stigma attached to the role also required certain personal qualities of mind and physique that set the drivers apart. Their work not only widened their sphere of movement and connected them with networks of news and petty transactions but pried them mentally from the introspective local bonds of the townland. It was a strategic position for ambitious opportunists and casual profiteers such as Cox. The qualifications for this detested role were few but well suited to Cox's talents, cunning, indifference to scorn or threat, and bilingualism. In the midst of the turmoil and misery of the forties, he browsed zestfully on a variety of opportunities that presented themselves in the gap between the lower deputies of the landlords and the subtenants of the townlands, subsequently establishing himself as a comfortable farmer in the area, still remembered for his shady dealing during the famine.

The Tenants

It is not possible to give a completely reliable estimate of the population of the townland in any given year before the emigration despite numerous surveys carried out between 1834 and 1848. These counts, taken on the spot by resident witnesses long familiar with the district, do not differ markedly as to the total number of tenants living on the estate, nor do they conflict with the estimates that can be derived from the 1841 census or Isaac Weld's *Statistical Survey of the County of Roscommon* of 1832. All give a figure of approximately five hundred occupiers living on the Crown lands, varying little from year to year until the famine. Taking into account the changes due to births and deaths, several partial crop failures and incidences of fever, marriages off and into the townland, a heavy accumulation of arrears for all the tenants, several temporary evictions and individual voluntary emigration, the townland's population seems to show a remarkable degree of stability for a community in such precarious economic straits during these turbulent years.

The apparent consensus of all observers on the number of people in the townland contains some mysteries, however, that leave room for a margin of doubt and raise some questions about the internal social structure of the townland. Between the time when they were the tenants of Lord Hartland and their emigration in the fall of 1847, a number of accounts of the townland's inhabitants were compiled in the form of rent books, tenant lists, and lists of those entitled to assisted emigration. The most thorough attempt to record all the occupiers appears in a "List of Tenants," compiled by Knox, presumably with the help of his driver, sometime between 1842 and 1846. It lists 101 "households" containing 476 persons, giving each a name, and the apparent heads of the households together with the names and ages of children and resident dependents. It is by far the most searching of the surviving counts made at any time of the residents of the estate and must have required a good deal of trekking from cabin to cabin, as well as prolonged face-to-face contact between the compiler and the people, which is why it could not have been the fainthearted Knox himself who compiled it. It is also likely that this list constituted the basis of the master list against which Knox checked the names of all recipients of the emigration bounty shortly afterward. The other lists he had available for this purpose, the rent books, enumerated only the "tenants-at-law" (that is, holding leases) who at any given time made up only 8 percent to 20 percent of all households, the rest falling into the category of "tenants-at-will."[12]

Following a near-universal practice, the larger tenants sublet, joined, and subdivided their holdings among the remaining households and individuals, often annually, to provide access to some land for all but not enough for any but a few to engage in commercial farming. The remaining 80 percent or more, including some who had been resident for decades, would not have been able to establish any legal claim whatever to their tiny holdings much less to the bounty the Crown finally offered in order to make the lands "perfectly untenanted." In their effort to resist eviction in the courts, even those whose names appeared year after year as the tenants of record were denied any right of tenure and could be ejected as mere intruders.[13] The fact that the majority of the remaining "trespassers" appeared on the emigrant lists, although their very existence was unrecognized in the law of the land, demonstrates only the Crown's anxiety to rid itself of the embarrassment caused by their presence, even at great cost.

The divide between town and townland is clear even in this highly localized effort of the landlord's agent to determine who was actually living on the six hundred odd acres within a few miles of his door. The compiler of the tenant list, no civil servant or land surveyor from Dublin but a local resident, freely admits that he had tacked on an extra twenty-eight people in his tally because he had "made a mistake of the whole lot," as though he had been counting migrating geese.[14] Another fifty-one were then crowded on the final page of his account with only their family name and number entered, perhaps because they refused to open their doors to the driver, or were otherwise inaccessible in the folds and ravines of the hilly land. Most of the missing were from among those who are recorded to have left in one of the "batches" sent off to the Dublin ferry in 1847 and 1848, the poorest and most obscure of the townland, either landless laborers or cottiers who held small plots in some years but not in others. As everywhere else in the country, these "conacre" peasants were at the lowest level of rural society and were the least likely to survive eviction or famine.

The names of the perennial tenants, varying from forty-two to eighty between 1834 and 1848, are given without such uncertainty, along with the names and ages of their families and dependents. Most of these were well known to John Cox or even to Knox, mostly men whom he actually met at the semiannual "gales" when the rents were settled, at least in the years when rents were paid. Many of the same names appear prominently among the "Defendants" who were first evicted and later reoccupied their holdings, among those identified by the agent as "ringleaders" of suspected plots and threats and instigators of the townland's "rent strike," as their refusal to pay the arrears demanded by the Crown had come to be called.[15] All of the fourteen Defendants were either tenants-of-record or the sons of such tenants on the estate in November of 1844 when charges were brought against them before the Court of Exchequer for illegally intruding on the lands from which they had been evicted eight years before. They were neither the only tenants-of-record, nor did they hold the largest plots of the townland, but at some point after 1836, when they were evicted as an example to the others and reentered their holdings, they chose to put their names to the suit against the Crown and identify themselves as leaders of the defiant community. It was to these that Knox referred in 1846 as "the most lawless and violent set of people in the County Roscommon." Knox also had declared at that time, just weeks before the first signs of the potato blight, that they were all in "a state of comparative affluence towards the neighbouring peasantry," most of them having provisions to dispose of and being worth from £20 to £100 each in the agent's estimation.[16]

Given the source and the prevalent illusions of his class about "buried gold" in the peasant's cabin, such estimates cannot be taken at face value. But it is clear that the Defendants were not among the poorest of the townland and that they did represent the main core of resistance and leadership. Apart from Knox's suspicions, there is clear enough evidence to suggest that at least some of the Defendants took the lead in organizing and enforcing the rent strike and enlisting the services of the attorney Hugh O'Ferrall,[17] a resident of nearby Ashbrook with a practice in Dublin. According to an affidavit drafted by Cox and submitted to the Clerk of the Quit Rents, an agreement had been made between O'Ferrall and the tenants in which they would pay the attorney 5s./acre/year for his services in their dispute with the Crown. All of the tenants but three (Maguire, Reilly, and the Reverend Thomas Lloyd) were party to the agreement, he said, and two of the Defendants, Richard Padian and Patrick Connor, acted as the collectors of the fund. He said that he had frequently seen O'Ferrall at Padian's house to receive the money collected—this money, Cox pointedly emphasized to his superiors, was always punctually paid up. Describing himself as the "driver or bailiff" and a native of the parish, Cox claimed to have "a general knowledge" of all the inhabitants. They had been duped by O'Ferrall into raising these sums, he thought, and would long since have become amenable but for the lawyer's false promises. O'Ferrall's son, another Hugh, and the son of one of the larger tenants, Edward Donellen, who acted as his clerks, were seen by Cox at six o'clock on a morning in January of 1846 collecting the funds and informing the tenants that their cause had been won and that "they would never again have to pay a penny of rent, provided they paid him the agreement of 5/s per acre."[18]

There is every reason to doubt specific charges and testimony coming from Cox about the townland. But there is no doubt that Cox was well informed at first hand about Ballykilcline and better placed than any other "outsider" to observe its inner workings. He had been a driver for Lord Hartland before Knox became the Crown Agent; his younger brother resided in the townland itself; and his "shebeen" was located along the road entering the townland, competing with another only a few steps away that was maintained by Hugh and Bernard McDermott, who were both Defendants and among the larger tenants. In an apparently thriving clandestine business, Maguire (an alleged informer in the townland and the carriage driver on the night of the Reverend Lloyd's spree through the countryside), was known to keep yet another such establishment nearby.[19] Cox also used every possible device to advance the clearance of the estate, profited greatly from carrying the tenants off, and exploited every opportunity the empty lands offered when they were vacant. All in all, John Cox seems to be something of a prototype of the Catholic middlemen who found opportunity rather than starvation in the great famine and joined the propertied classes of the following decades.

The dubious accuracy of Cox's self-interested alarms should not obscure the fact that agitation and conspiracy were afoot in Ballykilcline. The largely unrecorded obscurity of life within the townland, the relative scarcity of testimony from the mouths of the inhabitants themselves, and the often suspect evidence of witnesses like Cox or Knox make it difficult to wrest a sure picture of individual minds and motives among the tenants. But a few figures involved in the rent strike do stand out. Together with the lawyer, O'Ferrall, Richard Padian, and the Connor brothers (John, Patrick, and Michael) appear to have been the most active in organizing the rent strike. Cox was apparently right about these few, at least; apart from his own contention that they were the collectors of the "legal fund," the frequent appearance of their names on petitions and memorials and as the return addressees on appeals sent by the lesser cottiers suggests that they were, as Cox charged, among the "ringleaders" of the townland. Padian in particular, although only one of the middling tenants with ten acres of poor land, stands out as a leading figure among the Defendants and, along with young James Donnellen (whose family held nearly twenty-five acres),[20] was probably the community's main link with O'Ferrall. Even after they had lost the suit against the Crown's order of eviction and were daily expecting the appearance of the sheriff and constables, he was bold enough to put his name to the final petition, which was sent over the heads of both Knox and the Clerk of the Quit Rents directly to the Commissioners in London.

It is impossible to say what qualities of Padian's placed him in such a central role among his neighbors. The location of his cabin, where Cox claimed the meetings with O'Ferrall took place, at the crossroads of the Rooskey and the "Old" roads in the most isolated area of the estate would have afforded some concealment for their gatherings. But no more than sixty feet from the Padians' was the cabin of Patrick Reilly, who described himself as "a faithful subject for which I sufferd many injuries" and was probably one of two alleged informers in the townland. Padian and his small family, a wife, Mary, and two sons of six and four years, were also apparently unconnected by blood to any of the other families on the lands, unless very possibly through his wife; this also distinctly set him apart from all but three of the other male heads of families and all of the other Defendants. His was also the only household that contained a known lodger, as opposed to keeping dependant kin, widows, orphans, maiden sisters, or in-laws, which was quite common in the other households. The lodger was the forty-year-old Reverend Peter Geraghty, the only priest resident on the estate. He had neither church nor school, and with the Reverend Henry Brenan of nearby Kilglass claiming the people of Ballykilcline as his congregation, it is not clear what Geraghty's offical duties were, unless he was merely Brenan's curate. It is possible to imagine him as the enlightened and stoical priest encountered by Tocqueville in "Village X" in Galway: the teacher, advocate, and spiritual pillar of his community. There is no evidence that Geraghty was any of these things, but the presence of the forty-year-old churchless priest, presumably a man educated and literate to some degree, in the home of one of the rent strike's ringleaders during the prolonged crisis could hardly have been of no consequence in the tenants' struggle, particularly if Cox were right in charging that the house was the center of the agitation.

Brenan and Geraghty were frequently given as "people of substance" in the neighborhood who could provide testimonials for the writers of various petitions. So it seems that the presence of the priest in Padian's home would at least have enhanced Padian's standing among his neighbors, whether or not the priest were playing some surreptitious role, such as scribing the petitions, running some form of school, or in some other way influencing the mental life of the community. Such semiclandestine priests were, of course, one of the vestiges of the old Penal Laws and were often viewed by the Ascendancy and sometimes by the Catholic bishops as dangerous and iniquitous agitators, poisoning the peasant's mind against authority while surviving on the unsupervised income of sacramental fees and the generosity of their hosts. The pastor of Kilglass, Father Brenan, complained on at least one occasion of his loss of pastoral fees and dues, as he had also complained of a loss of income due to the emigration of his parishioners and the real or imagined encroachments of the Protestant clergy in the National School built near Rooskey in 1836. Whatever Father Geraghty's role in the townland's resistance, if any, his mere presence in the Padian household distinguishes it from the rest.

The influence of some of the other Defendants can be traced more easily along the lines of family and access to land. Hugh McDermott was one of these: holding the largest tenancy on the estate (thirty-six acres), jointly with his brother John, he was dispossessed along with the other defendants in 1836 and again in 1841 by the Sheriff of Roscommon. With his brother and his son, Bernard (twenty years old), he immediately reoccupied the land and paid no rent until the family emigrated on their own in 1844, the only Ballykilcline family to do so before the evictions.[21] Because his rent of nearly £22 per year was the highest of the tenants, his accumulated arrears of more than £200 also topped the list; ironically, his savings from withholding rent quite likely made it possible for him to emigrate with his family before the famine, when those less in debt could not! Hugh McDermott was then sixty-five years old, presiding over a household of thirteen, including his wife, Elizabeth, who was fifteen years younger, four sons ranging in age from twenty (Bernard) to six years, and seven daughters, the eldest a girl of eighteen and the youngest a child of one year.[22] In joint tenancy on the thirty-six acres was his younger brother, John McDermott (forty-six) with his wife, Nabby (forty), four sons and two daughters of from one to fourteen years in age; another brother, Thomas (forty), was also a tenant nearby on a smaller holding of seven acres, with a family of eight. At various times the McDermotts also held shares of other tenancies, including meadows and bog, with the Reynolds and Calligans, two other Defendants, as well as some of the lesser tenants, including even the abused and mistrusted Reilly.

Supported by both land and family and undiminished in vitality at the age of sixty-five, Hugh McDermott was one of the chief among those whom Knox described as "in a state of comparative affluence towards the neigh-bouring peasantry" and one of the "lawless and violent set of people" in the townland. McDermott's land was situated in the center of the estate about a half mile from the most densely settled sector of the townland. His was not only the largest but also the least subdivided farm on the estate; indeed, though he was one of the first to receive notice of eviction, McDermott came closest of any of the tenants to the model so often in-voked by the critics and improvers of the Irish land system: a solid tenant farmer of thirty or more undivided acres, raising grain and cattle for the market in addition to his potatoes. Ironically, the one figure in the townland who measured up to this model of order and prosperity was also a leading agitator against the Crown and the first to flee the country with his gains.

Equally prominent in terms of kin were the Connors, three of whom were among the Defendants: Michael, age sixty; Terence, forty; and John, thirty. The patriarch of this family, Patrick Connor, the oldest tenant, lived in Aughamore, the name used locally for the crowded southwestern sector of the lands, a place where the cabins huddled together and the lots were little more than kitchen gardens, a typical "rundale-clachan" settlement. In rundale-like fashion, the elder Connor held about eight acres scattered throughout the tiny subdivisions of Aughamore as well as a cottage set amid the cluster of cabins strung out along the Old Road nearest the crossroads and the Lloyd's Glebe House. None of the Connors were among the larger tenants individually, but the aggregate holdings of this large family, all scat-tered in archaic patches in the oldest part of the townland, seem to have conferred upon them sufficient status and means to play an influential, clan-destine role. Just before the final evictions, the Reverend Henry Brenan of Kilglass, in a letter appealing to the Commissioners that Patrick Connor, his son John, and John Stuart be allowed to stay on as "Tenants of 20 or 30 acres," vouched for their good behavior and industrious habits and of-fered that "they are considered by the people to have some money" and that they had declined to accept the offer of emigration "having means to live at home."[23] Patrick Connor, along with Padian, was also one of the collectors of the legal fund named by Cox. It may also be that he was the "person of the name of Patrick Connor [who] claimed to be entitled to the rents and profits" of the estate and cautioned the others, as one of the petitions claimed, against paying their rents "to any person but himself." This "pretender" was and still remains an elusive figure. But if, as Knox thought, the claim had been nothing more than peasant casuistry about ancient rights to forestall legal evictions by the Crown, the patriarchal Connor of Aughamore is as likely a candidate as can be found.

If McDermott came as close to being an independent tenant farmer as anyone on the lands, the Connor family represented something closer to the deplored stereotype of the large, congested household, working impossibly small parcels of land, endlessly divided and subdivided among the adult children. The elder Connor was a widower living with five of his sons, ranging in age from the eldest, John (one of the Defendants) who was twenty-eight, to Denis, twenty, and three daughters between twenty-three and twelve years of age. An older son, Terence (forty), was also a defendant and held six acres situated between Padian and McDermott along the road to Rooskey. Terence was one of the smaller tenants, paying a rent of only £3 15s. for marginal lands, but he may have been one of the links between Aughamore, the "infield" section of the estate, and the more isolated larger tenants of the outlying sections.[24] Patrick's brother and also a Defendant, Michael Connor, was also a widower with a number of unmarried adults in the household, two sons of thirty and twenty-four and a daughter of nineteen. His son Michael (twenty-one) was one of the two previous emigrants of Ballykilcline; he was said in the rent rolls to be "Married . . . in England harvesting."[25] Michael Connor's seven acres of land were also scattered around the old clachan area in small parcels.

The Connors were more deeply immersed than the McDermotts in the system of joint tenancies and subdivided strips in the townland. The generally larger tenants farther north also shared many joint holdings, but the archaic strip lots, which had once been periodically redistributed, did not extend to that part of the estate. Annual redistribution was apparently no longer practiced, but the widespread use of "fines" between one tenant and another still assured a fairly high degree of movement and mutuality in the cultivation of the strips. "Fines" might be paid by one tenant to another for the temporary use of parcels of land, for either tilling or grazing, quite often between members of the same family. Although the practice resembled the grossly exploitative "conacre" system (the leasing of subsistence-size plots for one season at exorbitant rents), the network of "fines" among the Ballykilcline tenants was more often an arrangement between equals or near equals that allowed some of the larger families like the Connors with little land to make the most of their labor. Other middling families, like the Magans or Winters, with slightly more land but older or fewer hands to work it, received small payments or labor at crucial times of the year. The system of "fines" existed independent of the tenancies of record and remained invisible until the time of emigration, when the Crown agents were surprised to receive a number of claims from the tenants for "compensation" for these unofficial payments due them from others being evicted.

The system of fines and the sharing of rents in the many joint holdings also recalls older practices in which elders or other persons of status in the townlands collected and passed on the rents for common lots and were thus inevitably drawn into apportioning shares, presiding over redistributions, settling quarrels, and generally guiding the internal workings of the community. Unlike many other peasant communities of Europe, there was in

Ireland no established or customary way of selecting individuals for these important roles or even of investing them with some symbol or title of office, nor was there any understanding that those whose judgment might be heeded in one season or on one issue would be respected on another occasion. It was another of the "throughother" characteristics of the townland. Like so much else in Irish peasant life, the process of choosing leadership had an anarchic quality that sometimes ended in chaos and frequently in dispute.[26] Attributes that might carry weight in mediating quarrels over land, like a reputation for fairness, wisdom, experience, or knowledge of custom, could decide whose judgment might be heard on one occasion, and a strong farmer, or the head of a large family or merely the cleverest or toughest might be preferred at another time. Naturally, the same individuals were often called upon as advocates in dealings with proprietors and authorities, as they were in Ballykilcline during the rent strike. But the qualities of wisdom and toughness were not necessarily to be found in the same individuals, so the collective action of the townland sometimes varied from petitions to threats, and from litigation to violence, depending upon the fluctuating charismas of its leading figures.

All surviving information about the townland strongly suggests that its leadership in both internal matters and in dealings with the outside was chosen, or imposed, from among the fourteen Defendants. And of these fourteen, five individuals in particular stand out as decisive figures in the ten years before the emigration: Patrick Connor, Hugh McDermott, Martin Padian, William Stewart, and Mark Nary. Of these five, Patrick Connor and Hugh McDermott seem to have exerted the most consistent influence over the other tenants, especially in the early years of the strike. Some consequence may also have derived from the surviving power of their names alone, the O'Connors and MacDermotts having once been the ruling families of the region. Of the rest, all but Padian were heads of large families, with either adult brothers or sons at the head of families of their own on the lands, and they were all among the longtime tenants-of-record. Except for Patrick Connor, the five also held ten acres or more—McDermott with by far the largest single holding in his name. The three sons of Mark Nary (Luke, James, and Edward) held slightly more than thirty acres jointly. Even Connor's modest eight acres is slightly deceiving, since his large family was deeply enmeshed in the web of joint holdings all over the townland. But a number of other tenants who were not Defendants nor visible as leading figures in the rent strike were also in possession of ten or more acres, so the size of their holdings alone does not seem to have entitled or inclined these five to take initiatives more than others. Any number of factors may have determined who was to speak for the all-but-invisible and all-but-powerless bulk of the community. Personality, fervor, eloquence, conviction, family name, or the sheer ambition to lead others may have propelled some of these and not others to take the risk of making themselves known to the authorities as "ringleaders."

The Microgeography of Ballykilcline

Speaking in parliament for Her Majesty's Commissioners of Woods and Forests, Lord Monteagle described the population of the Crown estate in Roscommon as "a mass of destitute paupers," meaning that even the most generous effort to reclaim them from indolence and poverty would be wasted. Just so the occupants must have seemed to almost any outside observer. But within the microscopic limits of Ballykilcline's social hierarchy there were some noticeable gaps in status that would have been of great importance to the people themselves, especially between the landless laborers at one end and the tenants of fourteen to thirty acres at the other. At the height of the townland's population in 1846, there existed some fifty-eight separate tenancies on the rent rolls, some "at-law" and some "at-will." Because the number of households recorded as resident at that time was ninety-eight, it appears that some forty families held no leases at that time. Although Knox's records, as we have seen, take no account of the access to land that kinship and the network of oral arrangements gave to nearly all of the occupants, it might still be fair to say that these forty households made up the townland's laboring class, whose livelihood depended primarily on the exchange of their labor and on their access to land by oral agreement. They numbered approximately two hundred individuals, or 40 percent of the townland's population. Of the fifty-eight tenancies, only seven were of ten or more acres, and five of these were joint tenancies. Only Hugh McDermott and Edward Donnellan (with just under fifteen acres) were tenants with individual holdings large enough to be described as farmers. Of these two, McDermott was one of the leading Defendants but, apart from his son's connection to O'Ferrall, Donnellen seems to have played only a passive role. Just beneath them in size of holdings were five groups who held jointly: John and Anne Mullera and John Carolan rented just under twelve acres together; Thomas and Edward McCormick shared fifteen acres; Patrick and James Deffily shared eleven acres; and Patrick and Martin Finn shared ten acres. None of these were among the ringleaders. But Bartly Connor and James Nary, two active Defendants, held eighteen acres jointly with the Foxes, one of whom was a servant in the Lloyd's household. Some evidence points to the young Connor and Nary as the firebrands of the townland, suspects in assaulting alleged informers and possibly also in various threats and anonymous messages to Knox. Some individuals were landless, to all appearances laborers relying on access to small lots that varied from year to year, were not excluded either from taking leading roles in collective community action or from sharing the thought of the "farmers" that they had rights to the land.

Three focuses of activity are visible on the estate. The one in Aughamore was dominated by the Connors and Stewarts. To the southwest, beyond the Celtic Ring Fort, was another cluster of settlement, described as "Kiltullivary or Bungariff," place-names that had no legal standing any more than Aughamore. In this corner of the estate, the Narys were now the only tenants of record, although they were intimately involved in joint tenancies with the occupants of Aughamore. Because the Crown Surveyors of 1836 still thought it pertinent to record the Gaelic place-names of this neighborhood, referring to it as "the Narry lands," this sector of the townland retained at least some vestige of self-conciousness until that time, especially since it was represented prominently in the leadership and agitation of the rent strike. The third nucleus of "activists" dwelt in the "outfield," in relatively isolated households to the northeast, including two of the most active, McDermott and Padian.

Complicating the local puzzle of conscious status and affiliation still further, some of the key figures in the defiance of the Crown were now the heads of families who had seen better times. Many Ballykilcline families overlapped into adjacent townlands through generations of intermarriage and subleasing, creating a continual movement of individuals among the townlands. An obviously older Richard Padian, for example, had held a substantial forty-three acres on a lease of adjacent lands granted by the first Baron Hartland in 1797, expiring in 1822. The Hanlys, who were among the poorer occupants of Ballykilcline by the 1840s (with five acres in joint tenure), had held long leases in neighboring Barrawalla on at least 150 acres that had also expired some twenty years before. Similarly, both the Connors and Narys had been much more substantial tenants (in the nearby parish of Farnbeg) until early in the 1820s, when their original leases expired, and they found themselves in default and unable to renew.[27] It is likely that the default of leases in the early twenties was due primarily to the general depression in prices that decimated farmers throughout the country after the Napoleonic Wars, reducing some from relative affluence to grinding poverty. The fact that some of these lands later fell into the hands of local gentlemen and farmers may also have left a residue of grievances in the minds of once prouder families.

Some, like the Connors and Hanlys, seem to have receded back into older family cores in the "infields" of Aughamore and Barrawalla on small joint holdings that tied them to the solidarity of the townland and, possibly, had brought the younger Padian through marriage to his marginal lot of seven acres. The differences between these "infield" and "outfield" cores of activity were not very great, but they do offer some insight into how the leadership of the community was shared during the rent strike.

If any of the tenants were possessed of the surplus of produce that Knox suspected, it was McDermott. Not only did he rent the largest undivided holding and owe the most in arrears but he was also the most diversified farmer, raising or sharing in five cows, a horse, and ten sheep. As we have seen, he also maintained a shebeen along the Old Road and therefore probably also worked an illicit still somewhere in the "outfield." He was the senior partner in at least three joint holdings, including some with younger brothers and cousins; he was owed "fines" from several of the smallholders for grazing; and, given the quantities of oats, hay, and potatoes harvested on his lands, he was also most likely the biggest employer of seasonal labor in the townland. With these resources as his footing, he was at the center of a network of clientage and interlocking arrangements that was easily convertible into a base for collective action. And all indications are that McDermott was possessed of a mind and temperament to suit his strong position. His early departure for America was most probably a sign among his neighbors that all was lost, though even with his evident strengths, it is unlikely that the townland's future would have been any less futile had he remained.[28]

Patrick Connor, to all appearances one of the small cottier-laborers of the district, who was always named with McDermott as one of the ringleaders, appears to have been the center of a different and older network of affiliation based in Aughamore. There were three households of Connors, all within the intimate nucleus of the old settlement. At the head of the three households were three aging patriarchs of a name that was hoary with age and legend in Roscommon. As with so much else in the tiny window that their action opened to us, it is not possible to say what this concentration of Connors in the ancient crossroads of Aughamore meant in the dynamics of the townland and its behavior during the struggle. Some hints point to Patrick Connor as the center of the conspiracy throughout its duration. From beginning to end, he was always named as one of the ringleaders. At least some of his family were literate. His name, along with McDermott's, was given as "security" for the good faith of others. He was said to be "in a state of comparative affluence" compared with his neighbors, although he had not held more than seven acres in his own name since the 1820s. Perhaps most suggestive of his frame of mind, he was one of only six heads of family who refused the emigrant bounty after all was lost, knowing that he and his many dependents would be ejected, starving, and in fever, in what he had called "the land of their nativity."[29]

According to the townland's earliest petition, it was also "someone of the name of Connor" who had told them to pay no rents to anyone but himself as the supposed "legal fund" was being collected clandestinely. In contrast to Hugh McDermott the emigrant and the seemingly intrepid Martin Padian, Connor's correspondence to Burke was apparently cast in his own hand (or at least not in that of the elusive "scribes" whose copperplate pens and phrasing speak for most of the other petitioners). Whether Patrick Connor of Aughamore was the Connor in question or, as appears possible, he had something to do with reviving the ancient claims of the O'Connors to the lands, the now threadbare patriarch was clearly one who would not allow his poverty to rob him of authority and respect among his neighbors.

5

"Rebellion" in Ballykilcline, 1836–1847

Why don't you take your hat off, fellow? Don't you know you are
speaking to a magistrate?" said the agent. "I know I'm not speaking
to the king, sir, . . . and I never takes off my hat but to them I can
respect and love. The Eye that sees all knows I've no right either to
respect or love an agent!"

"Rent-Day," a folk tale[1]

Nothing that can be called a personal account survives from the townland's conflict with the Crown. In the first few years, it is not even certain that they knew how they had suddenly become the Crown's tenants. For two generations they had looked upon the lords of Strokestown as their legitimate landlords, as had most of the neighboring townlands. But the coincidence of Maurice Mahon's lunacy with the expiration of the Crown lease temporarily freed them from any demands for rent. What illusion this emancipation may have created among them, or if it had begun under the mad Baron, is not known, except that their relations were apparently benign. They must have known of his condition, but there is no indication that anyone at Strokestown House thought to explain their changed status. Neither Denis Mahon nor his Galway cousin, who were now litigating for the estate, had a claim on Ballykilcline and demanded no rents. And after forty years of routinely receiving the paltry £200 a year through the Hartland lease, the Crown's Commissioners acted slowly before demanding payment of the rents directly from the tenants in 1836. By that time, some owed more than three years' rent to the estate. How far the tenants understood the change in their situation is unclear, but, knowing or unknowing, they were now Crown tenants and about to become visible to the royal bureaucracy. Almost nothing of their minds and lives would have survived but for this fact and for the decade-long conflict that followed.

It was characteristic of the eccentric system that governed Ireland that the portrayal of the "Ballykilcline rebellion" read in the House of Lords had originated with the wily Cox, who whispered his view of the situation to the cringing agent in his dingy office. The august setting of the ermined lords of the empire and the now neatly printed reports that Lord Monteagle had before him belied the source. Drawn up originally in George Knox's nervous hand as he sat barricaded against the night, the intelligence presented to the House by Monteagle was a bizarre contrast to the chaotic realities of the townland.[2]

The Crown's Commissioners were interested in knowing the minds of the occupants only in the way an adversary wants to know the disposition of the enemy, his leaders, his strength and intentions. But for this, as we have seen, they were forced to rely on the low and distant intermediaries whose vision was either blinded by aversion or distorted by self-interest. In this respect, at least, the Commissioners might be forgiven for misunderstanding the tenants' motives. For their part, the tenants had every reason to hide as much as possible from the view of outsiders and in some things even from kin and neighbors. Secrecy, subterfuge, and deception were among the few defenses available to them—intangible, unpoliceable resources against exposure. Having just emerged from a century of penal prohibition, these tactics had been brought to a high level of virtuosity by the peasantry of "hidden Ireland." The importance the peasantry attached to concealment may be gauged by the notorious place the culture has given to the informer, the weakest link in a fragile defense and the perennial cause of its defeats in the national folklore.

Facts from Ballykilcline

But not all could be hidden. However well they maintained their silence, the driver was unlikely to miss much of their assets or the identities of their leaders. But neither could he usually be trusted to pass on everything of value to his employers; since information was his coinage, profit and safety lay in filtering its flow in both directions. Knowing something of the trends and tendencies in the townlands and either exaggerating or muting them in advising the landlord could often serve a driver's interests. Cox was clearly eager to put the townland in the worst light, including inflating its resources in order to make the withholding of rents appear all the more brazen. For similar reasons, Knox was unlikely to question the driver's information. The record they created may be relied on to give an approximate account of the names and numbers of tenants, although they usually overlook the poorest: the squatters, lodgers, travelers, and others who moved in and out of the townland unseen. Often, such "strangers" on the lands were taken for agitators, sometimes rightly.

Apart from what came to him from the driver and his informers, the agent was generally blind to the townland's mental dynamics, the leadership, loyalties, and feuds, the concepts of rights and customs that would have offered him some understanding of its actions. Every landlord and agent in Ireland knew that the townlands possessed collective identities, reinforced by powerful family ties and interests. Identities were tacitly recognized in local usage, in addressing, recording, and sometimes punishing them as entities, as in the case of Doorty, the townland "banished" for harboring Mahon's killer. But virtually any action on their part that addressed the rights and access to the land collectively was invariably perceived as conspiracy and therefore became a police matter under the numerous emergency acts against illegal combinations.

Ballykilcline's tangible assets, consisting almost exclusively of the land, its crops, and animals, were carefully surveyed and logged, but even these were camouflaged as far as possible to elude the grasp of distraints and seizures. Agents and drivers knew of these ruses and worked on the common assumption that even the most visibly destitute and ragged had hidden resources and had been reared expertly in feigning pennilessness. Mutual mistrust prevailed over nearly all contact between them. Once the prospect of eviction arose, even exchanging courtesies with the deputies of the landlord—a conversation at the crossroads or a fulsome greeting in the marketplace—raised questions of loyalty in the eyes of the townland. On the other side, open sympathy or apologies for the distressed tenants, such as those expressed by squire Hogg or Father McDermott, came close to class betrayal, even to sedition. The atmosphere of suspicion was further charged by the general conviction that "Paddy's" bowing submissiveness and obsequious speech concealed a well of bitterness that awaited only a sign of weakness to overflow into violence.

The sequence of accumulating arrears and the threat of eviction contained an inherent potential for violent conflict everywhere. Virtually all the small tenants and cottiers of the country were indebted for small amounts from year to year—with the ever-present fear of eviction as the prod, most were in a perennial struggle to catch up with the payments due on each gale day. Except for a small minority of the stronger farmers, surpluses of convertible assets in cash, goods, cattle, or crops were rare, and for the majority completely unknown even in the best of times. When the arrears of at least two years had accumulated in the townland, few of the tenants would have been able to meet such a debt, even if they had wished to. Since the entire townland was then heavily indebted, the attempted evictions, the threats and violence, and finally their forced emigration followed in an inexorable progression.

The solidarity that the Defendants were able to maintain among themselves for a decade might be explained by the fact that the larger tenants were also the most heavily in arrears in their rents. By 1846, none of the tenants owed less than nine and a half years' rent, and some had paid nothing for twelve years. By that time, some of the larger holdings owed more than £200, an amount that none could conceivably have raised at once, even with their "buried gold." The smallest tenants were in no better state to settle their debt; Honora Winter, a widow living alone on less than half an acre, owed £46; the widow Ginty owed £29; and some families with fewer than five acres owed £50 or more, the equivalent of about eight years of a grown man's labor. The impossibility of their paying such amounts may have been the stimulus for going to O'Ferrall in the first place. Whether the idea of making a direct claim to the lands in the name of a shadowy "pretender" of the Connors' was his or theirs, it was their only alternative to begging before the agent. That ordeal was known to them all in both personal experience and folklore as a futile and humiliating ritual. As in the tale of Bill Doody, the supplicant approached the agent's door "hat in his hand, his eyes fixed on the ground, and his knees bending under him," knowing he would be refused.[3] If the biannual struggle to meet the rent was the cause of grief and grievances, arrears had always been the bane of the Irish landlord as well. The landlord's stringency in demanding them or his liberality in extending them very often decided the entire relationship between the classes and consequently the peace or turbulence of the neighborhood. Through both necessity and long practice, landlords who insisted on the consistent and prompt payment of rents were widely regarded as violating a benign established custom.

There is no record of serious disturbances on Lord Hartland's estate until after 1834. Nor is there a clear record of how far the old lord had let the tenants' arrears accrue in the years before. But by the time he was committed as a lunatic in 1836, the finances of the estate were already in a parlous state. By 1845, when the old man died and Denis Mahon took full possession, £13,000 in arrears had accumulated and three years of poor rates were due.[4] When Denis Mahon tried to restore the estate to solvency, first by "emigrating" thousands of the indebted peasantry and then by threatening eviction for nonpayment, he was assassinated. When the Crown, rather naively applying policies of estate management based on routine practice in England, demanded full payment of arrears in Ballykilcline, it met resistance, litigation, and violence.

Although it cannot be said that all Irish landlords were equally negligent, the many select committees of this period looking into the causes of distress on the land in Ireland agreed that the management of Irish estates was often backward and chaotic. On estates occupied by large numbers of pauper tenants, rents were often simply uncollectible in a chronically cash-poor economy no matter how harsh the measures employed. And neither the seizure of the tenants' assets nor wholesale evictions could recoup an estate's finances when heavy arrears had been accumulated. As the Encumbered Estates Act later recognized, such cases were inherently insoluble if the peace of the country were to be preserved.

By the fall gale of October 1841, the tenants of Ballykilcline owed £2,884 in arrears, in addition to an unknown amount in tithes and cesses. In that same month, a survey of the townland's assets was executed on orders from the Quit Rent Office, apparently in an effort to find how much of the debt might be reduced by confiscation of the tenants' movable property, a step recommended by Knox but never seriously considered by the Commissioners of Woods and Forests. At first sight, Knox's survey (if accurate) tended to confirm his suspicion that the tenants' resources were enough to make up at least a substantial fraction of the five years' arrears owed, from the sale of the goods in their possession. The forty-two recorded tenants of October 1841 had raised 174 stacks of oats, 33 cocks of hay, and 103 acres of potatoes, and possessed 66 cows, 7 horses, and 26 sheep—no hens, ducks, geese, turkeys, or (remarkably) pigs were noted.[5] If added to the approximately 100 to 150 acres of potatoes cultivated by the remaining cottier subtenants, who possessed little else, the total cash value of their resources might have amounted to half the rents they owed, at best, perhaps as much as £1,400. Even after five years of living rent free, the nearly five hundred occupants of the townland had thus accumulated an average capital of less than £3 per head (just 10 shillings short of the current transatlantic fare for one adult).

With such minute quantities of wealth involved, it might seem nearly meaningless to draw distinctions among the people based on their share of it. But such distinctions were real and perceptible within the townland and to a lesser degree even from the outside. The possession of a cow, for example, was a visible sign of relative substance that distinguished a few of the tenants-of-record. In the case of the larger tenants, Knox's estimate of their worth at between £20 and £100 may not have been far off, although it is not clear whether he believed that they had salted away these amounts in cash from their unpaid rents or had assets in goods of this value.[6] Rarely traveling in the townland, Knox was not able to make any such distinctions among its occupants by eye; all descriptions agree that the dwellings, dress, and other outward signs of "comparative affluence" offered little clue to the outsider. And Knox's books, enumerating the individual holdings, annual rents and arrears, and occasional details about the crops and livestock of each tenant, conveyed a relatively tidy arrangement of the property that only hinted at the underlying intricacy of the townland's economy and might easily have deceived the agent about the relative wealth and status of individual occupants.

The "Return of Crops and Cattle," which Knox presented to the Quit Rent Office in the fall of 1841, is an example of the incongruence of the written record and the realities of the land system as practiced by the peasantry.[7] The widespread practice of holding land and livestock jointly would have been quite familiar to any land agent; most deplored the custom as a hindrance to bookkeeping and a barrier to developing individual responsibility, although it was very widely tolerated. In cases where rents were seriously in arrears, it also was an obvious hindrance to establishing a clear account of which tenants owed exactly what part of the debt. Since most joint holdings were encumbered by informal and customary agreements, such arrangements removed much of the landlord's control over individual tenants, forcing him and his agents to deal with tenants collectively while the joint shareholders kept each individual's exact accountability in their own minds, concealed from those above. Thus, Thomas, Edward, and Patrick McCormick, together with John Hanly, John Clemons, and Luke Henry (neither of the latter residents of Ballykilcline) held some fifteen acres in 1841 and produced nine stacks of oats, two cocks of hay, and about five acres of potatoes jointly. The six also kept four cows and a horse and owed £76 5s. 9d. in arrears altogether. Apart from Hanly, these were apparently smallholders in adjoining townlands, a mixture of marginal cottiers and petty tenants with dispersed fields. Since their obligation was "off the books" and all but uncollectible, the advantage in their acting collectively with Hanly, the tenant-of-record, is obvious. What seemed like a "conspiracy" to the authorities was often merely customary practice or, when eviction threatened, a rallying of the silent economy of friends that made it difficult to single out vulnerable members of their class, some of whom had no assured access to the use of land besides these claims on friendship. Such arrangements were another vestige of the "throughotherness" of the old rundale system, operating now not only as a form of clientage and mutual aid but as a source of defense and solidarity against intrusion.

Most of the tenants were enmeshed in such joint holdings and oral agreements throughout the small estate. The "big farmers" like McDermott habitually engaged in joint holdings with no obvious need, perhaps as an act of patronage or favor to in-laws. Patrick Connor, with not much more than potato and kitchen gardens in his own name, was a center of a more egalitarian network of interdependency among the smallholders. The "fines" for temporary grazing rights or subdivisions with other indebted tenants on a year-by-year basis sometimes also included cottier laborers, squatters, and individuals from outside the townland of whom the land agent had no record or knowledge at all. From the outside, this maze of changing tacit arrangements often appeared as deliberate peasant intrigue to disguise the tenants' income and frustrate supervision. Thus, when the threats and violence actually began and reports of outside agitators in the neighborhood circulated among the people of property, the landlords and their middlemen were already used to seeing nearly any of the townland's activities as intrigues. In some part, at least, it was his inability to decipher these semiclandestine arrangements that frightened Knox and led him to believe that he was surrounded by a hostile and conspiratorial society of paupers without names. Of the same mind as the local low gentry like Sandys and Hogg, Knox was unable to understand the ferocious love with which these faceless peasants clung to their homes.

The Official View

There are at least two versions in the surviving records of how the Ballykilcline rent strike began. One is the official version, recorded and preserved in parliamentary papers, court records, and estate books. On the very day that the final sailing dates for the evicted tenants were posted in the townland, Thomas Spring-Rice, the first Baron Monteagle, made his report to the House of Lords. In it he gave the commissioners' view of events in Ballykilcline. The rents due from the tenants had been "tolerably punctually paid," he said, for the two years following the expiration of the Hartland lease in April of 1834. In the gales (that is, the semiannual rent days) of 1837, however, he said that there had been "great difficulty found getting rent and notices served upon all (about 80) occupiers," for one year's arrears. Fifty-two tenants surrendered possession after being served, and were immediately readmitted as "Care-takers, at an allowance of sixpence per Month," having signed an agreement to vacate when required. The remainder "positively refused" either to give up possession or to account for the arrears. Attempts made to collect the rents by the Crown's receivers in the following four years, to 1841, were completely ineffectual and the previously compliant fifty-two "now refused also to surrender possession."[8]

An "Information of Intrusion" was then filed by the Crown against eight occupiers who had paid no rent at all for the previous seven years, declaring the tenants "trespassers." This action also being defied for another two years, an injunction was then obtained against four of these offenders. Monteagle reported that the Crown agent finally succeeded in taking possession of their houses, but for reasons not then revealed, failed to have them pulled down. Shortly after, three of the four families "re-entered forcibly" and proceedings were then once again brought against them. A second information was then filed, this time against fourteen occupiers who "were ascertained to be the ring leaders of the conspiracy." In the midst of this ineffectual effort to bring the estate to rights, the tenants themselves had initiated a suit against the Crown, tried by the Court of Exchequer in Dublin, that finally ended in 1846 in the Crown's favor. In these eleven-year-long proceedings, Her Majesty's Commissioners of Woods and Forests succeeded in expelling just one of the occupiers and his family from Ballykilcline. It is unlikely that even these strayed very far.

These laborious and expensive proceedings were an embarrassment to the Commissioners and kept their agents in Ireland in a high state of frustration. All the proprieties of the law were being meticulously observed by the Crown in this dispute, to a much greater degree than most private landlords in similar conflicts. In fact, some of the Irish landlords and the Lord Lieutenant were beginning to complain that the Crown was setting a dangerous example, especially as violence against landlords began to show a marked increase in the autumn and winter of 1847, when six were shot to death and another gravely wounded.[9] In the two or three years preceding the clearance of Ballykilcline, the Crown had also come under fire from the local gentry, as Monteagle said, "for too great leniency and forbearance"; "frequent remonstrances were made by the Proprietors of the adjoining lands, that the worst consequences as regarded their tenantry resulted from the continued occupation by these persons without payment of rent, and in defiance of the rights of the Crown." Lord Clarendon, the Lord Lieutenant of Ireland, demanded of the Commissioners what action they proposed to take about these troublesome tenants. The matter now called for "decisive measures," said Clarendon, "for the expression of resistance and general insubordination on the part of the Crown tenants has been most injurious to the Peace of the County of Roscommon and has induced the disaffected to believe that such illegal combination can be carried on with perfect impunity."[10]

Another cause of embarrassment to Monteagle was that if he reported only the official actions taken by the commissioners, it was certain to seem that they had been remarkably lax in defending the interests of the Crown revenue. But if he tried to summarize the voluminous "intelligence" from their agents on the spot that had guided their action, the mass of arcane detail, stewed with obscure local quarrels and conflicts, was sure to baffle their lordships. The constant flow of such information from the Crown agents in Ireland was never fully digestible to the commissioners, any more than was most of the intelligence received from that source by the Home Office or the Irish Secretary. The vast testimony of various Irish "experts" given before the select committees, too, was often greeted with skepticism, disbelief, or indifference in London. Until the crises of the famine years, the annual report of the Commissioners of Woods and Forests was rarely questioned or debated in the House.

Following the decision against the tenants in the Court of Exchequer in 1846, the Crown offered to accept applications for new leases from the tenants in Ballykilcline. The surveyor Weale's advice of ten years before still applied: the Crown could not simply evict in Ireland without endangering the public peace. As a result, the final eviction process was suspended for some months while an effort was made to ascertain if the tenants did, in fact, have the means to pay the now-heavy arrears, or some part of them. Receiving the local agent's report on that matter, they then proposed to the tenants that two years' arrears be paid by the fourteen "ring leaders" (out of the ten years' now due) and one year's arrears by the remainder before new leases were drawn up. As of December of that year, Monteagle had to report, no proposals of any sort had been received from the tenants. One further month was allowed by the Lord Lieutenant of Ireland for the occupiers to send a spokesman to Dublin to negotiate a settlement in order to avoid the disturbing ceremony of eviction and the hooking down of roofs during Christmastime.[11] There was not yet any mention of hunger.

Still, there was no response from Ballykilcline through the end of January 1847, according to Monteagle: "In order to avoid even the semblance of harshness by the ejectment of these parties during the Winter, it was decided to delay enforcing the injunction till May." At that time, the commissioners had finally decided, the entire population of Ballykilcline would be "emigrated" to North America at Crown expense. There would be no forcible reoccupation this time because the cottages were to be "levelled to the ground" as soon as the occupants departed. Knox had all along urged sterner measures. Clearly speaking the feelings of the local gentry, he argued simply that if the rents were not paid the tenants should be ejected, especially those whom he had identified as the ringleaders. These had not only refused the rents and abused his bailiff but, by collecting money from the others to carry on legal proceedings against their rightful landlord, were the cause of the financial breakdown of the estate. He also felt that the Crown was ill-advised in offering new leases. Whether the arrears were paid up or not, he insisted, they "never would become satisfactory tenants." Knox had not originated the idea to emigrate the tenants but was evidently relieved by the prospect of emptying the townland entirely. Quoting Knox in his request for Treasury funds to pay the passage of the evicted tenants, Monteagle proposed that the Crown pay the expense of the tenants' "removal by emigration" if they surrendered possession and "level their houses," (presumably with their own hands).[12]

Although no challenge was raised to Monteagle's report, his summary of the events leading up to this decision leaves a number of questions unanswered: for example, why had the tenants "positively refused" to pay the rents when Lord Hartland gave up the estate; what had been the basis of their suit against the Crown; what focused the attention of the highest authorities—Dublin Castle and the House of Lords, and even the *Times* of London—on an insignificant settlement of recalcitrant peasants years before the sensational murder in the neighborhood; and why had the Crown's commissioners gone to such extraordinary lengths to appease the insignificant townland? More than £1,700 had been paid in costs to Brassington and Gale and substantial legal fees to the firm of Robinson and Son, not to mention the salaries of their agents and the various other intermediaries they employed. Added to the fact that the estate was finally sold in 1849 to William George Downing of Edenderry for only £5,500 (£4,000 less than its estimated valuation), the liquidation of the tiny estate produced a loss of at least £8,000 in the royal revenue. One might even add the remarkable award of 6d. a month to the recalcitrants themselves to act as "Care-takers" of their own homes after they had brazenly ignored legal notices! Now, an additional £2,500 (and more to come) was to be drawn from the Treasury to pay the passage to America for virtually all the delinquents, including the ringleaders and their families.

Lord Monteagle was himself an Irish landlord and had long been an advocate of the Wakefield policy of assisted emigration as a rational and humane solution for Ireland's problems, like Bentham's poorhouse, "a method not of cutting but of untying the Gordian knot" of congested estates.[13] But parliamentary opposition to it had balked for decades at "rewarding" the fecklessness of the Irish peasantry and its landlords with free emigration to the New World. Opposition from Canada to the Antipodes had also stiffened against "shovelling out paupers," shifting the burden of supporting indigents from Irish and English ratepayers to New World almshouses, as they regarded the policy of assisted emigration.[14] Even as the Crown's chief commissioner, Monteagle had not been at liberty to apply the policy until the first year of the famine, when opposition crumbled at the spectacle of mass public starvation. Even then, prodded by the reports of Knox and Cox that many of the tenants were still feigning poverty, the Commissioners were ambivalent. As late as the spring of 1847, they still hoped merely to reduce the townland population sufficiently to make it more attractive for sale rather than to adopt "the extreme measure of the entire dispossession by ejectment of the remaining population."[15] Only after the debacle between Major Mahon and Father McDermott and the subsequent assassination was it finally decided to clear the estate entirely. A month after Mahon's death, the commissioners announced that "the removal of the remaining occupiers will be essential to the future advantage of the estate by the emigration of those who are willing to go and the rest dispossessed."[16]

What had seemed for a decade to be a trifling irritant to the commissioners had escalated into a cause celebre by the murders in Roscommon. McDermott's alleged incitement was taken up and condemned in the House of Lords by the Earl of Shrewsbury, the leading Catholic peer, who called for a public rebuke of the provincial priest. First, the Bishop of Elphin and soon after Dr. McHale, the Archbishop of Tuam, took up the dispute with Shrewsbury in the press in language hardly less incendiary than McDermott's. In a letter to Shrewsbury published in the *Times*, the bishop was especially unrestrained in defending his priest:

> Can we every day behold scenes that would disgrace a Nero or a Caligula present themselves to our view without any attempt to throw the shield of the Gospel over the dying victims, and avert by every means that religion sanctions the deadly arrows that are daily and hourly aimed at the poor of God by inhuman and unfeeling oppressors?[17]

The latitude that the commissioners had once enjoyed in dealing with the estate had been lost, first by the suspicion of the authorities and the local landlords that the violence in Strokestown had been inspired by the Crown tenants and then by the appearance of an explosive sectarian conflict that extended not only to the House of Lords but even to the Holy See. The case also established a long-standing precedent when it was included in a brief brought by a delegation of the Lord Privy Seal, Lord Minto, to the Vatican demanding an injunction against the Irish clergy involving itself in political agitation.

Whether the tenants of Ballykilcline ever became aware of their association with these far-reaching affairs it is not possible to say, beyond what they must have heard from their own priest, Father Peter Geraghty, on the matter or concluded from the massing of troops and police through the fall and winter of 1847. None of those questioned, accused, or eventually executed for the murders of Mahon and Lloyd were apparently their kin, but they had been close neighbors and cotenants for more than a generation and could not have been unknown to them. They were already near desperation by the spring of that year, when Knox's plan for their mass ejection and emigration was made known to them, and they had begun to re-

direct their pleas and petitions upward to their Lordships the Commissioners, protesting among other things their innocence of any connection with
local conspiracies.

The results of fourteen years of management by the Crown's representatives were certainly unsatisfactory for the landlord. It is still to be seen
whether their free emigration was a satisfactory or unsatisfactory result for
the tenants. But their obdurate refusal to leave and the force required to
pry them out tends to suggest that even in the midst of famine, they faced
the prospect of departure with a loathing strong enough to risk rebellion,
doomed as that act was in Ireland.

The Tenants' View

Monteagle's account needs to be corrected on at least one point, that no
responses or proposals had been received from the tenants after the spring
of 1846, when they lost their suit. At about that time, two "Petitions" of
the tenants were sent, one delivered to the Commissioners in London by
The O'Conor Don, M.P. for North Roscommon, giving his residence as
"House of Commons, London." It was addressed to "Charles Gore" (that
is, Sir Charles Gore-Booth, one of the Commissioners) and included a note
from Hugh O'Ferrall describing himself as an "Agent" of No. 4 Chancery
Lane, Dublin. Pursuing a flanking path up through the layers of deputies,
O'Ferrall had apparently taken the petition directly from the tenants and
passed it on through his M.P., the patrinomial Gaelic heir of the Barony of
Balintobber, to deliver to the Commissioners. O'Ferrall had represented
the Ballykilcline tenants for several years by this time, had argued their case
in the Court of Chancery, defended the fourteen Defendants, and was regarded by George Knox as the instigator and "brains" behind the trouble.
He also kept a residence in Ashbrook, a few miles from Strokestown.

It is not always possible to determine the authorship of such "petitions"
and "memorials" as issued from Ireland in these years. They appear to fall
into three categories. There are some like the "Petition" delivered by The
O'Connor Don, whose form, script, and language are replete with the
archaic legal usage of the time, even more baroque in script and style than
was common in England. Some of these, including the May petition, might
be described as grandiose, mustering all the calligraphic skills available
to produce a document that might carry pleas or demands with dignity,
the magnificence of the object itself lending weight and justice to the
argument it contained. "The Humble Petition of Richard Padian and
the other persons in the occupation of the lands of Ballykilcline," as it
was entitled, could well have been the most magnificent written or printed
object ever to be seen in the townland, certainly the most imposing and
luxuriant ever to bear the name of one of its tenants. With its fanfare of
scrolls, flourishes, and curlicues, some Dublin Bartleby of O'Ferrall's seems
to have been flaunting his skills on an exceptionally fine quality of paper in
a good cause.

In a second and slightly more numerous category of "Memorials" were those composed also in a clean, dignified script that emanated from individuals or groups of tenants directly, usually on the inferior paper available in the town stores in the best hand available to them, sometimes a local priest or a sympathetic townsman or a well-tutored youth or one of the "ragged scholars" who infested the countryside. The most distinguishing features of this type are the poor quality of the paper and the economy of expression forced by its cost—they more often consist of one filled sheet rather than two, with rarely a square inch not covered with pleading and argumentation.

Lastly, there are a variety of beseeching or contentious "messages" received by the Crown's agents from individuals, apparently in their own hands or that of the most accomplished penman in the cabin or townland. Many of the latter are notable also by the even more stringent economy of paper, being merely remnants of clean sheets or torn-off segments or reverse sides of refuse sheets, with "last thoughts" or blessings crowded vertically in the margins.

The second petition of May 1846 was less grandiose than the first. It was also elegantly enscribed, but its unpolished phrases point more starkly to the defeated frame of mind among the tenants at this point (reproduced as is):

The Humble Petition of the Tenants of Ballykilcline parish of Kilglass County of Roscommon Ireland———
Most Respectfully Sheweth———
That your Petitioners humbly pray your honours will Interpose Humanely between her most Gracious Magesty the queen and your Petitioners by selling the said land and giving a lease thereof at a reasonable rent the same as was paid by Lord Hartland while held by him—your Petitioners are sincerely sorry and poignant at giving any obstruction to our Most Sovereign lady the queen but were infatuated by the false claim and pretension made on said Lands by one Patrick O'Connor who misguided your Petitioners and now ask pardon for their long Indulgence in Ignorance. Under said Circumstances petitioners humbly solicit and Deprecate in your Benevolence and Humanity you may be Graciously pleased to Interpose on the behalf of your petitioners who will accede to any rule or condition you may be Graciously pleased to comply with the desired Effect of this petition.

That your Petitioners beg to represent most Humbly that there are residing on Said Lands 459 Individuals of Moral Industrious habits exemplary Obedient and Implicit to their Landlady or Landlord which is the cause of bringing thim into contempt but are penitent—and regretful for any misunderstanding which has occured in the Event of the case in question.

Petitioners will for their Correctness give Undeniable Security if required and prays your great Estate will be pleased to send a man in trust to execute Leases should you deem this proposal meet and fit and meet your sanction and Approbation let Strokestown be the place appointed your Petitioners humbly pray to have a reply hereto forwarded in the affirmative or negative before hand and said Response be Directed to Mr. John Connor

Senior of Ballykilcline near Strokestown post office County of Roscommon
Ireland———
    Petitioners are too numerous for insertion———[18]

Coming on the heels of the court's decree, the petition lost what credence it might have had earlier. And the appearance of "the Pretender,"
Patrick O'Connor, for the first time also cast doubt on the the petitioners'
good faith. Their "infatuation" with his claim was certainly not believed.
In his report to James Burke, Knox insisted that the petition contained "not
one particle of truth. . . . . They never believed that a person of the name
of O'Connor had any real claim on the lands. . . ." It was merely a new
effort to obfuscate the entire issue and defy the Crown's rights. "They never
will become satisfactory tenants to the Crown," he said, "and if admitted
again similar proceedings will have to be instituted (de novo) against
them."[19]

In the final joint petition before their emigration, the occupants of
Ballykilcline described their last days on the lands, begging to be spared
their crops now that no hope remained of staying at home:

> That on the 26th of May your petitioners were turned out of their houses
> and dwellings; that they are now deprived of their cabins, and lying out in
> the open air with their starvation for want of food and raiment, and are thereby
> subject to fevers and disorders prevalent in the country. That your petition-
> ers if they are deprived of their crops and tillage will, with their families, be
> thrown on the world, and doomed to ruin and starvation, and they solemnly
> assure you that a part of the tenants so dispossessed are in a raging fever,
> lying in the open air.[20]

The combined force of the law and famine was also bringing peace to
the other townlands. By February of 1848, all occupants of the townland
of Doorty, where Denis Mahon had been shot, had been ejected without
resistance and three suspects in the murder—including James Hasty, a
shebeen-keeper—were charged and in custody in the Strokestown Bridewell,
where another escaped the hangman by dying of fever. This speedy result
was achieved by the head constable with the help of two sworn "approvers"
(that is, informers) of an adjoining townland who came forth in response
to an offer suggested by the agent Ross Mahon that "the tenants who are
anxious to stay . . . be allowed to do so if the murderers are surrendered."
That townland, Cornashina, had "memorialised" the new heir shortly before to be spared from the punitive evictions:

> Memorialists beg in Sorrow to present that they fear the act of the Cruel
> Murderer who took away the life of their Landlord is now revenging on them.
> Memorialists call their God to witness that they are innocent of the deed by
> act or knowledge; they beseech for the Lord's sake that the act of such sav-
> age wretches will not be the means of casting them and their large families
> to perish houseless by the ditchside in a cold and severe winter.[21]

The petitioners of Cornashina came twice before the agents Guinness
and Mahon, promising to make up their arrears and begging to be left on

the lands. They were finally persuaded to give evidence when told: "Prosecute to conviction the murderer of Major Mahon at the next assizes, and you shall have your farms." Hasty was hanged at Roscommon in August before a crowd of four thousand, confessing his guilt of all charges in a dying declaration, thanking his jailors and priests for their kindness, and denouncing "that accursed system of Molly Maguirism" that had brought about his damnation. Owen Beirne, the man convicted of the murder of the Reverend John Lloyd, was hanged the same day. To the dismay of Ross Mahon, the funerals of the hanged men were also well attended.[22]

A number of individual efforts to be left on the lands were yet to be made by a few of the tenants of Ballykilcline once their solidarity was utterly broken. At least two were allowed to remain, having been put at risk for giving information of their neighbors' intentions. But of some 493 individuals who appear in the last recorded count of the townland, 409 had received the emigation bounty by the end of May 1848 and booked for the steerages of Liverpool packets bound for New York.

Outrage and Riot in the Townland

Coercion was the law of the land in prefamine Ireland. No fewer than thirty-five "coercion acts" under various names were enacted or amended between 1800 and the famine, designed primarily to suppress conspiracy and collective action in the rural districts.[23] If the level of violence could be measured by the weight of law arrayed against it, then Ireland surely contained one of the most violent countrysides in Europe. Unlike peasant rioters of England and France, the agrarian population of Ireland rarely expressed their grievances violently in response to fluctuations or "forestalling" in the price of food. Their dependence on the potato and the resulting localism of the food supply accounts for some of this behavior. Instead, whatever patterns are discernible in the rural outrages corresponded more closely to their fears of eviction and the loss of access to land than to market-driven forces in the price of food or even of rents. Similarly, the flour mills and grain warehouses that were often the object of local grievances in England were rarely the target of peasant disturbances in rural Ireland. What "moral economy" they expressed about their rights to remain "in the land of their nativity" was rudimentary and lacked any broader perception of impersonal forces that threatened to encroach on them. This was the clear pattern of Ballykilcline's violence from the time of the first eviction notices: assaults and threats against local figures, including some of their own community, who were thought to threaten their hold on their lots and cabins and therefore also the continuance of the community.

Although beyond the ken of most peasants, the sequence of events that led to violence in Ireland was dependent on distant market forces, as were decisions like Mahon's to clear out the pauper tenantry. But in the townlands the provocation to violence or collective action most often occurred at their threshholds, when bailiffs and drivers raised their hammers to nail notices on the door or iron staples to lock them out. The eviction scene was dreadfully familiar to every peasant in Ireland. The responses resorted to, invariably called outrages by the police and the press, could be drawn only from the limited resources available to the tenants. But these "remedies" had been practiced for years and were well understood in every cabin. Boycotts, forced reentry, anonymous threats, night prowling, secret oaths, cattle maiming, arson, and "turning up" the land were such familiar occurrences to both the law and the peasantry that they were universally regarded as a distinguishing national feature, immortalized in the voluminous "Outrage Papers" of Dublin Castle. It was primarily these elusive weapons that the coercion acts were aimed at suppressing.

Assisted emigration was a relatively new element in this struggle. Most landlords who promoted it as a means of reducing overpopulated estates saw it as an enlightened alternative to eviction and one less likely to damage reputation or stir up local passions. Mahon's ill-fated assistance scheme showed that free emigration might also seem a less benign prospect in the eyes of the townlands than in the landlord's. The emigration of their neighbors and the threat of it looming over those remaining had incited the murder in Doorty. The Crown finally assisted the emigration of Ballykilcline for reasons similar to Mahon's, but only after years in which the townland had repeatedly defied and resisted all attempts at eviction. However more appealing the prospect of America became to millions of individuals in the next few decades, the thought of uprooting a whole community, erasing its place and dispersing its identity, was apparently considered unjust enough in some townlands to risk murder and the damnation of God through the mouths of their priests. That thought had begotten the strife in Ballykilcline and transformed a "tolerably well behaved" tenantry into "rebels." Inadvertently, the Crown had transformed the spasmodic outrages that commonly accompanied evictions into collective action, requiring solidarity and at least a nascent political consciousness. Above all, that result was due to the fact that the commissioners had made an essentially political decision, more openly in this instance than on other emigrating estates: assisted emigration was used for all to see as a device to maintain order and forestall disturbances. Indeed, it was largely because the Crown's policy was viewed by many as a surrender to lawlessness that the rent strike of the remote townland was honored in the neighborhood as a "rebellion."[24]

The Eviction Riots of 1844

The prolonged rent strike and lawsuit were an uncommon addition to the arsenal of peasant resistance and suggest some qualities in the townland that are worth noting. Such forms of collective action would seem to have required an unusually high level of organization and solidarity for rural Ireland in those years, as well as a degree of consciousness among its leaders that belies the description of "lawless banditti" given to them by their local critics. However spurious their claim that a "pretender" to the lands had "plunged them into a state of ignorance" was thought to be, their resort to the courts was a significant act of submission to the law of the land, although it too was treated as an act of conspiracy and insolence by the Crown authorities. Indeed, in a community that was seen as a dangerous model of defiance, perhaps the most conspicuous trait it displayed in its dealings with the law and the Ascendancy was the diffidence that dominated virtually all its open communications with them. The obsequious language of their petitions was rightly taken as the distinctive native genre of feigned deference. But for the most part, their actions during the strike that were described as outrages and rebellion by Knox and the police were remarkably legalistic and pacific, with some notable exceptions.

On other estates throughout the country, tenants threatened with eviction responded with far less moderation than the people of Ballykilcline. It was not the most congested, the most rack-rented, or the most destitute estate in Ireland. And, despite Knox's incessant calls for troops and police, it was far from being the most violent. The piecemeal descriptions of violent incidents that occurred during the strike leave most of the thoughts and passions behind them in the dark. Drawn mostly from the complaints by Knox, the actions that gave the Ballykilcline rent strike the status of a "rebellion" in Parliament and in the memory of its neighbors seem to have consisted primarily of ignoring or defying notices, real or imagined threats against the Crown agents, and assaults on their own neighbors. The two significant exceptions to this pattern were in their responses to armed intrusions into the townland and in their treatment of suspected informers.

The first word from Knox that the tenants were prone to violence was in the spring of 1844, when those who had reentered their cabins were to appear at the Petty Sessions in Rooskey to answer charges of trespass. Were it not for a strong escort of police, Knox claimed, the agent and his party "could not have passed through the Lands to the Court; I never met a more desperate Set of Characters."[25] A few weeks later, when trying to serve a printed notice that Knox was thenceforth to represent the Crown as its agent, "the most determined Resistance and Opposition were experienced . . . that but for the accidental Presence of a few Police, the Process-servers would have been murdered." Six of the "Ringleaders" were arrested and held to "heavy Bail" in the outburst till their appearance on charges. On the night before the trial, Knox informed Burke, "a brutal Murder had taken place . . . on a Person considered as an Informer to Government." He feared this had "a great Effect upon the Witnesses," but thought he could still depend on two of them to appear against the accused.[26]

The trial of the "Queen v. Patk. and Barthw. Narry and others, for forcible Entry and Detainer" took place at the Quarter Sessions in Strokestown before twenty-four grand jurors and three J.P.'s, including Squire Godfrey Hogg. Before the verdict, the prosecutor and magistrates agreed that conviction would carry a sentence of a year in prison for the six charged and a fine of £5 for the ringleaders.[27] Another local landholder, Charles Blakeney, Esq., appeared for the defense, with Hugh O'Farrell (as his name appeared in the proceedings) acting as solicitor. The county subsheriff testified that he had taken possession of the houses and lands of the Defendants the previous January, accompanied by "a large Force of Military, Cavalry and Infantry, and a strong Body of the Police, and that even so attended the Police were obliged to fix Bayonets and charge to prevent Violence from the Occupiers. . . ." The Queen's Bailiff Michael Ryan then drove "Iron Hasps and Staples in the Doors and fastening and securing them in the best Manner." At that point, the tenants "riotously and tumultuously collected together at the Head of a large Mob, swearing that the Moment the Military left the Place they would smash the Locks, break open the Doors, and again re-possess them, and that they would murder any Person who would attempt to prevent them." "Caretakers" hired to mind the four distrained houses refused to stay "through Fear and Terror of their Lives, from the Threats and Menaces of the Defendants." In his only visit unaccompanied by troops, Knox entered the townland three weeks later to post the notices of repossession of the houses, attended only by Cox and another local driver. This time, he said, they were set upon by the "Occupiers of Ballykilcline, who assembled in large Numbers, drove the Bailiffs from the Lands, who fled to the Police Barrack for Protection." According to Mr. Browne, counsellor for the Crown, the mob pursued them even there and compelled the police once again "to charge them, to protect them from Violence."[28]

Blakeney called no witnesses for the Defendants but objected to this testimony as coming entirely from interested parties in the Crown's employ. And in his address to the grand jury, apparently written largely by O'Ferrall, he advanced the extraordinary claim that the queen had no title to the lands of Ballykilcline, "and that Her resorting to this Law [that is, forcible entry] was to avoid a Trial of Her Title; that if She had a Title Her Advisers would have levelled the Houses of the Defendants when they took Possession. . . ." Even more startling to the commissioners were his concluding remarks, "that in the Days of Strafford [Thomas Wentworth, Earl of Strafford, Lord Deputy of Ireland, 1632–1641] the only Men in Ireland who voted against the Rights of the Crown were the Men of Roscommon," and he hoped the jury would do likewise in this case.[29]

The Court of Exchequer in Dublin would curtly dismiss this "vexatious" claim two years later. But the Defendants would have their fleeting moment of triumph when they were acquitted of the charge of forcible entry in July of 1844 "to the great Astonishment of the . . . Barrister and a large Bench of the Magistrates." Knox described this jury as "a Set of the lowest and most ignorant Men that could be impannelled, and a Disgrace to any Court of Justice." Not long after, charges of assault prepared by the Crown against the Defendants were also abandoned in despair at finding a "respectable Jury" in Roscommon, especially when the respectable jurors who were summoned declined to attend.[30]

That July of 1844, a year before the first signs of the blight appeared in Roscommon, was surely the apogee of hope and misplaced confidence in Ballykilcline. No arrears, perhaps no rents forever, victory over the Crown of England, its magistrates, justices, and police, the admiration of their neighbors and the fear of their enemies! Armed forays and bayonet charges into the townland ceased for more than a year after. No notices were posted and no doors were locked and stapled. Neither the Defendants, those who chased Knox to the police barrack, nor any who merely watched the turmoil from their doorways paid rents thereafter. Few Irish peasants ever enjoyed such an illusion of power even for a moment.

Dissension and the Blight

Unfortunately, the calm that followed their acquittal also hides most of the following year in the townland from view. Denis Mahon finally took possession of Strokestown House in this time and hired Ross Mahon to "put the land to rights." The Crown counsellors had also initiated new proceedings for ejectment, this time on the "Equity side" of the Court of Exchequer, "thereby getting rid of the Influence, the Feelings, and Prejudices of Juries." It must have been obvious to O'Ferrall and other friends of the townland that the Queen's magistrates in Dublin were bound to uphold the Crown's title and that no landlord could leave matters where they stood. But there is no indication that the tenants, unmolested by bailiffs or police, remained aware of impending danger or anxious about renewed notices and eviction.

The emigration of Hugh McDermott and his family soon after the acquittals suggests that not all were swept up in euphoria. Even if his intentions were known long before, the departure of the most prosperous figure among them and a leader of the "rebellion" must have cast some doubt on the future. By January 1846, renewed probing from outside in the form of writs of subpoena on O'Ferrall and the Defendants again stirred a series of outrages, both against the agent and now also against neighbors as well. With the authority of the Stipendiary Magistrate and an escort of constables, Knox's bailiffs once again began serving notices of dispossession in the townland, this time apparently without the ritual of iron nails and staples. Possibly for that reason, no tumult recurred but, according to Knox, "a numerous Body of armed Men" soon after conducted "a forcible breaking up of Land" belonging to Knox. As before, pleas for protection flowed from the agent who claimed to be receiving threatening notices and was "expecting to be attacked at my house every night."[31]

In the months following, a new barracks for twelve police was built on the "High Road," in the outfield near the cabins of Padian and Patrick Croghan. These were to be supported by a "Military party" of twenty-five troops "kept in constant Communication with the present Police Station at Kilglass." Notices were again served without resistance. In April the inevitable decree of the court, that the present tenants' occupation was "only permissive on the Part of the Crown" and could be terminated without notice, reached Ballykilcline. Whether because of the constant presence of the police or the bursting of their illusions, further resistance was mostly

covert and directed increasingly against dissident or mistrusted neighbors.
It is not known whether the previous year's crop of potatoes had been damaged by the first blight, but this new tendency to turn their violence inward seems to mark a distinct withering of the solidarity from which the
demonstration of two years before had sprung.[32]

Expurgated of the repeated alarms from Knox, the record of violent incidents in the townland from this time forward consisted of alleged threats
and assaults against the tenants themselves. Patrick Maguire, a marginal
tenant north of Aughamore, was to meet Knox to give evidence against
O'Ferrall but had been threatened with murder if seen at the agent's house.
He was publicly abused and threatened in Strokestown market and was sure
he would be murdered if his communication with Knox were known. Knox's
reports strongly suggest that Maguire was indeed his informant but do not
reveal what useful information this marginal laborer, neither a Defendant
nor even a tenant-of-record, might have to offer. Neither did Knox divulge
what threats or promises had been made to Maguire to make him risk his
life and family name.[33]

Before the townland was emigrated, after Knox had died of unknown
causes in the second year of famine, two other marginal tenants were said
to have been assaulted by their neighbors. Patrick Reilly, an occupant but
otherwise invisible in the townland record, was beaten by the tenants in
the square of Strokestown before numerous onlookers. The meaning of this
assault is lost in the record; Reilly had no known contact with the agent
either as informer or threatener. Knox's son, Thomas, who replaced his
father pro tem after his death, thought the affray must have sprung from
some obscure private quarrel unrelated to the rent strike. This seems to have
been one of the aspiring agent's few intelligent observations.[34]

One other reported act of violence appears in a petition sent by one "Mick.
Hoare" to Lord Morpeth in February 1848, at the time when the townland
had been more than half emptied by the departure of the first three batches
of emigrants. Hoare had been one of the cottiers on the estate, with his
wife and five children under the age of eleven. He was writing now from a
notorious Irish slum in London, at Anchor Hope Alley in St. George's East.
He protested that "so far from having joined in any vexatious legal proceedings against the Gov't," he was, in consequence of his having refused
to do so, visited by a set of ruffians, whose threats compelled him to seek a
temporary asylum in England. The truth of his situation, he said, could be
attested by Mr. John Cox, the "Bailiff." Hoare's petition was in fact one of
the many demands for "compensation" for having to surrender his land.
When asked, Knox guessed that, like the rest, it did not contain "One word
of Truth."[35]

The Level of Violence in Ballykilcline

Given the climate of violence widely said to exist in the countryside in these
years, Ballykilcline's misdemeanors seem quite modest. Knox's repeatedly

expressed fears for his own safety also appear to have cast doubt in the minds of the commissioners about the true state of affairs in the neighborhood, at least until Mahon's murder. It was to be expected that local landlords and their agents, all of them keenly aware in their own circles that the country people were "unsettled" in these bad years, would see their own predicament as being the most threatened. The fears of assault by night expressed by the well-guarded and elusive John Ross Mahon also gave credence to this siege mentality among the landlords and their deputies of the area.

Threats had been flying in both directions between landlord and tenant in the few years before the famine, already undermining whatever tranquility the district may once have enjoyed. The recent assaults that had occurred on adjoining lands had further inflamed fears on either side. It is also likely that Knox had not merely imagined the anonymous threatening letters received by him and his bailiff, although he never enclosed any in his reports. But neither Ross Mahon nor Knox could point to any confirmed instance on the estate in which life was in danger, apart from the alleged murder of a potential witness, until the assassination of Major Mahon. The only destruction of property Knox was able to report was the "turning up" of his rented fields—those sublet from Mahon for which Knox was himself still in debt.

In repeatedly refusing Knox's appeals for troops before 1846, Dublin Castle was merely assigning them the low priority that the events in Ballykilcline seemed to warrant till then. Knox's applications for military reinforcements, the undersecretary informed him, were "not sufficiently explanatory" of the imminent danger in view of the fact that no breach of the peace had actually taken place since the affray of 1844, in which no bodily harm had been done.[36] Battle hardened in the incessant disturbances of the country, the lord lieutenant and the skeptical veterans of the castle quite rightly detected the submerged panic of Knox's memos and received his alarms with detachment, as one of a myriad of demands that troops be dispatched to collect the rents that the land agents (the "service-for-fee" men as they were known in the Castle) had not the respect or gumption to take themselves. In the absence of a clear physical threat or insurrection in arms, such a collection service could hardly be provided for every profligate Irish landlord without a barrack in every townland.[37] Both Lord Clarendon and his successor as Lord Lieutenant at the time of the clearance of the Mahon estates, Lord Bessborough, regarded themselves as students of the country and models of progressive landlordism. They both despised the jittery bungling of such landlord agents as Knox and, except for assigning a few local constables to keep an eye on Cox, generally ignored his alarms till the murder had put the entire barony into a state of emergency.[38]

Even before his murder, Denis Mahon and the local gentry had raised the scattered assaults and unarmed threats from the long-subjected peasantry to the status of a *jacquerie* in the Irish countryside. It is apparent that few of the local gentlemen, excepting the Reverend Thomas Lloyd, set foot in the townland for most of the years of the rent strike, lending Ballykilcline an aura of terra incognita in which any sort of mischief might be imagined hatching among the cabins. Sandys claimed to fear for his life if his offer to lease the lands became known among the Defendants. The backwoods squire was also among those who had raised suspicions on several occasions, after the assault on the middleman-magistrate Irwin and the threats against Knox, that "strangers" were seen in the townland and that "Molly Maguires" (by now a catchall for any form of clandestine mischief), may have had something to do with the threats and beatings. Oddly enough, the same charges of "Molly Maguirism" were offered by some of the tenants against the Defendants in their last-ditch petitions to be left on the lands, as if confirming such rumors of conspiracy might somehow entitle them to the clemency of the authorities. In the same vein, James Hasty's scaffold testament damned "that accursed system of Molly Maguireism."[39]

Clearly, the tenants of Ballykilcline had been pariahs in the minds of the local elite and apparently among the townspeople of Strokestown for some years before the sensations of 1844. What was thought by tenants like themselves in the surrounding townlands is unknown, although it can be safely assumed that the progress of their rent strike, the leaders responsible, the amounts withheld, the reoccupation after eviction and the harassment of Knox and Cox were frequent subjects of conversation. At least in that sense, Ballykilcline had become a bad example in the neighborhood. Knox also thought that their defiance had already spread to other townlands: "to my own knowledge," he reported, "the Properties of Lord Hartland, Mr. Blakeney, and Mr. Balfe in the Locality of Ballykilcline have suffered severely from the Example of those Tenants, and are not paying their Rents as hitherto."[40] Inevitably, when the investigation into the murders began, with police and rumors overrunning the district, suspicions were again raised that the "lawless banditti" of the townland were somehow implicated, though no material link was ever brought forward by the agent or the police informers.

Despite the aura of irrational violence given to it in the official record, perhaps the most striking features of the "Ballykilcline rebellion" were its unusual duration and the apparent conviction of the tenants that the law would uphold their rights. The tenants had been under the threat of eviction from 1836 onward, yet all but a few had relied for their defense on passive resistance, that is, withholding rents, refusing to vacate their homes, resorting to the courts, and sending petitions. It was this "illegal combination" that had achieved the remarkable success of delaying their ejectment for nearly eleven years. Only in the spring of 1844, before their claim had been tried by the court and an armed party of strangers tried to bar them from their homes, had they openly resorted to force. Even then, their action appears to have been spontaneous and defensive. And a year later, when their eviction was imminent and inevitable, the tenants were submissive to the law and did eventually leave their homes without incident or outrage, except against those thought to be informers.

While the official count of outrages was higher than ever during the famine, there was a marked decrease in their proportion to the number of evictions as a whole.[41] The reason for this trend toward acquiescence on the part of the peasantry is easy enough to see in Ballykilcline: as even Knox was willing to concede by the summer of 1846, the population was now penniless, half-starved, and deeply demoralized. By December, Knox was finally able to venture again onto the townland for inspection, still accompanied by "a Police Magistrate & Military Force": "I went over the entire lands yesterday," he reported to the commissioners, "and must say that I found them a very different Tenantry from last year—certainly not three months provision with any of them, and their holdings neglected and unimproved."[42]

Any remaining hope of relief ended with the "Information of Intrusion" against them in April. It may not have been the failure of their suit against the Crown as much as the news of hunger from elsewhere that had broken their will to resist collectively. From then on, most of the petitions came from individual occupiers, cast in an almost ritual language of submission. Of course, it is impossible to say what course of action the tenants would have followed had the famine not intervened in the summer of 1846. But some of the conditions present at that time do suggest that Knox's fears of a more violent conspiracy may well have been borne out. First of all, as O'Ferrall sadly admitted, the law no longer offered any recourse—even if the arrears were forgiven, the tenants had no means of meeting current rents or taxes due for the foreseeable future, making general evictions inevitable. That prospect had all along made for unity in the townland and, in the event that the nearly five hundred residents were merely put out on the road by force, the likelihood of violence would have been high. And if any of the plans to replace the evictees with more solvent commercial farmers had been carried out, as the Commissioners had once considered doing, violence was equally certain. Four deliberate murders and numerous assaults had resulted from just such a clearance a few years before in nearby Ballinamuck, on the estate of Lord Lorton.[43]

Lord Clarendon's demand for "decisive measures" to preserve the peace in Roscommon after Mahon's assassination (in November of 1847) also suggests that any further attempt to resist eviction would have met with much sterner action on the part of the authorities than in the past. Not only murder and a heated sectarian conflict were on the minds of the population as the winter approached. The panic of the famine was abroad by then and Dublin Castle was taking a hard line, in tune with the disapproving gaze of London. Apart from the murders of great landlords, the long-held view across the political spectrum in London that the Irish land system was moribund had become disgust at the sight of its results—and eagerness to bring it to an end. Both lord lieutenants of the time, Clarendon and Bessborough, held lands in Ireland and were highly alert to the potential for violence in the situation. So, there would be no muzzle put on the military, the criminal courts, and the police. The dramatic rise in the number and severity of criminal sentences while the famine lasted gives a harrowing testimony to their intentions in policing Ireland in the midst of famine.

No more than a few families of Ballykilcline were capable of bearing the cost of emigrating after 1846, and fewer still had shown any inclination to leave voluntarily even when the means (including withheld rents) were available to them in some better years. Their resistance to eviction up till that time had also been resistance to emigration, free or forced, and had actually intensified for a time after the plan of emigration was announced. By the fall of 1847 there was little point in defending their right to remain, for even success would mean starvation.

6

Eviction

Their will be done and not mine.

James Connor of Ballykilcline

The tenants were to leave Strokestown in five "batches," the first four in groups just over one hundred in number and the last made up of stragglers, those who had at first refused the offer of a free passage to America or who could not make up their minds until all the rest had left. Refusal to emigrate would still mean eviction, however; the Commissioners' orders were "to serve Notice upon each of these persons that, in the event of their not accepting the offer of Emigration, they will be summarily dispossessed and their Houses demolished except such of them as Mr. Knox may certify as being proper to be retained upon the lands—."[1] There would be a great deal of stalling and changing of minds among the tenants and many futile efforts to persuade and plead exemption as each group saw the cabins begin to come down. At least some of them must have witnessed this final ceremony before they set out on the familiar hour's walk to Strokestown on the morning of their appointed day. There is no evidence or likelihood that any ever saw this over-the-shoulder sight again. When asked to recommend any "proper person" whose behavior warranted leave to stay on, Knox named only Patrick Maguire—an exemption that must have confirmed the suspicions of those neighbors who had beaten him, whoever they may have been.[2]

So many years had passed between the last time they paid their rents and the day they began the long trek to Dublin and the Liverpool ferry that it is easy to imagine them in that interval mistaking the passage of time for a promise of permanence. The sheer inertia and routine in the cycle of their daily existence embodied the reassurance and continuity of the past as it had always done. Births were celebrated, marriages were consummated, and deaths were mourned as always. Until the hunger began in the summer of 1846, nothing had tangibly changed in the townland's life. Even the alarms caused by new notices of eviction and the police forays that punctuated the calm had, by coming and going without apparent result, become a kind of routine themselves, dulling the dread of worse to come.

But it cannot be said that life in Ballykilcline had been entirely serene or orderly in the fifteen years between their change of landlord and the harrowing winter of 1847–1848, when the townland was dissolved and dispersed. Eviction had hung over the life of the community as a constant threat throughout these years, immediately imminent on several occasions with the eviction notices posted on the inhabitants' doors and the dates set for the bailiff's "emergency men" to appear at the townland's dwarf thresholds with their hooks, rams, and torches. There had been periodic threats of troops and notices as well as some internal dissension. Maguire, who was to lose five of his six children to famine and fever, and Patrick Reilly as well, had been branded as informers and both had been assaulted. Near the end, the early solidarity of the rent strike broke down into private pleading. Even a few of the Defendants, who had sternly chastised individual bargaining among their neighbors for years, secretly made invidious offers for the holdings of those who had been sent off first during the fall of 1847. Two of them, Stuart and Padian, somehow negotiated private "compensations" (token payments for small improvements made in their holdings) when all the rest had failed. So, before they had even set out on the most testing period of their life as a community, many of the illusions of mutual aid and collective security that had been fostered in the decade-long syncopation of calms and crises had been ground thin.

Nevertheless, there had been some years before when Connor, Padian, some of the Stuarts, and McDermott had apparently held rosy but deluded hopes of gaining outright title or long leases to the land, enabling them to stay in their homes indefinitely. That was what Squire Sandys claimed he had been told by them—that "they think and are Vain Sure—that they will have it as an Estate. . . ." Before the crisis brought on by the murder of Denis Mahon had doomed any remaining illusions, the inaction and timidity of the Crown Agent also encouraged them to think that they were not entirely defenseless against the threat of removal. The ultimate outcome of their struggle to remain they could hardly have imagined before the winter of 1846–1847. The ominous premonitions they expressed in their petitions, like that of the impoverished Maurice Fitzmorris, of becoming "strangers in the land that gave them birth," seem incongruously mild and abstract in contrast to the sheer physical enormities they would soon endure in starvation, pestilence, and exile. Since little in their experience allowed them to foresee the real calamities to come, the periods of calm between the crises are not too surprising. The time when nearly every family would expect to lose some of its members to emigration had not yet arrived, and the forced removal of whole townlands was a sight that none had yet seen.

The generally hopeful mood evident in the townland during the few years before 1846 may also be confirmed to some degree by the exceedingly small number who voluntarily emigrated during this period, although at least some of the larger tenants apparently had the means to do so before the famine. Some of them had withheld ten years' rents by this time and good harvests had been taken in several of these years; yet, as far as the record shows, no more than one family and two individuals of the nearly five hundred inhabitants had left the lands.[3] Of the leading families of Ballykilcline, only the McDermotts emigrated as a group before the famine. It was a significant loss of a strong family and a powerful figure in Hugh McDermott. The McDermotts had also been the most entrepreneurial family in the townland, its farms and holdings the most diversified and market-oriented. And together with Hugh McDermott's illicit shebeen, theirs was the only entity on the estate that might be said to have had a "cash flow." The departure of the McDermotts was in keeping with the general tendency of prefamine emigration to draw primarily from the more prosperous and enterprising tenant farmers—but their going seems to have had no effect on the solidarity of the remaining tenants or in inducing others to go, free or otherwise.[4]

Whatever gap in leadership McDermott's leaving may have created was almost immediately filled by Richard Padian, who became increasingly prominent as conditions worsened in 1846. His immediate interests and outlook were more closely akin to those of the bulk of the tenantry, to avoid eviction and gain some security of tenure, than to those of the more commercially minded McDermott. For a time, until two years of famine crushed all resistance, Padian's ascendancy represented a more prominent role for the smallholders and subtenants in the struggle.[5]

Whatever remained of routine and continuity was smashed in the calamities of 1847. Evictions were served on all the occupants (excepting Patrick Maguire and the Reverend Thomas Lloyd) in May of that year, along with a proclamation of the Crown's offer of free passage to America for all those who were willing to leave the country. Those who were unable to establish their identity as rightful tenants, like the landless laborers Geelan, McGanne, and Costello, or the "dependents" unrecorded in the rent rolls (including some women and children whose head of household had died of hunger or fever), would also be removed from the lands without the option to emigrate at Crown expense. At least twenty-two longtime residents of the townland fell into this category, as well as an unknown number of landless laborers "lodging" or squatting on the lands who disappear from the record at this point. Those of them without kin in the area with the means to take them in would have had little choice but to apply to the lethally overcrowded poorhouses, where thousands died and uncounted others from the countryside were seen to wait for weeks before their doors.

The panic that may have been lacking in their earlier fears of eviction began to show itself in the spring of 1847, though probably not because of the proclamation alone. They had been served notice before and had remained. Rumors of all kinds had circulated in the past about the landlord's intentions, that payment of one or two years' arrears would satisfy Knox, that only those who had led the strike would be forced to go, that only some would have to leave while others who could provide "security" (which they understood as testimony of "good will") would remain on holdings of twenty acres or more. But rumor became knowledge during May, when the first "batch" of Mahon's tenants, 490 of their neighbors and kin, were evicted and gathered in Strokestown to begin the journey by cart and foot to the Dublin ferries, eventually to board the *Virginius.* The ship's fate would not become known till August, but to witness the mass eviction and departure of their neighbors, the scenes that incited Father McDermott's incendiary outbursts from the pulpit, must have frozen all illusions of landlord bluff or last-minute help from the law.[6]

Within a week of the Mahon evictions, the subsheriff of Roscommon appeared in Ballykilcline in the company of a dozen constables, the bailiff, and his "emergency men" to evict the fourteen Defendants and their families. These ringleaders must have expected to be singled out in some way by the authorities, but the suddenness of the Crown's action took them unawares. The proclamation of a week before had not specified a date either for eviction or emigration, nor had it warned of any punitive action against the Defendants in particular. The tenants were also accustomed to the very slow pace at which the Crown authorities had always moved in the past. Rather surprisingly, there had also been no forewarning from the leaky chain of command that ended with Cox and his hired men, who must have been notified at least a few days before the event. The operation was conducted like a military raid. What store of crops and animals they still possessed after the hungriest winter of their lives were within plain sight when the sheriff's party arrived and were confiscated for arrears.

Embarrassed in Parliament several times before for their management of the estate, the Commissioners now reported that the cabins "were either levelled to the ground or rendered uninhabitable," with the exception of a few to house a party of twelve police to prevent another reoccupation.[7] This was done as Knox had recommended the year before, to rid the estate of the leading troublemakers and to make the remainder, as he put it, "amenable to the Crown." It had been his voice that had put before the distant commissioners the picture of a lawless conspiracy of violent men who would resist any effort to dislodge them. But even the agent had softened his view of the tenants since then, relieved of the fear that they had once inspired in him when he realized that the blight had already tamed whatever ferocity they had shown in the past. The agent was dead by now, but his alarming reports did climb slowly up through the pyramid of deputies and returned in the form of the sheriff's raid in May of the following year. No defiance was shown on the morning of the twenty-sixth as the Defendants' houses were leveled.

Instead, the only response was more petitions. One of these was received soon after by the commissioners and read in Parliament. The Defendants now pled,

That on the 26th of May your petitioners were turned out of their houses and dwellings; that they are now deprived of their cabins, and lying out in the open air with their wives and families, who are in a state of destitution and starvation for want of food and raiment, and are thereby subject to fevers and disorders prevalent in the country. That your petitioners if they are deprived of their crops and tillage will, with their families, be thrown on the world, and doomed to ruin and starvation, and they solemnly assure you that a part of the tenants so dispossessed are in a raging fever, lying in the open air.[8]

There were approximately sixty-two individuals among the Defendants' families who were evicted in May of 1847 and left to fend for themselves in the open during the five months before the first batches were to leave in the fall. The majority of them survived and were eventually permitted to emigrate with the rest, but at least twenty-three of them remained unaccounted for in the final emigrant lists.[9]

The meticulously copied order of Knox's "system of emigration," as he called it, began to fray at the edges almost immediately. In part this was because the agent was by now in the habit of managing the estate at arm's length, leaving many of the crucial details in Cox's hands. Burke was a more humane man, but he was still further removed. There were also many others in Dublin in the spring of 1847 who had not yet witnessed the horrors that the famine had brought to the townlands. It may have been out of charity, or out of ignorance of the extreme need now gripping Ballykilcline, or perhaps to insure against a scandalous scene during the actual evictions, that Burke arranged to have small quantities of cash put into the tenants' hands for their provisions on the road and the Liverpool ferry. This allowance of 12s. 6d. per head was apparently a last-minute thought on Burke's part and probably did help to avert the repugnant spectacle that had aroused local feelings the previous spring with the sudden eviction of the Defendants. But it clearly disrupted the ultimate plan of making the lands "perfectly untenanted." The townland was emptied of every family designated for emigration or eviction by the spring of 1848. But of the 498 individuals on the lands in 1846 and the 476 deemed to be eligible for the emigrant bounty, no more than 368 showed up on the docks of Liverpool.[10]

There were a number of reasons for the discrepancy. Indeed, it would have been more remarkable if none were to turn up missing among so many. Among any large number of Irish emigrants who set off for Liverpool in the famine years, there were always some who fell out or strayed from the line of march. In the winter and spring of 1847–1848 especially, the attrition was high along the roads to the big towns, which were clogged not only with the massive emigration but with a great wandering of individuals and families fleeing to the homes of relatives who were likely to be equally prostrate or tracking down rumors of food and shelter. The poorhouses, dispensaries, infirmaries, and churches were overwhelmed throughout Roscommon as everywhere in the country; hordes of beggars and dying lined the turnpikes and squatted under the hedges while thousands more lay in fever in their cabins, unable even to move.

The travelers from Ballykilcline, especially those slated to depart among the first three batches of September and October, may have been in at least slightly better condition than most of the other emigrants, however, because of the cash they had in their pockets from James Burke. Of the one hundred or more who failed to reach Liverpool, it must be presumed that at least a few either died or fell out en route some time after leaving Strokestown; most of the late "memorials" received by the Commissioners during that winter mention the presence of fever in the townland and, as Knox himself reluctantly conceded, even in the preceding year food had been in very short supply for two full seasons. Many of these had pleaded for their departure dates to be postponed till they or members of their family had recovered from fever or debility. Those desperate enough to leave on the carts while still in that condition greatly diminished their chances of surviving the entire voyage or even that part of it on road or ferry before meeting the ordeal of Liverpool and the ships. A conservative estimate of about one in five, even of those who were passed as fit enough for the voyage when examined at Liverpool that year, died on board or in the quarantines after landing.[11]

Another probable cause of the depletion in numbers also resulted from the arrangements for paying the travel expenses to Dublin. Although the 12s. 6d. per head was merely a fraction of the £4 10s. paid to H. & W. Scott for the passage (a high rate, especially for the three out-of-season sailings of September and October), the total sums of £3 to £6 that families of five or more found in their hands were sudden fortunes. It was unusual for the cottiers and laborers who made up the bulk of the tenants to hold such a quantity of ready cash in their hand at one time. At this juncture, the temptation to fill their bellies immediately would be great. For those who were to wait through the coming winter it would be irresistible. The first to leave were only a few days from the free provisions of the emigrant ships, if all went well. For the rest, the harshest starving months of December through March would come on the heels of the cash bounty, or the certain promise of it.

According to Burke's instructions, they would not have it in hand until their houses had been peaceably vacated and destroyed on the day of departure. But the neighborhood knew of the bounties coming. So, there could not have been much trouble in borrowing and running up debts on the grocer's cuff against the Crown's announced word. There was also a panic for food in that winter and many charges of gouging. There is no record of transactions of this kind. But, as we shall see, it was among those scheduled to leave after the long winter that the largest number of missing was recorded.

From the perspective of the Crown's commissioners or of Denis Mahon, whose evicted tenants had been innocent of any conspiracy, these arrangements were not only lawful but eminently humane: the Crown tenants who had defied all authority, abused the agent and bailiff, and withheld their rents for a decade, and who were thought to have had a hand in provoking the brutal murders and assaults in the district would be carried free of charge to a land of plenty at great cost. Or they could choose to remain in the country at their own risk. Many others in the area and most of Parliament thought the tenants' treatment was grossly indulgent.

The commissioners and Mahon, in unison with most other great landlords who chose the option of assisted emigration, had at first been appalled by the cost of the emigration programs being promoted by the agents and sought every saving possible in their dealings with the ship charterers, brokers, and provisioners. Tragedies like that of the *Virginius* were inevitable in the semicriminal chaos of the "steerage business," where a saving of a shilling a head (about £100 in the case of the *Virginius* passengers) was likely to produce misery and death among the assisted emigrants. Prominent agents like Guinness and Mahon or Stewart and Kincaid (who had managed the tragic clearances of the Palmerston estates) could hardly have been unaware of the dangers of the emigrant trade in these years. Any of Her Majesty's "emigrant agents" in Liverpool and the other major Atlantic outports would eagerly have given them the grisly chapter and verse of what might happen in the steerages as a result of their little economies—if they had been asked.[12]

The Strokestown and Ballykilcline tenants had known only a little of the potential dangers of their emigration as yet. But the alternative of simple eviction was a prospect all could envision, either from their own experience or the long word-of-mouth history attached to it. Even the Crown Commissioners showed themselves to be conscious of the abhorrent image that eviction in Ireland conjured in the public eye and had exercised extraordinary patience and restraint in their dealings with the Crown tenants to avoid it. In the eyes of the tenants, no act could have been crueler. A special nightmare language seems to have been reserved for describing the eviction scene: as the tenants of Cornashina put it to justify their giving information against their neighbors, even against the curse of that deed, they could not face the prospect of "casting them and their large families to perish houseless by the ditchside in a cold and severe winter. . . ."[13]

Sights throughout the neighborhood in the year of the Strokestown clearances left no doubt about the fate that awaited those who refused the emigrant bounty. The winter evictions on the estate of the Misses St. George of nearby Cloneash were described by the *Ballinasloe Star* (a paper not usually sympathetic to the tenantry). Mr. Malone, the subsheriff of Roscommon, brought a party of the Scotch Greys and infantry from Ballinasloe and leveled the residences of some of the Cloneash tenants. One poor family was taken out in fever and erected a little shed at the side of a ditch; on the next day it was likewise thrown down. Guinness and Mahon were also the agents of the St. Georges and had been unable to obtain the rents for the last three or four years. One of the men ejected was offered, before proceedings were taken, to be left in his holding if he would pay even one year's rent; when his house was being leveled by the sheriff, he offered three years' rent in cash (he owed four years). "Very properly," according to the *Star*, he was not permitted to remain in the tenancy.[14]

Such scenes were capable of stirring the deepest emotions of onlookers. They were living enactments of the cottier's perennial nightmare, by now the most familiar tableau in nationalist images of the Irish landlords' inhumanity. It would now be lived out amid a general starvation, in which one's neighbors and kin were nearly as desperate as the evictee. As in Father McDermott's denunciation of the Mahon evictions, dramatizations of the scene had also come to take on something of a formulaic language: "half-naked children" running from the cabin, mothers "prostrate on the threshold writhing in agony," desperate fathers "supplicating on their knees" and "wretched outcasts . . . perishing in a ditch."[15]

It is probably no coincidence that "ditches" figured frequently in descriptions and images of eviction. One of the sights most often depicted in both visual and written reports of the famine was of evicted families huddling in roadside drains and ditches over which they had constructed roofs of boughs and sod as temporary shelters, similar to the "shed" erected by the evicted tenants of Cloneash. Evicted families sheltering in ditches beside ruined cabins was the standard pictorialization of the horrors in Ireland featured by the *Illustrated London News* in the winter of 1848.[16] The well-honed technique of pulling and battering down the diminutive cabins had never been perfected to include keeping their former occupants from haunting the neighborhood afterward, waiting for some opportunity to resettle themselves as laborers or subtenants on adjoining lands. Both Hanly and Patrick Connor seem to have taken such a fall. In the past the dispossessed rarely traveled far from their former homes in search of a place to resettle, relying on the obligatory help of kin and the capacity of subdivision and conacre to absorb them into even deeper poverty. There were also few townlands without squatters, lodgers, and unrecorded tenants of one kind or another, individuals or whole families without recorded existence; when the final count of those eligible for emigration was made by the younger Knox, almost two dozen of this category were discovered in Ballykilcline. Surrounded by kin and a culture of hospitality, such intervals of homelessness had been survivable in the past. But by the spring of 1847, the conjunction of famine and mass evictions had overwhelmed these resources and made the ditch hut the last resort. It was that vision that captured the meaning of "becoming strangers in the land of their birth," as Connor put it.

The gathering of emaciated crowds from the countryside at the gates of the union poorhouses was a scene described by nearly all witnesses of the famine. These crowds were seen in Strokestown, Rooskey, and Carrick-on-Shannon, where more than a hundred waited for thirty places in the workhouse in the cold December of 1846, subsisting on irregular relief work at 8d. a day. Hardly any provincial town was free of starving beggars, hovering and often dying at the doors of the more fortunate. But even the last extremes of starvation failed to drive all its victims toward the towns' soup kitchens and poorhouses. The worst of the horrors of hunger and sickness even in infamous Skibbereen was discovered only when the derelict cabins and overgrown lanes of the surrounding townlands were entered by outsiders. The Cork magistrate, Nicholas Cummins, whose letter to the *Times* brought the name of Skibbereen to the world's attention, at first thought the townland to be deserted but soon after discovering "six famished and ghastly skeletons" moaning barely audibly in one of the hovels, he was surrounded by "at least 200 such phantoms, such frightful spectres as no words can describe,"[17] all of them apparently preferring to wait out their last hours where they had passed their lives, hidden in the townlands beyond the sight of strangers. Beside the vitality of "Village X," described by Tocquville a decade before, such scenes give one true measure of what was lost in the famine.

In the first eviction of the fourteen Defendants in 1836, it had been one thing to drive them from their cabins and another to drive them from the neighborhood, where they disappeared for a while before reoccupying their homes. In the final eviction, demolition of the townland's houses was now understood to be essential in cases like Ballykilcline's, where the tenantry had more than once before retaken possession of their dwellings surreptitiously after the bailiff and his men departed. This was a simple process, since the tenants traveled light, with few portable possessions, which were easily concealed in the neighborhood to wait for the coming of the night when they could reenter the cabins unopposed.

Once the tenants were back in possession, the eviction process had to be begun all over again. The evicted tenants had been like seawater leaching back through a makeshift dam, eluding the notices, injunctions, writs, and warrants with which the landlord and his agents tried to stem the flow. The favored expression among the propertied and law-abiding classes for this maddening behavior was "setting the law at defiance." It was also the main argument made by Knox to have a permanent police barracks erected on the lands. This was finally done in Ballykilcline at the expense of the Crown and on the Strokestown estate, where Major Mahon's successor was required to pay £1 per month for each constable kept in the barracks, in addition to the rent due to Owen Cox, who had built them on his land. But this was a service that the combined resources of Dublin Castle, the militia, and the constabulary were hardly able to provide for all of the country's embattled landlords without filling the countryside with an army of occupation.

The "Decline of Life" in Ballykilcline

The townland of Ballykilcline never became quite "perfectly untenanted." When the younger Knox had doled out the allotment of shillings to the 139 people in the batch who were the last to leave Strokestown in April 1848, only two households of the previous eighty-two had received permission to remain in the townland, those of Patrick Maguire and the Reverend Lloyd, whose right to stay had never been in question. Maguire, then in his early forties, was rewarded with a renewed lease to his less than three acres, forgiven his more than £15 of arrears, and permitted to remain as the only native tenant on the once congested estate.

The scene that Maguire must have witnessed from the door of his cabin could not have been consoling, even to one who had survived the worst that two years of famine had brought upon him. Five of his six children had died in the preceding two winters. His family now consisted of his wife, Catherine (thirty), and his eldest daughter, Bridget (fourteen). He was forty-three when the last of the townland was sent off the lands. He had been a laborer whose erratic wages of 8d. a day paid the rent on his small holding. Part of his work had been driving carts for Strokestown House and Johnny Cox. He was also on friendly terms with Lloyd, with whom he had shared at least one midnight spree as the parson's driver, careering through the countryside in a borrowed coach. Any of these associations may have been the cause of his downfall in the townland, which was sure he had given information on O'Ferrall's "legal fund" to the agent. If he had, it is very likely it had been filtered through Cox. Maguire had opposed the collection of the fund and, perhaps inadvertently in the form of a complaint, he had alerted the authorities to a criminal conspiracy among his immediate neighbors. That act was anathema in the townland and inevitably led to the ostrasizing of his family and violence against him.

Although those who had threatened and beaten Maguire publicly were now gone from the townland, not all of them had chosen to emigrate from the country. He was still an outcast with his wife and daughter in close proximity to his enemies' kin and friends scattered all over the neighboring estates and their townlands—in Barrawalla to the west, Knockhall to the northeast, and Lecarrue south and east. From their vantage point along the Old Road a few hundred yards north of Aughamore, the Maguires had an excellent view of the effaced landscape of the townland and could not have missed the doleful sight of the leveling as the bailiffs battered down roofs and walls, firing what thatch and flammable detritus of cabin poverty remained, leaving a smoldering debris at ground level. In Ballykilcline, the Crown's counsellors thought it would be best also to have "the Materials removed so as to prevent them being rebuilt."[18]

One can only imagine what the malignant winter months of 1847 had been like for the Maguires and their young daughter as the deaths and burials of the younger children came one by one, as one batch after another of the community were sent off after seeing their homes carted away as rubble, the last of them who had survived the worst famine winter treading in hunger and complete destitution toward Strokestown and the road to America, probably cursing Maguire's name. His once indistinguishable hovel was now quite conspicuous and exposed in the desolation. He had escaped the fate of the rest at a great price, but there was no more assurance than before that he would be able to meet the rents demanded by a new landlord.

Burke reminded the younger Knox that he was to see that all of the remaining cabins be "properly levelled."[19] Cox had been paid for performing this labor, as well as the £3 for injuries he claimed to have incurred in the process. But it is not clear how thoroughly he had done his work, for within two years, when the walkers for the next census passed through the former townland, they counted a population of forty-five people dwelling in eight houses on the same lands, some thirty to thirty-five individuals and six dwellings more than the Maguire and Lloyd families would account for. It was a dramatic decline from the previous congestion, but not what the commissioners had intended nor how they had described the property when it was purchased in 1849. The discrepancy may have occurred in several ways. After buying a "perfectly untenanted" estate at a bargain rate of £5,500, the new owner may have arranged quick leases to produce immediate income, much as the local squireen landlords were accustomed to doing before the famine. Or some few of the former occupants, either all or a part of the six "new" households, managed once again to elude Cox and the constables and reoccupy the townland—ironically, this may have been made possible by the 12s. 6d. in cash they had been given by the Quit Rent Office as travel expenses, enough to secure leases on small parcels from the new landlord.

The Time of Petitions

The sequence of moods that the tenants were now completing, from threats and violence to blarney and finally pleading, followed the caricature of the Irish countryman widely held in the metropolis. For the tenants under notice of eviction, it was a ritual taught by necessity, as their means of resistance crumbled. Even after witnessing the departure of their neighbors the preceding September and October, many of those waiting their turn to emigrate still harbored some hope that the Crown would relent. Their pleas were written in what had become the formulaic language of the "petition" and "memorial." After two winters of hunger, they cited illness or fear of abandoning helpless dependents as reasons to be left at home. In this all were alike, but their appeals used differing mixes of entreaty and argument.

John Stewart and Bernard Magan, who had taken no leading part in the strike, denounced the "lawless Banditti of persons" who had robbed them of £4 "in broad day, feloniously" and led them to their present fate. They declared they had not litigated against the Crown and had paid "two or three more years' rent" (that is, out of the previous eleven years) than those who had emigrated and received "compensation." They could not emigrate if they wished because their parents were too old to undertake a voyage and "owing their Parents a debt of Gratitude, could not attempt to leave them in their old age as a Burden on the Public—. . . ." (Stewart's mother was eighty and lived with his childless brother, Patrick). They begged to be left as tenants in "enlarged" holdings, "as they are ready & willing to become honest & punctual tenants—. . . . [and] desire to be restored to the land of their forefathers and the land of their birth. . . ."[20]

Patrick and John Connor, who were known by Burke to be among the "banditti," made the same plea nevertheless. Family members were in ill health and "were not fit substitutes for *the seas* & and Petrs could not in gratitude leave them behind and on whose existance are depending on yr. Petrs' Protection and Support." They too claimed not to have "put the Crown to any trouble and paid 2 yrs & 6 months beyond any part of the Tenants." The brothers "Pray yr Honours to permit as tenants them back into the land . . . having an anxiety to live in the land of their birth, and to become good and solvent Tenants in future—." The Connors had failed to appear as scheduled in the second batch of the previous September, but they had received the travel allowance (after their cabins were pulled down). Although Patrick Connor was now more than seventy years of age and a widowed father of nine (including a twelve-year-old daughter), he had apparently found shelter enough to survive the winter months, perhaps in one of the nearly invisible ditch huts in the hills northeast of the townland, an area where Knox never dared to venture, or in one of the households still awaiting their time to leave. The brothers gave "Ballykilcline near Ruskey" as an address for the commissioners to send their reply. Earmarked as "ringleaders," the Connors might have wished to avoid entering Strokestown while troops and police inspectors were still looking for suspected troublemakers, and Rooskey was a post-town where mail might be picked up without their having to pass through the heart of the townland, where they would once again have been regarded by the law as trespassers.[21]

The tenants' entreaties share some of the pathos of all dead letters. It was never the policy of the commissioners to reply directly to any petitions. At most, they would direct Burke to instruct the local agent to take some action or post a notice. In this case, the Connors' memorials reached the Quit Rent Office and went no further. The Royal Mail had not yet fully penetrated the frontier between town and townland and was still largely a one-way service as far as the tenants were concerned. Though most of their petitions begged for an early reply, few offered a "return address," apparently relying on word-of-mouth or repeated inquiries to learn of return mail at postal towns. It was possibly because no replies ever appeared that many other of the petitions bore their resemblance to prayers, to which no reply was expected.

One of the younger of the Connors, James (forty-five), who had lived quietly through the strike years with his wife, Honora, and three young children, wrote several memorials in his own hand that display both a tutored and rather formal literary skill and a taste for irony. Writing directly to the commissioners, he declared more truthfully than some of the others that he had never been a "refractory tenant":

> [H]e therefore hopes on that account that you will allow him compensation nearly equivalent to the sum it would cost the Crown to send out his family which on the lowest scale would amount to nearly £20. Memst. prays he may be allowed this compensation but memst. would prefer his farm on the lands of Ballykilcline—to any sum the Commmissioners might think just to award him as memst. would give a fair rent for his farm hoping that the Commissioners will grant this small Boon.

Like the others, Connor also pleaded ill health in his appeal; one of the reasons for the failure of some tenants to come forth for emigration was the presence of "famine fever," typhus, dysentery and dropsy, in the family. By February, Connor, addressing "John Burke Esqr., at Customhouse Dublin," said he had been resigned to leaving with the next batch, but was now unable:

> Honoured Sir
>
> on the 15th Inst: i attended the Agent and had my family returned for emigration agreeable to the rule you had made. Though my son [ten-year-old Martin] was only a few days out of fever he is now relapsed and will not be fit to go out at this time Therefore I humbly implore your tender Mercy that you will allow me untill the end of March next as it is the will of the allmighty to afflict him and could expect Nothing but death by his removal at this time
>
> > Sir your compliance will
> > much oblige your Most
> > Humble and obt. Servt.

Appended with an authoritative flourish was a confirmation from Cox, stating, "I Certify James Connors familly is favour [presumably meaning "fevered"], John Cox."

Later still, after the March batch had left, Connor pleaded again that his family was unfit to travel:

> That memst. is in an infirm state of health and likewise part of his family are after fever and at present incapable of going on sea to the danger of their own health and the great danger of the accompanying passengers. . . . [I]t does not answer his own state of health to emigrate at this season of the year.

It may be worth noting in this memorial that Connor reveals an awareness of the dangers of shipboard contagion and off-season sailings that was not common among the emigrants.

Writing in absolute futility on the day before he and his family were scheduled to depart, he again implored their lordships to reconsider because he still had a "sick youth" in the house:

> I would take compensation in preference and stop at home. Their will be done and not mine.
> > Memorialist as in Duty Bound will ever Pray—
> >
> > > James Connor[22]

Connor's daughter, Eleanor, had died at sixteen, leaving the houschold with two sons, the ten-year-old Martin and an infant whom the younger Knox had overlooked in the rent books, as well as his spinster sister. When the lists were posted for those to leave on 6 March, they included only three of his family, omitting the infant and Connor's sister. Writing again nearly three weeks after the appointed time, Connor protested that he had "2 sons, wife, self, and his *sister* [*sic*]," whom he had said had been removed from the house with fever. He thought that statement may have caused the omission: "She's lived with me these 22 yrs. and has no other dependents when I leave Ireland."[23]

The Connors had twice missed their departure time and would have to rely on the Crown's forbearance to be included in the last batch, scheduled to leave in mid-April, or face homelessness. Another of the large Connor clan, Bartly Connor and his family, had missed the October batch and made the same plea, "Some of my family took Sickness at the time," but now wished to be included in the last group: "[N]ow I hope your Honrs. will admit me to America When I go to Dublin."[24]

Within the limits allowed him, James Burke acted with compassion in response to the pleas of family illness and most of the tenants of record who failed to join the large batch scheduled to leave in March were permitted to emigrate in the following month. James Connor and his family, though without his ailing sister, were among these. There was little Burke could do, however, about the numerous claims for "compensation" he received, most of them referring to the 12s. 6d. he had allotted for the Dublin journey. Some of these were from recognized tenants who preferred to remain in the country even if evicted, and others were from petitioners completely unknown to him.

At a time of such extreme distress, with many unable to face the journey because of illness in the family, the prospect of the cash in hand was irresistible, even if it meant homelessness. The requests for compensation in lieu of emigration reached a peak in February, before the last two batches were scheduled to leave, apparently a time when the effects of hunger and fever were at their worst. Notices of the March clearance were posted early that month, prompting even those who intended to emigrate to plead for the allowance at once in order to relieve their hunger and to survive the few weeks remaining. Knowing that it would not be paid until their cabins had been leveled, a number of them claimed the cash anyway and spent the remaining interval as squatters in the open air. At least fifteen tenants who took the allowance in this way never appeared on the lists of those arriving in Dublin.[25]

Everyone in the locality was well aware that an uncertain number of landless laboring families were always resident in the townland, surviving on casual wages, as conacre tenants or as clients of the farmers. Thomas Geelan was one of the twenty-two whose families were in this category and were therefore not entitled to the emigrant bounty. He wrote a brief memorial to Burke (apparently in his own hand) begging to be included in the last batch, which was due to leave in mid-April. He had to leave his house in Ballykilcline because it was "not good," he said, and had moved to his father's on an adjoining estate. That, he thought, was why Cox had not "returned" his name in the emigrant list: "Therefore I trust you will condesend & have me emigrated as you have done to my neighbours." He asked that Burke reply to James Connor. Connor also interceded for

Ireland.

"Semi-underground dwellings" built into the side of an embankment, made of unmortared stone and turf. (Courtesy of *Ulster Folk and Transport Museum*)

A "bogtrotter's" cabin, Balintobber, Co. Roscommon, in the 1840s. Landless or evicted families often squatted in remote locations and below ground level to escape notice. *(Illustrated London News)*

Major Denis Mahon approximately a decade before his assassination. *(Courtesy of Strokestown Park House)*

A small farmer of the west before the famine, mounted and clothed in the fashion of an independent but not wealthy native leaseholder. *(Henry Collier,* The West of Ireland *[Dublin, 1862])*

Strokestown Park House, as it now appears, the site of the new National Famine Museum of Ireland. *(Courtesy of Strokestown Park House)*

The Gates of Strokestown House.

The Guthrie brothers, small farmers of Antrim in the 1890s. Sam and John (on the left) had been forty years old at the time of the famine. The younger brother, James, had been in his mid-twenties. *(Courtesy of Ulster Folk and Transport Museum)*

"A Kerry Man." Clearly a local native, but the slightly pretentious collar and hat suggest the man is not a farmer. Some country "deputies," such as the Drivers, may have borne such a mixed appearance. *(Courtesy of the Council of Trustees, National Library of Ireland)*

Evicted families petitioning before the landlord's gate at Castlebar, Co. Mayo, possibly communicating through the housemaid in the background. *(From the Wynne Collection, courtesy of the Council of Trustees, National Library of Ireland)*

(Opposite) "Gap Girls." Among the earliest stereo photographs taken in Ireland, probably in the early 1860s. The young women, who had been children during the famine, are selling refreshments to tourists in the Gap of Dunloe, Killarney. *(Courtesy of the Council of Trustees, National Library of Ireland)*

"Their will be done and not mine." Evicted at Clongorey, Co. Kildare, probably around 1880. To judge from the collapsed roofs of his neighbors, the old man was one of multiple recent evictions in this townland. *(From the Lawrence Collection, courtesy of the Council of Trustees, National Library of Ireland)*

Homeless but still in the townland after a general eviction, from about 1880.
(From the Lawrence Collection, courtesy of the Council of Trustees, National Library of Ireland)

The "clearance" of an Irish townland as imagined by the *Illustrated London News*.

Geelan's brother, Hugh, who had been a resident but had also left the townland. Acting as Hugh Geelan's scribe, Connor assured Burke "that his claim is equally just though both live at present on the Marquis of Westmeath [*sic*] contending for their father's possession . . . he Hugh Geelan hopes you will treat him as many others who had a claim."[26]

Patrick Riely, also writing in his own rough hand on a scrap of paper, begged to know "as the time for cultivation is passing round . . . that you please to say whither i be continued as tenant to Crown or not." He too swore he had been a "Faithful subject for which I sufferrd many injuries which the Rev. Thomas Lloyd can assertain if required." Riely had also reported being abused by the Defendants for opposing the collection of the "legal fund" and, like Maguire, may have received some promise from the agent or driver about preferred treatment. He had held his eight acres in the townland for forty years and swore (this time in an elaborately scribed petition) "that I have never countenanced by money, advice or otherwise any litigious opposition to the Crown." He had been "subjected to a series of ill usages," including a beating so severe he had been in sick bed for eighteen months, he said. At the agent's urging, he had also brought charges against the "ruffians" at great risk to himself—"as the county then stood it was a rather dangerous matter." He thought this record of fidelity entitled him to stay on one of the "enlarged holdings" he had heard about, perhaps thirty acres, he suggested.[27] Burke left young Knox to decide if Riely were a "proper person" to be granted the privilege of staying on, together with "any others not in opposition to the Crown and who may appear deserving of any consideration of this nature. . . . not only Maguire." But, whether out of the same hostility his father bore toward the townland or ulterior reasons to wish it entirely vacated, Knox never offered any other names of tenants he thought deserving. When again pressed by Burke in March to submit a definitive list of those who would be emigrating in the final batch, the younger Knox complained that "the Tenants take so much time to make up their minds, about Emigrating, that I cannot forward you the last list perfected . . . but they are all under notice."[28]

Confusion in the communications between Burke and the young Knox was as much responsible for tenants' slipping through the net of clearances as the deliberate maneuverings by some of them to evade emigration and remain on or near their former holdings. And, as always, the presence of Cox as the ultimate source of their information added still another level of uncertainty. As of Christmas 1847, 195 individuals were reported by him to be remaining in the townland. The fourth and next-to-last batch of evictees, containing 127 of the remaining residents, was scheduled to depart from Strokestown on the following sixth of March, after three more months of famine winter. Of these, Cox reported to Burke, 113 had actually turned up in Dublin and were put aboard the steamer for Liverpool. The missing 14, he said, had been given their allowance after their cabins had been destroyed and had been "removed" from the townland. Cox had been issued an allowance of nearly £8 from the Treasury to distribute among these missing travelers, two or three destitute families for whom the bounty could mean the difference between life and starvation, and had either given it to them before they disappeared into the landscape or had merely falsified the list and pocketed the difference. The chaos and panic of the time made either a possibility: once a particular batch of tenants were reported by Cox as removed from the lands, there was no mechanism to confirm that he had actually delivered the allowances into their hands until they arrived in Dublin. In the last two batches alone, at least 39 of those who were still alive in the spring of 1848 and entitled to the allowance never boarded the Liverpool ferries. Without including those whose names appeared on Cox's emigrant lists but were already buried in the folds of the townland, about £25 of Burke's well-intentioned largesse simply vanished.[29]

No small part of the uncertainty about who had gone and who remained may be ascribed to Cox and the nearly free hand he was given in arranging the clearances and departures, supervised only by Knox's haphazard son and the distant clerk of the quit rents. While neither the agent nor Cox was ever accused of diverting the funds provided by Burke, the sudden circulation of cash among the distressed tenants must have been a sore temptation to the driver. In the chaotic circumstances, there was practically nothing the Quit Rent Office could do to verify Cox's accounts or to determine what had become of the missing individuals. Another device employed by the driver to allay possible resistance to the evictions had a similar result. What Cox knew to be a charitable allowance to help them on the road to Dublin, many of the tenants took for "compensation," a word they had always used in their petitions as equivalent to "tenant right," the value of their improvements and "good will" in the land. It is clear that the tenants believed the allowances were being offered as an alternative to emigration, a reward for surrendering their holdings peacefully. On other Crown estates, in fact, the commissioners eventually conceded this point, at least tacitly, by offering tenants small cash payments if they would "provide for themselves elsewhere."[30] It seems that the driver did nothing to correct this misunderstanding, leaving his superiors perplexed and the tenants squabbling over the payments till the very end.

Thomas Geelan's case was typical of the confusion. He informed Burke that he had "paid a fine" (to someone unnamed) for one acre and had lived in the townland until his house "tumbled down"—"Mr. John Cox of Lagan, the Bailiff in the land" would testify to this. But since his name had not appeared on the emigrant list, he said, "I expect you will be so kind as to allow me a compensation as well as the Cabiners that have no land by so doing I am in duty bound for ever pray."[31] Geehan's family of ten, together with at least fourteen other landless "Cabiners," fell into the category of unrecorded occupants who had paid "fines" but were not entitled to allowances or emigration. On instructions from the commissioners, Burke had to refuse all claims from this category of resident, and in Knox's last report of the clearance they were described as "presumed to have left the lands."[32]

The Missing

Of the 476 residents of 1846, the Commissioners reported that 409 had been emigrated at Crown expense by May of 1848. The number was given with confidence, but conflicts between the various emigration lists and the last rent books suggest that the individual identities of the emigrants were less certain. Inevitably, as the famine panic worsened, with families and individuals moving in and out of the townland, Knox's "system" produced greater discrepancies between the orderly facts presented to Parliament and the monstrous confusion of the countryside. Yet another level of record-keeping deputies was added once the assisted emigration scheme went into operation: the Commissioners retained the firm of H. & W. Scott, ship agents of Dublin, who were responsible for the emigrants once they were delivered by Cox in Dublin till they boarded ship in Liverpool.[33] According to the ship agents, a total of 368 emigrants of Ballykilcline had arrived in Dublin by 18 April 1848, containing the last batch expected.

The missing may be accounted for in several ways. At least forty-one were members of families who expressly refused to emigrate and were dispossessed, their houses "demolished" as the Defendants' had been. For many of these families, this had been a life-or-death decision. With a few exceptions, none had expressed a wish to leave the townland before the decision was forced upon them. There might well have been some, most likely among the young and unmarried, who were more eager to emigrate. Others, like Hugh Geelan, came around to the idea only near the end, when no other hope remained. In most of the petitions, even free emigration is addressed in tones of defeat or resignation, a thought accepted only after extreme privations. As the subtenantry saw their choice, with no claim to their former homes or "compensation," they could either leave the lands peacefully as emigrants or be thrown into the road as beggars and wanderers.

At the request of the commissioners, the subsheriff of Roscommon again came to the townland at noon on 15 May, 1848, a year after the Defendants' eviction, to oversee the general demolition on the chance that some resistance might still be offered. Those remaining by this time were an unfriendly mixture of those who had opposed the rent strike (including Reilly, John Stewart, and Bernard Magan, with fifteen of their families) and two of the leading Defendants, Patrick and John Connor, who had somehow survived a year in the neighborhood after their houses had been leveled. In the end, no distinction was made between the compliant and the defiant, except for Maguire: the appeals of the loyal tenants were disregarded and they were dispossessed together with the Defendants, without compensation. An additional fifteen occupants had been given the travel allowances but, according to Cox, failed to appear in Dublin. It was from this group that at least parts of three families eventually succeeded in reoccupying their holdings more than a year later and remained thereafter as tenants of the new landlord.[34]

The record of Ballykilcline also contains evidence of widespread debility and fever among the residents in the winter of 1847–1848. No methodical count of the deaths and burials in the townland was made, and those noted in the surviving record appear only incidentally: Eleanor Connor, age sixteen, appears in an emigrant list of October and is missing in February; in the margin of another list, Knox scribbles "Dead Easter" beside the name of Patrick Coyle's thirty-year-old son, Dominick, and "dying" beside that of his other son, James (twenty-five); Catherine Connor is listed as the "wife" of John Connor in 1846 and a "widow" the following year. At least nine deaths from all causes may be positively identified in the petitions and emigrant lists of those who stayed on the lands until the last batch departed. But it must be assumed that not all of those who remained unaccounted for, numbering about forty-two, survived till the final clearance.

The number who perished due to famine, disease, or natural causes in the preceding two years can only be guessed because a number of families had also strayed from the townland during the killing winter of 1847–1848. Some, like the Geelans, reappeared before the end as applicants for the bounty, and others left no trace. But since this group included many of the poorest cottiers and landless laborers to begin with, it must be assumed that they would have been at great risk as homeless wayfarers or poorhouse inmates somewhere in the county. But even if none of the missing survived, Ballykilcline would have fared better than most of its neighbors, since in Roscommon as a whole the excess mortality during the famine was higher than in all but three other counties (Mayo, Sligo, and Galway). At least in this regard, assisted emigration and Burke's small allowances almost certainly protected them from the worst.[35]

By any of these measurements, the laborers and subtenants who vanished from the estate record and those with the smallest parcels had a poorer chance of survival than those who could still resort to the sale of their cows, pigs, and oats until the time of departure. With the fourteen Defendants landless and without their crops and animals since the spring of 1847, all but a few households in the townland were now at great risk. It was the second summer of extreme hunger and even the stronger farmers were forced to bleed their animals a pint or two at a time to strengthen the weakest and guard their turnips and cabbages against starving wanderers, including some of them their former neighbors. By most reports, hospitality and charity had still prevailed before 1847 among most of those with something to share, trusting that such a disaster could not befall them a second time. But the stench of the rotting stalks returned again the following July in those fields that were planted, the now familiar sickening, sulfurous smell that surely meant the end of the townland.

It has often been noted that mortality in the famine fell hardest on the most marginal of the rural population. In Ballykilcline, this class included at least those twenty-two of the Geelans' class who were resident but were denied the bounty or allowance because their names appeared on no rent rolls. Others, like James Connor's ailing sister, came to light only in the crisis, if at all, when friends and neighbors pleaded for them. There is no telling how many more such individuals resided in the townland, but at least twenty more appear incidentally in the surviving record: seven orphan girls and two teenage boys living among five households; two young girls and a blind daughter, Bridget, with the widow Fallon; two orphan girls and an unmarried sister of forty years of age with the laborer Michael Mulligan, recently widowed; two more girls with seventy-year-old Patrick Coyle, whose two sons had just died of fever. Father Peter Geraghty, the parishless priest, lived in the Padians' cabin. Three other landless individuals, identified only as a "Labourer," a "Shoemaker," and the "Schoolmaster," were unearthed by the agent as the townland was cleared.[36] It is impossible to say what, if any, part these individuals had played in the events of the past twelve years. On the other hand, given the folklore surrounding such figures, it is hard to envision the priest or the hedge-school master as completely mute or neutral bystanders in such a prolonged dispute. But implicated in the conspiracy or not, none of these were entitled to the emigrant bounty or any allowance in the rule set down by the commissioners. Before the end, however, James Burke was to take a number of compassionate liberties with these intructions and, to his great credit, make it possible for some of the most vulnerable to survive.

Though nearly imperceptible from the outside, all these individuals would have been familiar names and faces in the years before and undoubtedly played some great or small part in the internal life of the townland. There undoubtedly were others. No mention is made, for example, of musicians, senachies (storytellers), midwives, or foster children among them, although they probably existed in a community of this size. We learn from a marginal scribble in one of the rent books that Thomas McGanne was a "Mason, quite willing." But it is impossible to tell whose hand it was that composed the dozens of memorials and petitions in a skilled script and archaic turn of phrase. Some of these skills could have contributed to their chances of survival. The possession of grain and livestock assuredly helped the bigger farmers to get through the first potato failure. But in the blight of 1847, the landless were no longer any more vulnerable than those who tilled two or three acres, who were almost equally dependent on the potato. With the start of relief works in the neighborhood (the subject under discussion when Major Mahon and Father McDermott had their altercation), the single "Labourer" may have stood as good a chance as the fifteen-acre farmer he had once worked for, once his crop of oats had been sold and his cow bled to death or confiscated for arrears (which had apparently been Patrick Connor's fate). On the other hand, there were a number of cases in which weak or fevered individuals probably survived only through the care of their family, at least three of whom declined to leave, as John Stewart put it, "owing [them] . . . a debt of Gratitude."

Infirmity and great age, either of which commonly barred emigrants from boarding the Liverpool ships, were among the most dangerous handicaps. A number of families and individuals whose names do not appear on the emigrant lists were aged or kept aged parents in the household. John Toollin (eighty-six) lived with his wife Catherine (seventy-six) and was described as a small tenant for the previous forty years and "Cripple." Thomas and Mary Costelloe lived with his mother, Bridget (eighty), who had been born in Ballykilcline in 1766. Frank Stewart (seventy) and his wife (fifty) had lived alone on a petty holding on the goodwill of their neighbors. All of these were dispossessed and leave no trace. Bridget Fallon (twenty) had been blind for eight years and lived in the household of her widowed mother, Bridget (sixty), two brothers, a younger sister, and two orphan nieces, Mary (fourteen) and Catherine White (five). None but the widow and her daughter were entitled to the emigrant bounty, and the blind girl would have been rejected by the medical inspectors in Liverpool. A thirty-four-year-old son of the patriarch Denis Connor, one of the possible "pretenders" to the townland, was "Pleuritick" and unable to work. Both the old man and his crippled son were rejected as unfit for the voyage. The petitions also suggest that after two famine winters many had become well aware of the risks of protecting their weaker dependents by choosing to stay with them, yet there is no clue that any townland family abandoned their handicapped dependents.[37]

Women and Widows

In several senses the women and girls of the townland had always been among the missing. The census of 1841 counted 236 females and 237 males on the estate, 23 short of Cox's count, which included the "squatters." But when the townland was counted again in 1846, before famine mortality could fully account for it, only 199 females were listed as present and entitled to free emigration. The number of males remained much the same, less the absconding Michael Hoare, who had fled to London.[38] Several possibilities may be conjectured to explain the missing 37 females, but none of them very satisfactorily.

There had always been a substantial number of peasant women in domestic service in the country, nearly four times the number of men in that occupation in Roscommon. Three townland women were employed by the Reverend Thomas Lloyd alone, and it is likely that others had found similar employment in households in the Strokestown area. There were also four times the number of women paupers in the county than men. Some 3,023 women in the county were "servants & labourers" (compared to more than 46,000 men), a category that denoted farm workers rather than domestics; otherwise, there were few occupations outside the home to which they could resort. Some of the women missing in 1846, when the hunger was first felt, may have found refuge as servants in households not yet severely affected or survived from day to day in the relief works. In the poorest families, women were also more accustomed than men to seasonal begging in the bad years. Others may have resorted to the workhouse sooner than the men, for whom it apparently carried a greater stigma. The fate of these cannot be known, but even given an abnormally high mortality among the townland women, none of these alternatives can account for the missing.[39]

Two other alternatives seem to offer a more likely explanation: a higher rate of single emigration of women in the first throes of the hunger and a return of some of the female orphans and widowed dependents to the households of their birth as a way to relieve the families expecting eviction of an extra mouth to feed. The widespread evictions in the neighborhood of Strokestown seem to have had a similar effect of depleting the female population of the townlands disproportionately. In this, too, the town and townland differed. While Strokestown had lost about 26 percent of its population by 1851, it increased its slight majority of females (from 51 percent to 54 percent), as had the county in general. But in the surrounding townlands and Poor Law unions of North and South Kilglass, Rooskey, Knockhall, Lecarrow, and Ballyglass, the trend was very much the reverse. Women, especially single women between fifteen and forty years of age, were missing in all the nearby rural settlements by the time the hunger abated.[40]

While this local trend corresponds to the general pattern of famine emigration, it is far more pronounced, almost certainly due to the threat of eviction that hung over the area at the time of the Mahon clearances. But what it suggests about the mentality of the townland as a response to the threat is unclear. Few if any young women of the townland would have been able to emigrate on their own unless some families pooled what resources they had, perhaps from withheld rents or allowances, to send their daughters off. A small number of men were described as "off the lands harvesting" from time to time and others may have gone shorter distances "booleying" (that is, minding sheep and cattle) in the summer pastures. These were understood as temporary absences and implied no break with home or the past. There is also some hint in the records that women had been more accustomed to movement all along, either marrying off the lands or leaving for varying periods to enter service, while the males were more fixedly tied to the land by tradition and gender. In any case, the missing women remain as a possible indication that either in their own minds or in the community's their place on the land bound them less strongly than their brothers.

None of the townland records give any indication of either what role the women played or what views they held about the rent strike or emigration. Some may have been in the crowd that forced Knox to flee to the police barrack, but no report mentions them specifically. All the ringleaders and troublemakers named by Knox were adult males. All rent-book entries were in the name of the male head of family, except in the case of widows. All letters, memorials, and petitions were signed by male heads of families or in their name. There was one household of women only, where Bridget Conry, a widow of seventy, dwelt with her unmarried sister, Judith McDermott (sixty). No unmarried woman lived alone. Of the fourteen widows resident in 1846 (there were eleven more two years later), only one, Bridget Mahon (seventy), lived by herself. All other holdings in the name of a widow contained adult males. All spinsters but Miss McDermott lived as dependents in households headed by males. The presence of only two orphan boys in the townland, as compared to the seven girls, also suggests a more restricted sphere of independence for unattached females or at least a sense that boys could be allowed to fend for themselves at a younger age than the girls. This is also borne out by the fact that nearly seven times more boys under the age of fifteen worked outside the household as farm servants and laborers than did young girls of their age.[41]

None of this is surprising in the circumstances. The layers of evasion and anonymity that veiled the townland from the outside hid its women even more effectively. In different ways, both the culture of the townland and that of the legal structure above it tended to separate women from any formal economic or political identity, especially while the male head of family lived. The women of the Mahon family seem to have played virtually no part in the management of the estate, even when "poor Maurice" was incompetent. Bridget Conry and her sister in the townland and the Misses St. George of Cloneash are the only households in the record in which women held the leases and apparently managed their own holdings. Although there might well have been a few more, it seems that unaccompanied women, whether single or widowed, rarely were expected to maintain themselves without a male in residence. All of these circumstances tended to cast the women of the neighborhood, apparently of all classes, into a formal passivity that may or may not have disguised a more powerful role in fact, in the silent economy, in the cabin councils, or in the pecking order of deference and respect. Symbolic of their more passive position is the curious fact that although three times as many males of the neighborhood could write English (because they were kept under instruction longer), substantially more women could read it.[42] It was one of the few areas in which the two cultures were not fundamentally in conflict.

But there are some indications that both the town and the townland contained at least a marginal sphere of women, not one with open access to power but with some degree of independence. As we shall see, the town contained a small number of private schools operated by women on a fee-paying basis. Their incomes were at a subsistence level, but these teachers were autonomous and were clearly an integral part of the culture and social life of Strokestown, however marginal their status or dreary their private lives might have been. Always at the edge of poverty, the loss of income they must have suffered with the famine is likely to have made their lives little if any better than those of the landless laborers of the countryside.

There are also slight indications that some of the women of the townland, the widows in particular, carried greater weight than their near invisibility in the record suggests. Of the fourteen widows, at least six seem to have been de facto heads of households, with the land in their names and only unmarried sons and daughters under the age of thirty in residence. A number of the widows were also engaged in the system of joint holdings that prevailed among the smallholders. Both these factors necessarily meant that they were involved in the withholding of rents, the collection (or refusal) of the legal fund, and in the constant discussion and dispute that joint holdings always entailed. At least those widows with strong families, like Anne Flower or Honora Winter, need not have been entirely mute or demure in matters directly affecting their land and families. And if they were expected to pay their 5s. to O'Ferrall, it seems unlikely that they would have no part in the treatment of the dissidents and informers. They signed no petitions, but the notices nailed to their doors were in their names, in a sense giving them entitlement to a say in whatever collective action was to be taken. In the absence of a record of their own minds, it is impossible to know just what part the women of Ballykilcline played in the events that ended with the community's destruction. But that alone cannot be taken to mean that they were either silent or without influence in those events, perhaps even decisive influence.

The culture of which the townland was a part had always depended on some women of strong character despite their lack of prescriptive status or rights. In the absence of any firsthand expression from the widows of Ballykilcline, some sense of their thinking might be suggested from another in very similar circumstances. The Widow Loughan was a tenant of another Crown estate, Boughill, in Galway, which was about to undergo a clearance similar to Ballykilcline's. Hearing of the plan, the Widow Loughan sent a petition to the commissioners in a schooled but inelegant hand, apparently her own, entitled "The Humble Petition of the Widow Loughan of Boohil":

> Petitioner altho a widow does not plead poverty She thanks God. She is by her late Husband one of the oldest Residenters in the Village She has paid her rent at all times as punctual as any Ten't on the Land Therefore She now has to request that ye Gentlemen will Consider me and give no Ear to any underhand dealing if there should be any such But give her & her Son a Holding equally as any of the Tenants for which She will pay for Regular & fealing ye Gen't should consider her unworthy of the like. . . . She humbly Intreats ye will look to her and leave her Settled like any of the Tenants. For which She prays the Almighty may guide & direct ye in all your undertakings in this life and Eternal happinefs in the next.

As another widow of Roscommon, at the age of ninety-seven, once said, "I can be led, but never driven."[43]

The Remains of Ballykilcline

The Reverend Thomas Lloyd, his wife, Eleanor, and their three boys and four girls also remained on the empty lands. He had formerly kept five servants attending the land and the house. But of these, Thomas Wynne and Thomas Fox, common farmhands, Anne Stuart (fifty), the housekeeper and cook, and Maria Gill (twenty), the scullery girl, were all members of families who had been cleared and departed. Bernard Regan, a man of fifty, was another member of the household, apparently a domestic manservant who may have taken on the style of a butler on ceremonial occasions. It appears that at least Anne and Maria left with their families. Wynne and Fox, both young men of landless laboring families who were not entitled to free passage, simply disappear from the now slovenly records of the estate. By April 1848, there remained at least three Maguires and nine Lloyds on the lands, possibly as many as three male servants, Regan, and the young Wynne and Fox—between a dozen and fifteen people of the more than five hundred who had previously populated Ballykilcline.

These, at least, were the only ones with official leave to be there. But, with the clearance completed without incident and their final report made to Parliament, the commissioners relaxed their vigilance. Not long after, the "barracks" (two vacated cabins left standing for the purpose) that had been manned to insure against reoccupation was felt to be an unnecessary expense and was also abandoned. It was at this point, sometime during the summer or fall of 1848, that the three former tenant families and some few others who had survived the awful winter of 1847 reemerged from whatever shelter they had found in the interval and quietly settled back in their places before the new landlord took possession. By 1851, there remained some forty-five individuals living in eight dwellings on the former Crown estate.[44]

The immediate area hardly fared much better as the density of life radically changed in the countryside. The Strokestown Poor Law Union, an area of about 90,000 acres, had contained more than 50,000 people before the famine and just over 30,000 after. The town itself was reduced by 21 percent in the same interval. The smaller estates of Knockhall and Lecarrow shrank from 1,200 to 470 and from 147 to 58 occupants, respectively, even without a scheme of assisted emigration. Not only in their numbers but in the disposition of these remaining populations a dramatic change had also taken place in the landscape. The townland roads and paths were lined with vacant stone dwellings, their roofs collapsing. Where the clearances had occurred, even these traces were piles of rubble or bare ground that would soon be overgrown. Around the crossroads of Aughamore or Doorty, where the cabins of the old clachans had been nearly side by side, one could not before have raised a voice in anger or laughter without being overheard; now one could shout for help without a reply. Apart from the leveled townlands, the remaining households contained fewer members, fewer children, fewer women and young men, and, inevitably, more bachelors and more old men and women living alone. And although no count of the census walker would reveal it, there were almost certainly fewer musicians, hedge-school masters, and storytellers. The closed and intimate life of the old townland was over in this part of the Irish countryside.

Similar purges took place in countless townlands throughout the country during the famine, first of the tenantry, the subtenantry, the annual conacre tillers, and the landless laborers, and slowly thereafter of the marginal and indebted squirearchy. In the space of three or four years, hamlet after hamlet and settlement after settlement, many of them replete with pre-conquest histories of heroes and failed protest like Ballykilcline, lay in weedy ruins with only fading traces of their former vivacity. After the eviction, the management of the small estate, its former system of "deputies," fell into another sort of ruin, first descending to the ne'er-do-well young Knox and then to the bailiff's son, Thomas Cox, who earned small fees counting the departing batches at the very end. Once the younger Knox had completed the travel terms with H. & W. Scott of Dublin, his employment with the Crown ended—he had already been refused his commission in the constabulary and must have left his fastidious father's desk of pens and rent rolls a disgruntled young man with no immediate prospect of a living in the hostile neighborhood.

Johnny Cox, the last and lowest of the Crown's deputies, would also have only temporary employment under the Quit Rent Office, to arrange for the provisioning and clothing of the emigrants and their conveyance into the hands of the shipping agents in Dublin. This task would also be complete by April of 1848, after which all trace of Cox vanishes from the record like the townland itself, although it is safe to suppose that Cox made the most of this last opportunity (he was commissioned to spend nearly £300 of the Crown's funds under loose supervision in outfitting and carrying the emigrants) and also that a man of his proven talents as an enforcer and provider of misleading information was unlikely to be long unemployed in rural Ireland.[45]

II

7

Knowledge and Isolation

"A Child of the Dust Must Not Be Proud"
John Leahy's "Copy Book"

The famine emigrants' understanding and visualization of the outside world is not well understood. Even their conception of Ireland itself on the eve of their departure is uncertain. It can be safely assumed that even the far-removed cottiers of Kerry or Donegal had some perceptions of their place on the globe. Among these would be a precise knowledge of the local distances and topography encompassed by experience as well as an elaborate and deeply disseminated oral and religious tradition that located more distant places of historical and religious significance and linked them with the history of the people. But a consciousness and acceptance of unity on the part of the peasantry or a sense of identity with national symbols and institutions cannot be taken for granted. In other European countries where a national culture was thought to have extended its influence far more widely than that in Ireland, the peripheral peasantries remained only marginally integrated into the nation by the end of the century.[1]

The long experience of colonialism had also prolonged the isolation of rural Ireland from many of the changes occurring in the metropolises of western Europe, as though a heavy curtain blocked their view. No wars had been fought in the name of the nation or any indigenous dynasty. Its popular revolts reached only separated pockets of the countryside. No native coinage had been struck bearing symbols of the people's history. Even the native religion had been only quasi-communicant for more than a century, requiring a "devotional revolution" after the famine to restore it to practices recognizable to the Roman Church.[2] But virtually any adult man or woman in Ireland in the 1840s, it seems safe to say, was quite conscious of Ireland as a distinct entity, as an island flanked to the east by at least two large and powerful nations that had figured intimately in their history and

to the west by a great ocean on which their holy men had traveled and from
which the worst of their weather came, although even this was still shrouded
in ancient myths and superstition that attached a degree of dread to the
prospect of crossing it.

Songs, tales, folklore, and hagiography transmitted a mental geography
of western Europe that was rich in detail and association and replete with
place-names from the voyages of the abbots to Napoleon's retreats. But
for all the wealth this oral tradition contained in history and imagination,
it offered very little to the emigrants with which to measure space in time
and distance and even less to anticipate the conditions and hazards they
were likely to meet along the route out of the country and across the Atlantic.
For this kind of useful knowledge, emigrants such as those from Ballykilcline
had scanty sources at their own disposal.

Very few of them had traveled and returned. At least one is known to
have been "in England harvesting," as one of Cox's scrawls in the rent
roll noted. Their legal entanglement with the Crown brought five of the
Defendants to a Dublin court.[3] One other had an aunt resident in
Liverpool and another had fled to London shortly before the final eviction. The McDermott family left in 1844 and may have written. Travelers were always sought after for news. Any of these may have been a source
of information about the outside before their departure. But these links
were mostly of very recent origin and could hardly have carried the flood
of fact and fancy, or the all-important remittances, that the coming chain
of migration would soon produce. In the long run the emigrant letter
would become the townlands' American library, but that time had not
yet arrived in Ballykilcline.

It is also doubtful that the emigrant posters and guides that confettied
the countryside in the 1850s were yet a common source of information for
the townland emigrants. The most widely distributed of the emigrant guides,
Sidney's Emigrant Journal, Chambers's *The Emigrant's Manual*, and Vere
Foster's *Work and Wages; or, the Penny Emigrants's Guide to the United
States and Canada* (of which 250,000 were distributed freely), could be
commonly found only after the last of the townland departed and reached
their peak several years later. Some copies of *Sidney's* may have reached
Strokestown shortly before, but if the emigrants had seen any printed information of their destination earlier it would most likely have been the
posters and sailing announcements that had been circulated by the Dublin
and Liverpool emigrant and ship agents since the midthirties. It was said
that these could sometimes be found decorating Irish cottage walls by the
early fifties, but that even then their appeal was mainly aesthetic, meaning
little more than "Chinese notices on a tea chest."[4] There is no doubt that
in the decade before the famine the quantity of printed material relating to
emigration was entering the country on an ever-widening scale. Since the
Crown agent had begun bruiting the plan of emigration, it is also likely
that such material had reached as far as Strokestown from the presses of
Dublin and Liverpool. But from the town to the minds of the townland

was in some ways a much greater distance yet, obstructed by mutual suspicion on any matter relating to their leaving.

Many barriers lay between the small farmers and laborers of Ireland and the receipt of practical knowledge of the outside world. The distance in miles between even the more remote townlands and the country's centers of commerce and communication were not great in comparison to those of town and country in the rest of Europe. Irish rural communities were also less physically isolated from one another than were most European villages because of the density of settlement in the countryside—at least among equals, human contact in rural Ireland was as close as the land could support. The isolation experienced by the rural laborers in Ireland resulted less from their "outward" distance from the centers of information than from a "downward" remoteness brought about by the all but impenetrable stratification of the society and its economy. Even in relatively accessible districts like Ballykilcline, we have seen how broad was the gap between the clerk of the quit rents and George Knox at one end and that between him and the tenants at the other. Regular contact across it was limited to a few intermediaries like Cox and McDermott, and the bulk of the cottiers and the town's elite were separated by suspicion and ignorance of each other even when they were not in open hostility.

That gap was also maintained by differences in language, culture, and economy. Even in the 1930s, nearly a century after the bulk of the Irish-speaking, nearly landless laborers had disappeared from the landscape, the economic life of the small farmer could be described as "a livelihood little connected with the outside world." What connection existed relied mainly on the farmers' role in the production of food exports, especially the endless movement of cattle from west to east, from the small farms where beef was very rarely eaten to the "ranches" of the big commercial farmers, who then sold to the shippers and factors who supplied the English market. With the sale of a few calves at the fairs, along with what remained of his milch cow's yield, the small farmer's "business" with the outside world was over except for his account with the shopkeeper. That account, for imported tea, tobacco, sugar, and the flour that had displaced the potato, was settled with the small cash proceeds of his "cattle business." Beyond that annual cycle of subsistence commerce, the small farmer of the twentieth century returned to much the same "livelihood from within" that had encompassed the lives of the townland at the time of the famine.[5]

Information also traveled with trade before the famine and, although its range was widening, it still reached into the townlands selectively. The "farmer" who was able to graze a few cows and fatten calves or yearlings haggled over weights and prices at the fairs, received credit in the town shops, paid wages for labor, and mingled with the commercial farmers and others like himself in the process. And although, like McDermott, he might be personally indistinguishable from his poorer neighbors in the townland, he was within the outer perimeter of the world of cash and calculation and able to make some choices based on at least a limited knowledge of its workings. In this sense, it is probably no coincidence that Hugh McDermott was both one of the leading Defendants and the first to emigrate, since both were acts of calculation. For most of the rest, the mental isolation of the townland had to be penetrated from the outside, sometimes by force. In Ballykilcline, the intrusion was almost invariably from Strokestown. The flow of writs, notices, and threats that emanated from the town alone was enough to create a certain degree of suspicion of any form of communication from the same source. But in a variety of other ways a consciousness of the changes taking place in the outside world had been encroaching on the townland before it disappeared.

Schools and the Townlands

The first National School in the area of Ballykilcline was built near the town of Rooskey in 1836, just two miles away. The National School would eventually reach most rural children. But more important at this time were the independent, itinerant teachers known as hedge-masters and the fee-paying "academies" of various kinds operating in provincial towns like Strokestown. The presence of the one unnamed "Schoolmaster" in the townland and the priest, Father Peter Geraghty, may have figured much more importantly than their almost accidental mention in the record suggests.

No hint remains to suggest whether Geraghty bore any resemblance to the priest of Tocqueville's "Village X," a teacher, commiserator, and advocate of the community, except that he lodged with one of the leading Defendants. Less still is known of the "Schoolmaster," except that he rented no house or land, paid no rent, and must have relied on the goodwill of the country people. Only his calling was listed in the roll, suggesting he was a bachelor of undetermined age whose occupation was not primarily manual. Unlike Geraghty, he was part of no household. Such circumstances would describe most of the native "hedge-school" masters, so named for the clandestine classrooms in which they once taught.[6] Such figures were known to play decisive roles in other rural communities as advisers, scribes, or agitators but could just as often have been mere scolds or freeloaders. It is also possible that he was one of the Strokestown academy teachers, genteel colleagues of the hedge-master. Both were a part of the "hidden Ireland" that was slowly retreating into near-oblivion before the famine.

Isaac Weld's *Statistical Survey of the County of Roscommon* of 1832 offers the best available record of these town schools.[7] It leaves us a valuable cameo of the education available to the children of provincial Ireland before the coming of the National Schools, although it never allows us to see into the classrooms themselves. It is a picture of thriving penury: a town of merely fifteen hundred mostly poor people maintaining ten fee-paying schools, more than enough to accommodate all the town's children of school age. With 359 pupils enrolled, they apparently included a sizable number of children from the surrounding countryside as well, at least some of them from townland families. Few of these "storefront" free enterprises would long survive the coming of the National Schools and the loss of clients during the famine. But in the decades before, they provided a surprisingly far-reaching access to literacy in the country town and its environs.[8]

When and how these schools came into existence in the town is not known; how the six men and four women who taught in them were themselves educated is not known; how the fees were paid, or if and when they were paid is not known. And how some of the masters and mistresses survived on £3 a year or 2s. 6d. a quarter can only be guessed.[9]

Some of these schools bear a family resemblance to the ancient hedge schools. In some, the tuition fees were clearly insufficient to support a living; the Elphin Street master, claiming forty pupils, for example, would not have brought in enough at 10s. a quarter to cover the £6 rent for the house in which his classes were held (and in which he almost certainly lived as well). Like the hedge-school masters, many such freelance teachers might rely more for their upkeep on "gratuities" from their pupils' parents, such as potatoes, butter, milk, and turf, than on their fees.[10] Teachers were commonly paid for the writing of letters and petitions; for drafting wills, agreements, and accounts; and, in such a bustling market town, perhaps for service as occasional clerks and copyists for merchants and agents. It is only barely possible that some of these teachers also did manual or servile labor, but such a last resort would have been only in the most dire need, given the honorific status the teacher enjoyed among the people.

In the case of hedge-school masters in the townlands, their notorious hauteur may have been enough to keep their hands uncallused. All the casual resources of the learned were cultivated by the hedge-school masters as well. Even in the previous century, when the native schoolmaster was subject, as Lecky put it, to "universal, unqualified, and unlimited proscription," the hedge scholars existed astride the clandestine and the legal frontier, hunted subversives by night and petty clerks of the bureaucracy by day. It should not be surprising, then, that Weld's survey, taken merely three years after emancipation, should show a continued mixture of marginal, freelance instruction supplemented by clerical piecework and barter. Provincial teaching was no longer a forbidden and secret vocation, but it was not yet a profession.

In contrast to the hedge-school masters, two of the town teachers were Protestants and four of them were women. Except for the lone Protestant mistress, the women who taught school in Strokestown were clearly on the lower end of the pay scale—only one of the six men declared an "emolument" below theirs. Reading, writing, and domestic arts like sewing and needlework were the subjects offered by most of the women teachers. With an unequal training themselves, many were not prepared to teach arithmetic, which clearly paid higher fees.[11] But even this low standing among the women teachers probably flatters their real status; the various forms of supplementary income available to the men with clerical skills were almost certainly not available to them, or not as readily. Thus, the annual income declared by the schoolmistresses is likely to have been a good deal closer to their real means than in the case of the male teachers, putting at least two of them on the very edge of poverty, even as this was measured in the neighborhood—unless their incomes were supported by marriage or some other form of employment in town, these women teachers were as poor as the townland tenants.[12] To a large degree this hierarchy of male and female merely mirrored the gender expectations of the sons and daughters of both town and the townland. Mistresses were paid less than masters, and girls' instruction moved on to "domestic skills" while the boys were kept at their slates—possibly one of the reasons that they were more likely than girls to write as adults.

The distribution of students suggests rather strongly that parental choices were *not* necessarily made on strictly sectarian grounds. Much more notable than sectarian division is the general integration of pupils of each denomination in this provincial town. Only one school, the smallest, was without a Protestant child; the most distinctly Protestant school, supported by the Church of Ireland parish, still contained a *majority* of Catholic children. The remainder, both the free and fee-paying schools, contained between 9 percent and 24 percent of Protestant pupils, approximating the overall proportion of Protestant children of school age in the town.

The bare numbers of the Weld survey, however, shed only a mottled light. It is clear enough to show that the supposed sectarian divide of rural Ireland in these years was blurred in the Strokestown schools. On the other hand, little can be said about the curriculum presented to the children of either sect or sex beyond what the mixed nature of the classes strongly suggests. It is most unlikely that the Protestant parents who enrolled their children in the schools run by Catholic teachers would have extended their tolerance to instruction in the Roman catechism. In contrast, Catholic parents apparently tolerated reading from the King James version by or in the presence of their children in the endowed schools, either because of the lower costs or some other advantage not noted by Weld, such as a superior master or some condition imposed by their employer or landlord. In either case, sectarian factors in the schools were clearly negotiable enough to accommodate most parents' sensitivities. The collective result was that most of the children apparently received instruction that was primarily secular from common texts and lesson books readily available at that time.

Hedge Schools

The Strokestown schools do not correspond very closely to the hedge-school prototype of the solitary master rehearsing his pupils in barn or bothy, living on the hospitality of the cottagers, and occasionally lambasting his rivals in Latin verse, but their essential function and style seem similar in a more domesticated town setting. Significant differences may have existed in the character and prerogatives of the teachers, such as in the permissible bounds of arrogance or inebriation, in which the hedge-school master is said to have enjoyed a wide latitude. But a resemblance is most apparent in the relationship of the teacher to the population. In contrast to the National Schools, the masters operated in an unregulated, free-enterprise environment, dependent for a livelihood on their own merits and the goodwill of their patrons. Much the same is reported by all sources about the country hedge-school masters; rivals could deprive an unpopular master of pupils and income; masters might be reduced to laboring or forced to move on by competition or by the inability or refusal of the clients to pay the fees. William Carleton's hedge-school master, Pat Frayne, left the neighborhood after his first day for lack of pupils and did not return again for four or five years.[13] Among these sometimes haughty individualists, it was also not unknown that scandal or an oversharp tongue could lose a teacher his living. But their fate was governed by their pupils' families rather than the state.

The accounts of the Strokestown "school system" also illustrate the precariousness of the profession in the early part of the century: ten masters teaching 359 children are maintained by the town for little more than £100 per year! Even the widely acknowledged love of learning in this impoverished peasant world would not have been enough to maintain a native school system that sustained a fair degree of literacy for nearly two centuries unless a startling power to reproduce teaching scholars had not made their services extremely cheap. This achievement must be credited in large part to the deeply rooted mystique of the teacher and the esteem in which learning was held by the population. P. J. Dowling, the historian of the hedge school, reckoned the hedge-school master's salary at from £20 to £50 a year early in the century. He used Mason's *Parochial Survey* as the basis of this estimate, computing from Mason's complex and largely fanciful "shopping list" of the hedge-school curriculum: spelling at 1s. 8d. to 2s. 2d. a quarter; reading at 2s.; writing at 2s. 2d. to 3s. 3d.; arithmetic at 4s. 4d. to 7s; and luxurious Latin at 11s. Like so many other outside observations of "hidden Ireland" in these years, this was a fantasy of clandestine discipline that the hedge-school masters were never able to achieve even if they had sought to. The poet Thomas Ruadh O'Sullivan's complaint "It was my shame/To be teaching children for sixpence a quarter" is probably a more accurate estimate of the fees of the country masters. And teachers' incomes of £6 a year reported in the Parochial Returns of 1824 give a more realistic idea of the status of the ordinary country scholars eking out a living in the townlands, that is, surviving at about the same level of material life as the small subtenants and laborers, besides the more intangible rewards of respect and influence they may have enjoyed.[14]

The hedge-school masters are depicted by their critics as well as their admirers as figures of prestige and status in the rural communities in which they traveled. William Carleton, Daniel O'Connell, and most others recalling their experience with them confirm the masters' imposing image in the minds of the people. But perhaps the best summary of their role and activity among the population is provided by one of their most hostile critics in a shrill but insightful diatribe:

The country schoolmaster is independent of all system and control; he is himself one of the people, imbued with the same prejudices, influenced by the same feelings, subject to the same habits; to his little store of learning he generally adds some traditionary tales of his country, of a character to keep alive discontent. He is the scribe, as well as the chronicler and the pedagogue of his little circle; he writes their letters, and derives from this no small degree of influence and profit, but he has open to him another source of deeper interest and greater emolument, which he seldom has virtue enough to leave unexplored. He is the centre of the mystery of rustic iniquity, the cheap attorney of the neighbourhood, and, furnished with his little book of precedents, the fabricator of false leases and surreptitious deeds and conveyances. Possessed of important secrets and of useful acquirements, he is courted and caressed; a cordial reception and the usual allowance of whiskey greets his approach, and he completes his character by adding inebriety to his other accomplishments. Such is frequently the rural schoolmaster, a personage whom poetry would adorn with primeval innocence and all the flowers of her garland! So true it is that ignorance is not simplicity, nor rudeness honesty.[15]

How many of the country schoolmasters were "the centre of the mystery of rustic iniquity" is not something easily determined. Some undoubtedly were all or some of the things this critic imagines: senachie, priest, scribe, lawyer, political agitator, and clay-footed folk hero. The aura of scandal that always hovered over this figure probably also carried a memory of endearing mischief and peccadillos in the minds of the people—the silver-tongued peasant-scholar, a seducer, a leech, or a harmless fraud, but protected by tradition and demanding a minimum of respect, even if given with a wink. Along with boy-soldiers and fleeing rebels, the ragged scholar was one of their picaros, prone to trouble from excess in thought and deed.

The same figure possessed a brighter side that was less profane. A century of persecution had drawn a halo of martyrdom around the ragged scholar's head, and underground life among the dim huts of the townlands had established a confidential and protective understanding between them and the country people, as it had also done between the people and the priests, even if this relationship was not always serene. But in times of evictions and arrears, there was great need for the scribe and adviser who in many cases was inevitably the schoolmaster. He and sometimes his students were the masters of words and of writing among those who fed and housed them, many of whom had never received a letter or written a word since copying their lessons. Oliver Goldsmith wrote of the village schoolmaster of *The Deserted Village*, "Lands he could measure, terms and tides preseage." The role he played was essential, especially if he were a man of good memory and shrewdness rather than the clown or the fraud.

In the circumscribed townland communities his role frequently brought the writer of letters and petitions into the most intimate family business: disputes over inheritances or dowries; measurements of land in Irish and Statute acres; the paperwork of remittances, taxes, and tithes; pleas and memorials to landlords; petitions to the bishop for annulments and dispensations. All of these functions required some knowledge of form, precedent, and argumentation, which might lead a stranger to believe that the scribe was in fact the mover and cause rather than the intermediary. As we have seen in the Ballykilcline petitions, the intermediary's role was often that of an adversary of landed property, "the fabricator of false leases and surreptitious deeds and conveyances." The Connors' claims to the lands of Ballykilcline were seen by the Crown agents and the law to be of this ilk, written in the hand of the lawyer O'Ferrall and his clerk but emanating from ragged troublemakers at a lower level. It was at least widely believed that the schoolmaster's hand was behind many of the petitions and threatening letters that flowed in profusion from the townlands before the famine.[16]

Unfortunately, it is not possible to tell whether the townland's scribes were also its schoolmasters. There is also no evidence that the Strokestown schoolmasters and schoolmistresses filled any or all of the functions attributed to the hedge-school teacher. But before the full emergence of the National School, no fixed line should be drawn between the town and country teacher. As Dowling rightly asserts, they had shared the same history of illegality and persecution, they taught much the same curriculum, and a great many of the town teachers had themselves been educated in the hedge schools.[17] Equally important, most of the children they taught would not have been distinguishable from the children of the townland, many of whom were enrolled in the town schools anyway. Thus, in most respects the teachers of the fee-paying town schools might be regarded as domesticated hedge-school masters, practicing in an environment altered mainly by the mixed denomination of their students and their proximity to the watchful eyes of strangers.

As to what these teachers imparted to their pupils, a good deal is known in some areas and very little in others. All taught the basics of reading, writing, spelling, and arithmetic from a limited selection of primers in circulation: the *Rational Spelling Book*; Wall's *Hibernian Preceptor*; and Voster's, Gough's, Thompson's, and, later, Deighan's *Arithmetic*. No such universal textbooks existed in the sensitive subject of history, though it may be assumed that it intruded into lessons according to each master's lights. But the place of geography is even more elusive. Texts in geography were available, two by noted Irish masters, Deighan's and Lynch's, but due to their prohibitive cost, these appear to have had a very limited circulation and the subject does not seem to have been included in the ordinary curriculum of the provincial schools. Indeed, the cost of books was frequently the decisive factor in determining the text in which children would both learn and practice their reading. In an area like north Roscommon, the price of texts ranged from 1s. 6d. to more than 3s., a good deal more the the daily wage of an adult farm laborer. Given the paltry incomes of teachers, the possession of a few texts or favorite classics was possible only at real personal sacrifice. Teachers, nevertheless, were most often in the majority on the lists of subscribers kept by publishers. For the general population, the possession of a few books was something to be proud of. In such circumstances it was common for the masters to employ whatever printed matter happened to be available in their baggage or in the cottier's cabin.[18]

In some rare cases, a classic work of literature or history might be found on a laborer's shelf in the townland cabins. But for the most part country readers might possess cheap reprints from the publishers of "sixpenny books" in Dublin, Cork, and Limerick, hawked in the market towns by itinerant peddlers. Various lists of their titles were compiled from time to time in the early part of the century by amused or suspicious observers of Irish country habits, including Edward Gibbon Wakefield and William Carleton. The reading habits of the common people were also deplored by the improvement societies, such as the Hibernian Bible Society, which provided bibles for prisons, workhouses, hospitals, and orphanages in various parts of the country, and the Association for Discountenancing Vice and Promoting the Knowledge and Practice of the Christian Religion. One such observer, Hely Dutton, whose *Survey of Clare* was influential in forming opinion on this matter, published a list that seems specially designed to arouse anxieties among the respectable classes. Referring to the reading he found in use in the hedge schools of County Clare, he claimed that

> the state of education may be easily appreciated, when it is known that, with the exception of a few universal spelling books, the general cottage classics are:
>
>   History of the Seven Champions of Christendom
>   Montelion, Knight of the Oracle
>   Parisimus and Parismenes
>   Irish Rogues and Rapparees
>   Freney, a notorious robber, teaching them the most dangerous mode of
>   robbing
>   The most celebrated pirates
>   Jack the Bachelor, a noted smuggler
>   Fair Rosamund and Jane Shore, two prostitutes
>   Donna Rosina, a Spanish Courtesan
>   Ovid's Art of Love
>   History of Witches and Apparitions
>   The Devil and Dr. Faustus
>   Moll Flanders—highly edifying, no doubt
>   New System of Boxing, by Mendoza, etc. etc.[19]

Dutton's bizarre list of "cottage classics" was apparently taken quite seriously by Wakefield and by a number of other authorities on the condition of Ireland. Indeed, alarming reports of this kind about the "secret mind" of the native Irish were almost common enough to constitute a minor genre of their own. In a similar vein, for example, was the popular tract of "Signor Pastorini," the wildly anti-Protestant tract speciously attributed to the Roman Catholic clergy and secret societies in the teens and early twenties.[20] Such authorities provided the bulk of the "intelligence" from Ireland, along with the spokesmen of bible and improving societies, to the parliamentary committees looking into Irish education. The distorted images they created undoubtedly contributed to the severely disciplinary and corrective character of the National School system that emerged.

However hostile or friendly, most outside observers remarked on the apparent avidity of the country people for books and learning. Most ignored the clearest available evidence of this, which was their unbroken willingness to maintain and fill their own schools and support their own scholars generation after generation, despite their poverty. Contemporary critics of native schooling like Dutton and Wakefield saw only mischief and superstition in what the masters were teaching. And, like Carleton, some of the Irish who passed through the country schools had little better to say about them. But as the hedge school was gradually displaced by the National School and receded into a folk memory, its image greatly improved. It seems clear that in the decade before the National Schools, inexpensive books of a wider variety were becoming increasingly accessible in the countryside and provincial towns, partly owing to the efforts of the Kildare Place Society and the Cheap Book Society, which published, printed, and promoted a list of low-priced reprints of classics and novels of good quality and uncontroversial nature.

Fairly typical of modern views of the old hedge school is the one offered by Kevin Danaher, who drew his information from an old schoolmaster of Limerick who took his description from an aged priest who had been a hedge-school pupil just before the famine:

> [T]the little picture of the past remains bright and clear. The old thatched farmhouse with the bright fire in the kitchen. The priest and the poor scholar vieing with each other in learning. The little circle of attentive young men. The farmer's children listening and picking up a bit of the classics here and there—they had had their lessons in the three R's from the poor scholar earlier in the day. The flow of erudition, Latin, Greek, Rhetoric, Philosophy and Mathematics. The farmer and his good wife looking on in admiration and the servant boys and girls amazed at so much wisdom.[21]

The hedge school portrayed by P. J. Dowling is not much different: one of its more illustrious products, Patrick Lynch, himself a master at Carrick-on-Suir (a few miles from Ballykilcline), is said to have been taught by a Clare hedge-school master who knew no English but was able to learn the classics through the medium of the Irish language, "acquiring . . . an excellent knowledge of Greek, Latin and Hebrew." Lynch himself later wrote prolifically on a wide variety of subjects, mostly in the form of teaching manuals: "The Pentaglot Preceptor: or Elementary Institutes of the English, Latin, Greek, Hebrew, and Irish Languages, Vol.I, containing a complete Grammar of the English Tongue"; "The Classical Student's Metrical Mnemonics, containing in Familiar Verse, all the necessary Definitions and Rules of the English, Latin, Greek and Hebrew Languages"; and "A Geographical and Statistical Survey of the Terraqueous Globe including a comprehensive Compend of the History, Antiquities and Topography of Ireland—Embellished with a Curious Map of Eire—For the Use of Schools and Adult Persons," as well as an "Introduction to Practical Astronomy," an Irish grammar, and a life of Saint Patrick.

It is probably safe to assume that the great majority of the schools and masters in the country and the provincial towns were of a quality somewhere between the two images of rustic iniquity and high erudition. It is to be expected that a tradition of heroic persecution would keep a seditious temper alive among the schoolmasters, but the parents were paying scarce shillings for the sake of their children's literacy and the dignity that learning, even a little, conferred—that distinction was second only to holding land in the microstatus of townland society. The result was a self-perpetuating subculture that nurtured the peasantry's grasp on literacy, sustained the lore and literature in the native language, and supported a permanent cadre of learned scholars, independent of both the state and the church. All indications are that the emigrants of Ballykilcline included a substantial number of literate individuals and perhaps a few of greater learning. But there is very little to suggest that they had learned much of practical utility in any language about the outside world from the books and masters. Even the ragged scholars among them were like travelers from some antiquity, learned but innocent of most of the world beyond their sight.

National Schools

While the evidence of popular literacy in the English countryside would be taken as a sign of hope and promise, Parliament and the National Commissioners of Education regarded it with alarm in Ireland. Like so many other experiments in reform during the era, the reformed schoolroom was to be given its first test in Ireland, more or less frankly for the purpose of suppressing subversion and instilling obedience. When the National Schools emerged, with their bleak and severe architecture and their exaggerated Victorian sternness, they immediately began to carry out the same mission by sanitizing and demystifying Irish history, muting the oral tradition, deemphasizing the Irish language, and extolling an extreme puritanical code of deference, obedience, and chastity. From the first, the local school officials were also given latitude to exercise powers well beyond the classrooms: the masters' contacts with the community were closely monitored; the children's standing in school was sometimes tied to their parents' good conduct; and local priests were enlisted as part of the disciplinary relationship between the schools and the community.

The National School at Rooskey would not have directly affected any of the Ballykilcline emigrants who were older than about twenty-five years in 1848, since it had opened its doors twelve years earlier only to children under fourteen. But some portion of these would have spent some years under its discipline and received a view of the world in stark contrast to that of their elders.

Pobble O'Keefe-Kingwilliamstown

No record of the Rooskey National School remains, but the record of the Crown estate of Pobble O'Keefe in Cork shows something of the intentions of the Commissioners of National Education and also some of the obstacles they confronted in their plan. The Kingwilliamstown National School was established under a parliamentary grant and opened for classes in the summer of 1836. No record remains of its sister institution near Ballykilcline, but Pobble O'Keefe's response to the all-but-free new school suggests that not all the townland pupils flocked to its doors.[22]

The townland of Pobble O'Keefe on the five-thousand-acre Crown estate of Kingwilliamstown, in the barony of Duhallow differed from Ballykilcline in some significant ways mainly because of its location in an area of Cork remote from the network of market towns and turnpikes. But, except for the "rebellion" that distinguished the Roscommon townland, its experience in the decade and a half before the famine was quite similar. The middleman's lease of ninety-nine years under the Crown had also lapsed in the early 1830s, bringing the townland under the direct management of the Commissioners of Woods and Forests. In this case, too, the commissioners had tried various methods of "improving" the lands without much success and finally decided to assist the emigration of a large part of the population.[23] Among the improvements encouraged by the commissioners was the establishment of a National School, leaving a firsthand record of the design and progress of the school not available for Ballykilcline. According to the Crown agent for the townland, a local engineer by the name of Michael Boyan, the population on the lands consisted of 479 persons (later counts varied), including 84 children under the age of fourteen who were expected to be enrolled in the school's five grades. In the report of attendance for the August-through-October term of 1836, the supervisor estimated that twenty to twenty-five "attended regularly" (that is, from three to six days a week) and that about 50 percent of the total attended "casually" (that is, averaging fewer than two days a week), either missing whole weeks in sequence or turning up once or twice a week. Even this modest attendance declined as the season progressed. Thus, on a given day during term, the great majority of the children of the townland would be found in their fields or cabins and not in the new school. The attendance improved slightly by 1841 (averaging fifteen boys and thirteen girls), but the school was never able to attract even half of the neighborhood children despite its negligable fee of a penny a month.[24]

The Commissioners and the Crown Agent took a view very much like Dutton's and Wakefield's to account for the school's failure: the people were recalcitrant peasants benighted by superstition and myth, with no true interest in learning of a proper and useful sort. The bustling attendance in the Strokestown schools, which charged much higher fees, seems to contradict this opinion, unless there were striking differences in the attitudes of the Roscommon and Cork cottiers toward their children's education.

Did parents keep the children at home for their labor? The declining attendance during the harvest suggests that they did. It was also reported that
enrollments in the upper grades of twelve- to fourteen-year-olds were lowest of all. Of course, this was a problem confronted everywhere that
children's labor was of value, but it fails to explain why more than half the
children avoided the Kingwilliamstown school at all times, whether there
was work to do at home or not.

The hedge schools, meeting in a flexible synchronization with the seasons, often in the evening, and working on a "retail" principle—2s. for
reading, 1s. 8d. for spelling, and so on—avoided this conflict. Indeed, it
appears that a hedge school was already in operation in the townland or its
vicinity. Like Ballykilcline, the population of Pobble O'Keefe gave ample
evidence of at least a core of literacy in numerous letters and petitions to
the authorities regarding eviction and emigration. The great variety of
writing styles and qualities in Ballykilcline's petitions suggests a wider literacy than in the Cork townland—as the resident engineer and surveyor of
Pobble O'Keefe put it, "[T]here . . . [was] no person above the condition
of a cottier tenant resident within several miles of the school."[25]

Yet a rustic and oddly antique literacy flourished in this remote community, as the "memorials" and letters amply demonstrate. Two of the tenants, Denis Daniel and Denis Mathew Denahy (who were to emigrate to
Buffalo not long after), addressed one such memorial to Lord Duncannon
after receiving their second notice of eviction in May of 1837. They pleaded
that there was "every reason you won't digress from [the] kind and charitable feeling of your Ld.s ancestors." Denis Daniel and Denis Mathew described themselves as "the father of seven helpless young children and the
latter of five that they are now reduced to the lowest ebb of poverty." Weale,
the same Crown surveyor employed in Roscommon, had forbidden them
to lime their fields or thatch their cottages, "which induced them to think
that Mr. James Weale's determination was to dispossess them of the land
of their Nativity." When Weale died soon after, that threat seemed to
recede—until the notice of eviction arrived, as the petitioners explained:
"A false convalescence mistaken for the recovery of their farms awakened
their joy, but turning their graziers off the lands soon replunged Petrs. into
grief and diffused an universal gloom over their joy."[26]

Many letters less artfully phrased reached the Commissioners of Woods
and Forests from the mountain townland. One of the cottiers, Michael
O'Connor, a poor three-acre tenant, was apparently on better terms with
Weale and was apparently another literate rustic of the community. He wrote
to Weale, "I lent you Keating's *History of Ireland*. . . . You said you'd return
it Christmas with a few shillings." Weale noted on the letter that instead of
returning the seventeenth-century classic (which would have had considerable cash value), he "gave him a set of Barron's publications," selling new
at 6d. apiece.[27]

The frequent use of *X*'s on the rolls of relief works in the neighborhood
suggests that many of the laborers were illiterate. But it may be assumed

that there were others in this predominantly Irish-speaking townland who could write in English but did not petition the authorities. These traces of native literacy in English were not the product of the National Schools, which were not yet established, nor of the kind of town fee-paying academies that we found in Strokestown, since there were none nearer than Kanturk. Only the hedge school can account for their eloquence, an eloquence that may be less surprising even in such remoteness when it is remembered that the townland was in the heart of Gaelic Munster and along the well-worn track of the poet-scholars of Cork, where "learning in rags" had reached its pinnacle of expression in the previous century.[28]

Two latter-day exponents of that tradition make an appearance, unfortunately brief, in the Kingwilliamstown record. The first, Daniel McSwiney, wrote to "A. Wales" (that is, Weale) when he heard of the proposed new school, introducing himself as an "Irish teacher." He "presumed the patronage" of Weale to teach the Scripture "in our Vernacular Idiom in Williamstown," where, he wrote, he had "no doubt there would be much good effected by that means." He suggested a "Trial." Another, John O'Reilly, addressing James Weale of "Willamstown" offered that he "feels delicate to say a word tending to self-praise, save a reference to others." Nevertheless, he was obliged to inform Weale that "besides his knowledge of Mathematics he flatters himself to say that he knows his native language to perfection."[29] Not surprisingly, neither was hired—it is unlikely even that Weale replied, since the Irish language was not being considered as part of the curriculum. The plan was to be frankly adversarial to the existing learning and living habits of the population. This, more than any supposed local indifference to schooling, probably accounts for the poor showing the school made among the people.

Weale drew up a plan of "Regulations" for the commissioners' approval and for the guidance of Boyan, the resident engineer, who was also to be the school's supervisor, hiring the teachers and enforcing the regulations.[30] Strict account was to be kept of the tuitions, and falling in arrears was to bring instant expulsion, presumably as the first lesson to be brought home to the pupils' parents. In the first "Division," containing the elementary curriculum, three absences in a row would cause the child to be expelled for one month or pay a fine of 2d., unless Boyan approved an exception. There was to be no penalty for irregular attendance in the upper two forms, but admission required a "ticket" from the engineer, who, the plan stipulated, "will be guided in granting such tickets by the Character of the parents." Any conduct of the child "or her parents or friends" that might make it advisable to bar the child from school was also to be considered by Boyan.

There was a calendar of attendance to suit the late dawns and early dusks of winter, primarily to save fuel and candles. Children were to be admitted to school at ten o'clock "and not after, on any pretence whatever." In contrast to the Strokestown "academies," the masters and boys would be segregated from the mistress and girls in two apartments in the school ("Boys" and "Girls" entrances remained standard in the National School for the rest of the century). Children without shoes and stockings had to assemble one half hour before ten, presumably to be washed or given footwear on loan. Children "with uncombed hair, or dirty legs, arms or person" were not to be admitted. The roll was to be taken at 10:10 A.M. and delivered to Boyan before 11:00 A.M. Minor cases of misbehavior were to be punished with "Home memorizing" of from forty to three hundred words taken from the National School *Stock Books* and recited "standing on the Black Stool." Finally, reversing the often combative relationship of schoolmaster and clergy, the most serious of the children's offenses were to be "delivered to the Priest on the following Sunday," presumably for the priest to consider a public scolding of the malefactor.

The rules governing the teachers were equally austere and intrusive, as though they would need as much watching as the children. Boyan was to conduct an inspection monthly and to deduct any "broken glass" from the teacher's salary, "whether willfully or accidentally broken by anyone." Use of the school building "for any purpose other than the instruction of the children" would mean immediate dismissal. Immediate dismissal was also to be imposed for several other infractions: for debts contracted and un-paid for more than fourteen days; for any visitors in the school not autho-rized by Boyan *or by the clergy;* for admitting into the schoolroom "any printed books or Tracts, writings, prints or Pictures other than those sup-plied by the National Board"; and for accepting presents of any kind from the children, their parents, or friends. The last of these was clearly aimed at preventing the "economy" of the hedge school from gaining entrance to the new institution.

The regimen of the school was a complete contrast to anything the popu-lation had experienced before and may have been enough in itself to dis-courage the tenants from entrusting their children to it. Apart from the lib-erties it proscribed, the school regulations aimed at and ultimately succeeded in transferring popular control of schooling to the local representative of the landed interest, in the person of Boyan, and to the clergy, who not only shared disciplinary authority over the children, the teachers, and the cur-riculum but were assured what amounted to compulsory religious instruc-tion in public education. Roman Catholic, Anglican, and Presbyterian clergy were guaranteed access to the children of their denominations in prescribed hours of instruction during the school week. Even with this guarantee, most of the Protestant hierarchy (and the Presbyterian Synods of Ulster with vehemence) opposed cooperation with the National School, leaving the great bulk of the early enrollments to Catholic children and a powerful share of influence over the schools to the Roman clergy.[31] The screened and closely watched new teachers would have little scope for "rustic iniquity."

The minutiae of Weale's regulations assured that punishable infractions would be routine occurrences. The fact that Boyan, whose other duties included collecting rents, serving evictions, and supervising the public works, was also empowered to hold the children and teachers hostage to the good conduct of the parents went strongly against the grain of the townland tradition of education. Whatever mischief the hedge master might do to annoy a troublesome parent, he could hardly have barred the twelve children of the Denahy family, for example, for the fathers' dispute with the landlord. Many of the parents were also employed by the resident engineer in the local quarry and road works. With his new power as school inspector added to his role as rent collector and employer, the parents might well have thought it unwise to put their children under his control as well.[32]

The early history of the school strongly suggests it was a place that earned no affection from either masters or pupils. Teachers came and went with great rapidity, some absconding in midterm from Boyan's surveillance and the bleak and lonely life of a single man or woman who did not find the exclusive company of Irish-speaking children satisfying.

Lessons

The first lesson in "Descriptive Geography" in the *Fourth Book of Lessons* for National Schools concludes with the following passage, which might have been one of those errant children were required to recite from memory standing on the "Black Stool": "The people of Ireland are a clever, lively people; formerly, very much given to drink, and very ignorant: but now it is believed that they are one of the soberest nations of Europe; and it will be their own fault if they are not also one of the best educated."[33] The plan of the *Lesson Books* varied little from the time of their first appearance. They were meant to provide the masters with a uniform elementary curriculum, proceeding from Natural History, through Descriptive Geography, Scriptural History, Political Economy, and "Miscellaneous Lessons," which usually included brief explications of practical subjects like Printing, the law of Gravity, Astronomy, "the Microscopic world," and various "Moral Tales" purportedly taken from life. The master was advised that every sentence could be made an exercise in grammar and appendices of Sacred Poetry and Latin and Greek derivations, which were to be given special attention in each lesson, ended each volume.[34]

Thus, to introduce the lessons "Natural History, or Kingdoms in Nature," the pupils were given "Linnaeus, the great Swedish naturalist," describing "the three kingdoms of nature—the animal, the vegetable, and the mineral. . . ." The teacher was to see that the pupils could spell every word, read the sentence "with proper pronunciation and accent" and to examine them on it as follows:

(Q.) Who was Linnaeus?
(A.) A Swedish naturalist.
(Q.) From what Latin root is *naturalist* formed?
(A.) *Natura*, nature. . . .
(Q.) What part of speech is *naturalist*?
(A.) A noun.

(Q.) What kind of naturalist was Linnaeus?
(A.) Great.

(Q.) What part of speech is *great*? . . . [etc.]

(Q.) Where was Linnaeus born?
(A.) In Sweden.

(Q.) Where is Sweden?
(A.) In the north of Europe.
  "Point it out on the map. . . . [etc.]"

The Natural History lesson is unremarkable for the time, emphasizing the natural order and the "Omnipresence of God" (a verse that ends with "vegetable kingdom"), and overlooking the subject of reproduction. But perhaps the most useful part of the students' Natural History is contained in the lesson on gold:

> Gold being limited in supply . . . is extremely valuable, and is therefore coined for money. One small piece, the size of a shilling, and called a sovereign, from having the Queen's head stamped on it, is worth 20 shillings, or 240 pence; because the copper of which *one* penny is made is twelve times less valuable than one silver shilling, and 240 times less valuable than 20 shillings or one sovereign.
>
> A pound weight of gold is worth about 50 sovereigns.

With sovereigns as rare as oranges in these rural districts, it should not be assumed that the children's parents could make all of these computations.

Frauds practiced on emigrants during their journey were often the result of their inexperience with cash, especially in handling paper currency and negotiable paper like passage tickets.[35] The Irish Poor Law Commissioners often noted this widespread ignorance of money in the rural districts. One witness, speaking of the West in 1847, describes the extremes to which this innocence sometimes went:

> Money is, in truth, not to be found in almost any part of the country and its value is so little known or understood in consequence of its total disuse, that it is no uncommon thing for a peasant who becomes possessed of a bank note to pledge it at a pawnbroker's for so many shillings as he may want, and pay the interest on the loan.[36]

There might well be some exaggeration in such reports, but large numbers of the cottier-laborer classes of the townlands clearly had had little experience with cash beyond the value of silver shillings, in which they paid their rents, and the copper pence in which they received their wages. Golden sovereigns were mostly symbols, "strokes of luck," "pots of gold," or perhaps the treasured remainder of a rich dowry, something to be "hoarded" but not spent. The relative absence of the currency-related crimes—coining, clipping, or counterfeiting—in the countryside suggests the same money innocence in the bulk of the rural population.[37]

Every section of the National School texts provides some clear indication of what effect the commissioners and the authors they selected hoped to produce in the minds and characters of the Irish children.[38] Almost no collateral knowledge (as of cultivation or manners) was taken for granted, and where it was, the tone of the lessons was corrective. All books meticulously avoid the Irish language and history—except, once again, to correct misguided myths and notions. But for the prospective emigrants of Pobble O'Keefe and Ballykilcline, perhaps the most significant part of their experience with these schools was what was taught under the headings of "Geography" and "Political Economy."

The Geography lesson, written by the Reverend James Carlile, a Presbyterian and the chief commissioner of education, begins with western Europe and proceeds on a highly selective "tour" of the world, moving eastward to Russia and the Near East, Africa, Asia, and America, and ending in Guiana (possibly meaning New Guinea), New Holland, and New Zealand. The "tour" was to "begin from home" and was to be illustrated with maps of England, Ireland, Palestine (for scriptural history), Europe, and the world. It was expressly decreed that the lessons were to be given from the assigned text and "*from no other source.*" The lesson "The British Islands" begins:

> The island of Great Britain, which is composed of England, Scotland, and Wales, and the Island of Ireland, form . . . the British Empire in Europe. The people of these islands have one and the same language (all at least who are educated), one and the same laws; and though they differ in their religious worship, they all serve the same God, and call themselves by the name of Christ. All this is enough to make them brethren, in spite of many disagreements and faults which history tells of them in their intercourse with each other, when the strong oppressed the weak, and the weak hated the strong; but a better knowledge of their duty will give future history better things to record.[39]

Proceeding in this hope, the masters conducted a "tour" of Ireland and the world that took many curious turns. Each step was illustrated with the maps provided, almost certainly the first such pictorialization of the world around them that the townland children had seen up to this time. All but a few of their parents would have been equally ignorant of the relative positions of the places the lesson described, or of the distances between them, since geography received little attention in the hedge schools and maps were all but nonexistent.

The lesson continues through the four provinces of Ireland in which Dublin, and then Belfast, are featured. Dublin's public buildings are described—the Courts of Law, the Customs House, the Bank, the Mansion House, but not Dublin Castle. Its many charitable institutions are noted, especially its hospitals, "where the most skilful physicians and surgeons attend." The "famous hospitable for incurables" (that is, lunatics) is described as "a large dwelling in the midst of a pleasant garden, where persons who have an incurable disease are taken in to live, where they are kindly and skilfully tended, and enjoy the comforts of easy circumstances and kind companions." From the hospitals it goes on to Phoenix Park and its zoological gardens, where "it is a treat permitted occasionally to the scholars of public schools to walk. . . ." The school board recommended that all such lessons be punctuated with emphases on new words appearing in the text along with their Latin and Greek derivations: "Hospes, hospit-is, a guest; as hospitable, hospital"; "Char-is, (Gr.) love; as charity." The pupils would recite these derivations in unison and aloud and were examined on them at a later date.

The description of Dublin, where the children of Ballykilcline would later find themselves, possibly wondering as to the whereabouts of Phoenix Park, ends with a brief account of its manufactures (poplin, velvet, and glass). But it dwells at much greater length on the sad decline of the city's industry:

> [T]here were once many more manufactories, but the workmen, not satis-fied (Satis, enough; as satisfy) with good wages, refused to work at a lower price than they should themselves appoint, which the masters being unable to afford, the establishments were broken up, and the proprietors took their money and machinery elsewhere.[40]

Wales and Scotland are visited. The Welsh "are a remarkably clean, active, industrious people—their houses and persons are very neat, and they are so careful never to lose a moment of their time, that they carry their knitting with them where-ever they go. . . ." The Scots "are a steady, industrious people, and schools are so universal among them that it is hardly possible to find any one who cannot read, write, and cast accounts." England itself is covered rather briefly and modestly, with emphasis on its rich fields, in-dustrious towns, and busy ports; any mention of Irish residing there is notably missing. The only mention of Liverpool is that it "is well known as a famous trading seaport."[41]

The continental nations are treated quite cursorily, beginning with what is quite probably an accurate summary of popular English stereotypes of the time. "The first thing you would see on crossing the straits and landing at Calais, would be crowds of fishwomen standing about the pier or quay, all dressed in dark stuff petticoats, with gilt ear-rings, and wearing hand-kerchiefs over their heads, or white caps, and all chattering away in French." The only divergence from this routine is a relatively long lesson on Peter the Great, praising his desire to learn shipbuilding and his building of "Petersburgh" for the sake of his people's prosperity, for which he "well deserved the title of *Great*."

Various other parts of the globe—Turkey, Africa, India, China—are cov-ered in the same selective manner, but the most notable feature of the over-seas tour is the treatment of the United States and New South Wales. Curiously, the United States is given less attention than most of the lesser nations of Europe, including Switzerland, despite its obvious relevance and prominence in Ireland. The lesson informs the pupil about the conquest and division of the New World in one short paragraph, concluding, in 1783, when "the descendants of the English who inhabited the centre of North America separated themselves from Great Britain, and formed themselves into an independent republic, called the *United States.*" Its geography is summarized tersely: "The *United States* are partly wild, full of forests, mountains, and lakes; and partly flat and cultivated. The inhabitants are of British descent, and all speak English. The principal towns are New York, Boston, and Philadelphia—all in the eastern or cultivated states." No further mention is made of the habits and character of the population, except for the North American Indians, who are examined at length and in admiring detail, reminiscent of eighteenth-century images: "though they have not been taught to hallow God's name as we have, they set an example which some among us might do well to follow."

The Commissioners of National Education clearly intended that Irish children know much more about New South Wales and give accordingly a more voluble, and cautionary, description of the famous penal colony. The sufferings of those sent off for their crimes in Great Britain and Ireland are great, the children are warned. Despite the fine climate, rich soils, and remarkable fauna, the colony "is neither a pleasant nor a safe country to live in, for the greatest part of the settlers are men who were wicked in their own country, and become still more so here from the influence of bad examples amongst them. Nothing is so corrupting as bad company. . . ." Again, no concept of distance is given. It is also not mentioned that an inordinate proportion of these malefactors had spent their youth in Ireland.

At appropriate intervals, the lessons in each subject are illustrated either with moral tales or sermonizing verses from obscure English authors. To conclude the lessons in descriptive geography, the commissioners chose a patriotic poem by one "Montgomery," entitled "A Voyage Round the World." Like the other verse selections, "Voyage" is suitable for exercising the children's memory (twenty-four stanzas) or for small punishments. But, perhaps by oversight, it also contains passages that the commissioners would probably not wish to become the focus of a lesson; the poet hired by the commissioners had various axes of his own to grind. Thus, on passing "O'er Canadian woods and lakes" he sings an old Tory lament:

> These my spirit soon forsakes.
> Land of exiled liberty,
> Where our fathers once were free,
> Brave New England, hail to thee.

In passing through the West Indies, he is an abolitionist:

> No—a curse is on the soil;
> Bonds and scourges, tears and toil,
> Man degrade, and earth despoil.
>   Horror-struck I turn away,
>   Coasting down the Mexique bay;
>   Slavery there hath lost the day.

And when he reaches India, where, as the children have learned only a few pages before, the population is "subject to, or dependent on, the British sway, amounts to nearly one hundred and twenty-five millions," he is almost subversive:

> Either India next is seen,
> With the Ganges stretch'd between;
> Ah! what horrors here have been.
>   War, disguised as commerce, came;
>   Britain, carrying sword and flame,
>   Won an empire,—lost her name.[42]

It is tempting to imagine what some of the masters and mistresses might have made or said of the decline of Dublin's manufacture or "War, disguised as commerce." No doubt some subversive spirits were able to slip through the board's selection and practice a quiet sedition in the schools without detection, but it seems evident that the National School was not the place where the country people learned rebellion in these years, or for a long time thereafter.

Political Economy

Although there were still active Bible societies and missions in the Irish countryside, the prospect of converting the Catholic peasantry had long been a dead letter as an article of government policy. But the "Irish Education Experiment," as the National School was called, might be seen as a renewed effort to bring the island out of its barbarism, now not through a spiritual conversion from the error of Rome as much as through a conversion of mind and morals from the errors of the Gael.

In no area was this more evident than in the lessons described as "Political Economy." They rested on certain assumptions about the culture from which the children came that are commonly found in European colonial ideologies of the time: that the native populations possessed no discernible system of organizing their economic life; that they were unable on their own to produce anything beyond permanent scarcity; that they could be stimulated to work only by the immediate prospect of hunger; and that their consequent lack of reverence for private property was at the root of their factious and unruly society. The same axioms applied elsewhere, especially in India, but nowhere in the empire did that effort to reeducate the peasantry rely so doggedly on the precepts of classical political economy as in Ireland.[43] If we could recreate the moment in the rustic schoolhouse in which the lessons were given to the unkempt and shoeless children of Pobble O'Keefe or Ballykilcline, we would behold a scene more akin to revolutionary China than to any schoolroom in western Europe. In effect, these lessons were designed to drive a wedge between the rural generations by denigrating the values and practices of the children's parents and replacing them with an irrefutable natural law that governed the behavior of all rational men.

The prominence of political economy in the National School curriculum was due largely to the influence of Richard Whately, the Church of Ireland Archbishop of Dublin, a devotee of conversion through the Scriptures and one of the prime movers of the National School in its first three decades.[44] The children of the upper form, ages twelve to fourteen, for whom these lessons were designed, were lectured and examined on the following subjects: "On Value," "On Wages," "Rich and Poor," "On Capital," "On Taxes," "Letting and Hiring," and the "Division of Labour."

The central point of the first lesson, "On Value," is that for an article to contain value it must have at least three properties: it must be "desirable, as being of use"; it must be "limited in supply—that is, it is not what everyone can have for nothing"; and it must be "transferable—that is, one person can part with it to another." Thus, the great value of precious metals and stones derives from their being desirable, scarce, and transferable, in contrast to common stone, air, or good health. Two pointed emphases are given that make up the moral message of the lesson. On desirability:

> There is no harm in people's desiring to be well dressed according to their station in life; but it is a pity that so many should be fond of expensive finery above their station, which often brings them to poverty. And often they spend money on ornaments, which would be better laid out in buying good useful clothes and furniture, and in keeping them clean. A mixture of finery with rags and dirt is a most disgusting sight.[45]

And on the relation of labor to value:

> When anything that is desirable is to be had by labour, and is not to be had without labour, of course we find men labouring to obtain it; and things that are of very great value will usually be found to have cost very great labour. This has led some persons to suppose that it is the labour which has been bestowed on anything that *gives* it value; but this is quite a mistake. It is not the labour which anything has cost that causes it to sell for a higher price; but, on the contrary, it is its selling for a higher price that causes men to labour in procuring it.[46]

The vital subject of land is glaringly absent from the lesson "On Value." Of course, even the children in congested Ireland understood that land was "desirable" and "limited in supply." But the pupils of the fourth form were given no guidance in the meaning of "transferable" as applied to land. It was understood clearly enough that landlords and farmers dealt in land as they would in cattle or grain. But if the pupils were asked to recite or copy these lessons at home most would have been hard put to explain to their parents how that practice, still an alien morality in the townland, was the source of the land's value.

Even more sharply antithetical to the moral economy of the townland was the lesson "On Capital." It was clearly intended as the central precept to be conveyed on the subject of political economy: "When men are left quite free to employ their capital as each thinks best for his own advantage, he will almost always benefit the public, though he may have no such design or thought."[47]

The lessons on wages, the classes, and letting and hiring must sometimes have seemed outlandish even to many of the early town-bred masters, as they instructed the ten or fifteen country ragmuffins in the reasons for their parents' poverty:

> [L]abourers often suffer great hardships, from which they might save them-
> selves by looking forward beyond the present day. They are apt to complain
> of others, when they ought rather to blame their own imprudence. If, when
> a man is earning good wages, he spends all as fast as he gets it in thoughtless
> intemperence, instead of laying by something against hard times, he may
> afterwards have to suffer great want when he is out of work, or when wages
> are lower: but then he must not blame others for this, but his own improvi-
> dence.[48]

Most of the lessons are illustrated by a prescribed tale. The one in "On Wages" was probably the most familiar and casually cruel of the fables of capitalism in these years, the story of "The Grasshopper and the Bees," which ends, "[T]hose who do nothing but drink, and dance, and sing, in the summer, must expect to starve in the winter."[49]

The most challenging of the lessons for the new National School master in this predicament must have been "Lesson VIII—On Taxes, Part II," in which he or she was asked to explicate the national debt to the cottiers' children! This infamous conundrum is attacked in the following manner. It is first explained that "during our long and costly wars . . . ," much more was spent than could be raised by taxes, requiring the government to borrow money of "rich merchants and others," promising to pay interest till the debt was repaid—"which most of it has not been, and perhaps never will be." Thus, the lenders were awarded annuities—"property in the funds"—or the right to receive so much a year out of the taxes raised by Government. The children may have been quite surprised to learn that "when a poor man has saved up a little money, he generally puts it into the funds . . . ; he is then one of the government creditors, and receives his share of the taxes." Therefore, if the debt were abolished without repayment "many, even of the labouring classes, would lose their all; and the nation would not be relieved of the burden; since it would be only robbing one set of our countrymen for the benefit of another set." The authors betray some dismay at the task of conveying the sense of this arrangement to the children: "We may be sorry that so much money was formerly spent on gunpowder, which was fired off, and on soldiers' coats, and ships, which were worn out, but nothing we can now do can recal [*sic*] this, any more than last year's snow." Nevertheless, the lesson ends hopefully: "[T]he taxes find their way back into many a poor man's cottage who never suspects it."[50]

Finally, in the second lesson of "Letting and Hiring," the delicate matter of the land is introduced. The way is prepared at the end of the preceding lesson through a dexterous exegesis of the Mosaic law forbidding usury among the sons of Jacob; despite this taboo, the text points out, the Israelites "were allowed by God's law to receive interest on the loan of money, or of anything else lent to a stranger. . . ." This shows, the children were told, that there can be nothing wrong in receiving interest or any other kind of hire, "for the law expressly charges them not to oppress or wrong the strangers, but to treat them not only justly, but kindly and charitably."

Only in the barbarous and benighted parts of the world were other practices followed: "There are some countries in the world, indeed, inhabited by half-savage tribes, such as the Tartars, where land is not private property, but is all one great common on which every man turns out his cattle to feed." The lesson's point follows inexorably:

In order, therefore, that the land should be properly cultivated, it must be private property: and if a piece of land is your property, you ought to be at liberty to dispose of it like any other property; either to sell it, or to cultivate it yourself, or to employ a bailiff and labourers to cultivate it for you, or to let it to a farmer.[51]

The discussion of land in America is both curious and revealing. America is introduced to illustrate the principle of scarcity—"limited in supply"—which is then applied to explain to the class the reasons for the high rents in their own country: "[I]n many of the uncleared parts of America, land may be had for nothing, though the soil is good and will bear plentiful crops." But there the land is so abundant, and the people so few, that anyone may have as much as he chooses to clear. Thus, land in the wilds of America is of no value, "because, though it is very fertile, there is enough, and much more than enough, for every one who wants it." Thus, as Irish land "grows scarcer in proportion to the number of people, that is, as the people multiply, the owners of it find that they can obtain a higher and higher rent." Whatever the kindness or meanness of the landlord, there was nothing that could be done to raise wages or reduce rents so long as these iron laws ruled: "[T]he farmer . . . would get the same price for his corn as he does now; the only difference would be, that he would be so much richer, and the landlord so much the poorer: the labourers, and the rest of the people, would be no better off than before." And the class was told not to credit those who say that if rents were lower the farmers could afford to pay higher wages to the labourers, because "those who talk so, confound together a *payment* and a *gift*."[52]

It is difficult to know whether the twelve- and fourteen-year-old children of the 1830s understood the portrayal of the "labourers" in the lessons was to apply to their own parents. The letters from the tenants refer repeatedly to their own prudence and industriousness, suggesting that they at least were conscious of the value attached to these virtues by those above them and were anxious to reassure all landlords and authorities that they possessed them, that the petitioners lived by these values even if many of their neighbors did not. The intent of the commissioners is also uncertain. The description of laborers as "improvident," "intemperate," or "thoughtless" implies some intent to reform that behavior, but it is not clear whether the commissioners were merely scolding the parents through the children or believed that by inspiring shame in the children they would create a gulf of habit and belief between the generations.

The National School curriculum contained a variety of messages, but perhaps none rang more clearly in the ears of this first generation of National School children than the note of shame and subservience that was palpable in nearly all aspects of the school regimen. Their bodies and clothing were examined for dirt and disease on entering each morning. They stood in borrowed shoes if they came without their own. Their speech and manners were relentlessly corrected. Punishments, like reciting from "the Black Stool," also emphasized public humiliation as the main disciplinary tool, as did the threat that transgressions of the children might be brought on the heads of the parents. Foremost, the children's experience was a lesson in powerlessness, both their own and their parents'.

The most routine of punishments assigned in the school was the copying of moral sayings. John Leahy, who managed the school in Kingwilliamstown in 1839, left a "Copy Book" of these to be used by the teachers for this purpose that conveys the point to be made in the children's minds— they were to be copied sixteen times each:

> Bear with patients [*sic*] unavoidable evils.
> Omitting to do good is committing of evil.
> Justice to all men friendship to a few.
> Opportunity lost cannot be recalled.
> Emulation produces miraculous action.
> Banishment to all orangemen [*sic!*].
> Learning and manners are charming companions.
> Beaty [*sic*] is transitory and perishing.[53]

Leahy's copying list was clearly unauthorized and may never have been sentenced on a single bewildered child. But one preferred by the National School commissioners to be recited and copied in thousands of schoolrooms, probably by tens of thousands of punishable boys and girls of the townlands, carried a meaning that neither the children nor their families could have mistaken in the hard times that preceded their leaving: "A Child of the Dust Must Not Be Proud."

8

The Way Out

Hurra for the land of liberty I will be with you on friday morning
Bound for it adieu to the land of Land Lord tireny and oppression

> I am Sir yours
> gratefully
> William Dermody[1]

After years of struggle to remain, it is still likely that some of the Ballykilcline tenants shared the sentiments of the merry Mr. Dermody when the time came for them to leave. If not all of the defeated ringleaders, at least some of the children and almost surely many of the women would not mourn the place that had become the scene of their misery and dread in the past two years. Those who left first, in the batches of September and October of 1847, would have included the most willing. Some of the last to go had pleaded sickness or old age in the family or simply could not make up their minds till the last moment. Those who waited through another winter had seen their close relatives leave in the earlier batches, although the Clerk of the Quit Rents took pains to see that families left together as far as possible. For the rest, the gradual emptying of the townland between the fall and spring and the prospect of a lonely eviction must have acted as a powerful inducement to abandon any thought of staying.

Not very much more may be said as to what was in the minds of these emigrants as their assigned dates of departure approached. Almost all who had left a record of their thoughts in the preceding two years expressed strong resistance to emigrating, and some also knew something of and feared the dangers of the journey itself. With few exceptions, these were the thoughts only of the male heads of families expressed in the written petitions and memorials, many of them from the Defendants. However lowly their status, the townland was a realm in which their place and identity was clear and secure. The women's thoughts are less evident, but they had much

159

less to lose both materially and psychologically by the dispersion of the community. Although their knowledge of what awaited them was still quite limited, they seemed to sense that emigration would force many radical alterations in the community and their personal role in it.

The expressions of "patriotism" in their language also referred primarily to their strong attachment to the townland itself and its immediate landscape. What they asserted as their rights on the land were also expressed in terms of "the land of nativity," in which the land and the townland were congruent and inseparable. In their profoundly localized mentality, the intimately familiar spaces and shapes of their everyday surroundings more than any abstract idea of Ireland as a nation contained the meaning expressed in their petitions as "the land of their birth." What would later become "the myth of exile" was an emigrant nationalism, suffused with bitter hindsight. But as they took the first steps on the road out and in the preceding months of distressful waiting among the emptying cabins, the sensations of loss were of their only place of belonging, a living grief not yet abstracted by time and distance.

There could have been no doubt in their minds that the future would be very different from the past. Had they not been leaving in great distress but of their own will, that prospect might have been welcome to both young and old and they might have set off on the journey, like Mr. Dermody, with a "hurra." But their march to Dublin would be like a defeated army. Their strongest figures, who thought themselves able to defy the power of the law, had been exposed as helpless and deluded. Parting them from the townland would now strip them of their only remaining claim to authority and respect in the eyes of their dependents, and possibly in their own. Hunger and the fear of eviction had reduced them to secret beseechers and writers of hopeless petitions. In these, the false and resentful humility that would become a permanent part of their demeanor as emigrants was already visible.

Town and Townland

For the emigrants of Ballykilcline, the journey began in the market square of Strokestown, as it had for the Mahon tenants the previous spring, an event that at least some of them must have witnessed. There were other ways to leave the townland unobserved if an emigrant were traveling freely and on foot. Hugh McDermott and his family of thirteen had probably avoided passing through Strokestown when they emigrated before the famine, since he was escaping with years of rent unpaid. But those who were about to leave at the Crown's expense were told to assemble in the town to be counted, provisioned, and given their allowances for the trip.

Under the supervision of Cox and the younger Knox, the first batch of 111 were assembled in the early morning of the fifth of September, when the light was just arising. On this occasion, the agent and driver were joined by James Burke, the clerk of the quit rents himself, checking the count of children and adults in his rolls for those who were missing or unauthorized and those who might be rejected in Liverpool as unfit for the voyage. At such moments, it was also to be expected that the constable of Roscommon and a number of police would also be in attendance.

No eyewitness account remains of the assembly, but given the circumstances, some atmosphere of captivity was likely to be present: a large number of "rebels," rounded up, inspected, and counted by their enemies, undoubtedly watched by some number of townspeople and segregated from their relatives and friends who were present to see them off, being sent off to distances from which they would never return. Among the others from the townland present were those who would be at the center of a similar scene themselves in a few weeks.[2] There were certainly the priests, Fathers Geraghty and Brenan (who also demanded "compensation" for the lost income that went with his parishioners), and the combative dean of Strokestown, Father McDermott, offering prayers and blessings for the journey. It is not known whether the highly public scene took on any of the mournful rituals of the "American" or "Emigrant" wake, as such partings were now coming to be called. Even if there were no keening, it is unlikely that no expression of grief arose from among the spectators as their friends or loved ones set off.

That Strokestown was the site of the their departure may also have been of meaning to those present. It was their first "outside" and their first experience as aliens, exposed now without a place of refuge. The town and square designed by the first Baron Hartland, scion of a defunct line and M.P. of the defunct Irish Parliament, to symbolize the order and prosperity he intended to bring to the area, now witnessed the futility of that hope. The emigrants waited in sight of the great gate of Strokestown House, which had been the embodiment of the power that had ruled them for generations. The broad market square had been the place where their sometimes plentiful crops and animals were bought and sold and where their rents and cesses were recorded as paid or unpaid on gale days. The courthouse, the constabulary, and the agents' offices had been the source from which the bailiffs, drivers and police had received their orders to enter the townland and post the notices of eviction that no longer could be resisted. All present knew this.

The spectacle of the assembled emigrants of Ballykilcline in Strokestown market clearly demonstrated the power of the town over the townland. But all had seen the town before on happier occasions. On fair days the market town had provided some of the main punctuations in their yearly round and had been their main contact with the outside world. Throughout the country such towns provided much excitement for the countrymen, with the crush of cattle and wagons in the main street, peddlers of ribbons, trinkets, and old clothes, children ricocheting among the legs of men and cattle, beggars (in ever greater numbers), tinkers, musicians, booted men on horseback, farmers and factors haggling in the public houses, and, the largest numbers, peasant men and women in town to find and pay the shillings they owed and, in good seasons, to purchase their ounces of tea and tobacco in the shops.

As all witnesses attest, such gatherings in the country towns before the famine were highly animated, raucous scenes with greetings, hawking, and the voices of man and animals filling the air. The usual presence of the constabulary, sometimes reinforced by troops, also reflected the reputation such gatherings held for violence, especially for the well-publicized brawls and faction fights that occasionally disrupted the country fairs. But, in contrast to such market and fair days in England and on the continent, they were not generally known as the site of collective actions or protests on the part of the local peasantry. In Strokestown, despite the constant demands by Knox for troops, there was no instance in all the years of bitter dispute, mounting arrears, and evictions of the tenants assembling in the town to voice their grievances or to challenge the authorities.

The Strokestown fair was held on the first Tuesdays of May, June, October, and November in addition to the weekly Saturday market, both numerously attended, more than doubling the town's resident population, and giving a bustling appearance to the place.[3] As the first Baron Hartland had conceived it, the main street had the dimensions of a market "piazza" more than of a mere provincial street. Barrels of wheat were loaded on carts for the Sligo mills or for Richmond Harbour on the Royal Canal and export to Dublin and England. Eels, Shannon River and saltwater fish, and "laver" (seaweed from Sligo) were sold from the carts or exchanged for small quantities of local linen, linen yarn, flannel webs, and woollen stockings worked by both the women in town and in the townland cottages. The semi-underground local economy of the fairs always included potatoes and turf carried barefoot in groaning back-frames and reed baskets, mostly by women and children, or dragged for miles on "slide-cars" or "slipes." These ironless and wheelless vehicles were easily constructed of two stick rails and a base about 5′ × 5′ × 3′, bound with rushes, and were used for pulling loads of turf over bog. Both could also be seen carrying household goods or small children and the aged when the people were on the road.

The driving of pigs was a prerogative of the men. As far away as the Liverpool docks, where many of these porkers would ultimately find themselves, "Paddys" were renowned for their delicate ways with pigs, gently prodding them to obedience with reed wands. In the country the household pigs were often called by names given them by the children who would hardly ever see them butchered and eaten. Patrick Connor, Richard Padian, and Luke Nary would have assumed this dignified role on the way to town, anticipating the haggling and hopefully inflating the prices they would win from the farmers and factors. Red-aproned women bearing eggs counted more like coinage than food and the hard-won yellow butter that sweetened every cabin meal were another hidden market that neither Knox nor Cox could quantify and that was therefore safe from their distraints.

The heavier loads of grains, dairy goods, and truck that made up the main commercial products of the market were carried by heavier carts and wagons driven mostly by hired men, as were most of the cattle. The most common carts in use in the countryside (which are most in evidence in photos from about twenty years later) were described as "low-backed cars" mounted on solid wooden wheels and a turning axle of wood, secured to the cart by two iron hoops. They tilted backward when loaded or mounted from behind, like chariots. Their carrying capacity was limited not only by this construction but by the combined weight of the ass or mule drawing it and the weight of the driver and yoke. Though simple to construct and maintain, such a cart represented a significant capital investment, requiring hardwoods and ironwork not easily accessible to the occupants of the townland, who anyway lacked most of the tools to work such materials. These were among the vehicles that would carry the townland emigrants and their goods on the road to Dublin. Cox's possession of at least one dozen of them to let for this service might therefore qualify him as a small capitalist in transport (and might also have had something to do with his being fined for taking "bog deal" from the lands). The heavier wagons, called "land carriages," were four-wheeled and flatbedded for carrying heavy commercial cargoes, such as market quantities of grain, milk, pigs, poultry, or potatoes. Drawn by teams of horses or mules, these were more often owned by merchants of the larger towns employing nonlocal skinners, and would not normally be visible in the neighborhood except on market and fair days.[4]

Even at the height of the famine, carts and wagons of the same kind continued to carry out a steady flow of local products from similar markets all over the country, most of it heading eastward. The sight infuriated John Mitchel, and William Cobbett railed at Parliament for allowing it.[5] The continuing passivity of the growing crowds in the towns is even more remarkable amid this concentration of plenty in plain sight being prepared and loaded for removal. It is worth noting, however, that most of the produce handled at the markets and exported from the Strokestown fair, especially the wheat and cattle, was neither raised in the townlands nor was it a usual part of their diet. Most of the local cash crops were raised on the large estates and private farms of the surrounding area. The cottiers and small tenants worked these lands seasonally as laborers but only a few, as we have seen, possessed enough acreage to cultivate cash crops. Despite their overwhelming numbers when gathered in town, their share of the market as either sellers or buyers was quite small. Cottage spinning was apparently not followed by many in the townlands, and apart from small quantities of butter and eggs, the input of the cottiers and small tenants consisted mainly of potatoes, turf, and garden produce for the town itself, which they brought in for the weekly market, and the pigs fattened on their own winter diet to be sold on gale days.

The tenants' relations with Strokestown were thus of a mixed kind, as secondary producers and petty consumers. As tenants and agricultural

laborers, they were the base of the crumbling land system but were marginal to the town economy, supplying only some of its household provisions and fuel, and possibly some of the cloth for the town laboring class.
They were tied more directly to the town market as cottage producers, casual
laborers, domestic servants, and microconsumers of the goods that passed
through it primarily from the outside. But none of these were roles that
offered any potential influence or power over the local market. Even those
who had been absorbed as unskilled workers in the town's brewery, its dress-
ing and dying mill, its market transport, shops, and sculleries were on the
margins of town life. In addition to the 100 houses in the town that Weld
describes as "above the rank of cabins," there were another 160 that contained the bulk of the town's resident population of about fifteen hundred.
Even in Limerick, £4 a year was considered a high wage for unskilled labor,
according to the Devon Commission. Thus, added to the idle multitudes
within an hour's walk, Strokestown was glutted with labor that could be
hired at only slightly higher rates than in the country (10d. a day for men),
that is, enough if paid regularly only to assure subsistence and minute addictive supplies of tobacco, tea, sugar, and porter.

The Strokestown fair days gave a deceptively prosperous appearance to
the neighborhood in the years just prior to the famine, the hectic activity
of the square cloaking the fact that the carts and wagons were more heavily
laden on leaving the town than entering, siphoning from the countryside
much of what was necessary to sustain its life. Empty of the crowds and
stalls, the inanimate skeleton of the town was exposed: a spacious avenue
lined by facing rows of attached two-story stone houses, 224 in all including those along the turnpike, most roofed with Welsh slate hauled over-
land from Sligo town or with the local sandstone from Slievebawn. North-
eastward from the crossroad formed by the narrower road to Longford the
stone pillars and ornamental iron gate of the demesne still stand. Within
sight through the gate is Strokestown Park House, a sprawling neo-Palladian
structure of the 1730s with an Ionic portico, a high flat roof trimmed with
a balustrade, and two advancing wings. In a grove entirely of imported flora
on the grounds, cut off from the main street by the gates and walls, stands
one of the three churches of Strokestown. It was described in 1832 as

> the roofless ruins of an old church, some of the windows of which retain their
> ancient mullions, and in others some of modern workmanship have been sup-
> plied; the enclosed area has been selected for the site of a family mausoleum:
> the surrounding grounds are very beautiful. The church forms a regular oc-
> tagon, and is a handsome building of limestone, with a tower and spire, in
> the Gothic style.[6]

Facing Strokestown House's gate at the opposite end of the avenue was
the "new church" (Thomas Lloyd's parish) on the town's high ground.
Biweekly petty sessions and quarter sessions also sat in Strokestown for the
northern half of the county; a sessions house and bridewell "on the new
plan" were erected in the 1820s containing the keeper's rooms, day room,

and prisoners' cells. On the street level of some of the houses were small shops (one containing the town post) and three public houses. On the avenue was also the constabulary police station, a well-endowed dispensary under the dirction of Dr. Shanley (who had been in the carriage with Major Mahon when he was shot) and the Crown Agent's office. The common tenants and servants of the town lived in approximately 140 diminutive one-story "artisan dwellings" off the main thoroughfare, screened by the stone facades.[7]

For most of those in the surrounding townlands, Strokestown was merely the broad street encompassed by these structures. With the exception of the Roman Catholic church in which Father McDermott preached and the ten small fee-paying schools, the rural people conducted their business and pleasures outdoors in sun or rain, mostly barefooted and uncapped, distinguishing them on sight from all but the lowest town servants and workers. The small local brewery supplied the three public houses licensed by the magistrate, in which the more substantial farmers, tradesmen, merchants, and gentlemen sheltered to do business and pay for their recreation in cash. Local peasant men and women rarely entered indoors without a purpose or on errand as servants.

The town was likely to be saturated with taxed and untaxed stimulants throughout fair days, especially when they were embellished with the added attraction of fights and races, such as the races "supported by private subscription" that werc held each spring on the course at Ballynafad at the base of Slieve Bawn, south of the town. Such occasions in Irish country towns were soaked in vivacity at their best—the scene described by numerous travelers who admired their lax and archaic merriness. Viewed through the windows of the constabulary, which were the eyes through which Dublin Castle saw events in the country, the same stimulated crowds were the bane of civil society and a constant threat to the peace. At such market fairs as Strokestown's, many of which became the scenc of "donnybrooks" and faction fights, most brought their drink with them from the country, consuming enough during the long fair days to percolate the outdoor crowd under the anxious eyes of the constabulary and quieter residents, sometimes ending by filling the small jail for the night. To some of the well-shod men in the town, like Knox or Ross Mahon, such crowds contained many men whose intentions they feared, milling, drinking, and arguing within feet of their doors in a language barbarous to their ears.

Knox's fear and loathing of the people of the townlands could not have been shared by all the town dwellers. Strokestown was not yet two generations old, and some of its inhabitants were themselves still at least sometime agricultural laborers, sharing most of the material and working conditions of the townlands and probably still tied to country families by blood, as they still are. At least some of the townland children also appeared routinely at the day schools. Some, like the Lloyd's scullery maid, lived apart from their immediate family in outside employment. Many others must have been familiar faces as they passed in and out of the town as laborers and servants. "Handyman" labor outside the townland, mostly hauling and digging, was also commonly done for small amounts of cash or goods or to repay debts. Less frequently, various townspeople had business in the townland or were brought there by ties of kinship. Before the famine, in fair weather, the roads of the midlands were busy with people on foot and cart moving between town and country.

But most of these interactions were conducted as if through a palpable membrane dividing the two cultures. Exchanges through it were prescribed by long-established practice and the rhythm of the calendar of gale and market days, holidays, and seasonal work patterns. Conventions and ritual behavior also governed human relations between the cultures, false deference on one side and wavering authority on the other. To communicate through the membrane also required some decoding in both directions. For most of the townland this was not so much a problem of translating Irish to English as of expressing thmselves in a language of submission learned only partly and unwillingly. When their letters and petitions slip from the archaically florid pretenses of "The Memorialist Sheweth" and "Your Humble Servant," it is clear that they are disguising their language in communicating with the town, perhaps not only to avoid overt insolence but to cloak the anger that repeatedly shows its face even in the most obsequious petitions.

Now Emigrants

Describing a crowd of waiting emigrants on the Long Wharf in Galway Harbor during the famine, the protagonist of Walter Macken's novel *Silent People* "marvelled at the silence of them": "Never before could you have been in an Irish crowd like this and not be greeted and shouted at. There would be jokes and obscenities flying. Calling and shouting."[8] In contrast to their history before and after the journey, the demeanor of Irish peasant crowds in transit during the famine years was almost invariably described as passive, diffident, and quiet. As they passed through the places en route that were increasingly strange to the sight of them, their silence was more often seen as furtive and dangerous, even when they were visibly helpless with weakness and disease. The meaning of the silence to their minds is less easy to understand. All knew that there were law defiers among them who might yet be sought by various authorities and their deputies. They must also have understood what the sight of near-starving throngs might have meant to the well-clad and still-prosperous citizens of the eastern towns and the capital. It could not have taken long for them to see that they were objects of mixed fear and pity as they traveled eastward out of the country.

Dublin and then Liverpool would be the first and the last of Europe's great cities that the emigrants would see as they set out on the road from Strokestown in the fall of 1847. This had been by far the most heavily traveled route out of the country to all destinations for the emigrants of the

preceding two decades. A much smaller number sailed directly from the
Irish ports. Dublin, Galway, Londonderry, Cork, and Waterford all had
developed miniatures of Liverpool's mammoth emigrant trade before the
famine. Sligo was the only city of the old world the Mahon tenants would
ever see. The names of all of these had some place and association in the
folklore of the country, and even Liverpool might not have conjured up
any feeling of dread until their actual departure from home was imminent.
The great port's name was familiar in the songs of the country and the stories of travelers for at least a century. But only in the past twenty years or so
could it have carried a sinister meaning in the minds of most Irish peasants,
unless they had learned of its place in the slave trade.

The emigrants were not told the route long in advance, and with little or
no experience of printed maps, compass points, or timetables they could
hardly have visualized all the distances and terrains they would cross in the
journey, but these must have become matters of great interest in the
townland in the few months of hunger and waiting before their day of departure. In the plan of travel when it was divulged to them, the names of
the towns and cities on the route punctuated the legs of the journey to
come—Longford, Edgeworthstown, Mullingar, Dublin, Liverpool, New
York—beginning in Strokestown. These place-names had a presence in their
mental geography, the nearer with more concrete and the farther with more
fanciful meanings attached to them, but very little of it from first- or even
secondhand experience but for Strokestown itself.

The first towns they would encounter would surely have been familiar to
some of the older males of the community at first hand from previous travel
as harvesters or migrant laborers; their route eastward, as far as Mullingar
and Meath, followed well-worn tracks of seasonal migration and cattle
droving.[9] But there is no sign that any had been farther than Dublin and
returned. What may have been envisaged in the townland about this part
of their journey, their first experience of the great cities, is likely to have
been largely imaginary or received at second hand. For the young people
under the age of eighteen who would be leaving, what foreknowledge of
their route they may have accquired in the National School, the fee-paying
academies, or hedge schools is still more uncertain. Any of these may well
have helped them cope with the experience by merely increasing the number of literates among them, but their education was not likely to have prepared them for either the practical or emotional obstacles such a journey
would present.

All of the emigrants of Ballykilcline had been assigned the same plan of
travel, from Strokestown along the turnpike to Longford, Mullingar, and
Dublin, where they would board the ferries at Eden's Quay on the Liffey
bound for Liverpool. In the same year, several hundred other Crown tenants from Cork and Galway who had received the emigrant bounty passed
through Mallow on the way to Cork City and the ferry, also bound for
Liverpool. The physical aspects of this leg of the journey can be reconstructed fairly clearly: traveling twenty miles a day on foot or aboard two-

wheeled carts, they would not see the outskirts of Dublin for more than four days, if all went well and the weather were fair. Thousands had trodden this Dublin road before as migrant workers, expecting to return soon, and more recently as emigrants, knowing they would not.

The Crown emigrants were provided with clothing, shoes, and cash for provisions along the way, though it is not known how much they had been able to conserve of their "allowance" without depleting it earlier for food or borrowing against it. It is certain that most were debilitated from at least a year of hunger, and some probably still suffered from the fevers and dysentery that were rife in the townland during the previous winter. Of the 257 who left in the first two batches, there were at least 8 who were over seventy years of age, one of whom would be turned back at Liverpool as unfit for the journey. There were nearly fifty children under the age of six. Some of their food would have been carried with them, bought in Strokestown at inflated prices, and milk and buttermilk would be purchased in the towns along the route by those who could, also at prices that their own numbers would surely have pressed upward.[10] With hordes of others from the townlands trekking the same route and thousands dying along its sides, the roads leading from the interior to the outports in the spring of 1848 were a sight that nearly all observers carried away as their most lasting memory of the famine.

There were some limited sources available to the people of the townland about certain aspects of the cities they would encounter. But not surprisingly, it was their relationship with Strokestown that emerges most clearly in the record before their leaving. The town contained and embodied most of the symbols they associated with their domination: the landlord, the agent, the law, the established church, and the record of their debt. Their presence in it was usually furtive when alone, and when they entered in crowds the town was on alert. In the famine exodus, their appearance in the towns and cities along the route most often produced a similar antipathy. Even the most well-disposed citizens of these towns were uniformly shocked by the appearance of the famine emigrants as they passed through, and most shunned any contact with them, partly from the fear of infection but also from a less reasoning aversion to the sight of their helplessness and degradation. The consciousness of the travelers is less well recorded. But nearly all descriptions note their silence.

The Plan of Travel

The first caravan of carts gathered at the Strokestown crossroads in an early morning of the first week of September 1847, two months before the murder of Major Mahon. Two more groups would leave during the fall and two more in the spring. The dates had been set to correspond to the sailing schedules of five chartered emigrant ships bound for New York out of Liverpool: the *Channing*, the *Creole*, the *Metoka*, the *Progress*, and the *Roscius*.[11] Separate Treasury grants ranging from £900 to £1,500 were forwarded to Knox to cover the cost of passage and expenses for the road and ferries to Liverpool. Knox and Burke had made the detailed arrangements with H. & W. Scott, ship brokers of Dublin, who had been chosen by the Quit Rent Office. Deputies of the ship agents were to pick up the emigrants as they reached Dublin on Cox's carts and see them on the ferry to Liverpool, where they were to be met by Daniel Kenny, another deputy of Scott's and put them aboard ship for New York. All expenditures were strictly accounted, including outfitting the emigrants in Strokestown, the carting costs to Dublin, the ferry fares, the passage money, commissions to each deputy along the way, provisioning for the voyage, and the required "head money" on landing in New York ($1 per head to assure against their becoming wards of the state as soon as they disembarked).

The costs and organization of this clearance were not typical even of the large-scale assisted emigration schemes of the great private estates, such as Mahon's, Palmerston's, or the Fitzwilliam's. On paper at least, it seems that the people of Ballykilcline were to enjoy the protection of the Crown from the now-notorious dangers of the emigrant route, from their cabins to the New York docks, where they could be forgotten with relief.

Provisions

Not many evicted tenants set off from their cabins as well provisioned as those of the Crown estates. In the original plan devised by the commissioners and the clerk of the quit rents, the tenants of each of the Crown estates in Roscommon, Galway, and Cork were to be provided with transportation to Dublin, a small quantity of cash for that part of the journey, and fully-found provisions once they were aboard ship in Liverpool, as well as the head money on disembarking in New York. These arrangements were generous even by the standards of the most progressive private landlords who assisted their tenants' emigration. Counting the transatlantic fare, the Treasury expended nearly seven years of Ballykilcline's former rents, £2,451.[12] Similar expenses were paid out by the Commissioners over the next two years to remove the tenants of four other Crown estates in Cork, Galway, and Kings counties before the lands could be sold.[13]

To these very substantial sums were added smaller amounts as each batch of former tenants were actually assembled to begin their journey. Some of these are recorded in petty bills and vouchers from Roscommon and Galway merchants for sundry other "necessities" lacking among the travelers but apparently not anticipated by the commissioners. One of the more suggestive both of the emigrants' condition and the commissioners' concerns is a bill from one John Harrison, an outfitter of Galway, for £181 2s. 10d. to cover the cost of clothing and shoes for 261 of the emigrants (apparently the first two batches). Eighty-eight of the women were provided with a "gown", two "pettycoats", two chemises, two caps, and a shawl—girls under nine years did not receive the caps. Fifty-eight men were given cloth caps, a "Body coat," vest, and trousers of "Frize" (frieze); boys between fourteen and eighteen received a jacket, vest, and trousers of the same cloth; and the younger boys the same outfit made of "cord," without the vest. The forty-four boys of nine years or less were topped with "Glengary Caps." Eighteen boys under six years wore "dresses," as was the prevailing custom.

More than £35 in shoes were ordered by the Crown Agent for the two batches who were to leave in March and April. It is unlikely that more than a few of the tenants were accustomed to wearing shoes whether at work or play. Barefoot since childhood, their feet were well accustomed to the sharp stones and winter mud of the roads. To judge from the rather sketchy evidence touching on the subject, shoes were rare enough in the townlands to be something of an honorific symbol, like the hats worn mainly by adult men and heads of households as a mark of standing, and rarely adorned the feet of women or children. At a price from 5s. to 7s., a pair of plain brogues was the equal of nearly two weeks' wages for the male farm laborer when in work, which at least partly explains the importance attached to them. But shoelessness also carried a value of another sort, a proof in a woman or child of willingness to bear pain and cold, which was perhaps tacitly taken for granted in men, as well as an acceptance of a code of humility. The £35 spent by the Crown could have provided as many as 140 pairs of shoes. With only fifty-eight adult men in the batches for whom the shoes were intended, the sudden flood of new shoes and other luxuries provided for all meant that in this part of their preparation they had already made a meaningful break from the past before they taken the first step from home.[14]

No mention is made of how such problems as shoe sizes were handled or what sort of complications may have arisen when the 257 individuals were assembled to sort these luxuries or with what expressions of gratitude or sullenness they received them. But various scenes can be imagined. It has also not been recorded just how, where, or when these garments were distributed among the emigrants—whether they were merely dumped at the crossroads or distributed at an assembly in Strokestown market in view of the townspeople, or even if they ever received them from the hands of Cox or Thomas Knox at all. A count had been made of the ages and sexes of the emigrants, but for obvious practical reasons no effort was made to accommodate variables of size in their feet and bodies. Given the style of the driver and the predatory habits of the emigrant provisioning business, it can also not be known whether Harrison of Galway had not merely arranged to rid his stock of oversized petticoats and unmatchable brogues. But misfits would hardly have mattered, since the recipients were well accustomed to odd bits of clothing and hand-me-downs. In the end, the Crown paid the provisioners without complaint—it came within a few pounds of the townland's annual rents.[15]

In spite of the expense, Burke and the Commissioners undoubtedly felt relief at the peaceful departure of the tenants. Their eagerness to reach that result is visible in the final arrangements for the removal. Their original plan, which was devised in the spring of 1847 after receipt of the "Bill of Distress" from the court, was orderly and judicious in its overall outline and no expense was spared to assure the safe passage of the emigrants. There was nothing amiss with this plan on paper. But the Commissioners in London were strangers to Irish rural life, including traveling by foot or cart, by more than mere miles. What might have served Lord Morpeth as a perfectly workable itinerary for a holiday in France—a train or coach to Dover, an outside airy cabin, good food, warm bunks on the Channel ferry, and a holiday destination in good season—could not have been enacted by hundreds of Roscommon peasants, driven from their homes, having an uncertain idea of their destination or of the route, its hazards or length, and carrying only imaginary hope, if any, of ever returning home. Even with the plentiful resources of the Treasury and the best intentions, the practical flaws in the commissioners' plan were evident in Ballykilcline even before any departures took place and the suffering had already begun.

The Road

The turnpike that crosses Strokestown's market street within a few yards of the gothic gate of the Hartland demesne met the road to the Atlantic about sixty miles west, at Killala, passing through Tulsk, Frenchpark, Ballaghadereen, Charlestown, and Swinford. The more heavily traveled route to the port of Sligo turned north through Tulsk and Elphin and met the Sligo-Longford turnpike at Boyle, whence it ran north to the Atlantic at Sligo Bay, a distance of about fifty miles. The completion of the Grand and Royal Canals had diminished the share of the western Irish ports in this traffic, but many goods from the west midlands still followed this secondary route into the English markets. Parliament had established an Emigrant Agent in both Sligo and Galway town in 1833 to oversee the departure of transatlantic passengers, but the numbers leaving from the western ports of Ireland to North America were a relatively small part of the emigrant traffic, despite the directness of the route. Palmerston's unlucky tenants had left by this route for Canada. Their fate had been one of the reasons the Commissioners chose to avoid it, knowing that the lower fares of the Irish ports reflected even shoddier conditions for the emigrants than in the Liverpool trade.

Irresistibly and largely without choice, emigrants followed where trade had gone before, and the main stream of that flow went by land or canal to Dublin, Belfast, Waterford, and smaller eastern ports and from there to Liverpool and the ports of the west of England and Scotland. The road from Strokestown to Dublin ran east by southeast through Longford and Mullingar, a distance of about ninety miles, and entered Dublin along the north bank of the Liffey around Lucan. On the road to Dublin the emigrants were under the care and orders of Cox, their "luggage," infants, and infirm aboard his carts, the women and children clad in their new shawls and Glengary caps. Those leaving in October and November were subject to the cold rains and chill winds on the road, many were already suffering from malnutrition, some were feverish or recently recovered from fever and other illnesses of the body or mind. Each of Cox's trains of carts and its hundred-odd pilgrims on foot would have passed from the Lucan Road into the Chapelizod with the river on their right and Phoenix Park (containing the Zoological Gardens the National School children had heard described) to their left. If they arrived in daylight, they would have had a fine view of their capital city. As they trudged along the north bank of the river, along Ellis, Arran, and Ormand Quays, they would come within the very shadow of the Courts of Justice, where O'Ferrall had pleaded and lost their case. If the day were clear, they would have been able to glimpse the spire of Christ Church Cathedral. And, as they passed the Grattan Bridge, they would have an angular view across the river of the gates and walls of Dublin Castle itself, before reaching Bachelor's Walk and their final destination in Ireland: the ferry landing at Eden's Quay.

From the quay they would board the Liverpool sailing ferries, their first sea voyage, as deck passengers in the Irish Sea. If they reached the Liverpool docks intact and on schedule, the five groups of peasant travelers would then enter the parasitic gauntlet of the great waterfront, their fate utterly dependent on the almost whimsical sailing times of the Liverpool emigrant trade,[16] before beginning the longest and often the most harrowing leg of the journey in the already infamous steerages. Of the 496 men, women, and children whose names appeared on the various rent rolls of the estate during the previous year, no more than 298 disembarked between November 1847 and July 1848 on the ramshackle wooden piers of lower Manhattan island. It is possible that their numbers were much fewer than that.

On foot, in fine weather, an unencumbered young man or woman might have covered the distance to Dublin without camping more than three nights on the road before entering the city's suburbs. At worst, he or she would spend the nights on the "long meadow," the grassy verge that on each side of every road separated it from the stone wall or hedge bordering the fields beyond. Many eyewitnesses of the winter of 1848–1849 describe the pathetic scenes to be found along these verges, of starving stragglers and wanderers, casual burials, and exposed corpses, all suffused with the smell of the decaying potato fields. In most months of the year, a coat, a hat, and shoes would have been a great comfort as protection from the mud and sharp stones and from the universal dampness, ground frosts, and wet winds of the roadside. In normal times, the hazards of human origin on the Irish roads were all but negligible. A widow walking with a bag of gold was certainly safer from assault on almost any Irish country road than on the busy turnpikes that connected the great cities of England and Europe. For these travelers, the real dangers of tramping the roads of midcentury Ireland were the country's moody weather and its political economy, which made for many bad years and often set the people on the road very poorly prepared for the journey.

Each batch of emigrants leaving Ballykilcline included a number of young men and women between the ages of sixteen and twenty-five who at least formerly had been hearty and able-bodied. But each group of travelers also included infants, aged dependents, and others who needed assistance. This first walking stage of the transatlantic journey amounted to about 1,800 to 2,000 steps per mile for a sturdy adult—a total of some 140,000 strides to Dublin. As for the many thousands of harvesters of the previous century whose feet had hammered the road into its existing shape, the company of their fellow travelers and an accumulated knowledge of where and to what the road led would also have shortened the miles and improved the chances of surviving the marathon, as would the expectation of returning in the not-too-distant future to familiar places and the welcome of friends and family.

From the descriptions of the crowds of Irish countrymen tramping off the Liverpool ferries bound for the English harvests, the age-old journey might often have been a fairly jolly jaunt despite the sore feet and soaking rains—and perhaps a welcome adventure from the boredom and constraints of townland life. Herman Melville's depiction of such a crowd of harvesters of 1849 contains an uncharacteristic touch of farce but also conveys what sort of group spirit such gang migrations of seasonal laborers might have possessed when in good health and traveling singly. Passing the gates of the Brunswick Dock in Liverpool, he describes hearing "a tramp, as of a drove of buffaloes," filling the street behind him: "Flourishing their shillelahs, they looked like an irruption of barbarians." "'Sing Langolee, and the Lakes of Killarney,'" cried one fellow, tossing his stick into the air, as he danced in his brogans at the head of the rabble. "And so they went! capering, merry as pipers."[17]

Most of these migrant work gangs were younger men and women on their own, understandably happy to escape the misery at home. But by no means all emigrants trekking this road in the famine years were described in such jolly spirits. The key to the difference was probably the absence of dependents and the hope of returning among the harvesters. Both of these factors worked painfully against the five batches of one hundred or so emigrants from Ballykilcline who assembled at the Strokestown crossing through the autumn of 1847 and the following spring. The first three batches, each booked for ships scheduled to sail from Liverpool in one to three weeks hence if all went well, were gathered in the early mornings of their appointed days to have their names checked off on the young Knox's "Emigrant List" and were assigned to one of Cox's carts, which would carry some of the bulkier loads as well as some of the feeblest of the travelers the ninety miles to Dublin.

While a great many other emigrants traveled the same route entirely on foot, the emigrants of Ballykilcline were favored on this leg of the journey. The alternative for most other emigrants of their class was to tramp the road as near-penniless wayfarers, some begging along the way, not knowing if the passage tickets they held in their pockets were any guarantee they would reach their destination. The notorious hazards of the road at this time may have been less both in fact and imagination for the Ballykilcline emigrants because they were assisted Crown tenants, traveling under supervision and guaranteed their passage. Otherwise, they could not be distinguished from the refugees of a thousand other townlands who wandered the Irish roads in this worst year of the famine. Unlike most, they were also traveling in large groups of family and friends, which may have relieved some feelings of vulnerability and offered a psychic protection against the increasing strangeness of their surroundings. They had been informed of at least some of the Crown's arrangements to "escort" them each step of the way to the gangplanks of the Liverpool ships, first by Cox and then by Daniel Kenny, a deputy of H.& W. Scott, who was to meet them at the Dublin ferry. Some of them would not have welcomed Cox's presence even for a few days, but the Crown's itinerary must have offered a greater sense of order and security than most other peasant migrants enjoyed.

The emigrants' protection against potential abuses had been a primary concern of the Commissioners' plan. But at least one of the batches had some trouble before leaving Dublin. The contingent of 127 who were to meet the Dublin-Liverpool ferry on 8 March 1848 was missing 14 of its number when counted at the quayside; the absentees had been paid their allowance but had disappeared somewhere between Strokestown and Dublin. By the time the contingent boarded the ferry, 2 more had gone missing, leaving 111 who would finally leave the country.[18] Some of the missing may have stayed in the neighborhood, as others had done through preference or obligation, but it is likely that some of those traveling in weakened condition or illness were buried in their own country.

In a sense, before they set eyes on the sea, Cox had become the emigrants' first navigator, the captain of the carts. In the days and nights on the road his power over the tenants was greater than ever before. Both the legitimate role he had been assigned and the powers he took upon himself as guide and guardian of the travelers left many chances for abuse, some of which he apparently failed to resist. Those about to embark for Liverpool lodged complaints of mistreatment against him immediately on arriving in Dublin, after the four-day trip from Strokestown under his care. No particulars of their charges survive, but Cox had ample opportunity to profit from his position as driver during this leg of the journey. He knew that at least some of his charges carried the Crown's cash allowances; he was in command of the carts, of where and when the small caravan stopped to rest, and, if necessary, of who might have to be left behind as stragglers or impediments to the fixed schedule. Having made the same trip at least three times before, he may also have established his own arrangements with vendors along the way in regard to the purchase of provisions. His many enterprises in the townland had always lurked in extemporized deals of this kind, and it was apparently on this score that the March emigrants' complaints were made.

Their protests had apparently been addressed orally to Burke or his delegates in Dublin. But there may have been some dissension, since fifteen of the group put their names to an "Affadavit" swearing they had been "kindly treated" and were "well satisfied with the ship 'Channing.'" What circumstances prompted the writing and signing of the affidavit as the emigrants waited to board are unclear, though it was likely part of the arrangement with the ship agents to defend against any future charges of mistreatment. Perhaps most telling was a postscript added by John McGann, one of the smaller cottiers who had not been prominent in the rent strike, which swore that "all the complaints that were got up were for the purpose of injuring Johny Cox."[19]

The assisted emigrants of Pobble O'Keefe, who embarked for Liverpool on the Cork ferry the following year, also had troubles with their escort—which may illustrate one kind of abuse such travelers were vulnerable to. The Crown Agent for Pobble O'Keefe had also hired the local bailiff and his carmen to carry a group of just over one hundred to the ferry. They arrived on a rainy September Friday and were waiting to board the next morning when six or eight men seized the carts carrying their "luggage," claiming to have "Civil bill Decrees" against them for outstanding debts, and posted "Advertisements" to sell the contents of the ten carts the next day at noon, exactly the time scheduled for the ferry to sail. The scene that ensued on dockside in a heavy rain was a last chaotic conflict of old townland enemies. Daniel Kelleher had tried to escape the creditors by rail via Mallow and Dublin to Liverpool, but lost his possessions and his sister's feather bed. The ship agent's deputy called in the police, who just succeeded in wresting the luggage from the bailiff's men as the ferry was about to leave. According to the deputy,

> [W]hen all this disagreeable work was over it was 12 o'clock and I had only time to get the Luggage on board the Steamer, and two Cart loads of Sea Store, Bacon, Butter & Biscuit when the Bell rang & the Steamer moved off from the Quay, leaving a Cart load of groceries consisting of 60 parcels of Coffee, Tea & Sugar on the Quay. Three minutes time would be sufficient to put them on board but Captain Pile of the *Nimrod* Steamer would not wait, I was very sorry for this disappointment. I also expected to be able to pay for the Groceries as the day was very wet & the sugar & coffee must have been much injured. 8 to 12 Saturday morning which I intended . . . to buy clothes for the Emigrants was taken up settling between Emigrants & their creditors and on that account I had to sail down from Cork to Queenstown with the Emigrants in the Steamer & I distributed £14:11 to the most destitute of them to buy clothes in Liverpool.[20]

Apart from Miss Kelleher's feather bed, apparently a prized luxury, the contents of the emigrants' luggage can only be guessed. But it was apparently the more valuable and negotiable provisions that most attracted the attention of the bailiffs and their men. Their loss could have grave results on the journey yet to come, especially if they represented what remained of the travel allowances. Whether Cox had been guilty of similar predations as a parting gesture is unknown. But the emigrants' complaints suggest at least that escort out of the country by the Crown's deputies was at best a mixed blessing.

It is also suggestive of the physical and mental condition of the emigrants by this time that such small and unarmed gangs of predators were able to cow and exploit their much larger numbers once outside the townland. In these first few days, the former townland tenants had experienced the first realities of their emigration. Many of their numbers were already missing. In the famine winter of 1847, it is all but certain that some who failed to board ship in Liverpool either slipped out of the march near home or perished from some cause on the road, ending their journey at some point to join the thousands of other aimless or hopeless spectres lining the "long meadow." Like all other travelers in Ireland at this time, none of the emigrants could have failed to notice the unburied corpses, the emaciated families, and the universal beggardom thronging the main roads and towns. At least three adults of Pobble O'Keefe are known to have died before reaching Liverpool and another was rejected at the gangplank, and these casualties were only recorded because Boyan the Crown agent demanded their fares be refunded.[21]

It was also the emigrants' first prolonged experience among a predominance of strangers, knowing that they themselves would remain strangers wherever they were perhaps for years to come. By the time they reached the ferry slips, at the latest, all would also have seen the first signs of enmity and disgust their appearance inspired. The callous and demeaning treatment at the hands of strangers was also a foretaste of the extreme vulnerability they now bore. Many even more predatory strangers waited at each stage of the journey ahead, on the ferries, in Liverpool, and on the New York docks. But the first in the gauntlet were faces well known to them, old enemies apparently even more emboldened and hostile as the distance from the townland lengthened.

The Liverpool Ferries

Once they had set foot aboard the ferry, the emigrants were free of their old adversaries of the land and entered the outer edges of a system far more powerful and complex, whose extent and workings were still further beyond their experience and understanding. In one sense, they were also temporarily beyond the authority of the Commissioners, or even of Parliament itself. The Colonial Office had long before established a system of regulation and inspection for the Atlantic emigrant ships, after numerous scandals revealed the outrages and needless mortality in the trade.[22] But the myriad of sail and steam-powered vessels that ferried the great majority of emigrants to Liverpool still operated in the Irish Sea as freely as Barbary pirates in the Mediterranean.

Inspection of the Irish ferries had been considered by the Colonial Office some ten years before, also after public outcries against the abuse of their passengers. Since the movement of people from the British Isles overseas had formerly been seen primarily as part of the process of populating the colonies, its control was given to the Colonial Office, which created the Colonial Land and Emigration Commission to supervise it. When the traffic in the Irish Sea began to swell with emigrants, they proposed that this trade should also come under supervision. But the uncounted thousands of vessels plying the seas between the islands were part of the "inland trade" and therefore came under the jurisdiction of the Board of Trade, the department that oversaw the traffic in goods. Not unnaturally, the board declined to extend its responsibilities to the notoriously troublesome human part of the traffic. As a result, a bureaucratic gap was created in which the more than a million who traveled the Irish ferries in the famine years went unprotected and largely uncounted.[23]

Aboard the exotic assortment of vessels that carried the bulk of the emigrants, from open fishing boats and slow-moving coal barges to the fast cross-channel packets, human amenities were entirely missing for all but first-class passengers. Since none of the vessels were designed primarily for this traffic, all but cabin passengers were supercargo, stowed wherever their primary goods allowed, on deck or in the holds. Like the master of the steamer that carried the Pobble O'Keefe emigrants, many ferry captains and crews in the trade often treated such passengers as they would stowaways, even though their fares added a handsome new source of profit. Their trade was as old as the kingdom itself. No count was ever made, but the intercoastal and cross-channel vessels that took up the carrying of emigrants numbered in many thousands by the mid-nineteenth century, and they were only a part of the even larger number of vessels whose incessant scurrying between the two islands tied them together. Unlike the Atlantic emigrant ships, they were not required to provide any minimum of space, provisions, or hygiene to their passengers nor even to report the numbers carried. Those who traveled on them merely disappeared from public view temporarily, as though crossing St. George's Channel by tunnel.

The most trying conditions in the ferry passage were those commonly suffered by the so-called deck passengers, the category in which all but a privileged few "cabin passengers" who paid nearly treble the fare for the relative comfort and safety of an inside passage, across the Irish Sea.[24] Small numbers of these were emigrants with means, but most were part of the regular flow of merchants and gentry who were long accustomed to the crossing. Even with the amenities of dry bunks and plentiful food and drink, these crossings of the Irish Sea were infamously trying when winds were adverse, causing lengthy delays for sailing vessels and routine seasickness even on the steamers, especially when the sea was in one of its frequent turmoils. To these discomforts was now added the visible presence on deck of crowds of destitute and diseased fellow travelers. The sounds and smells of those even less fortunate who were carried in the holds also could not be ignored.

The famine was a windfall to the owners of almost any vessel that could cross the Irish Sea, one that was greedily raked in by masters and owners of thousands of vessels of all kinds; in a period of five consecutive years they were to transport close to two hundred thousand emigrants a year, more than three hundred thousand in 1847 alone. At 5s. a passenger (half the steamer rate) even the larger vessels of hundreds of tons built for the profitable grain and cattle trade found the emigrant supercargo a bonanza. Even a vessel of fifty tons might cram enough emigrants on deck and in crannies below to produce £50 in cash above its usual profit—for owner-captains it might equal a whole season's income, and for hired skippers an undreamed-of bonus easily concealed. And if all went well, the irritation of crowded decks and seasick peasants might last only a day or two's sailing. Steam packets like the *William Fawcett* out of Dublin, 500 tons and 160 horse-power, built to carry insured cargo as well as passengers of three classes, advertised sailing times of eighty hours to London, thirty-six to Plymouth, thirty to Falmouth, and less than a day to Liverpool (presumably with wind and sea cooperating). The more numerous and more lumbering sailing vessels could take three days and nights in the worst weather before disgorging their cargoes on the Merseyside.[25]

The seaborne trade from Ireland carried a large share of the lifeblood of Britain in the hulls of the Irish Sea fleet. Its vital business had never been seriously interrupted by Britain's enemies. Dozens of major port cities and hundreds of busy small harbors, thousands of vessels crisscrossing its surface day and night in all seasons, the dense commercial network of the inland sea bound the islands together like the veins and arteries of a living organism. Its flow of tonnage was overwhelmingly eastward, food from the fields of Ireland to the hungry urban populations of England. The quantities being carried out during the famine years especially were and remain a subject that raised passions: the estimate made by John Mitchel, the eloquent polemicist of "Young Ireland," that more than a third of the country's food production (at a value of £15 million) was exported to England in each of those hungry years may have had more rhetorical power than accuracy.[26] But the magnitude of the trade carried in these vessels was clearly very large and the traffic incessant. The "Customs Bills of Entry" recorded in Liverpool from the manifests of all incoming vessels reflect both the multitude of carriers and the types of cargoes with which the ferry passengers crossed. There were some ships, both sail and steam, of a size comparable to the Atlantic emigrant ships (of 150 tons or more), but the great majority were sailing vessels between 50 and 120 tons. Dozens arrived daily in Liverpool, but it must be assumed that many small vessels called unrecorded day and night, some with passengers, at the many anchorages on the Lancashire and Cheshire coasts.[27]

Famine refugees were being offloaded in numbers large enough to alarm the coastal towns from Glasgow to Cardiff. The most vulnerable of these were naturally those with no itinerary but to escape the hunger by sea aboard any outgoing vessel, to "the nearest place that wasn't Ireland." A great many of these vessels landed in Liverpool. But many others merely unloaded their passengers at their accustomed ports of call to become unwelcome burdens on the parish, perhaps for years. Their numbers and their dispersion among the western coastal towns made regulation far more difficult than smuggling had ever been. Once in England, destitute refugees either collapsed before the nearest poorhouse or wandered from parish to parish seeking outdoor relief or casual work, which many were entirely unfit to do. Because of their long-established traffic with the Irish ports, the coastal towns of Wales were particularly hard hit by the influx of Irish paupers. The magistrates and guardians of Cardiff demanded that the Home Office instruct the Coast Guard to put an end to "the improper landing of Irish Paupers along the Coast" and bring to justice the masters engaged in the traffic:

> Cardiff is full of Irish lodging houses and every tide adds to the number of these poor wretched creatures who throng here. They are brought over in the Coal Vessels as *live ballast* to save port dues, and other similar interruptions to this odious domestic slave trade. The shippers make no provision for them and the roadsides are covered by parties who are said to sleep under hedges and in ditches. Deaths from cold and want in the open fields and roadsides are frequent.[28]

Masters of such vessels were condemned as profiteers. The Cardiff Union offered a reward of £10, posted throughout the town, "to any Person or Persons who shall give such information to the undersigned [the Board of Guardians], as will lead to the conviction of any COMMANDER of a VESSEL, who shall illegally LAND any IRISH PASSENGERS on the coast between Aberthaw and the River Rumney." Outbreaks of cholera and typhus were linked to the appearance of the refugees. Some parishes erected roadblocks to halt the movement of wandering crowds of the destitute Irish. There was rioting in Liverpool, Wellington, Birkenhead, and Holyhead—and on the job sites along the railways and excavations along the west coast—directed against Irish laborers and newcomers.[29]

Action by the local authorities to control the traffic was of little or no avail. Even the Government Emigrant Agents of the major ports had no control over the incoming passenger traffic and were barely able to make their cursory inspections of the enormous flow of outbound emigrant ships. Most of the inspection of the cross-channel trade was in the hands of the Customs House, whose business was the manifests of goods rather than passengers entering the country. One of the midsize class of trader that dabbled in the emigrant traffic arriving in Liverpool in 1848 was the *Pride of Erin*, from Dundalk, carrying 218 ferkins and 50 boxes of butter, whisky (no quantity given), 124 bags of meal and barley, 50 boxes of eggs and fowl, 196 cows, 19 sheep, and 385 pigs. The *Erin*, from Dublin, carried 3 cows, 7 horses, 256 pigs, along with "12 bales Rags," an entry that does not appear in the manifests before the famine. The *Forget Me Not*, 116 tons out of Limerick, unloaded 1,186 bushels of wheat, 100 bushels of Indian corn, and "26 bags of Hair for W. Jackson & Son" of Liverpool.[30] Whether *Forget Me Not*'s usual business was in carrying passengers, grain, and "sundries" across the channel or its masters merely improvised as opportunities arose is unclear, for not long after offloading its cargo at the Prince's Dock it weighed anchor for Australia filled with emigrants, a very frail vessel in which to round the Horn or cross the vast oceans of the Southern Hemisphere.[31]

The cross-channel cargoes merely reflect the long-standing relationship between the two islands, one consuming more food than it now produced and the other filling the gap with the "surplus" of its fields and meadows. The heavy preponderance of wheat, beef, and pork in the manifests suggests one of the peculiar features of the relationship between the two islands, in that these foods were hardly eaten by those who had raised them. The pigs, with whom the Irish cottier had long been especially associated in folklore and caricature as his housemates and rent payers, were now his shipmates as well. So tightly packed in the holds that they required constant "stirring up" by their attendant to prevent suffocation, the pigs' presence a few feet below the deck passengers was more than symbolic of their former companionship, since many of the creatures had undoubtedly been the source of the emigrants' ferry fares in the first place.[32] Although the cattle and wheat more usually originated from the commercial farmers and graziers, some part of the butter, eggs, and fowl had also been provided by the townland peasants and made up a part of the economy that now carried them away. Although it had long drained the common Irish diet of its meat and bread, this commerce was still reciprocal and helped provide the cash both to keep the cottier in possession of his plot as well as his means to escape from it when the time came.

But the rags, hair, and Indian corn were new entries in the ledger of the trade, bleak symbols of the new depth of poverty in Ireland and a harsh demonstration of the lesson in political economy. The Limerick master or owners of the *Forget Me Not* (carrying twenty-six "bags" of hair and one hundred bushels of Indian corn) were practicing its simplest precepts. Possibly in Limerick, they had come upon some "spillage" of the corn distributed in 1848 by the American or British Famine Relief Committees, organized by the Quakers and paid for by far-flung popular contributions, from Cincinnati pubs to Philadelphia or Manchester meetinghouses. As the *Fourth Book of Lessons* in the National School had said, "It had value and was desirable." The rags and hair were also cargoes of opportunity, sprung from some unknown source of dire need in the townlands, following the same routes and carried beside the emigrants to Liverpool. Before now, rags had been part of the westward import trade to Ireland, a source of the picaresque, oft-caricatured "native" style of dress. If the "bales" of rags were measured as was cotton, the *Erin*'s cargo amounted to four tons of cloth no longer usable or needed as clothing by their former wearers, bound for the pulp mill—possibly one that provided the paper on which eviction notices or parliamentary reports were printed on. Presumably, the "bags" of hair came from the living and could have been destined for a variety of purposes in the milliner's, costumier's or wigmaker's trade. Deck passengers could not have mistaken the sounds and aroma of the emigrant pigs in the holds below, but they may not have been aware of the contents of these bales and bags upon which they may have perched during the crossing.

Some features of these vessels are conspicuous even in the spotty record that remains of their movement.[33] Many ships in the Atlantic trade took on emigrants for North America as a "paying ballast" on the return voyage in holds now empty of cotton, tobacco, or timber. But edibles from Ireland moved in the same direction as the emigrants, so only deck space could be allotted to passengers. Tarpaulins or damaged sails were ordinarily provided to cover the huddled deck passengers from rain and sea. Even on large vessels deck passage could be a desperate trial for the sick and weakened in the frequent foul weather, but the larger ships and faster steamers, by speed or stability, were probably less likely to endanger life. Some large vessels, like the *Mountaineer*, 176 tons out of Swansea, carried cargoes of copper, patent metal, tin plates, and nails in great quantities outward and returned with grain and emigrants. But these were fewer than the vessels like *Erin* or the *Forget Me Not*, which carried food and sundries, the most common cargoes in the manifests.

The ferry fares of 10s. paid by the Crown for assisted emigrants were at least twice what most other emigrants paid on their own aboard such vessels. Bargain fares on smaller craft often took their toll on the passengers, but even by steamer the crossing could be traumatic for those on deck. Julius Besnard, who had charge of the Pobble O'Keefe emigrants, protested the state of his charges on landing in Liverpool:

> [N]o language at my command can describe the scenes I have witnessed there; the people were positively prostrated . . . from the inclemency of the weather . . . seasick all the way . . . drenched from the sea and rain . . . suffering from cold at night . . . debilitated . . . scarcely able to walk after they got out of the steamers. . . . In fact, I consider the manner in which passengers are con veyed from Irish to English ports disgraceful, dangerous, and inhuman.[34]

Even the ordinarily reserved reports of the district military authorities to the Home Office warned that "the destitution of those arriving is fearful."[35]

As bad as the relatively short crossings from Dublin or Belfast could be for deck passengers and those carried in the "casual" trade, the voyage to Liverpool from the western ports were often far worse. Those who chose the nearest ports from their homes and embarked at Sligo, Limerick, Galway, Londonderry, and the other western ports on vessels in the coastal trade often had to tranship along the way to link up with vessels tied more directly to the Liverpool network before they headed west again across the Atlantic. This could be a prolonged and hazardous voyage aboard heavy-laden coasting vessels whose principal concern was not passengers but bulk cargoes of fish, slates, coal, livestock, wool, and corn collected from many such inland markets as Strokestown. Added to the natural perils of navigating the notorious coastal waters of Ireland, these conditions made this way out the trail of some of the worst shipwrecks and human disasters of the emigrant trade.

The steamer *Londonderry* left from Sligo at 8:00 A.M. on 1 December 1849, bound for Liverpool with a cargo of cattle. Sailing in the most dangerous season of the year, it also carried 178 emigrants divided between the deck and the steerage, where the cattle were also stowed. According to the *Londonderry Journal,* when it tied up at that city's docks two days later, on a Sunday morning, "the astounding intelligense suddenly spread that an immense number of the passengers whose corses were on board, had perished by suffocation during the voyage." The town's magistrates were assembled and began an inspection of the ship. Dead bullocks had to be cleared from the deck. The body of a child was found on the quarterdeck, and an additional three adult "corses" were found in the engine room. The remainder, seventy-two men, women, and children were found below decks: "The steerage presented a most hideous spectacle of mortality, from which proceeded such a stench as to render close inspection impossible."

The events of the two-day voyage from Sligo were pieced together from testimony taken from the 102 survivors. As a storm rose, the deck passengers were forced below by the mates and crew, and the hatchways were closed over them. One testified that one of the crew "called him an Irish _____ & forced him down." The steerage was too crowded to sit, he said (it was later determined that each passenger had about two square feet of space when all were in the steerage). The lights guttered and eventually went out, producing a panic in which blows were struck among passengers trying to reach the ladders and force the hatches. "There was not a twentieth part of sufficient room below decks, he said, and the people were pulling each other by the hair of the head, and were moving to and fro in a mass. . . ." He had been traveling with a sister, who, he asserted, went mad before dying beside him. At some point later he remembered an old man's crying "very loud" through the decks, "Captain, Captain, Captain, for God's sake come & save us and have mercy on us."

A young girl from Ballina who "thought herself to be 12 or 14" testified that she became lost in the crush but was traveling with her mother and four children, all of whom died in the steerage. In the panic, rumor spread that there were "robbers" among them. She saw women beaten with "sticks," and she feared that the family's money would be taken. She remembered that her mother, who was lame and weak and could not climb the ladder herself, carried £32, a £20 note sewn in her jacket and two sovereigns and ten small notes "in a blue purse tied with a ribbon about her neck." It had become very hot in the tightly packed space, and the crowd was calling through the hatches all through the night for water and release. At some point during the night, a sailor was heard to remark in response, "[T]hey are only Irishmen fighting among themselves." The Captain, Alexander Johnston, and the mates, Richard Hughes and Ninian Crawford, were charged with manslaughter by the Londonderry magistrate.[36]

It was the good fortune of the Ballykilcline emigrants to be carried on what might be called the "honorable" ferry trade, aboard vessels prepared to carry human cargo. Although they had had no choice in the timing or route of their journey, Burke and the commissioners had at least devised an itinerary and destination that guided their movements as far as the Staten Island quarantine in sight of Manhattan Island. Only after that would their movements be their own. Even for the Commissioners, the choice of route was largely determined at each stage by the established currents of the inter-coastal and Atlantic maritime trade. At least a century of habit and commerce favoring the flow of cargo of all kinds along the route traveled by most emigrants had made the word "Liverpool" on a ship's transom the most familiar sight of sailors on all the world's oceans.

The tens of thousands of voluntary emigrants who scrambled aboard the casual trade of the inland sea had even less control of their routes. These were not governed by the passengers but by the cargoes below and dispersed the emigrants throughout the western ports of England, where they either gravitated toward the "Little Irelands" growing in each or fanned out inland wherever work or poor relief beckoned them. Inevitably, the mainstream of this traffic also brought many of these to Liverpool, not as passengers for the outgoing ships but as settlers unable to go any further. Major General Sir William Warre, who was responsible for keeping the peace of the North and Midland Districts in 1848, viewed this exodus from the famine as an insoluble threat to tranquility in England. He estimated the flow into Liverpool at one thousand a week at the minimum. Of these, he thought about fifteen in a hundred were "sent back," like the elder Connor, as unfit either to travel further or to perform useful work in England: "Those who are not sent back generally spread themselves over the country or remain solely dependent on the Charity of the inhabitants of Liverpool."[37]

As they approached this stage of the journey, the batches of emigrants from Ballykilcline would be seeing their countrymen in ever-increasing numbers, most of them in a condition much worse than their own and in settings increasingly hostile and beyond their control. The impressions left on them can only be surmised. In speech and appearance their fellow travelers were unmistakably like themselves. All were moving in the same direction as if driven by a wind. During this part of the journey, once they boarded the ferries and left Ireland behind, their circumstances were all but identical: crowded and counted at quaysides; herded aboard by strangers who saw no distinctions among them; stowed as cargo on deck or in the holds; witnessing the misery and sickness of the others; and, by most accounts, uniformly passive or in panics when they sensed danger, as in the holds of the *Londonderry*. Except for the unluckiest of them, this part of their emigration was objectively much the same experience for all.

9

Liverpool and the Celtic Sea

The Exodus still continues. With what eager rapidity one multitude
follows another. They have no king, yet their muster is prompt and
their march is regular. The great army moves on, its footsteps leading
to the sea. . . .

> J. Buck, "The Forget-Me-Not; or,
> Last Hours on the Mersey,"
> sermon aboard the *Clasmerden*.[1]

Liverpool was a much less distant magnet than America, exerting its pull
not on the minds of prospective emigrants but on their bodies, drawing them
into its domain whether they wished to be there or not and taking its toll on
each of them whether they stayed or merely passed through. By 1848 it was
as intrinsic to the great emigration from Ireland as the potato or the failing
land system itself. At least two of every three emigrants from Ireland during
the 1830s and 1840s passed through Liverpool whether their ultimate destination was Manchester, London, New York, Quebec, or the Antipodes. To
their number were added the bulk of Scots, Welsh, and English migrants
into the North and the midlands, including the many unfortunates swept
out of the poorhouses and prisons in the great "shovelling out of paupers"
that followed the reform of the Poor Law. And behind these, already, were
growing numbers of westward migrants from the continent transshipping
from North Sea, Baltic, and even Mediterranean ports as Liverpool began
to corner the market on the Atlantic passenger trade.[2]

   Seen from a distance, the logic of this route was compelling: the most
heavily traveled shipping lanes of the Irish Sea led mostly to Liverpool; the
roads, rails, and canals from the Merseyside led to work and wages inland,
and the Liverpool docks had become the main gateway to the Atlantic for
most of those leaving the British Isles.[3] The Irish Sea was Liverpool's realm.
The peoples and goods of its periphery moved to its commands. But at

ground level the movement of people through the port had little appearance of order. As the volume of emigrants began to swell in the early thirties, first tens and then hundreds of thousands entered the Liverpool dockland each year as though sluicing through a funnel's neck, at the mercy of the flow, unable to control the pace or often even the direction of movement as it took them from one leg of their journey to the next. Those who fell out of the "march to the sea" because they had been weakened by recent experience or were short of the cash and knowledge needed to negotiate this gauntlet often suffered the worse fate. Awaiting them was the voracious criminal world that infested the waterfront alleys of Rotten-row, Gibraltar-place, Booble-alley, Oriel Street, and the hundreds of putrid cellars that received the thousands who strayed. In each of these bleak crannies of the waterfront lurked "a company of miscreant misanthropes, bent upon doing all the malice to mankind in their power."[4]

After the emigrants had survived the dangerous passage from ferry to steerage, their choices were dictated by the impersonal rhythms of the great port. Tides, winds, and seasons had once set these rhythms absolutely, controlling the timing and capacities of the port's traffic. But steam and monumental feats of earthmoving, building, and hydraulic engineering were now breaking that hold, releasing the full power of the port over the movement of goods in and out—and with that also came its power over the movement of populations. Shipping tonnages increased more than thirteen times in the second half of the previous century, to four hundred thousand tons inward and outward by 1800, another six times that volume by 1825, and four times that again by midcentury. The passenger trade had always been a junior part of this boom, but it too increased steadily on the back of the cargo traffic until Liverpool's name became synonymous with emigration and the Atlantic crossing.[5] According to Edward Walkinshaw, a shady ticket broker, Radical pamphleteer, and promoter of assisted emigration, all this was thanks to "the true principles of Political Economy," the same force that had brought Ireland's "superabundant population" to his door in Exchange Alley North, cash in hand.[6]

The Reverend J. Buck of the Bethel Union Mission Society saw an even more powerful "invisible hand" guiding the steps of the emigrants to Liverpool: "Like Cyrus of old, they hear a voice they know not, calling them by name, and feel a hand they know not, girding them for the enterprise; hence the promptness of their start, and the determination of their progress, and the unity of their whole movement."[7] He was aware that men like Walkinshaw provided the means that moved the migrating masses simply for profit, but "the movement itself we believe to be divine," he declared on the deck of the *Clasmerden*. It was a common thought among the Liverpudlians of the time, offering a means of understanding the magnitude of what they were witnessing, both the hellish suffering all around them and the huge bounty of wealth that the movement brought with it. Seeing the horrors around him, the evangelical Buck was less certain that all his fellow citizens listened to the same voice:

Whether Liverpool be awake to the divinity that is in the movement or no, is altogether another matter; but certainly it is wide awake to the commercial advantages to be reaped by assisting it, the finest ships in the world, and the most profuse expenditure, being supplied to forward this great emigration movement . . . and securing corresponding profits to itself, Liverpool being likely to become, "par excellence," the great emigration depot.[8]

Whether it was guided by providence or political economy, the "great emigration movement" was the most prodigious seaborne enterprise in human history: thousands of ships bearing millions of passengers over a thousand leagues of ocean. More remarkable still, till after midcentury this feat was performed not by the new technology of steam and steel but by the artifacts of a previous age. Sailing ships, many of them lumbering through their last voyages, some originally built to carry slaves, were now paying a final dividend to their masters in the carrying of peasants from Europe to North America. In the near future, as the task was taken over by the steamers of the Black Ball, Cunard, Inman, and White Star lines, carrying thousands at a time and subsidized by the Royal Mail, the enterprise would hum with orderly speed, safety, and even comfort for most of the passengers, a metamorphosis of coffin ship into luxury liner. Deaths in steerage from infection and abuse diminished, and wholesale drownings became celebrated tragedies. But by the spring of 1848, when the flow of famine refugees approached its peak, all observers who were not themselves engaged in it saw in the Liverpool enterprise only chaos and suffering.[9]

Compared with London, the Liverpool of 1848 was an adolescent metropolis, brazen with success and callous toward weakness. It had been the bully of the litter of eighteenth-century port cities, weaned on the slave trade and fattened on its lion's share of tobacco, sugar, and cotton.[10] Between 1847 and 1853, at the height of the emigrant traffic, the town was receiving annually a migrant influx equal to its entire resident population of only a few years before. The grim human results had only become a subject of public alarm some two decades before, as the numbers of migrants either sojourning or settling in its precincts began to produce civic disorders for which its fledgling municipal authorities were ill-prepared. Londoners had known beggary and want in their streets for centuries, but the sheer size of the city helped mute the presence of the new waves of immigrants during these migratory decades. Liverpool's experience was different in many other ways from that of the other great towns where migrants from the periphery settled. Despite the numbers who would land and remain to make it the most Irish city in England, one whose dialect even today is hard to distinguish from Dublin's, most of the distressed classes who haunted its streets and alleys were wayfarers, transients who would never become part of its still-unformed society. Transiency aggravated both their physical distress and the animosity they encountered. By the time the famine emigration reached the Merseyside, its inhabitants were more hardened to the spectacle of public suffering than those of any city in the kingdom.

Herman Melville's penetrating sketches of Liverpool's streets in these years, often quoted but without a Liverpool Hogarth to illustrate the human catastrophe that was occurring, does more justice than any other eyewitness testimony to the sight: "In these haunts, beggary went on before me wherever I walked, and dogged me unceasingly at the heels. Poverty, poverty, poverty, in almost endless vistas: and want and woe staggered arm in arm along these miserable streets."[11] Just recently arrived from New York, the young Melville may have taken half the population of the Liverpool waterfront as paupers by their ragged dress and ill-fed bodies. Because of its tremendous surplus of labor, the extent of utter pauperism was certainly greater and more chronic in Liverpool than in New York. But it was also the measure of poverty and the irregularity of wages that differed on either side of the Atlantic, blurring the distinction between the casual laborer and the beggar. In Liverpool, Friday's laborer was often Monday's pauper. Newly arrived and ticketed emigrants one day could find themselves at the poorhouse door soon after, lost by the thousands in the frauds and chaos of the emigrant trade. These were all categories in which the Irish were to be found in disproportionate numbers in the late 1840s. From the point of view of the city's economy, no distinction need be made among them, except that an outsize pool of manual labor was needed, in part to help move the surplus population out. Its business and the livelihood of a large part of its population was to haul, warehouse, and route this mass of pauperism in and out quickly, along tributaries opened by centuries of cargo traffic.

In its sheer volume and consequence in the world, the dominion of the Liverpool maritime trade was unrivaled. At its height in midcentury, the city's boosters claimed that more than half the ships on the seven seas bore "Liverpool" on their transoms.[12] The unique character of Liverpool when the emigrants of Ballykilcline passed through was shaped by this boom, which brought with it an uncontrolled rush of incoming humanity, primarily from the hinterlands of the Celtic sea. Liverpool's population had already swollen beyond the control of the municipal authorities by the 1830s, rising by nearly 60 percent in that decade, from 165,000 to 286,000. The politically divided council and Poor Law authorities operated in an almost continuous state of alarm and overburden throughout these two decades under the pressure of cholera and typhus, typhoid, petty crime, homelessness, vagabondage, beggary, sectarian riot, brawling, alcoholism, corruption, venereal disease, lunacy, Chartism, bankruptcy, and mounting poor rates. By 1842 Liverpool was condemned as the "unhealthiest town in England," described by Dr. Duncan of Liverpool, one of the era's leading public health reformers, as "the black spot on the Mersey."[13]

All these conditions continued to worsen before the tidal wave of famine refugees reached the Liverpool waterfront. Estimates made in the ensuing chaos are indefinite, but in the six years between 1847 and 1853 as many as a million Irish arrived in the city as transients or settlers, of whom 586,000 were designated as "paupers," meaning they were expected to become wards of the parish if they remained.[14] Most of these escaped the town by sea or land, but the police, the night watch, the collectors and disposers of waste, the workhouses, poorhouses, almshouses, night asylums, clinics, orphanages, jails, prisons, and reformatories were not absorbent enough to clear the spillage of the migration from the city's streets. Neither were the madhouses and graveyards capacious enough to keep the attrition of the migrants from public view. The escapees from the stricken Irish countryside were by no means the only casualties of the Liverpool enterprise, but poverty, slum life, and disease from this time forward became inseparable from Irish names and accents in the city's consciousness.

Liverpool and Ireland

Liverpool contained none of the symbols that identified Victorian London as the center of a world empire. Even though its interests and influence were worldwide, its politics and culture were provincial, dominated by narrow factions and sects. What pomp there was in its public buildings and plazas was brashly commercial, without London's grand parades or vistas where its power might be flaunted in public ceremony. The greatest monument to its power, the massive dock system, was frankly unceremonious, a place of commerce and hard labor. But to the degree that the British Empire was a flow of goods and people as well as of power, Liverpool was certainly its second city, the pump through which most of what nourished its people and industry flowed both in and out. In 1845 alone, more than twenty thousand ships loaded and unloaded at its docks, not to mention the uncounted number of small vessels whose comings and goings were hardly noticed individually, although no observer fails to mention their constant "teeming" in the Mersey estuary.[15]

Although its ships and seamen were to be seen in all the world's ports, Liverpool had acquired this place first of all because of its dominance in the Irish Sea, especially in the lopsided traffic with Ireland. In the preceding thirty years it had become the depot of the Irish export trade, the main distribution point from which the produce of the Irish land system moved into the English market. Ultimately, it was from this source that the incomes keeping the Irish land system afloat originated. As the entrepot of the Irish trade with England, it translated fluctuations in the prices and demand for Irish produce, influencing choices on the use of land in Ireland and therefore on the peasantry's access to it, the rents they paid for it, and the wages they earned for tilling it. As Engels put it, "Today England needs grain quickly and dependably—Ireland is just perfect for wheat-growing. Tomorrow England needs meat—Ireland is only fit for cattle pastures." The responses of most Irish landlords to this influence were far from spasmodic, nor were they always rational, but adjusting to the demands of the Liverpool provisions market almost always meant changes in the townlands: relative prosperity when agricultural wages were available; hard times, evictions, and emigration when grain prices fell.[16]

Once pried from the land, few emigrants had any choice but to set out from the market towns to the ports along the main tributaries of the existing flow of the export trade. The network of transport and middlemen that had been established to carry the grain and livestock of the Strokestown market to the docks and warehouses of Liverpool was soon duplicated by a system of moving emigrants along the same lines. The "deputies of deputies" who had previously managed the movement of goods from the countryside moved easily into the business of managing the movement of people, following the same routes and often using the same interlocutors between the townland and the Liverpool dock.

On the Crown estates, the downward chain of command—as between the commissioners and Johnny Cox—was intended to manage the gathering and marketing of the land's produce and the surplus of the townland lots. After collecting the rents, it was the deputies' main purpose, as it was for stewards of private estates. All absentee landlords, like the Lords Westmeath or Palmerston, employed similar intermediaries between themselves and the market. The Crown Agent, Boyan, managed the produce of Pobble O'Keefe from the hiring of harvesters to the sale of the produce to the brokers of Cork City, under the supervision of the Clerk of the Quit Rents. Ross Mahon, and through him the Dublin land agencies of Stewart and Kincaid and Guinness and Mahon (later to become the Guinness Bank), performed the same function for the Mahons of Strokestown, who were resident landlords.

The firms chosen by Burke and Mahon to manage the shipping of their tenants, Shaw and Sons of Dublin and Harnden and Company of Cork City, were established grain and cattle shippers before taking up the emigrant traffic.[17] Not surprisingly, when commissioned to move the Crown tenants, they merely funneled this new cargo into the system long established in carrying the old. Increasingly, the two converged on the Liverpool docks, most often aboard the same vessels. The sight was recommended for tourists' entertainment by *The Picturesque Handbook to Liverpool*: "Should an Irish packet have just arrived at the time our visitor is at this dock [the Clarence], he will be much amused at the odd scene their decks exhibit! At the stern will be seen, as usual, a freight of bipeds, old and young, holding converse in a jargon that it would be difficult to interpret; whilst the rest of the deck will be crowded with a medley of sheep, pigs, and oxen."[18]

Although Liverpool achieved a near-monopoly of this traffic, there was a great competitive scrambling for emigrants in the Irish ports. Alternative routes were still in use in the 1840s, crossing to Glasgow, London, or New York directly from Irish ports, bypassing Liverpool. The western ports of Sligo, Limerick, and Galway also had their shippers and ticket agents, each with some kind of network inland drawing emigrants from the countryside, but these were mostly quite modest, improvised enterprises. Both local and national newspapers printed offers of commissions from these shipping agents for anyone "possessing the confidence of the emigrating classes" in the interior. Commissions of 5s. for adults and 2s. 6d. for children were paid to local promoters to act as ticket agents. A Mr. Spaight of Limerick advertised regularly in the *Limerick Chronicle*, claiming to have agents operating for him in Nenagh, Cloughjordan, Ennis, Killaloe, Ballingeer, Birr, Tarbert, and Tipperary.[19]

The same Crown Agent, John Besnard of Cork, who transacted the emigration of Pobble O'Keefe also recruited such subagents as far off as Carlow by mail circulars. Most seem to have been dabblers in the emigrant commission business, earning a pound for each family of seven they ticketed. Judging from the unfortunate droves who found out in Liverpool that their tickets were worthless, many commission agents were frauds or were themselves deceived by port agents like Spaight or Besnard who knew very well the conditions in Liverpool. These inland deputy-agents were both townsmen and farmers. One, a Thomas Edwards of Carlow recruited by Besnard, was a desperately indebted petty landlord, a failed tea merchant and coach agent who now hoped for salvation from the emigrant commissions: "O that it would please the Lord to cause me to have such success as to enable me to pay my rent," he wrote after receiving his packet of ticket applications and posters from Besnard. He prayed that "my new employment prove the means of delivering me from my difficulties." With luck, he hoped the emigration business might even afford him the means of marrying Lucy Marchant, whom he mooned over daily in his diary. The few emigrants he succeeded in recruiting from Carlow would also find themselves in the Liverpool vortex, ticketed by the melancholy Edwards, booked by Besnard, an agent of Harnden and Co., whose business had long tied them to the Liverpool shippers and brokers. These loose networks stretched out across the provincial towns and markets from all the ports, both serving and propelling the movement outward. There is no telling how many Besnards, Edwardses, and Spaights they employed, but as one Dublin engineer complained, "[E]very tree corner and pump in Dublin and for 50 miles about bore handbills, telling people that only fools remained in Ireland."[20]

Like the western ports of England, the lesser Irish ports were unable to resist the network in goods and emigrants drawing traffic eastward toward the inland sea and the maw of Liverpool. What remained of their competition was mostly in the reduced fares and schedules, as well as the dangerous conditions with which they were now widely associated. The *Limerick Chronicle* played instead on local loyalties by featuring the "Limerick men" among the emigrant ship captains, speaking of these stalwart figures with "bluff comaraderie." The *Waterford Mail* conducted a lurid campaign on behalf of its shipping advertisers against the Liverpool trade, echoing a growing spate of outraged reports about the treatment of Irish emigrants in Liverpool appearing in national papers like the *Freeman's Journal* and *The Nation*. But all was of little avail against the widening grip of Liverpool on the emigrant trade, founded firmly upon its dominance of the cargo traffic. As the founder of the City of Dublin Company, one of the first steam lines between Ireland and England, testified before a parliamentary inquiry, Irish graziers and grain factors had long before begun to deal directly with Liverpool merchants, bypassing even the Dublin market "no longer necessitating keeping large capital in trade" in Ireland. The Irish share of the trade was depleting not only in shipping but in shipbuilding, according to the same testimony, despite the universally lower wages. The City of Dublin Company spent £40,000 to £50,000 annually in shipbuilding in Liverpool, he said, but was "deterred from building a single vessel in the port of Dublin" where the company's capital was subscribed because of "the delays and risks of combination" among the Irish workers. In the end, the company became a firm based in Liverpool.[21]

By 1848 the emigrant and provisions trade of Liverpool was thus integrally linked in the system of extracting goods, labor, and capital from Ireland. The chronic shortage of cash and capital that hobbled industry and investment in Ireland resulted at least in part from this influence, as did the pressures that forced landlords to evict and townland peasants to consider emigration. The emigrant trade was also a relatively low-risk investment for the Liverpool merchants and shipowners, who could often suffer crushing losses and heavy insurance costs in the Indian and American trade. While it is true that the distant magnet of American wages ultimately governed the pace of emigration, it was through Liverpool and its networks in Ireland that the emigrant was first reached by the impulses to leave.

The Inland Sea

The Liverpool of 1848 had been created by the momentum of the same impersonal forces that were transforming all of Atlantic civilization by the mid-nineteenth century. After London itself, no other city had fed so greedily on the colonial trade of the previous century. Its rise to the position of the second city of the empire was founded on the success of its aggressive merchant community in cornering a lion's share of the trade in slaves, rum, tobacco, sugar, salt, and cotton, in addition to its share of Irish provisions. In this sense, it was perhaps the most colonial of Atlantic cities, integrating the extraction and distribution of goods from the old and new colonies and elbowing out its competitors among the older English port cities that had thrived in the earlier stages of these colonial ventures. More remarkable still was its success in adapting to the profound shifts in the world economy that followed, toward North and South America, West Africa, and India, after the decline of the slave and triangular trades and the abolition of the East India Company's monopoly in 1814. Its dominant position between American cotton and the Manchester mills was also a crucial part of this success, but this too had been made possible by its primacy over the other English ports and its near-hegemony in the movement of goods and people within the Irish Sea and its hinterlands.

Liverpool's success in adapting to these global changes entrenched its dominance for the rest of the century as the entrepot of both goods and human migration in the Atlantic economy. Seen from the outside, this triumph gave it the aura of a world metropolis—prosperous, progressive, and in control of its fate. But this exalted international aura contrasted sharply with the character of its internal life. Three factors in particular that contributed to its commercial success were also responsible for the chaos and factiousness of its civic life: the exploding volume of its internal and overseas traffic; the seasonality of work and wages dependent on its maritime, excavating, and building trades; and the boom-and-bust volatility of investment and speculation both large and small in the movement of cargo and passengers through and to the town from every direction, to and from the four ancient kingdoms bordering the inland sea, and literally to and from the four corners of the earth.

Much more than ancient and populous London, Liverpool resembled a New World city. Its character in midcentury was formed by the interaction of its narrow commercial elites with ever-growing masses of strangers; it was constantly being reshaped by the addition of newcomers who made up a proportionally larger share of its population than any other city of the eastern Atlantic seaboard. All these were signs of its boomtown prosperity, as they were of New York or San Francisco in the same years, but the former slave port and now the mercantile hub of a great empire bore the chaos and afflictions of both the Old World and the New together in its streets. The outrageous contradictions witnessed by all observers—between great wealth and hopeless destitution, bustling streets lined with dying beggars, avant-garde technology and backbreaking toil, unceasing work everywhere and idleness everywhere—were the result of its unique local economy as it responded in jerking leaps to the city's rise to the great Atlantic port.

Of the four main ports of the Irish Sea, including Belfast, Glasgow, and Dublin, Liverpool exerted by far the greatest influence over the movement of the peoples of the hinterlands, particularly those of the "Celtic fringe." The ancient migratory route between Belfast and Glasgow continued to carry a heavy flow of Ulster emigrants, both seasonal and permanent. Many of these, too, eventually had found their way to the Merseyside and made up a powerful Protestant working class in the maritime, cargo-handling, and building trades. But for most of them Glasgow was only a way into the wages of the Clydeside and the North rather than the first leg of a journey to more distant destinations. For the great majority of those leaving all the ports of the inland sea, Liverpool was the almost irresistible magnet whatever their ultimate destination—especially for the superabundant Celtic agrarians uprooted each year with no direction in mind but away from home. Since most of these migrants were general laborers or servants seeking wages in any work that offered itself, they can hardly be said to have had destinations in mind before leaving home. Liverpool was also the place where many first learned their destinations from the employers' agents, jobbers, and straw bosses who recruited labor for all parts of the country. The difficulty in discovering what destinations were in the minds of the migrants passing into and through the port in the 1840s is that as the migration of labor swelled, a larger proportion of it was swept directly outward as Liverpool became increasingly "the Gateway to the Atlantic" rather than the entrance to the English labor market.[22]

In the 1840s, East Lancashire's conurbation was the "big smoke" of the North for Scots, Welsh, and English, as well as the overwhelming majority of Irish trekking laborers whether their next destination were east or west, north or south: harvesting in Lincolnshire; excavating canals or rail lines everywhere; seeking mill work in Manchester or Bolton; hod carrying, casual labor, or domestic service in London; or drawing and hauling in the great port itself.[23] Night and day, in all weather there was also an incessant coming and going of coastal vessels crowding the sea-lanes between Liverpool and all coastal points north to Glasgow, Belfast, and Derry; west to Dublin, Waterford, and Cork; and south to Swansea, Cardiff, Bristol, and London.

Virtually every one of the hundreds of towns along both coasts of the Irish Sea routinely sent or received vessels known in Liverpool, together with their local crews who knew both the majesty and the horrors of the great port firsthand. While it was far from isolated from the rest of Britain or the wider world economy, the maritime population surrounding the Irish Sea was a distinct entity in many aspects of its internal economy, its culture, and even its language, and had been so for centuries before the rise of Liverpool as a world port. In this sense, this quasi-enclosed inland sea bears some resemblance to other vigorous maritime cultures that had formerly arisen in the Aegean, the Baltic, and the Mediterranean. The exchange of goods, people, and language at a sustained level over a long period of time helped to create established routes of movement and habitual ties of commerce, occupation, and even family across and along the coasts. The rise of Liverpool first established it as the dominant core of this subeconomy, one might say its Athens or Venice, and simultaneously made it the main conduit between the peoples of the Irish Sea and the rest of the world. Its power within this geographical orbit was not the only force that propelled the large emigration from it, but when the great migration of the nineteenth century began, it assured that disproportionate numbers would be drawn from this inner sphere of Liverpool's influence, the predominantly Celtic hinterlands of the Irish Sea. By the 1840s, this sphere was Liverpool's private empire.

Thus, Liverpool looked toward an inner and outer world. The great majority of those who hauled the cargo on its docks, crewed the vessels that crowded its river, and tenanted its slums were born around the inner sea and spoke with its predominantly Celtic accents while its great shipowners, bankers, and cotton brokers turned their minds in the direction of their business, along the far-reaching spokes of the world maritime trade of which they had become the hub and the masters. Although many of those who now commanded the city's wealth had themselves emerged from the hinterlands, most especially from the lowlands of Scotland, by the mid-nine-

teenth century the city's social economy and that of the rapidly industrial-
izing region surrounding it presented stark contrasts. It would probably
not be too much to say that the commerce and industry of the region within
one hundred miles of Liverpool represented the most dynamic core of world
capitalism of the era. In the movement of ships and cargo, the management of Liverpool port was an exemplar of modernity to the rest of the
maritime world. The immense traffic in goods and people that passed
through its docks and warehouses daily, hauled by muscle and counted by
a thousand clerks' pens, was made possible by colossal feats of building and
design that became models for the great enterprises in hydraulic engineering to come in the Suez and Panama canals and the Brooklyn Bridge. More
capital, labor, and technical innovation went into the construction of its
dock system at this time than into the great port of London or probably
into any seaport in the world. In this regard, the port of Liverpool stood
alone in the world as yet without a serious rival. Its mighty stone and iron
docks, which Melville likened to the walls of China and the great pyramids,
might truly have been called the first of the "eighth wonders of the world"
so enamored by the Victorians.[24]

At the same time, pouring through this spectacle of dynamism and innovation in their tens of thousands annually were the living artifacts of the
agrarian past, a great many of them the last remaining peasants, graziers,
and transhumants of the British Isles. Besides the large demand for casual
labor on the docks, their presence was required in the monumental excava-
tion, quarrying, and building of the port's infrastructure of docks and rails,
the kind of work in shifting earth and stone for which nearly all had been
raised in the stony Celtic hinterlands to which earlier colonial expansions
had forced them. Like the ships and cargoes being moved according to the
mechanical rhythms of the docks, these recruits from the hinterland also
had to be disciplined to the port's complex system of movement and engineering. In the process, whether as day laborers or steerage passengers,
individual identity had to be submerged in a collective effort whose rhythms
demanded alternating periods of intense action and enforced idleness, something else for which most of the migrants seem to have been prepared by
their own cultures, especially those from the Irish townlands.[25]

Entering Liverpool

The only tangible hint that remains of the state of mind of the Ballykilcline
tenants after their departure was the complaint of "short provisions" directed
at Cox by the first "batch" of 1848. It was merely a parting shot at their
old enemy from the former tenants, which could have had only a symbolic
effect because they were at sea by the time it was received. As it may have
been intended to do, their final complaint infuriated the Commissioners.
Their only response was to instruct Burke to "hold the corn of Ballykilcline"
till the price rose, when it would be sold in partial payment of arrears, quite

possibly to follow in the footsteps of those who had raised it, at least as far as Liverpool.[26]

Their complaint was the last communication from the former occupants of Ballykilcline. Like nearly all of the many thousands who passed through the great "emigration depot" in these years, none of the tenants left another word about their experience after leaving the townland. Of course, in their case there were no letters home to an empty townland, and their circumstances in passing through Liverpool were hardly conducive to written reflections.

Just as the first close view of the New World for most emigrants was of lower Manhattan as their ship entered the Narrows of New York harbor, their first sight of the Old World outside Ireland was of Liverpool as the ferry entered the Mersey. A euphoric folklore of deliverance and great expectations has made the entrance to New York harbor, especially after the erection of the Statue of Liberty, a shrine to emigrant memories and the journey to reach it a pilgrimage. Even without the fabulous embellishments that the New World landing eventually took on, it seems fair to say that most experienced it on balance as a joyful moment or at least held it vividly in memory as the end of an ordeal or the beginning of a new life. The entrance to Liverpool during the famine exodus bears no such aura. There are few references to it, joyful or gloomy, in emigrant diaries, stories, and accounts, although it was certainly the most spectacular sight of their lives to that point and few other visitors of the time failed to miss its remarkable character. For all but a few, it was their first sight of the inner core of the civilization that had ruled them for centuries, not unlike that of the conquered Gauls entering Rome. At least in its material character, it was also a more wonderful revelation to a townland peasant than was New York of the power that the outside world had then acquired over nature, more stunning by far than any picture of that world presented to them in the National School geography lesson. Peasants who had never seen seagoing ships of sail or steam now saw hundreds in motion at once. They had just left a world in which a few cabins of piled stones and turf were the center of life and now saw gigantic geometrical walls of granite, thousands of multistoried buildings lining the shore, and crowds more numerous at a single glance than all the strangers they had seen in a lifetime. Compared to this, New York's ramshackle East River docks and waterfront were a backwater. Yet few recollections of the first sight of Liverpool during the famine exodus survive, as if it were a memory best forgotten.

It is unlikely that in any other place in the world of the 1840s was the contrast of economic vitality and utter destitution more manifest than in Liverpool. And only some modern cities, such as Rio, Mexico City, or Manila, present such a discordance of the modern and the archaic in its material and human dimensions. The port and city of Liverpool in 1848 contained most of the features of the great cities the emigrants would encounter later in their journey, as well as certain traits and qualities that made it unique in its time for the Irish emigrant. Visible immediately to the emigrants were its monstrous docks and warehouses, its fleets of puffing steamers and tall-masted ships from all corners of the earth, its crowded streets, the incessant sounds of labor on the waterfront. Old sailors said they could smell Liverpool over the horizon. To the inland peasant its aromas were mostly new, except for the reek of live cattle from the holds and docksheds: the brine, bilge water, and pungent tar of hundreds of wooden ships; the horrific stench of sewage and worse released at low tide that gave it the name "Black Spot on the Mersey"; the smoke of thousands of domestic coal fires; and already the distinctive odor of railway cinder and creosoted ties. Whether they could identify the meaning of these sights and the sources of these scents as the ferry approached the quay, their senses could have left little doubt that they were now entering a world in which many of the familiar things of nature had been altered beyond their recognition.

There were also many things invisible or mysterious to them that nevertheless controlled their fate directly, most of them having to do with the physical and commercial operations that were the raison d'être of the port— the management of ships and cargo and the human disciplines required to keep them moving. Given the already defeated state of mind and body in which they had set out and the limited knowledge they had yet acquired of the outside world, the profligate display of physical power and technical marvels that opened before them might have heightened the feelings of impotence that had overtaken even the strongest of them in their last year in the townland. If any further proof were needed of their own weakness and the futility of their resistance, the awesome impersonal energy that the great port exuded before their eyes must have riveted it in their minds. Once they had landed on the city's streets, they could not have missed either the "want and woe" of the crowds of emigrants like themselves who had just preceded them or the palpable hostility of the people, compared by one who had arrived in these years as a child to a "stony-hearted step-mother."[27]

The Liverpool System

Before incoming vessels reached the Mersey's mouth their approach to the coasts of Lancashire and Cheshire could be espied and transmitted to Liverpool from Holyhead in less than a minute by a semaphore telegraph established in 1827, "One of the most ingenious inventions ever designed for the purpose of carrying on a communication with distant persons," as the *Picturesque Hand-Book to Liverpool* described it. On one occasion, a ship-sighting query was made from Liverpool and an answer received in thirty-five seconds across a space of seventy-two miles, nearly the distance from Strokestown to Dublin. Placed at an average distance of eight and a half miles apart between Liverpool and Holyhead, the telegraph sent ahead "the ordinary intelligence of what ships were in sight" in an average of five minutes.[28] Among its many useful functions, the telegraph fed information to the Dock Board that helped speed the turnaround time, the discharging, receiving, weighing, and loading of ships in the elaborate dock system. Merchant ships represented large capital investments to the shipowners, who demanded that no time be lost lying offshore or moored in the river. Steam vessels had to be distinguished from sail, and entrance priorities established that could mean long delays for the lesser ships and meaner cargoes, including most of the Irish ferries. The constant building and redesigning of the docks at great expense of public funds and labor strove to keep up with this growing demand for space and speed. Liverpool's dockers were also said to age rapidly under the weight of keeping traffic and goods moving at maximum pace; in the opinion of the *Lancet*, "no-one could be a dock-worker for five years and escape disfigurement." The telegraph sometimes alerted the Customshouse officers, also overwhelmed and demoralized by the volume. It communicated also with the exchanges, causing flurries of buying and selling as information affected prices and investors waited for news of ships and cargoes arriving from points near and far.[29]

Some of the larger Irish ferries were announced through this method, not out of interest in the emigrants but in the cargoes they carried. Notice of the time and displacement of steam vessels especially was useful to the masters of the appropriate docks in avoiding delays and congestion in the harbor while wet docks were cleared, water levels adjusted to the river's tide and hands assembled to begin offloading. The passengers were entirely passive in these procedures, few of them more aware of the system they were entering than the cattle below decks. Perhaps not much more decipherable were the first sights and sounds they encountered.

Entering the mouth of the Mersey on the morning tide a year after the Roscommon emigrants, Herman Melville first saw through the mist great buoys and distant objects on shore, "vague and shadowy shapes, like Ossian's ghosts." Leaning over the side of the *Highlander*, he first heard the sound of the port's famous Bell Buoy, a "doleful, dismal" ringing in time with the rolling of the sea. As the mist cleared and the town came into his view, he beheld "lofty ranges of dingy warehouses . . . very deficient in the elements of the marvellous," reminding him from a distance of the ramshackle warehouses he had seen along South Street in New York. For many years before the telegraph appeared other bells signaled the arrival of ships, ringing from the Old Church of Saint Nicholas in Chapel Street: "Thirty or forty years ago, these bells were rung upon the arrival of every Liverpool ship from a foreign voyage. How forcibly does this illustrate the increase of the commerce of the town! Were the same custom now observed, the bells would seldom have a chance to cease."[30]

Only on closer sight did the extraordinary power of the port begin to reveal itself. In striking contrast to the disorder of the city's social order, its mighty docks and warehouses were among the modern wonders of the world, at the highest state of the art in the movement of ships and cargo. For miles along the eastern bank of the Mersey stood dock after dock "like a chain of immense fortresses," their names famous among merchants and seafarers the world over: Prince's, George's, Salt-House, Clarence, Brunswick, Trafalgar, Waterloo, Albert, Victoria, King's, and Queen's, and a maze of lesser structures serving every type and quantity of cargo. In what Melville described as "a grand parliament of masts," the densely packed hulls, spars, and timbers of the ships being maneuvered through the complex system represented all the forests of the globe: "Here, under the beneficent sway of the Genius of Commerce, all climes and countries embrace; and yard-arm touches yard-arm in brotherly love."[31]

In contrast to the "land system" from which the emigrants emerged, the greatest care in design and management was devoted to the Liverpool docks, with the capacity and efficiency of cargo handling increasing as new ones were built and older ones improved. Expanding the main source of the city's burgeoning wealth, the Mersey Docks and Harbour Board and its engineers were engaged in a virtually ceaseless struggle to construct new dock capacity to match the unprecedented growth of shipping traffic since the end of the Napoleonic Wars. Since 1834 alone, the Waterloo, Trafalgar, Victoria, Coburg, Prince's, and Albert docks, as well as eight smaller or specialized docks, together with their quays, piers, transit sheds, and gates, had been added to the waterfront. These, as Melville noted, were not the mere wooden wharves and shambling piers of South Street; to him, they were marvels of man's newfound energy and ingenuity:

> [T]he sight of these mighty docks filled my young mind with wonder and delight. . . . [I]n Liverpool, I beheld long China walls of masonry: vast piers of stone and a succession of granite-rimmed docks, completely inclosed, and many of them communicating. . . . The extent and solidity of these structures, seemed equal to what I had read of the old Pyramids of Egypt.[32]

The great docks erected in the thirty years before the famine may well be compared to such monuments of bygone empires. Like them, many Liverpool docks bore the names of monarchs, princes, and battles, but the colossal expense of wealth and labor that went into them was no act of piety, nor were they mere memorials. Of all the public structures in England they were perhaps the frankest symbol of the new empire that had come into being: above all, their purpose was profit and if they exalted any deity it was the Moloch of commerce.

Each extension of the dock system over the preceding century reflected a new stage in the expansion of the empire and in Liverpool's rise from a coastal town to a world port until, with the addition of the great Albert Dock in 1846, their quays and warehouses lined the Mersey shore for seven miles.[33] No account has yet been made of the expenditure of human labor in the creation of these mighty structures, labor of much the same kind as would be employed in excavating the water-bound sites of the great canals and bridges of the next generation. Like the fedayeen of the Nile, crowds of diggers and haulers had to be assembled to move earth and ponderous blocks of granite and sandstone, most of it carried to the dock sites from

Cheshire and North Wales or dredged from the Mersey's own bed to contain and manipulate its tides. According to the Chief Constable, who was hard-pressed to maintain order among these laboring crowds, some four thousand Irishmen were working at one moment on the dock extensions in the North End alone. The large numbers of laborers working in the area and the even larger numbers of Irish seeking work each morning produced mounting turbulence, which at one point prompted the authorities to swear in twenty thousand special constables to reinforce the two thousand regular troops camped at Everton.[34]

The principal dock engineer of the time, Jesse Hartley, was responsible for the design of the new dock system, whose many functions would have been well beyond the ken of the manual laborers. Every square yard of the structures was designed within the larger purpose of speeding the movement of ships and cargoes, controlling the water levels, and counting the transit of dutiable goods, though Hartley's touch gave them the appearance of medieval fortresses, castellated, and battlemented behemoths that advertised power and security to all who approached.

To the great majority of incoming migrants only an ominous chaos would be visible in the bustling activity controlled by this complex arrangement. Although it had been only a week or less since they had last walked the narrow dirt paths of the townlands, they were now entering a landscape that might have been centuries away. In one of the many startling contrasts that characterized the Liverpool waterfront, its highly rationalized inanimate landscape was peopled to an extraordinary degree by wanderers, casual workers, and paupers, most of them recently removed from the land and many of them homeless, squatting among its quays and dock walls oblivious to the purposes of their surroundings. Most of what they saw of the port and its people during their sojourn was arbitrary power, exercised over them even by the lowliest crewman or functionary, and the lawless chaos of the demiworld of emigrant brokers, lodging houses, and their bullies. Not all of the emigrants would fall victim to the criminals, but all would see their victims among the beggars haunting the streets, too much like themselves to mistake.

If the annual thousands of straggling paupers were like grit in the works of the port, a percentage of each year's newcomers was culled haphazardly from their thousands to become an essential part of that machinery, refilling the reserve pool of unskilled and casual workers. All, both migrant workers and emigrant passengers, had been invited there by Liverpool's commerce for their labor as well as their fares. But their presence was a source of great annoyance to the public and the authorities: the police and magistrates viewed them with disgust, no local jury was friendly, and the Poor Law guardians wanted only to remove them from the parish as quickly as possible.

While Melville condemned the "Sodomlike" corruption of the city for the suffering he witnessed on its streets, the American consul, Nathaniel Hawthorne, was more inclined to a view of the emigrants already widespread among the native population of the city. Describing the scene at the docks, he betrays a personal revulsion to the sight of Irish peasants that had already taken root in Liverpool. This much might have been expected from their most recent experience, but that the same aversion was present in American eyes could not have been known to them: "The people are as numerous as maggots in cheese [Hawthorne noted of the dock scene]; you behold them, disgusting, and all moving about, as when you raise a plank or log that has long lain on the ground, and find many vivacious bugs and insects beneath it."[35]

Liverpool Streets: "Via Dolorosa"

What Liverpool thought of the famine emigrants is painfully clear. But only reasonable guesses may be made about the emigrants' understanding of what was happening to them based on what we have seen of their mentality in the few years preceding their departure. Both official and private observers have left a copiously detailed record of the migration. The subjective impressions of bystanders at the scene are also rich in detail and sometimes, as in the young Melville's humane and analytical eye, capture moments of insight into the emotions of the emigrants caught in the Liverpool maelstrom. There is no English Melville who reproduced the scene of misery on its streets with the compassion of the young American, and no Mayhew of Liverpool to search through the cellars and alleys to record the lives they contained. Other Americans, like Hawthorne, felt little sympathy for the suffering and leave only an ominous forecast of the patrician disgust and racial prejudice that awaited the emigrants in the land of promise.

Even with Melville's extraordinarily vivid picture of the city, the second-hand literary testimonies leave us at best a remote view of the subjective experience of the millions of individuals for whom the port of Liverpool was the first sight and the first impression of the world outside Ireland. And even the most humanitarian local officials, such as the half-pay naval lieutenants appointed as emigrant officers, speak of the Irish crowds as they might of mistreated creatures of another species, barely able to imagine them as distinguishable individuals whose inner thoughts they might understand. The most passionate of these, Lieutenant Robert Low, who had besieged the Colonial Office in the 1830s with a voluminous outraged correspondence over the abuse of emigrants, saw himself as something of a sheepdog fending off the city's wolves. But even he was incapable of seeing the emigrants' *via dolorosa*, as he called it, through their eyes. The term was not only a burst of Low's compassion and outrage but a sober appraisal of the crimes and sorrows he had observed and recorded conscientiously for years, powerless to protect the victims or to punish their tormentors. From his superiors at the Colonial Office his repeated reports describing the suffering produced by the villainy of the emigrant trade earned him only a rebuke of "mistaken kindness" and the contempt of the ship brokers.[36]

Lieutenant Low and his successor had struggled for more than a decade against the predators of the emigrant trade with little success, leaving the system even more dangerous for emigrants in 1848 than it had been before the state had begun to regulate it some twenty years before. But while there was still no shortage of scoundrels high and low waiting to prey on any stranger in Liverpool, the refugees from Ireland brought vulnerabilities of mind and body with them that made them more defenseless victims than others, turning what might have been minor setbacks for other travelers— brief delays, loss of baggage, or seasickness—into fatal tragedies. Traveling in family groups with infants and aged together could be another handi- cap, multiplying the risks of sickness and delays and sometimes confront- ing parents or children with dreadful choices between abandonment and survival if one or more of them faltered. The swarms of orphans relieved by the parish and found begging in the streets were one measure of this bur- den, whether their parents had left them at the poorhouse door or died trying to keep them alive. The abundance of individual cases of emigrant families found dying together suggests the latter was the more common experience in Liverpool, as it was in the Irish countryside.

The lieutenants who were appointed to inspect and regulate the emigrant trade agreed that most of those disembarking from the Irish ferries arrived unticketed, despite the invariable warnings of emigrant guides and manu- als to make bookings in advance, making them easy game in the gauntlet of dockland predators.[37] Many factors may have accounted for the vulner- abilities of the emigrants on entering Liverpool, but most commonly it was sheer poverty and their ignorance of the pitfalls inherent in the system that made the place so dangerous for them. The greatest danger awaited any who were merely escaping starvation, whose resources or forethought took them no further than the Liverpool landing, trusting to luck, labor, or the English Poor Law to see them through. This may have been a tolerable risk for healthy young men and women traveling alone, but the plight of those traveling in families who fell victim to the hazards of the waterfront were scarcely believed when witnesses reported it. Melville recorded such a scene as he strolled the docks amid the crowds of emigrants:

> Often, I witnessed some curious, and many very sad scenes; and especially I remembered encountering a pale, ragged man, rushing along frantically, and striving to throw off his wife and children, who clung to his arms and legs; and, in God's name, conjured him not to desert them. He seemed bent upon rushing down to the water, and drowning himself, in some despair, and cra- ziness of wretchedness.[38]

While family ties were a great source of strength in the townland and would again be in America, they were more often the source of tribulation en route. Of the many misfortunes that might overtake a malnourished family traveling in a plague year, perhaps the most frequent and dreaded was fever. Whether in a child, a parent, or dependent, it posed heartbreaking dilemmas. A sailing date missed nursing a sick child might mean remaining in Liverpool till nothing was left—all had seen the crowds of paupers and beggars who had suffered similar setbacks. Nearly seventy-five hundred died of typhus and dysentery in 1847, more than half of them in the predominantly Irish wards. The health officer estimated that typhus alone accounted for some twelve hundred widows and four thousand orphans in that year. The fever sheds, night asylums, and lazarettos were overflowing, but to their daily death toll was added perhaps a larger number who chose to die privately, sometimes whole families, in obscure cellars and courts. At least three pleas of fever in the family were received from Ballykilcline on the eve of their departure, and there is little doubt that some of the stricken were among the later batches arriving in Liverpool. It is not known whether any of the eight who went missing in Liverpool died of fever, but the fate of some families with fever among them could be appalling. Patrick Culkin, once a schoolmaster, had been marooned as a pauper in the town with his wife and three children. When the parish relieving officer discovered them in a cellar, Culkin lay in bed beside his dead wife, and his eldest daughter was laid out on a table, having died of cholera. When the officer returned to remove the corpses, Culkin had cut the throats of his two younger children and had barely failed in taking his own life. Many cases equally harrowing were found by the health officers and reported in the press and official exposés, not always compassionately, which illustrates the potential cost of carrying close family ties into this dangerous phase of the emigration system.[39]

Disease was as intrinsic to the emigration system as robbery, a result of the hunger that drove emigrants from the townlands, of the exposure to the elements en route, and especially of the disastrous crowding that was inescapable in the journey out, in ditches and hostels, under tarpaulins on the ferry decks, and in the steerage of the emigrant ship. But it was poverty above all that made them susceptible to the physical and spiritual triage of Liverpool. The material poverty of the townland, its "utter squalor" as Weale the Crown surveyor put it, was visible to any passerby, but for years its stark reality had been modestly hidden from daily exposure to strangers. Once in Liverpool, the abjectness of that poverty was made naked in the light of day. Melville had seen poverty before on the New York waterfront but was stunned by the extremity of it in Liverpool.

It also struck Melville that the pauper crowds of Liverpool were entirely white-skinned, in contrast to the large towns in the "free states" of America where "negroes almost always form a considerable portion of the destitute." "All were whites; and with the exception of the Irish, were natives of the soil . . . ; as much Englishmen, as the dukes in the House of Lords." The emigrant Irish peasants who formed the bulk of these crowds held the black man's place in Liverpool. In one of the ugly ironies of the colonial system that had moved the African and the Irishman from their homes, the American black man was freer in the onetime capital of the slave trade than in the democracy of his birth. Melville marveled at the sight of his ship's black steward, "dressed handsomely, and walking arm in arm with a good-looking English woman." In New York, he thought, "such a couple would have been lucky to escape with whole limbs." Indeed, owing to the friendly reception and immunities extended to them in this town, "the black cooks and stewards of American ships are very attached to the place and like to make voyages to it."[40]

More than anything else, it was the public destitution of native-born whites and the even more extreme want of the Irish in Liverpool that reminded him that he was not in his own land. The horrors that shocked the young American were commonplace in the daily lives of Liverpudlians, as familiar as the smell of tar and coal. There were many in the town—humanitarians, Quakers, Marist fathers, and the usual eccentric mixture of Victorian missions and charities—who devoted themselves to the bodies and souls of the emigrants and native paupers alike, sometimes at the risk of their own lives. There were staunch abolitionists who were quite undisturbed by the suffering under their noses. But many more natives of the town, in all classes, reviled the image of the priest-ridden Irish peasants—the brutish "Paddy" and the slatternly "Bridie"—even before they saw them pass in thousands through their own streets. Invariably, apologists for the emigrant trade also excused the misery as the working of divine providence and the improvidence of the emigrants. Even the priests assigned from afar to minister to their suffering coreligionists sometimes found it hard to find their common ground, horrified to find how far Catholic Ireland had drifted from the bosom of the church. Said one Marist father to his superior in Lyon, of some seven or eight thousand Catholics in Spitalfields, excepting "several" of the more prosperous families, "all the others live without any Religion." In varying degrees, virtually all agreed that the emigrants had brought their holocaust on themselves.[41]

No effort was made to give a total to the loss of life among the emigrants in transit through the port; the fetid Irish wards of the North End invariably suffered the highest mortality in the cholera and typhus epidemics, but it was impossible to say whether the victims had been there for a day, a month, or a year. Numerous but uncounted deaths from starvation and consumption, discovered by the public "scavengers" or the night watch, often made the immediate cause of death unclear. Halfpennies were paid weekly to private burial societies to avoid a pauper's burial—sometimes in a "resurrection box," in which a false bottom allowed the burial of many at low cost—but corpses were retrieved from the river daily and displayed naked behind bars open to the street in the "Drowned House," where they might be identified by loved ones if they wished to assume the cost of burial. Such deaths were rarely even casually investigated unless there were signs of violence—even then, the coroner and police knew that it was both the best and the worst of sailors' ports and were well used to dead strangers.[42]

A host of other tragedies short of death were there for all to see in Liverpool's streets. Recently arrived Irish wandering the streets were easily recognized in their dress, manner, and condition. Crowds of paupers, a great many of them visibly Irish, lined the waterfront thoroughfares—these were among the first of their countrymen the newly landed saw abroad. Begging had become a scourge of the town, and though it was practiced by many others, had become especially associated with the famine refugees. Beggars of every kind, aggressive and deceitful or truly hopeless, dogged the citizen in every street and alley. Melville's "Dock-Wall Beggars" offers the most vivid picture of "the remarkable army of paupers" that beset the docks every day, especially at noon when hundreds of sailors and stevedores left through the dock gates on their way to their dinner. Beggars chose this hour to meet the emerging seamen:

> The first time that I passed through this long lane of pauperism, it seemed hard to believe that such an array of misery could be furnished by any town in the world. Old women, rather mummies, drying up with slow starving and age; young girls, incurably sick, who ought to have been in the hospital; sturdy men, with the gallows in their eyes, and a whining lie in their mouths; young boys, hollow-eyed and decrepit; and puny mothers, holding up puny babes in the glare of the sun, formed the main features of the scene.[43]

Young Melville was in the town for only six weeks and recorded only what he saw with his own eyes as he wandered its streets. Even his powers were strained to encompass the "enormities" he saw routinely practiced against strangers in the town. But the emigrant and medical officers, philanthropists and bystanders who witnessed the passage of the famine emigrants produced a similar catalogue of horrors in reports to the press and Parliament that firmly establishes early Victorian Liverpool as one of the century's capitals of atrocity: organized daylight robbery on the quays, forced imprisonment in lodging houses, unburied corpses of whole families in unlit cellars, multiple suicides, mercy killings, and a plague of madness that filled the asylums and clinics to overflowing with emigrants crippled in mind and body.[44]

"Milesians": How Liverpool Saw the Irish

The English cities into which the famine exodus flowed experienced repeated panics over infectious disease, rising crime, congested housing, and over-crowded poorhouses. Never before had public attention been drawn so incessantly to the grim details of early-Victorian city life. Liverpool's problems were by no means due only to the migrating Irish, since the time was one of unprecedented internal migration and population growth in general. But the bedraggled hordes fleeing from Ireland made an irresistible scapegoat for public fears and official impotence. Many of the refugees did in fact carry contagion. Large numbers fell immediately on public relief. Desperate for work of any kind, they did undercut local wages and they did appear in disproportionate numbers before the magistrates. The same could be said for all the cities into which the migration flowed, but with the largest proportion of Irish-born already among its resident population, Liverpool above all cities became the scene of the most intense public reaction.

The exact number and condition of the Irish entering Liverpool in each year of the famine is uncertain. Edward Rushton, the stipendiary magistrate, ordered the police to count the incoming passengers from the Irish ferries as they landed at the Clarence Dock, which was the main terminal of the Irish ferries. The results he reported for the year 1847 amounted to 296,231, of which he estimated 130,000 emigrated soon after landing (among them the first three batches from Ballykilcline); some 50,000 arrived "on business"; and the remainder (116,231) were paupers, "half naked and starving, landed for the most part during the winter, and becoming imme diately on landing, applicants for parochial relief."[45] Since this surveillance focused only on the regular steamer traffic and took no account of entries to the city by land from the casual trade across the channel, its count must be considered as a minimum estimate.

Dr. Henry Duncan, the crusading medical officer of health, offered an estimate doubling Rushton's: some 296,000 Irish alone, mostly paupers, landed in just the first six months of the year. The most recent estimate finds that more than 586,000 paupers, distinguished by the police from emigrants and cabin passengers by their complete lack of baggage, landed at the docks during the famine migration. Even taking Rushton's minimal estimate, no people in the Atlantic world saw as much of the Irish emigrant in his most distressed condition as did the people of Liverpool.[46]

Even before the famine brought the poorest and most distressed classes of Irish peasants to the city, the ferocious passions of the large Orange Order of Liverpool had made sectarian riots an annual disgrace of the town, and escalating fears of Irish pauperism and criminality had produced more bru-talizing racial images of the newcomers than could be found anywhere else in the kingdom. "It is remarkable and no less remarkable than true," said the *Liverpool Herald*, a leading Orange newspaper, "that the lower order of Irish papists are the filthiest beings in the habitable globe, they abound in dirt and vermin and have no care for anything but self gratification that would degrade the brute creation. . . ." The brutalized condition of the newcomers merely confirmed such long-held images among the bigots of the city. But it also fostered similar feelings among the general public.

One whose motives were not in question, the Dr. Duncan who had cru-saded for years to improve the inhuman and unhealthy conditions of the city, inadvertently gave authority to the sectarian stereotypes. Writing in a style typical of the "social inquiry" of the time, which combined clinical language with highly speculative moral observations, he observed of the Irish patients in his dispensary, "What other people would consider com-forts, they appear to have no desire for they merely seem to care for that which will support animal existence. Frequently there are 4 or 5 beds in a room just large enough to hold them & 4 or 5 persons sleep in each bed— There is no distinction of age or sex."[47] When he warned the home secre-tary of "the most severe and desolating epidemic" of typhus facing the city in the spring of 1847, the press and public officials coined the name "the Irish fever" as a catchall for all the diseases that the Irish were then dying of in the packed streets, tenements, and cellars of the North End. The diseases that Duncan associated with the overcrowding, poor sewerage, and water supply of the Irish wards the press and public personified in the Irish themselves, transposing the causes from the unhealthy environments described by Duncan to the inherent moral defects of the afflicted.[48]

Even the progressive Edward Rushton warned of "the great danger, moral as well as physical" that the influx of "the miserable Irish people into such towns as Liverpool" posed for its citizens and perhaps for the entire nation. By the time the famine emigrants began arriving, the city's social problems were also personified in the press and the popular culture by the Irish migrants. To a large degree, the denizens of the Irish slums and their migrating compatriots of the 1840s had replaced the native underclasses as "the Other" in English urban culture, embodying all the pathologies of violence, unreason, and contagion that so obsessed the early Victorians. Though most had known contempt and suspicion before, few of the emigrants could have anticipated the reception that awaited them in either the English or American cities, especially in Liverpool, which almost certainly was the most hostile place most of the emigrants would ever encounter on either side of the Atlantic.[49]

Liverpool had been primed for the racial hostility of the late 1840s by the cholera epidemic of 1831, which had stricken it harder than any other English city. It would not be known till much later that the cholera had come not from the oldest and nearest of the colonies but from the furthest frontiers, carried in the bowels of His Majesty's soldiers returning from the East and lurked in the city's own water supply rather than on the bodies of the emigrants, as many thought. It was an as-yet-invisible "ecological break" marked by the crossing of European colonialism with an eastern microbe, which returned to wreak a kind of revenge on the colonizers.[50] Again in 1847 with the outbreak of typhus and the reappearance of cholera two years later, the incoming Irish were seen as the source; they were in fact carrying the typhus rikettsia on their bodies this time, but they were associated with the disease intuitively, by reason of their rags and otherness rather than with the deadly lice. Ignorant of the nature of the dreaded infections, many also took the symptoms of mere deprivation and exposure, the consumption, ophthalmia, and diarrhea that beset the emigrants, as signs of infection and reacted with a general revulsion to contact or even close proximity with the sufferers.

This was the response of many of the towns of Lancashire, Cheshire, and the West Riding through which the emigrants passed during both epidemics, where notices were posted banning Irish paupers and rewards offered for information about any captains who landed them secretly. When the cholera scare was at its peak, the Home Office was receiving constant reports of civil disturbances in the northern districts in which the cholera and the immigrants were linked: in Preston, York, Sunderland, and Wellington there had been incidents between English and Irish workers in which the mixture of wage competition and the fear of infection had produced a threat to the peace. Regular troops were needed to quell "serious disturbances" in Wellington, where quarrels broke out between English and Irish navvies and were "made tranquil" only when the Irish were dismissed or "sent to other parts of the line." Major General Sir William Warre, whose military district included Liverpool, thought the source of the disturbances was the number of Irish pouring through the western ports: in Liverpool alone, he estimated the Irish arriving (by pure military guesswork) between January of 1849 and the previous November at 11,253, and the number of those "sent back" for fear of infection at about 155 a week. He recommended a more stringent policy of exclusion both at the docks and in the worksites as a means of controlling the riots.[51]

Glasgow, Manchester, and London, which contained respectively the largest proportions of Irish-born residents after Liverpool, experienced most of the same crises after the cholera epidemic, heightening a national frenzy of introspection coinciding with the great Poor Law Inquiry then in session.[52] Among the many results of this often sensationalized scrutiny of poverty was the emergence of a new stereotype of the Irish suited to the time, now all but devoid of the humorous childlike foibles of the old "Paddy." Debasing the heroic founding myth of Gaelic Ireland, in which the sons of Miled, venerated for their poetry and reason, displaced the demigod Danaans, Thomas Carlyle drew this venomous image of the Irish in England:

> The wild Milesian features, looking false ingenuity, restlessness, unreason, misery, and mockery, salute you on highways and byways. He is the sorest evil this country has to strive with. In his rags and laughing savagery, he is there to undertake all work that can be done by mere strength of hand and back—for wages that will purchase him potatoes. He needs only salt for condiment, he lodges to his mind in any pig-hutch or dog-hutch, roosts in outhouses, and wears a suit of tatters. . . . There abides he, in his squalor and unreason, in his falsity and drunken violence, as the ready-made nucleus of degradation and disorder.[53]

Friedrich Engels thought Carlyle's caricature slightly "one-sided" but otherwise "perfectly right": "The worst dwellings are good enough for them; their clothing causes them little trouble, so long as it holds together by a single thread; shoes they know not; their food consists of potatoes and potatoes only; whatever they earn beyond these needs they spend upon drink. What does such a race want with high wages?"

The Irish stereotype took on a new moral dimension transposed from the physical traits and living conditions in which the immigrants were most often found.

> The worst quarters of all the large towns are inhabited by Irishmen. Whenever a district is distinguished for especial filth and especial ruinousness, the explorer may safely count upon meeting chiefly those Celtic faces which one

recognises at the first glance as different from the Saxon physiognomy of the native, and the singing, aspirate brogue which the true Irishman never loses.[54]

The poverty of the English working class, in Engels's eyes, was the result of injustice and exploitation, but the Irish carried their poverty with them, living content "in measureless filth and stench . . . penned in as if with a purpose, this race must really have reached the lowest stage of humanity." The Irishman's squalor was also thought to be as contagious as the diseases he carried:

> Filth and drunkenness, too, they have brought with them. The lack of cleanliness, which is not so injurious in the country, where population is scattered, and which is the Irishman's second nature, becomes terrifying and gravely dangerous through its concentration here in the great cities. The Milesian deposits all garbage and filth before his house door here, as he was accustomed to do at home, and so accumulates the pools and dirt-heaps which disfigure the working-people's quarters and poison the air. He builds a pig-sty against the house wall as he did at home, and if he is prevented from doing this, he lets the pig sleep in the room with himself. . . . The Irishman loves his pig as the Arab loves his horse, with the difference that he sells it when it is fat enough to kill. Otherwise, he eats and sleeps with it, his children play with it, ride upon it, roll in the dirt with it, as ony one may see a thousand times repeated in all the great towns of England.[55]

Through the spreading fog of bigotry and the fear of infection, some of the traits of "character" commonly associated with the newcomers are discernible. As if drawing insight into the newcomers' minds by reading their bodies, a kind of popular associational "anthropology" began to emerge. The public health autorities learned empirically that cholera was somehow related to the density of habitation and to "filth"—a catchall word for the sight and smell of unwashed bodies, congested dwellings and their "effluvia," the most common euphemism for all the forms of waste and detritus that both flowed and stank. They found a preponderance of both in the Irish quarters of Liverpool and Manchester and attributed the cause of infection to the supposed indifference of the Irish to personal cleanliness and the "comfort" they enjoyed living in dirt. Dysentery and diarrhea, two of the most common causes of death in the Little Irelands, acquired the same associations, as if the sickening miasma they produced were the natural and preferred atmosphere of the Irish peasant.

Another lasting feature in this racial imagery was the Irishman's addiction to drink. In an age of prodigious alcoholic consumption, Liverpool's fondness for drink was infamous. Its ardent temperance preachers, railing at dock gates and street corners, were helpless against the more than twenty-six hundred *licensed* houses thriving in the town as early as 1831, beside the unknowable number of urban shebeens.[56] Yet Irish drinking required special diagnosis: the Irish had been weaned by their mothers on porter and spirits; it was used as their pharmacopoeia for all ailments, from teething to rheumatism; it was also confirmation of a weak will and intemperate nature. Drink was the Irishman's "firewater," affecting his mind in ways distinct and more dangerous than all others. As one authority of the town propounded, "Spirits produce a greater effect on Irish than others. It makes them in fact insane when under its influence and they are then so violent as to be regardless of the consequences of their acts."[57]

The typhus epidemic in Liverpool in 1847 added several new twists to this reading of body and mind. The police posted by Rushton to meet the incoming Irish ferries were confident they could distinguish the status and intentions of the travelers by their possessions: the one-third of those descending the gangplanks with "nothing but the rags on their backs" were those most likely not only to remain in the town on parochial relief but also to present the main threat of infection.

A "suit of tatters, the getting on or off of which is said to be a difficult operation, transacted only on festivals and the high tides of the calendar," was Carlyle's caricature of Irish rags. Engels also thought that Irish rags were sui generis and easily distinguished from those of the English pauper. The honest workingman's clothing was usually ragged, he thought, from the necessity of pawning the best pieces.

> But among very large numbers, especially among the Irish, the prevailing clothing consists of perfect rags often beyond all mending, or so patched that the original colour can no longer be detected. Yet the English and Anglo-Irish go on patching, and have carried this art to a remarkable pitch. . . . But the true, transplanted Irish hardly ever patch except in the extremist necessity, when the garment would otherwise fall apart. Ordinarily the rags of the shirt protrude through the rents in the coat and trousers.[58]

That such distinctions of fashion were visible enough to distinguish "the true, transplanted Irish" from their English fellow paupers is not at all unlikely. If not due merely to the long period of weathering and rough treatment that the emigrants' garments had undergone, the very different social meaning of "rags" in the two cultures might have accounted for what such observers saw as carelessness among the Irish in regard to appearance. By the same token, the perverse application by Rushton's police of "rags make the man" corresponded to the prevailing meanings given to clothing in England: those disembarking with baggage, that is a reserve of clothing, were assumed to be moving on presumably with tickets or cash in their pockets, having given thought to the future. What the Crown had felt to be the bare necessities, special children's clothes like the girls' smocks and boys' Glengary caps, the women's bonnets, men's waistcoats and shoes for all, were precisely those marks that distinguished the true emigrant from the incoming pauper at the Liverpool docks. Those without such outward signs of civility, in "perfect rags" and unburdened, were immediately identified as a threat to the health and order of the city or at best a potential burden on the poor rates.[59]

If rags were a window on the wearer's character, a particular symbol of depravity was contained in the word "nakedness," or "half-nakedness" as it was most commonly applied to the Irish. It was taken to mean almost any exposure of the skin beyond the head and hands and held Puritan connotations of savagery, shamelessness, and affinity with beasts. When applied to the empire's darker-skinned, tropical, and semitropical subjects, nakedness still suggested bestiality but it also contained some older allusions of innocence or endearing simplicity. Melville saw an expression of these meanings on the Liverpool docks where Sunday crowds of well-dressed people came as spectators to see the "Lascar"[60] sailors of, say, the Indiaman *Irrawaddy* of Bombay, in the port to unload a cargo of cotton. Clad like Gunga Din, "with nothin much before and rather less than 'alf o' that be'ind," the Lascar seamen "hopped about aloft . . . showing much dexterity and seamanship." People climbed the shrouds of nearby vessels to enjoy the display while "old women with umbrellas . . . stood on the quay staring at the Lascars, even when they desired to be private." These inquisitive old ladies seemed to regard the strange sailors as a species of wild animal, "whom they might gaze at with as much impunity, as at leopards in the Zoological Gardens."[61]

The images of white Irish nakedness were akin to those held by the dockside spectators; the Irish too were often seen as being so alien to the native onlooker that the simplest forms of communication were sometimes impossible and the most basic social courtesies suspended. But, perhaps because of the uncomfortable affinity their color conveyed, a different gauge and a particular loathing was attached to Irish nakedness. It was seen neither as innocent nor exotic. While a dark-skinned nursing mother might conjure a scene of heathen but "natural" beauty, the exposed white breast of an Irish mother in the streets of the city was read as proof of depravity. The hordes of begging waifs who haunted the town were more often seen as abandonées than as orphans of disease.

Melville's woman of Launcelot's-Hey, a dark alley lined with "dingy, prison-like cotton warehouses," dying for days with her two daughters in a vault fifteen feet below the street, "her blue arms folded to her livid bosom two shrunken things like children," her "soul-sickening wail" known to all around, epitomizes the dehumanization of the city at this time. When the young American appealed to those nearest by, an old-woman rubbish picker said she had "not time to attend to beggars and their brats." Asking another where to take the woman, he was told, "to the church-yard." When reminded that they were alive and not dead, the old woman replied, "Then she'll never die. . . . She's been down there these three days, with nothing to eat; that I know myself." Finally approaching a policeman to help them, he was told, "There, now, Jack, go on board your ship . . . and leave these matters to the town."[62]

Liverpool's casual tolerance of suffering had had generations of breeding in the slave trade and the trekking of destitute agrarians from the poorest parts of the kingdom. A majority of its population in 1848 was constituted by these earlier immigrants: Scots, Ulstermen, Welsh, and Irish who had come as manual laborers and occupied the congested slum wards into which the new migrants were now crowding. In no other place were these factious Celtic elements brought together in such numbers and intimacy. Contact between them was accompanied by a level of violence higher than anywhere else.

As the hub of Celtic migration, Liverpool was also the arena in which long-cultivated sectarian hatreds, kept stoked by the Orange Lodges, went almost unrestrained by law or civility. Of all places the emigrants would encounter, the streets of Liverpool seethed most furiously with these archaic passions, and in no other place were the emigrés of the townlands more defenseless. The Orangemen of Liverpool added a rage to the face that greeted the newcomers that stifled all sympathy, much as many emigrants were later to show toward the American blacks of New York or Philadelphia. Much of the most egregious imaging of the "Paddy" as the unreasoning and idolatrous brute emanated from this quarter, adding an ancient venom to local prejudices and further deadening the humane instincts of the town.

The Liverpool Mirror

What did this first landscape outside Ireland mean to the townland emigrants? How did they translate what they saw there—the brutal survivalism, the efficacy of force, the abuse of power, and the casual dishonesty—into their experience? How indelible was this first revelation of the "New World"? Did this initial training in powerlessness reinforce the fatalism they brought from home? How burdensome was their longing for home? Were some more vulnerable to the despair that filled the Liverpool streets and others seduced by its lawlessness? Did the open loathing of its people and the tyrannies of the emigration system become a lasting part of their social conscience and identity? Answers to such questions are difficult to find in the sparse testimony they left of Liverpool in these years. But there are many indications that at least some of them began to perceive themselves within hours of their landing as Liverpool saw them, as though beholding their own image for the first time.

Not many of the emigrants passing through Liverpool are likely to have read the gross depictions of themselves that filled the newspapers, much less the testimony of the health officers or select committee witnesses. But the milieu of revulsion focusing on them from the moment they landed could hardly have been missed, probably not even by the children. Hostility on unequal terms they had long known in Strokestown—if it could not be defeated it had at least been defied or evaded. Even that vain assertion of humanity was impossible in Liverpool, where the culture equated them with beasts and the workings of "the great emigration depot" held them in close captivity. James Connor's final cry of surrender—"Their will be done and not mine"—was merely a submission to the force of the law and the landlord, which he still saw as the will of men, distant and hostile, but still human. The coup de grace of the potato blight was also seen in terms of familiar if not knowable causes, a scourge of God or fate assisted by human greed. But what awaited him and the others once in the orbit of Liverpool could neither be resisted, appealed to, nor attributed to a human cause within their understanding.

The passage through the Liverpool funnel was also the most common experience of the famine emigrants. One might even say it was their first truly "national" experience. The sight of the exodus was concentrated and magnified in the few square miles of the waterfront where, in a sense, all of Ireland's townlands met for the first time and witnessed the commonality of their fate. Whatever the circumstances of their leaving home or their ultimate destination, the vast majority of emigrants were unmistakably linked by characteristics that identified them as one in the eyes of Liverpool if not yet in their own. Rags, disease, and the ravages of hunger were among the signs attached to them, as we have seen. For Rushton's police, baggage was the telling sign. The health officers looked for symptoms of "Irish fever." Adult males of the most ordinary appearance in Ballykilcline were the ape-like "Milesian" brutes of Victorian caricature. Above all, the symbols of Irishness in Liverpool were the signs of a poverty so extreme that, when found in the heart of the empire, it was seen as a fall from civilization and likened to savagery.

Most emigrants were well accustomed to material poverty at home. It was because they carried it lightly that Engels thought they took "comfort" in their poverty. They often described themselves in their petitions as "poor" or "in great want," without apparent shame, to invoke their claim on the sympathy and charity of the landlord or the law. In the townland, the same claim was made against the generosity of even the poorest households and carried no stigma. Certainly, Irish begging was no new sight to the emigrants. Some of the poorer laborers and their families may well have been forced to it at times in the past, in bad summers when there was little work and no income. But it would be wrong to describe such seasonal begging in Ireland as a last extremity in all cases, a last alternative to starvation. Even after the establishment of the Irish Poor Law, casual begging filled much of the void that the old system of outdoor relief had done in England. In contrast to England, where the vagrancy laws had increasingly criminalized it, begging was casually tolerated by the Irish authorities and the public as a fixture of traditional culture. Indeed, the "jolly beggarman" was held in the folklore in a class with the "ragged scholar," the hedge master or the traveling musician, a rascal, wily or ridiculous but following a craft that enriched the daily rounds of life. In Ballykilcline in lean years, no more than twelve of the larger tenants had enough resources to survive the months till the next crop appeared if local wages were unavailable. The remaining eighty families, more than three-fourths of the townland, who depended on wages to maintain themselves through the dearth, were subject to extreme want in the bad years. These were the begging seasons for the poorest families, when their women and children might wander as far as the male harvesters, living off the generosity of the countryside.

In Liverpool poverty was viewed quite differently by the public and the law, making it an almost unrecognizable experience for the Irish pauper. Pennilessness in the townland, interrupted now and then by small windfalls of cash or credit, was taken for granted as the natural condition of life rather than a punishment brought on oneself by some moral failing. Since nearly all endured it to varying degrees, their poverty was neither a cause for shame nor a stigma attached to class or birth. More important still, all knew that in the eyes of outsiders they were all poor. Indeed, poverty as much as religion, language, or nationality seems to have been at the core of the townland's identity, governing not only its dealings with the outside but many of the relations among the tenants themselves. In this milieu, it was easier for a poor man to earn the respect and trust of his neighbors than it was for a prosperous farmer, who lived further apart from these ties as his property grew. An acceptance of their all-but-uniform poverty was also a tacit axiom of their moral economy in matters of debts and owing and in the high virtue attached to charity and personal generosity. Similar assumptions account for the presence in half their households of widows, orphans, handicapped, and other dependent individuals who could not survive by themselves and therefore had private moral claims on their benefactors.

In Liverpool, the poverty of the emigrants was visible in their bodies, in their rags, and malnutrition. Toothlessness, matted hair, body smells, and other missing vanities also set them apart. But, according to some observers Irish poverty could be distinguished from that of other paupers as something more than just a lack of cash, something as evident in their gait and demeanor as in their obvious need. "Passive," "resigned," "stunned," and "mute" were descriptions most commonly given to distinguish Irish emigrants along the docks. The authorities, especially the unenviable health and parish relieving officers, were repeatedly frustrated by the tendency of sick or starving emigrants to hide themselves from view in the cellars and tenements, as though fearing to approach even those who meant to help them. There was some reason to remain unseen, since Irish-born paupers could be brought before the magistrates and immediately returned to Ireland under the Poor Removal Acts. Short of that dreaded prospect, the sick could be removed from the family for quarantine or "treatment" in the fever sheds. Inadvertently, the law also gave the lodging-house keepers and their intermediaries a new means of threatening their guests with exposure and repatriation. The laws and regulations aimed at emigrants, as well as the discretionary powers of health and parish officers, tended to reinforce the ingrained habits of isolation and secrecy with which the emigrants had long used to cloak themselves from scrutiny. In the townland, all deputies of the law or authorities were to be shunned—indeed, many succeeded in evading them and some lived entirely out of their sight for years. But anonymity was no longer possible, since in Liverpool the law or the threat of it was everywhere in the person not only of every official but of almost any native citizen.[63]

It is unlikely that most of the newly arriving emigrants understood the variety of proceedings of the law that could derail their hopes and plans: discovery by the relieving officers might be followed in a few hours by a summary hearing before the magistrates and forced removal along the same route they had just survived, as deck passengers back across the Irish Sea. Medical or ship's officers could reject one or all in a family without appeal moments before they boarded. Health officers could order immediate quarantine in the fever sheds or the hulks moored in the river to isolate the infected. Doctors or beadles could remove "lunatics" from the poorhouses to the crowded asylum at Rainhill, where the wards were filled with hundreds who were diagnosed as suffering from "mental paralysis."[64]

A large minority were also handicapped by language or illiteracy. The Irish accents of both native- and Irish-born could be heard throughout the city, distinguishing their bearers' place of origin or even their religious identity to each other. But speaking Irish above a whisper outside the Irish wards instantly marked the emigrant to both the authorities and the swarms of predators. More than half of the native population of the city was also illiterate, but new arrivals from Ireland were at greater risk of exploitation from this cause in the unfamiliar workings of the emigration system, in which reliable information and directions about ship movements, delays, and regulations were essential. At least in these circumstances, the literate children were more likely to be a help than a burden to many emigrant families; indeed, the value and status of the young adults had almost certainly risen as the distance from the townland lengthened and the powers of the elders diminished.

Another large but unknown number arrived in Liverpool with their tickets or their fares only and were completely unprepared for even slight setbacks. The routine delays in sailing dates were especially dangerous for these and accounted for the thousands caught in the gauntlet of official and criminal coercion from which few emerged unscathed and many totally penniless. Many were also vulnerable to the devious practices of the freelance banditti who infested the lower levels of the emigrant trade, being as unused to complicated transactions as they were to schedules or lodging houses. These easily fell afoul of money changers, offering to "dollar" their English coin into American currency of less or no value, or of lodging-house keepers who might keep a family "on the cuff" for food and shelter and strip them bare when payment came due, by force if threats failed. Many of the petty frauds practiced on them were common bullying: baggage would be stolen by the runners and "commissions" demanded for its return; half-fare children's tickets were sold to illiterate adults who would then be turned away at the gangplank. Worthless out-of-date tickets were casually altered and bought by the gullible or desperate. Others were refused passage because they lacked the additional one dollar "head money" required at American ports. In their rush to fill the steerages, brokers were known to book emigrants for New York on vessels bound for Baltimore or Boston, or even New Orleans, assuring them that these places were only hours apart. The fleecing of "greenhorns" was widely practiced in all big cities in Europe and America, often as in Liverpool by those who had survived a similar experience themselves not long before. It soon became a kind of initiation rite for migrant peasants in the new moral niceties of city life. But Liverpool's well-earned fame for this skullduggery could probably not have been achieved but for the overabundance of fresh and easy victims, a role the townland emigrant of 1848 was suited for as if by order.[65]

The exposure of their weakness had begun at the moment they were assembled in the Strokestown square and proceeded daily on the road to Liverpool as they were marched and herded under the eyes of strangers, all now reduced to homeless paupers whatever their former standing had been. Patriarchs and independent widows who had ruled adult families on the land became burdensome dependents when severed from their holdings, and together with infants and children under five suffered the highest rates of attrition en route. James Connor's father, a patriarch of one of the largest and oldest townland families, was rejected as "too old and debilitated" by a reputable captain who merely wished to reduce the risk of mortality aboard his ship during the crossing. Such descriptions tell us little about the old man's actual condition, since the same description was sometimes used of men or women of less than forty years of age as reason for rejection.[66] Hundreds of similarly described emigrants were "repatriated" weekly from Liverpool alone, some of them no doubt creating bits of the scenes of "want and woe" described by Melville. Of the nearly 300,000 who arrived in 1847, some 15,000 were removed to Ireland under the new Poor Law Removal Act.[67]

The moment of the elder Connor's rejection can only be imagined, but its bare essentials suggest something of the absolute dominion that the emigration system of Liverpool, in the persons of its numerous deputies, had achieved over Ireland. As the head of the large Connor family of Ballykilcline, the seventy-year-old Connor Og may well have been the anonymous "rightful heir" in whose name the tenants' claim to the lands was brought. He left with the first of the two spring batches of 1848, scheduled to board the *Channing* for New York, together with his wife, Catherine, and two brothers, each with his own large family of three generations. Bribes were sometimes offered to ships' officers by the shipping agents (like Harnden & Co.) to accept such aged or infirm passengers in order to salvage the agent's commissions, but the authority of such lofty figures as ship captains and medical officers was beyond appeal to any ordinary emigrant. Ticketed families could either board or remain with those rejected at the dock, perhaps to sink among the horde of beggars they had all seen haunting the waterfront. They could resort to the deadly poorhouses to join thousands of their unlucky countrymen or be returned to Dublin at public expense, after another bracing passage on deck. Many others were justifiably barred from boarding as risks of contagion. These were bound for the fever sheds, the overflowing temporary shelters built to house and quarantine fever victims. In these, said the Reverend John Johns, a missionary who died of typhus fever soon after, the sufferers "seemed resigned beyond natural resignation." With or without infection, thousands of others crept into Liverpool's notorious cellars and lodging houses. In one count Liverpool contained seventy-seven hundred of these small enterprises, into which their runners and keepers had swept twenty-seven thousand people, in which as many as forty Irish, some healthy, some in fever and dying, and others already dead, were found in muddy unlit underground spaces of twelve by fifteen feet. Johns described them as "the causes and concealment of scenes incompatible with the well-being of society."[68]

All of these fates were suffered by thousands of rejected or impoverished emigrants and their families each year. Not knowing what might await the old couple should they be stranded in Liverpool, the Connors no doubt enacted one of the many bitter scenes of separation at quayside. But because the Crown tenants were still under the protection of the commissioners, they were at least saved from abandonment in Liverpool. The old man was left behind at the dock but was joined by his wife and both were booked to sail later in the *Jane Glasson* and were maintained at Crown expense in the meantime. Such agonized scenes of separation were apparently common enough that they aroused little sympathy or even notice among the functionaries of the emigration system.[69]

10

The Crossing: "Just Over a River"

They were the most simple people I had ever seen. They seemed to have no adequate idea of distances; and to them, America must have seemed as a place just over a river. Every morning some of them came on deck, to see how much nearer we were: and one old man would stand for hours together, looking straight off from the bows, as if he expected to see New York city every minute, when, perhaps, we were yet two thousand miles distant, and steering, moreover, against a head wind.[1]

Herman Melville, Redburn

Out of Liverpool after three days of fog and rain, "Land ho!" was cried aboard the *Highlander*. Melville described the emigrants as grieved and crestfallen when they were informed that the land to the north was their former home, now in sight again after more than a week of journeying by land and sea. Rumors spread in the steerage that the ship was bound for the East Indies, whatever that may have conveyed to the emigrants. A mischievous seaman told the emigrants they were to be taken to "Barbary" and sold as slaves. There was a fiddler and a wandering, orphan Italian boy with a melodeon aboard this ship, and some merriment on deck in the early days of the voyage. But many remained in the steerage the whole of the way, groaning with the "irresistible wrestler" of seasickness from the first hour. As weeks passed, the poorer passengers began to wander in the ship looking for food, not having laid in enough provisions. "An almost famine" followed. Emigrants waylaid the steward on his way from the cookhouse to the cabin deck. They beset the sailors "like beggars in the streets." Wrangling and fighting broke out daily among them over the smallest bits of food or comfort. "Thus it is," wrote the young Melville, "that the very hardships to which such beings are subjected, instead of uniting them, only

217

tends, by imbittering their tempers, to set them against each other; and thus by themselves drive the strongest rivet in the chain, by which their social superiors hold them subject." In bad weather, with the hatches closed, the air in the steerage soon became "pestilential," already the idiom for the special reek of the emigrant steerage. The first cases of fever appeared on the sixth day and burials at sea commenced shortly after. There were two births aboard: "The first cry of these infants, was almost simultaneous with the splash of its father's body in the sea."[2]

Although it appears in a novel and is more artful than all others, Melville's account of the voyage is the closest thing to a captain's log of the experience, compassionate but clear-eyed and ringing with truth. His depiction of the voyage of the *Highlander*, as his depiction of the Liverpool docks, corresponds quite closely to most other firsthand accounts; it is far from the worst of the "coffin-ship" voyages but more melancholy than the majority of lucky crossings over summer seas in well-manned, well-founded ships. The luckier passengers aboard fast and taut "clippers" could take away treasured memories of concertinas and dancing under the stars. But most of such voyages were of a later time, after most of the aged and lumbering hulks of the famine ships had themselves gone to the bottom.[3]

The miserable epic of the Atlantic crossing in these years has been told so often and well that it hardly seems necessary to recount its dreadful details.[4] Flanked by the scenes of Skibbereen and Grosse Isle at either end of the voyage, the "coffin ship" stands as the center panel of the famine triptych, depicting bondage and fever in the steerage, wailing children and mothers' pleas from the darkness below decks, heartless captains and brutal crews, shipwreck, pestilence, and burial at sea. In its own smaller scale, the memory of the emigrant steerage has long been held, like the slaves' "middle passage" and the trains of the Holocaust, as an icon of Ireland's oppression. Having in fact been the emigrants' one universal experience, it is among the most evocative and long-nurtured images of "the myth of exile" and of the emigrants' severance from the past. And occupying that place in the emigrants' memory, the "coffin ship" has also carried much of the burden of both truth and distortion in the way their descendants memorialize this part of their history.

While the mortality of the emigrant voyage cannot be compared in magnitude to the colossal atrocities of slavery and genocide, the incidence during the famine emigration of death and suffering at sea and shortly after landing was appalling enough to stun its witnesses, revolt humanitarians, and enrage even the most moderate Irish nationalists on both sides of the Atlantic. The level of attrition aboard emigrant ships from English and Irish ports had been steadily rising in the preceding three decades, enough to prompt both the United States Congress and eventually the Parliament in London to impose regulatory codes to protect the health and lives of passengers. Widely publicized disasters due to shipwreck, stormy voyages, drunken captains and crews, and poorly provisioned, overcrowded, and unseaworthy vessels did much to attract this attention to the emigrant trade. More important, the public and the authorities in the North American ports were alarmed by the prevalence of infectious disease among the immigrants, especially after the arrival of cholera on their side of the Atlantic in 1832. As in Liverpool, the association of disease with the immigrants had thus been primed before the tragic appearance of typhus among the famine emigrants. The calamity of the Grosse Isle quarantine in 1847 clearly demonstrated that such fears were more warranted in America than in Liverpool, after the emigrants had spent weeks in steerage.[5]

Emigrant mortality rose sharply in the famine years, both on British and the more tightly regulated and generally better fitted and manned American carriers for a number of reasons. The suddenly increased volume of emigrants was too great a temptation for emigrant agents and brokers to resist extending the already lengthening sailing season into the more dangerous winter months, producing longer and more turbulent crossings and leaving weakened passengers to face North American winters harsher than any they had known, often with the scantiest protection from the cold. The most lethal year for emigrants was 1847, as it was for those who remained at home. Even in that sorrowful year, casualties varied greatly from one emigrant ship to another. The majority of ships arriving in Canada and the United States made harbor with their passengers intact and in reasonably sound health; others, like those carrying the emigrants of the Mahon and Palmerston estates, buried a third or more of their steerages at sea and disgorged staggering near-corpses at the dock, many of them only to die in the quarantines and hospitals ashore.[6]

The news from Quebec that had stirred the Bishop of Elphin to denounce Major Mahon from the altar, and perhaps also put the thought of murder in the minds of his tenants, was far from unusual in that year. The *Agnes* arrived with 427 passengers but disembarked only 150 after a quarantine of fifteen days. Almost 45 percent of the steerage passengers of the *Ceylon*, out of Liverpool bound for New York, were buried at sea before reaching the quarantine at Staten Island. Dr. John Griscom, a counterpart of Liverpool's Harvey as a pioneer of public health, entered the *Ceylon*'s steerage to find scores of "emaciated half-nude figures," suffering from typhus, "some . . . just rising from their berths for the first time since leaving Liverpool having been suffered to lie there all the voyage wallowing in their own filth." The *Loosthank* lost 33 percent before entering quarantine. Arriving at the end of October, Lord Palmerston's tenants aboard the *Lord Ashburton* were missing more than a hundred of those who had sailed from his Sligo estates. The survivors were described as nearly naked and had to be clothed before decency would allow them to land, including one woman who was entirely naked and was wrapped in a sheet before going ashore. Two other ships chartered by Palmerston, the *Richard Watson* and the *Aeolus*, unloaded their emigrants "almost in a state of nudity." in a New Brunswick November, with the St. Lawrence iced over.[7]

Though many of the worst "coffin ships" had sailed from Irish ports, the Liverpool influence was felt in these too, having reduced its competitors to underpricing fares and reducing standards at the expense of passengers' comfort and safety. That the worst horrors of the famine emigration were enacted in the Canadian quarantines also resulted in part from conditions prevailing in Ireland. Some landlords chose Irish ports and the Canadian route because these were less costly; the choices had resulted in the scandals of the Mahon and Palmerston clearances that sent off their tenants directly from the poorest townlands of the West. However ragged and reduced many of the outbound emigrants were on the docks of Cork or Sligo, they were still identifiable as remnants of the native peasantry, a familiar if not welcome sight in port towns. But even those not yet wasted by hunger when they boarded scandalized observers when they landed in Quebec or New York. Here, too, the words "ragged" and "naked" appear in most descriptions, sometimes apparently referring to extreme cases but probably as often to those clothed merely as they had always been, shoeless and bareheaded. To explain the appearance of their former tenants on landing, some, including Palmerston, retorted to their North American critics that their tenants were "the poorer class of farmer, very little better than paupers" and their dress of "the inferior kind of clothing to which the inhabitants of the west of Ireland are accustomed."[8]

Once aboard ship, no emigrant had much control of his or her fate. That now lay in the hands of the ship, its crew, and the sea. Death and suffering in steerage was more indiscriminate than the triage at home, making little or no distinction between farmer and laborer as it had in the townlands. The forensic causes of death differed, more succumbing to seasickness, dysentery, and fevers and fewer to pure hunger in the emigrant ship than in the townlands. Against the scourge of microbes, no foresight or preparation in the way of food, clothing, or even cleanliness offered much protection. Nearly uniform ship disciplines and the economies of space required similar uniformities in the stowage and confinement of passengers in the emigrant ships to those of the slave trade. The families of farmers and cottiers died inches apart, within each other's intimate reeks and pleadings below decks. The once-important distinctions of character, family, and deference among them were invisible to the ships' crews or health inspectors, whose job it was to order, inspect, and count them. The steerage was a form of captivity, of absolute powerlessness, that even the poorest had not known before and that reduced many who once thought themselves strong to the level of their children. If seen as a separate, temporary nation afloat, it might be said that the inmates of the emigrant steerages were suffering a second famine, one that was quite blind to the name or history of its victims. The anonymity they had nurtured in the townlands as their protection was made nearly absolute in the darkness below decks, replaced by the universal face of famine, stricken, mute, and alien to onlookers. As in the pitiful *Londonderry*, those packed below decks became a moaning throng, distinguishable only by their strength or weakness. "Some of these poor people must have been so used to the most abasing calamities," Melville thought on entering the steerage of the *Highlander*, "that the atmosphere of a lazar-house almost seemed their natural air."[9]

Spillage and Evasion

The fates of the Ballykilcline emigrants up to their landing in New York, as far as it can be determined, show no pattern of attrition except among the elderly and the very young. This was the common result of famine everywhere, and the concentration of infection and debility in the steerages tended to raise the mortality of these vulnerable age groups still further. Even this is uncertain in regard to the Ballykilcline emigrants, since their individual traces become still more elusive than in the townland once they were put in motion. All but one of the five ships carrying the former tenants appear to have enjoyed uneventful passages with fair winds and few casualties. The first batch sailed on the *Roscius*, leaving Liverpool on 8 September 1847, carrying 252 passengers in all. Sailings at that time of year were often long and hazardous, but the *Roscius* arrived at the Staten Island quarantine on 22 October after a crossing of forty-four days, apparently with all its passengers intact, or at least alive. Of the five ships, the *Roscius* was to have carried the second-largest number of the Crown tenants, reported in the Quit Rent Office account as 111 "souls." As we have seen, some tenants took their allowances in those hungry months and disappeared from the estate record; others were counted by the agents as arriving in Dublin or Liverpool, but apparently never boarded their assigned ship. Comparing the number said to have vacated their holdings with those disembarking in New York, the *Roscius* group showed immediately a pattern that would repeat itself to a greater or lesser degree in each of the subsequent batches. Although she reported no losses at sea, the *Roscius* disembarked only forty-three of the Crown emigrants in New York, leaving some sixty-eight men, women, and children missing somewhere between Strokestown and Staten Island.[10]

The second-largest batch from Ballykilcline was assigned to the *Channing*, leaving Liverpool on the following sixth of March and arriving in New York on 18 April 1848. A batch of 113 had originally been assigned to the *Channing*, and all were reported to have arrived in Liverpool. A boy, John Farrell, "was taken charge of" by his grandmother, who resided in Liverpool, and the captain of the *Channing* refused to board Francis Stewart (sixty-one) because of his "aged appearance." Counting as they boarded, Lieutenant Hodder (the successor to Lieutenant Low as government emigrant agent in Liverpool) reported that 110 of the Crown tenants (just one missing) were aboard the ship, bound for New York.

The case of the *Channing*, which carried those who made a parting complaint about Cox and the ship's provisions, offers a more mysterious instance of "spillage" than the *Roscius*. The Crown paid the Messrs. Scott, the ship agents, for the fares of seventy-seven adults and thirty-three children to sail in the *Channing*; all were reported aboard by Hodder as the ship left the Mersey dock, but (allowing for some mispelling of names in the manifest) at most only seventy-two passengers bearing the names of Ballykilcline landed at New York. Yet the *Channing*'s captain reported only one "died-at-sea," the four-year-old son of John and Sarah Mullera of Ballykilcline, leaving some thirty-six of the emigrants missing!

Smaller but remarkably similar discrepancies also appear in the manifests of the ships that left the following spring, amounting to 104 additional tenants gone missing between the townland and the New World.[11] The last two batches to sail, in the *Metoka* and the *Progress* at the height of the spring sailing season of 1848, arrived apparently without incident. The old man, Francis Stewart, was first returned to Dublin and there "forwarded" aboard the *Laconic*. The Messrs. Scott reported that he arrived safely in New York but "died in hospital" after landing.[12]

It was the *Jane Glasson*, departing latest in the sailing season (13 October 1847) in the worst year of emigrant losses, that appears to have had the closest experience to Melville's *Highlander*, and leaves still further questions about "spillage" in the Crown's emigration scheme. Like all the others, 119 of them took the allowances on condition to vacate their holdings on the assigned dates, in their case, thirty-five days after the *Roscius* emigrants. But of the 261 passengers declared by the captain of the *Jane Glasson* when it arrived in New York in late November, supposed to include the largest batch of Crown tenants, no more than five bore the names of tenants of Ballykilcline! There is no doubt that the *Jane Glasson* had a harder crossing than the rest: twelve in its steerage were reported as "died-at-sea," including the seventy-year-old John Connor, a Mrs. "Kinclla [*sic*]," a nineteen-year-old dressmaker and her infant daughter who were traveling alone, a thirty-three-year-old weaver, and eight others of unknown age or occupation, including several male and female infants. This was not an inordinate attrition for ships sailing this late in the season. But it was not unknown for British emigrant ships to overload their steerage and remove passengers from the lists as they died. It is also known that Connor's wife, Catherine, sailed with him and was reported by the Scotts' agents in New York to have "died on the voyage," but she does not appear on the manifest, suggesting that something of the kind may have been done on the *Jane Glasson*.[13] But no tampering with passenger lists aboard ship can account for the hundred or more missing Crown emigrants. Instead, such a large discrepancy suggests that either the surviving passenger list for the *Jane Glasson* is unusually incomplete or that many of the missing never boarded her.

While it is not possible to be exact in summarizing the "untenanting" of Ballykilcline, some of its results may be seen clearly enough through the glaring contradictions between the reported departures and the record of arrivals in New York. The last count of the legal tenantry of the estate in 1846 recorded 396 men, women, and children among eighty-two households. By September of 1847, only 326 of these had received the travel allowances and the dole of clothing, and were approved for the Atlantic fares, presumably reflecting the mortality to that point. Of these, just 224 were reported to have arrived and boarded ship in Liverpool, 110 by the government emigrant agent and the rest by the Messrs. Scott. At this point, 172 of those living on the lands in the previous year were now missing, neither known to have sailed nor among the few who remained as tenants of record on the estate.

There is an apparent rhythm in the choices taken by the tenants that influenced both their fate as emigrants and whether or not they ultimately left. The months of September and October saw the worst suffering from hunger and fever in the townland, a time when the 12s. allowances being offered to cover the provisions and journey to Dublin would have been most irresistible. Some of the larger tenant-farmers, including eight of the Defendants, chose to accept passage on the very first ship, the *Roscius,* and arrived before the approach of winter in New York. More than half of them, mostly of the poorest class, never boarded the ship, but those who did enjoyed a relatively quick passage and spent the winter and spring in New York rather than in the ravaged townland. Similarly, most of the remaining leaders and larger farmers waited till the following spring, some after offering various pleas and propositions to the Crown, and sailed in good weather with few losses aboard the *Channing.* A portion of them also absconded with the allowances, and some, like the Reynolds, even succeeded in reoccupying the lands and remain to this day. But the majority of those who left first or had the resources to survive till fair weather returned appear to have made calculated choices, informed decisions to improve their chances at sea or in the first months of their resettlement. Most of the intended emigrants for the *Jane Glasson* seem to represent another category of thinking, largely among the more marginal of the tenants, in which sickness, fatalism, and desperation overcame wisdom or the hope of remaining blinded them to its risks. Given the relatively high excess mortality of the Roscommon population in the remaining years of the famine, it is highly likely that the 172 missing lost more of their number who would have survived as immigrant New Yorkers.[14] At least to that degree, the determination to remain was made far more dangerous than any threat the bailiff may have posed in the past.

But not all of the missing should be seen as merely passive victims. Since they were no longer of interest to the Crown's agents once they had surrendered their holdings, neither the fate nor the thinking of the more than half who apparently remained in the country, dead or alive, can be determined. The Crown's method of achieving a "perfectly untenanted" property seemed far more rigorous from the Quit Rent Office than it did in the confusion of the countryside in the fall of 1847. It left a variety of deceptions open to any who wished to slip through the emigration scheme and even to enhance their chances of survival afterward. As in the past, one of their assets in dealings with the Crown was the elusiveness and confusion of their identities; even with their agent on the spot and Cox observing them at close quarters, the commissioners had all along received substantially varying reports both of the tenants' names and their numbers. The discordance among those reported to have left with each batch, those counted boarding their ships, and those actually landing in New York appears to reflect not only the continued inefficacy of the agency system but perhaps something of a final virtuoso performance of disguise on the part of those intent on remaining on their own terms.

The case of the *Jane Glasson* in particular suggests one way in which such a sleight-of-hand may have been accomplished and at the same time reveals the persistence, even the improvement, of the "throughother" devices that the townland had made use of in its earlier crises. The Crown paid for 119 fares, provisions, and allowances for this group and they were reported as arriving in Dublin on schedule. But when their names were taken from the ship's captain in New York, only 5 can be identified as former tenants. Of the possible explanations, a massive private fraud by Cox or the respectable Messrs. Scott or an unreported last-minute change of ships, the more plausible is that a large-scale shuffling of identities was orchestrated among the people of the townlands at some point en route, most likely in the immediate vicinity, by replacing tenants choosing to stay with others ineligible for the bounty but eager to emigrate. Only the age, condition, and numbers of the steerage passengers would be of any interest to the ship's officer at the gangplank. The Scotts' agents in Liverpool had never seen the emigrants before. But Cox was certain to notice any substitutions on such a scale on the road out. What, if any, role he played in this apparent ruse is lost in the gap between Strokestown and Dublin. No refunds on this scale were asked or made from the shipping agent. No changes in the ship assignments were reported in the surviving record. Given the variety of personal obstacles repeated in the last petitions and the evident eagerness of their neighbors for the bounty, it is easy enough to imagine a brisk, hidden business in trading places during the hungry months between eviction and the days of departure. Unless the driver had mended his ways, as he may have amid the horrors, his collusion in the deception would have been essential as the only person after Strokestown who both knew the identities in Ballykilcline and could confirm them to the agents of the Messrs. Scott.

A variety of motives might have been behind the deceptions. Deaths among the tenants awaiting departure and the quiet substitution of relatives and friends might account for a portion of the missing, especially among those assigned to the spring departures. Some individual adults missing from the manifests may have chosen to stay for their own reasons and either given or sold their "identities" to their neighbors, if not for cash then for the goodwill of their holdings, that is, the right to replace them as tenants-at-will on surrounding lands. We know from the petitions from local townlands that there were many in the area who were eager for the bounty. Others, as we have seen, wished to remain to care for disabled family members, in which case whole families might have been substituted. Together, such quiet arrangements may have accounted for a portion of the missing. In the absence of another explanation, the large numerical gap between those officially assisted and those who actually arrived seems unaccountable except by the presence of yet another conspiracy in Ballykilcline to remain where and what they were.

Over the succeeding decades, the material fortunes of those who remained may have differed greatly from those who emigrated. Certainly, their physical surroundings would differ greatly whether the emigrants went no farther than Manhattan Island or set off for the California gold fields. The townland was also transformed, if not entirely eradicated, reduced from a densely peopled, self-conscious community to a few isolated cabins more hidden than ever. Nearly all the features of their surroundings from this time on suggest a widening gap of memory and understanding between them. But the aging grandson of John Reynolds the Defendant retained in his mind the names and characters, even the size and location of family holdings, of old Ballykilcline, securely preserved in the retelling of the story for more than a century. Only if we could hear the recounting of the "Repulse of the Bailiffs" or the "Dousing of Cox" in the third-floor rear of Jacob's Ladder or Little Water street of the Five Points would we also know what part their past remained a part of the emigrants' future.[15]

Ballykilcline in America

With fares overseas from Europe to America declining rapidly in the decade before the famine, the outward flow was already beginning to sweep larger numbers from within the Irish townlands. Among these were the McDermotts of Ballykilcline and Guineys of Pobble O'Keefe, not "farmers" in the usual sense that word conveyed in prefamine Ireland (commercialized leaseholders of some social pretension) but townland tenants with more regular contact with the local market than most of their neighbors. In cases like theirs, it is not clear that their still-marginal intercourse with the market, sustained by a few acres of grains or mostly jointly held dairy pastures, had yet peeled them away from the static defensiveness of townland society, beyond the fact of their leaving it voluntarily before it became a matter of life and death. The Guineys' distinction consisted of their role as low-level deputies of the local land agent as straw bosses of road and quarry laborers, a position acquired merely by virtue of being literate among the illiterate. On the other hand, Hugh McDermott's main intercourse with the outside was not as a deputy of the land system but as one of its subverters. At first sight, this seems to put him among the defenders of the Gaelic "old regime" of the townland, defending notions of ancient rights and a moral economy that was doomed. But there is also as much reason to believe that he risked exposing his identity as a Defendant because he had the most to lose either by eviction or demands for his large arrears. If so, his timely emigration would also seem an act of cool calculation with thought more for the future than for the past.

At the risk of imparting meanings to his actions that he did not give to them himself, it makes some sense to see figures like McDermott as the most typical of the prefamine townland emigrants. As the first to emigrate voluntarily, leaving two brothers with large families in the townland and an unknown number of close relatives married among the adjoining communities, he was apparently prepared to be a pathfinder for any who might follow later. In another sense, his decision to leave might also be seen as at least partially political. Whatever hopes he may have held earlier about the prospects of the rent strike and the lawsuit, he left at the point that such measures were obviously doomed. Unfortunately, although he was clearly among the prime movers of the resistance, he wrote no pleas or petitions that might reveal his language or reasoning. It is not even certain that Hugh McDermott was either bilingual or an Irish speaker. But of all the Defendants, his actions seem to represent both the most personally assertive as well as the best-informed: aggressive when the forces the townland faced seemed least determined and cognizant of futility when the full power of the landlord was finally revealed. These appear to be the responses of a rational man weighing his own power against that of necessity as it loomed before him one step at a time. Such qualities would be a great advantage no matter where in the New World he finally settled.

One would have to have eavesdropped on the nighttime conspiracies in Padian's cabin to know how McDermott's reasoning vied with that of James Connor, Stewart, Reynolds, the violent Narys, or perhaps with that of Father Geraghty. Although one can sense his importance in Padian's cabin, nothing is known of the priest's part in the "Ballykilcline rebellion" nor about his future following the demise of his "congregation." All the other Defendants eventually emigrated with the exception of Reynolds, whose descendants still live in the obscurity of the townland's former "outfield," apparently among those who had been able to slip through the emigration scheme. The aging Stewart and his wife died in the last stages of the journey. James Connor we know to have been deeply resistant to leaving, but he arrived safely in America with his family in the spring of 1848.

Without tracing their fortunes for years after their arrival, it is impossible to know whether the remnant of the townland reconstituted itself in some way in the New World. It would be gratifying to know what became of the rump of Ballykilcline after their landing in New York, whether their bonds of family, kinship, and recent experience inclined them to resettle as a kind of remnant of the townland, reconstructing their defenses against a new "outside". Did their prolonged collective experience and their emigration as a community incline them more than others to recreate and exploit those bonds in the New World or to settle together or work in occupations that gave them greater strength than working with strangers? Did the mostly older leaders of the rent strike reassume positions of leadership in New York's wildly differing environment or did their failures reduce their standing and influence? Did the trials of the journey itself raise others, perhaps younger or less prosperous in the townland, to replace them as voices to be heeded in their new surroundings? Were the Defendants more likely than these to feel "exiled" or more attached to the past because of the respect and status they had lost? The large numbers of old ragged men to be found cadging drinks in the shebeens of the Sixth Ward, dying in the Bellevue wards, and confined in the lunatic asylum on Blackwell's Island, most headed for communal burial in potter's field, suggest a fate that awaited at least some of them in America.[16]

It would be just as interesting to know whether and how long they tended to mistrust the Anglo-Saxon authorities and to keep their business hidden; whether the more commercialized among them were more or less likely to be enterprising or more apt to seek places on the land; whether their years of collective action translated into political or labor activism; how their autonomous educational traditions and their experience with the National School adapted to the public schools of America; and much more. These are essentially questions about the persistence of their consciousness and behavior as a community. How informative would it be to have some of the answers to these questions? How much might they tell us about the Irish ingredients in the stew that formed the antebellum republic on the eve of its bloodiest trial? Would the experience of Ballykilcline in America offer us a better understanding of the part the masses of famine emigrants played in the making of antebellum New York, about their mixed allegiance to the Republic in the coming war over the union and slavery? With no experience of citizenship, did their idea of freedom consist simply of being left alone?

The male children under fourteen who traveled as "half-souls" almost certainly were among those tempted by the recruits' "bonus" of $300, an amount equivalent to nearly ten years' wages at the rate of 8d. a day that their fathers earned at home. Few had ever seen an African before leaving home, but many had traveled in the same dark confinement as the slaves in the Atlantic crossing. Why did so many feel no commonality with the former slave in what they had experienced? Were the volatile Narys among the mobs that terrorized the blacks of Manhattan in the summer of 1863? Any of these questions and many more might be asked about the famine emigrants in America, especially about those from the usually mute townlands, whose histories most often only begin as Americans as though born from the sea.

Given the circumstances of their leaving, it is not surprising that no "letters from America" survive from the Ballykilcline emigrants. One letter of 1864 from the widow Maria Murray, a former tenant of Major Mahon's then residing in Albany, tells us only that she had been assisted to leave by "the honourable Sir Ross Mahon," while some of her children remained in the Strokestown poorhouse.[17] But a few of the former tenants of Pobble O'Keefe and Boughill left traces of their thoughts after leaving. Enclosing a handsome remittance of four pounds, perhaps the savings of months of hard labor, Margaret McCarthy asked the crown agent, Michael Boyan, to forward her letter to her father in Pobble O'Keefe. She was clearly a loving daughter and urged her father to bring the family out: "I must only say that this is a good place and A good Country for if one place does not Suit A man he can go to Another and very easy please himself. . . ." She did warn them that there were "Dangers upon Dangers Attending Comeing here" and offered detailed advice about preparing for the voyage. Her mother was to bring "all her bed Close" and "Smoothing iron," as well as her "Kittle" and oven with "handles to them." Her father was also to bring whiskey with him for the ship's cook and "Some Sailors that you may think would do you any good to give them a Glass once in a time and it may be no harm." The first two or three days of the voyage would be the worst, she warned them. Her father was to "Take Courage and be Determined and bold" but to mind his temper and take care not to "speak angry to any or hasty [since] the Mildest Man has the best chance on board."[18]

Whatever the hardships, they were to be "Clearing away from that place all together and the Sooner the Better." "Come you all Together Couragiously and bid adiu to that lovely place the land of our Birth, that place where the young and old joined Together in one Common Union, both night and day Engaged in Innocent Amusement."

Despite the obvious signs of nostalgia in her letter, Miss McCarthy apparently felt no regret of her leaving, aside from the parting from family and friends. She was "proud and happy to Be away from where the County Charges man or the poor Rates man or any other Rates man would have the Satisfaction of once Inpounding my cow or any other article of mine." Any man or woman without a family "are fools," she thought, "that would not venture and Come to this plentyful Country where no man or woman ever Hungerd or ever will and where you will not be Seen Naked. . . ."

Michael Byrne, formerly of Boughill in Galway, found work immediately "in the rail road line" in upstate New York earning 5s. a day: "And instead of being chained with poverty in Boughill I am crowned with glory. . . ."[19] Daniel Guiney's report from Buffalo to his friends at home in Pobble O'Keefe was also one of a land of plenty, a place "full of Orchards and Woods" and "the finest fields of Clover that ever wer seen." He marveled at the Indian corn "growing here like woods" and the "fine large Stock of Cattle 40 and 50 Cows together." "We could see six and 7 score of Sheep and 12 or 14 horses togather you may be sure that we seen great many wonders."[20]

It is self-evident that those most likely to extol the plenty of America were those who had enjoyed some degree of success and satisfaction, the release from the humiliations and the constant fear of ruin in the townland. Many emigrant letters also dwell on the small pleasures of regular food and decent clothing in America, enough for many to bless the day of their leaving. Differences of age or gender could often alter the feelings of the new emigrant, as could parting from family and friends who remained at home. It is not as clear that these feelings differed similarly between "voluntary" and "involuntary" emigrants or between those who paid their own passage and those assisted by the Crown. Certainly, many letters from assisted emigrants spoke nothing but praise and gratitude to the Crown agents who sent them, like those few who defended Cox to the Commissioners.

On this score, at least, the sentiments of the Ballykilcline emigrants may have departed from those of others. Those who sailed arrived in large groups together, having gone through the emigrant experience almost as an intact community and therefore may have been subject to a more collective mentality than others. And given their years of resistance to leaving, their sense of exile may well have been more intense than most and the sensation of freedom and release from the "land of landlord tyrany" may have been dulled by bitterness at the loss of their struggle. One would especially like to know whether the stoical James Connor found more or less scope to "do his own will" in the American democracy than he had as a subject and tenant of the Crown. Perhaps some future genealogist or finder of lost persons will find this task worthwhile.

Epilogue

Identity and Emigration

There were a large number of steerage passengers occupying the main deck, forward of the shaft. Many of them were Irish, late immigrants, but the large majority were slaves, going on to New Orleans to be sold, or moving with their masters to Texas. There was a fiddle or two among them, and they were very merry, dancing and singing. A few, however, refused to join in the amusement, and looked very disconsolate. A large proportion of them were boys and girls, under twenty years of age.

Frederick Law Olmsted, *The Cotton Kingdom*[1]

There are many circumstances that seem to be unique to the Irish peasantry in these years, especially its dependence on the potato and the catastrophe it suffered as a result. The famine gave the exodus from Ireland an aura of panic that was not common among European migrants, at least till the 1930s. It is the quality of fleeing that has given the famine migration a more involuntary character than the emigration before and after. The disgust its details inspires and the odor of racial hatred surrounding the emigrants' treatment also suggests that it should be seen as a special category of migration, a movement in "coffin ships" that bears more resemblance to the slave trade or the boxcars of the Holocaust than to the routine crossings of a later age. But, aside from its atrocious injustices, the social contours and the timing of Irish peasant migration from the land in the midcentury appear to correspond roughly to the movement of peoples in Britain and many parts of western Europe at about the same time. Its main destinations, toward the industrial cores of Britain and North America, also suggest purposes similar to voluntary movements. In comparing it to the massive internal migration of other Europeans, it is probably more important that all were moving away from the place of their birth than that some remained within their national borders while others crossed an ocean to become part of a new nation not yet fully formed.

Because Ireland contributed an inordinate share to the great Atlantic migration and had also been the most deeply penetrated of all colonial societies, the emigration of the Irish peasantry tests a variety of general theories that apply to these two momentous historical events of the nineteenth century. But understanding the microcosm of events that made up these phenomena in Ireland is as filled with pitfalls as the history of great nations. Ireland's smallness and its modest importance in shaping the world's history do not make the task any easier, as one might first imagine. Whether Ballykilcline "typifies" the peasantry of prefamine Ireland, for example, depends very much on how close to the ground the historical record allows us to go. At the level of the Ascendancy, or of political institutions and commerce, there seem to be great variations in the official contexts within which the peasantry lived. The same variety can be found, for example, in domestic building styles, in the persistence of "rundale" townlands, or in organized forms of peasant resistance. All of these were of great importance for those who remained and would continue to distinguish different regions of the country for years to come. But the great majority of the emigrants in these years were in effect stripped of their outward diversity and reduced to the axioms of their culture. In these intangibles, they appear to have shared as much simplicity and uniformity as the baggage they carried.

The townland's traces have allowed us some passing sights into its material existence and even briefer glimpses of individual occupants' thoughts and character, as though we were examining the artifacts of an ancient and vanished civilization. But they do not admit us into its inner life. We cannot stand at Padian's door and listen to the nighttime dialogues of the Defendants, as we might hear a parliamentary debate, although we know that they took place. These blanks blot out most of the conscious life of the townland peasants, making them appear more passive in retrospect than they were. The obscurity of human agency among them may even have inclined us to embrace notions about the country's history that we would reject as absurd caricatures if applied to the nations and cultures that shook and shaped the rest of the world. This is probably because most of Western history has been based on our study of power and our effort to understand change and its causes. Ireland has never had power. And, as for the mostly calamitous changes that mark its history, they have generally been ascribed either to intrusions from outside or to intractable cultural traits that have hindered its material progress and bound the country to an essentially inert and passive history as a nation.

Despite their apparent incongruity, there seems to be a great weight of truth in both these propositions. Many of the features of townland life were clearly vestiges of the past, social and communal values that may have preserved its internal moral order but did little to help its material survival in the long run. This seems especially true of the persistence of its "through-other" moral economy that impeded initiative and practical accommodations with the changing realities of the world around it. To that degree, it might be said that the townland imposed its history on itself. It is also self-evident that its lack of the conventional powers to resist subjection kept rural Ireland on the extractive periphery of Europe, blocked from direct access to the economic and technical family of nations that western Europe was becoming in the two centuries before the famine. And unlike any other Roman Catholic people in Europe, they were also virtually cut off from their mother church for more than a century, leaving many of them barely recognizable to their coreligionists when they surfaced in the metropolis.[2]

These circumstances certainly contributed to the many "hidden" qualities persisting in the native culture at the time of the famine, in its politics and economy, but even more strikingly in the inward-looking identities and stratagems adopted by the peasantry to prolong its existence. We have seen also that some of these traits at least set out on the Atlantic journey with the emigrants, perhaps surviving for generations into the future. There is even less doubt that they persisted stubbornly in the postfamine townlands. The bizarre revelations of the hidden lives of the Galway townland of Maamtrasna in the 1880s still mystified outsiders when a sudden light was thrown upon them following a sensational and grisly murder. The murdered family of John Joyce, a small farmer, was found on the earthen floor of their one-room cabin, a structure of $22' \times 10'$ without window or chimney housing seven people together with their cattle—a house, said the lord lieutenant, that "would not be used for pigs in England." Even more than the physical setting, the indecipherable confusion of feuds and codes of silence that lay behind the crime baffled all understanding, even of close and sympathetic outsiders, and ended in the hanging of at least one innocent.[3] To the degree that their habits of evasion and anonymity may have been acquired under the long and close colonial rule or were merely the result of rural Ireland's inertia, it might be said that even at that late date the cultural gulf created by the great imbalance of power with England had a lasting impact on the character of the country and its people.

Ireland's prolonged colonial experience also presupposes a high degree of penetration from the world power that came not only to dominate the legal, political, and economic institutions of the society but to successfully replace the native language with its own in most of the population. As in most other colonies, efforts to convert the peasantry from its traditional religion had largely failed. But in comparison to any other of Britain's colonies, the public life of the Irish people was more intimately governed by the colonial Ascendancy, if only because the Ascendancy in Ireland was a much denser presence than anywhere else and had been in place longer. Culminating in the Act of Union, this near erasure of the country's civic identity has certainly been near the heart of nationalist sentiment ever since. But it may be a lesson to be learned about colonialism that even apparently complete domination of civic life over very long periods of time was insufficient to dissolve the anathema of native culture and that the most successful resistance to intrusion was devised by the most ostensibly weakest layers of the native population, not by the intelligentsia and organized political movements but by the subjugated peasantry. This was a colonizer's Gordian knot that perennially frustrated the law and the landlord, as in the rent strike of Ballykilcline, a tangle of evasions, dodges, and fluid identities that often defied the order that colonial rule required everywhere.

There are a number of larger contexts in which the emigration of Ballykilcline might be placed. It was a cameo instance of the "destruction of the peasantry" that both "modernization" theorists and most Marxist historians once applied to the early industrial phase of capitalist development. There seems little doubt that the assisted emigration schemes of the Crown and private landlords was at least in part a deliberate effort to "rationalize" their productive properties and that in the process they helped produce a mobile "reserve army of labor" to provide the muscle power of industrialization, cheap and unskilled "hands" to dig, haul, and construct. As parliamentary Blue Books often noted, the townland Irish were the cheapest labor in western Europe. But, as the late E. P. Thompson rightly adds, "Irish labour was essential for the Industrial Revolution, not only— and perhaps not primarily—because it was 'cheap' . . . but because the Irish peasantry had escaped the imprint of Baxter and Wesley." That is, it was still accustomed to "pre-industrial labour-rhythms" that were well-suited to the work required at the base of industrial society, "a spendthrift expense of sheer physical energy" with alternations of intensive labor and "boisterous relaxation." Thompson's contention that the backbreaking work thus performed by the Irish laborer was now beyond the *physical* as well as the temperamental tolerances of English labor is quite suspect. But it seems almost self-evident that very large numbers of hungry and movable manual workers were essential at this historical moment in both Britain and the eastern United States and that the townland emigrants fit the bill to perfection: no Europeans were hungrier at the time, their legal grip on the land had already been broken, and their poverty made even the paltriest wages seductive.[4]

In *The Unbound Prometheus,* David Landes suggests a slightly different perspective in which the experience of Ballykilcline also appears to belong, where the "surplus humanity" required for industrial development emerges from the geographical "periphery" rather than from the native "core" by way of enclosure or rural depopulation. This perspective has had particular appeal as it applies to the "Celtic fringe," although it ignores the fact that at least as much of the hewing and hauling to build the infrastructure of industrial England (such as the great Liverpool dock system) was done by nonimmigrant labor. But there is little question that the largest pool of surplus labor of this era did reside in the Celtic periphery and was employed everywhere in distinct and largely segregated roles well-suited to its traditional skills and mentalities, especially in the near-universal use of Irish laborers in gangs of shovelers.[5]

Brinley Thomas's classic exposition of an "Atlantic economy" in which emigration ebbed and flowed between Britain and North America in synchronized tides of supply and demand also has appeal in explaining the larger historical forces behind the movement of people from the townlands to the building sites of Lancashire or New York. But the alert responses of potential emigrants to transatlantic wage fluctuations, as to the American recession of 1837, were more characteristic of the better-informed, opportunist, and English-speaking small farmers, craftsmen, and townspeople who made up the mainstream of prefamine migrants than it was of most townland occupants. Like the peasants of the "backward" regions of France or Italy, these were "moved by reasons that are local, special, and often incomprehensible to an outsider."[6] The poorest of them responded almost exclusively to local stimuli and moved first toward England, remaining within the "Liverpool system." Like McDermott, most of the rest were still only on the periphery of Thomas's "Atlantic system," still too distant in knowledge and inclination to react so quickly to the news from America. One might say these emigrated voluntarily, but only in the face of a disaster they were able to discern a little more clearly than their neighbors. The Atlantic economy would soon encompass the next generations of emigrants, but it would never be one in which all movement was perfectly voluntary and informed. In the famine era, it offers little help in explaining the emigration of the townland peasantry.[7]

One inadequacy of these frameworks, perhaps necessarily, is that they view the midcentury emigration largely from the top downward, shedding little light on the consciousness of the main participants, how the emigrants experienced and understood the history in which they were caught up. Nor do they help to reveal the mental predicaments in which the colonized peasant found himself for generations or the learned, internalized responses to contact with the outside he had invented to cope with them. This is where I found James Scott's analysis of the forms of colonial resistance, in *The Weapons of the Weak*, more helpful in understanding the "the situations of the colonized," those essentially political and character-subverting social predicaments that Albert Memmi, in *The Colonizer and the Colonized*, revealed to be the subjective core of the colonial experience.[8] Accordingly, what seems most lacking in the macro-explanations of the migration is any insight into the *interaction* of mind and circumstance, either before, during, or after their removal.

The Irish diaspora in North America followed a less coherent pattern than the Liverpool system had imposed on their route out of Ireland. Their tendency to settle in the urban ghettos and industrial towns of the East is well known, though still not fully understood.[9] Under various names, "Little Irelands" sprang up in most large towns, as they had in Britain, many of them "shantytowns" that retained a resemblance to the townlands in their poverty and disorder, as well as in their relative isolation from native civil society. But in New York, Boston, or Chicago there was little to sustain this isolation for long, and there were many more ways to escape it, both physically and mentally, as though an ancient barrier had been lowered if not yet destroyed.

Nativism, poverty, and the need for cohesion still limited the immigrants' choices, and many would remain in essentially Irish surroundings, among fellow immigrants sharing a familiar speech and similar values, for the remainder of their lives. In mind though not in body, these never left home. Many thousands of others were quickly drawn outward by the lure of American wages. These would eventually make up the main flow of immigrants, completing the transformation from Irish peasant to American worker. While it might be said that this process finally destroyed the townland as a community, it did not necessarily replace it with a new source of identity.

All had shared in a common experience at the moment of their departure, beginning with their separation from the "context of recognitions," as Eric Leed put it in his *Mind of the Traveller.* For most European peasants, this context was more or less congruent with the society and landscape of the village; in prefamine Ireland it was circumscribed more intangibly by the cultural membranes dividing the townland from the surrounding colonial milieu. In separating from this context, Leed suggests, the traveler becomes objectified, autonomous, and outside the relations that had once identified him as an individual and possessed him of a name and a history that bound him to the place.[10]

It is in this subjective respect, even more than in their isolation from the material life of the European metropolis, that the people of Ballykilcline were "hidden." Until the prospect of removal penetrated the townland, the consciousness of self, both personal and communal, was almost entirely inward looking and, as E. Estyn Evans aptly put it, "throughother." Thus, it might be said that the townland was mirrorless in both its physical and mental life, highly conscious of its collective identity but still only dimly aware of its objective existence or its "appearance." Of course, individuals in the townland possessed egos, but these were restrained to a remarkable degree by collective taboos against vanity and selfishness. In Ballykilcline, these restraints were eroded only on the eve of their departure. First the thought and then the reality of their emigration forced their gaze upon themselves as separate entities, as though for the first time. Such an "unfocused self-image" has been noted in other communities far more isolated physically from outsiders than was the Irish townland. But the "downward isolation" in which Ballykilcline concealed itself within an hour's walk of "civilization" appears to have been nearly as effective in dimming its view of itself as extreme geographical remoteness. Frederick Barth's observations on the Baktaman of New Guinea and Eric Leed's elegant glosses on them suggest that isolation produces "incomplete" self-images among remote communities and that both personal and collective identities arise only after discovering the outside, either through intrusion from it or from venturing into it. "Through being removed," Leed writes, "one may come to see one's native culture—which once provided the lenses and meanings through which one looked out upon the world—as an object, a thing, a unified, describable phenomenon." Among emigrants who were also victims, that sight was sometimes accompanied by shame.[11]

Most actually saw the land of their nativity fading into the sea as they sailed westward. For the famine emigrants, it was a revelation unimaginable just weeks before, sudden and experienced by masses of them simultaneously, shipload after shipload, year after year. Peering from the stern rather than the bow of the emigrant ship, that backward glance at the incongruous palms and gaily painted houses along the shore near Skibbereen was not only their last sight of Ireland but the first sight of themselves.

Notes

[Since this book was written, the Public Record Office has become the National Archives of Ireland, in Bishop Street, Dublin.]

Introduction

1. Daniel Corkery, *The Hidden Ireland: A Study of Gaelic Munster in the Eighteenth Century* (Dublin: M. H. Gill & Son, 1925).
2. Eilish Ellis, ed., "Letters from the Quit Rent Office," *Analecta Hibernia* 22 (1960).
3. William Carleton, *Traits and Stories of the Irish Peasantry*, vol. 1 (London: William Tegg, 1865), "Introduction" 11–111.

Chapter 1

1. Alexis de Tocqueville, *Journeys to England and Ireland* (New York: Anchor Books, 1968), pp. 154–55. At that point in his tour of Ireland in 1835, Tocqueville was passing through Tuam, County Galway, which he calls "county Connaught."
2. Thomas McErlean, "The Irish Townland System of Landscape Organisation," in Terence Reeves-Smyth and Fred Hamond, eds., *Landscape Archaeology in Ireland* (British Archaeological Reports, Oxford, 1983), p. 334; Cahal Dallat, "Townlands—Their Origin and Significance," in Tony Canavan, ed., *Every Stoney Acre Has a Name: A Celebration of the Townland in Ulster* (Federation for Local Ulster Studies, Belfast, 1991), p. 3; Canon P. Power, "The Place-names of Decies" (Cork: Cork University Press, 1952), p. 40.
3. Tocqueville, *Journeys*, pp. 154–55.
4. Ibid. Tocqueville traveled in Ireland in the summer of 1835 with his friend Gustave de Beaumont, who published his own observations on the country in *L'Irlande sociale, politique et religieuse* in 1839.

5. Tocqueville, *Journeys*, pp. 160–61.

6. Daniel Corkery, *The Hidden Ireland: A Study of Gaelic Munster in the Eighteenth Century* (M. H. Gill & Son, 1925), pp. 11–13.

7. Seamus Heaney, "Preface," in Tony Canavan, ed., *Every Stoney Acre Has a Name* (Federation for Local Ulster Studies, Belfast, 1991), p. xi; McErlean, "Irish Townland System," p. 335; J. Grandlund, "Folk and Farm," in *Royal Society of Antiquaries of Ireland* (Dublin: Kilkenny Archaeological Society, 1976), p. 89.

8. E. Estyn Evans, *The Personality of Ireland: Habitat, Heritage and History* (Cambridge: Cambridge University Press, 1973), p. 60. See also Desmond McCourt, "The Dynamic Quality of Irish Rural Settlement," in R. H. Buchanan et al., eds., *Man and His Habitat* (London: Routledge and Kegan Paul, 1971).

9. Probably the readiest introduction to the history of the townland, the "baile," the "rundale village," and the "clachan," all of them varieties of native settlement, can be found in E. Estyn Evans, *Irish Heritage: The Landscape, the People and Their Work* (Dundalk: Dundalgan Press, 1949), esp., "Village and Booley," pp. 47–57; also Evans, *Personality of Ireland*, p. 91; P. Robinson, "Irish Settlement in Tyrone before the Ulster Plantation," *Ulster Folklore* 22 (1976). See also R. H. Buchanan, "Rural Settlement in Ireland," in Stephens and Glassock, eds., *Irish Geographical Studies* (1970); McCourt, "Dynamic Quality"; *Parliamentary Papers*, 1843, vol. 24, Griffith's Valuation Report, "Accounts and Papers' Valuations" (Ireland).

10. Evans, *Personality of Ireland*, pp. 90ff.

11. For the layers of society created by the repeated conquests of the country, see C. Brady and R. Gillespie, eds., *Natives and Newcomers: The Making of Irish Colonial Society, 1534–1641* (Dublin: Irish Academic Press, 1986).

12. In the boundary sketches preceding the Ordnance Survey, the geologist Richard Griffith recognized the discordance between townland and estate boundaries, trying as far as possible to "keep the two from clashing." J. H. Andrews, *History in the Ordnance Map: An Introduction for Irish Readers* (Kerry: David Archer, 1993), p. 12.

13. Evans, *Personality of Ireland*, p. 91. See especially Eric Wolf, *Peasants* (Englewood Cliffs, N.J.: Prentice-Hall, 1966) and *Peasant Wars of the Twentieth Century* (New York: Harper & Row, 1969), for comparison to characteristic villages of western Europe. See M. Agulhon, *The Republic in the Village* (New York: Cambridge University Press, 1982), and Ralph Samuel, ed., *Village Life and Labour* (London: Routledge, Kegan Paul, 1975), for contrasts to the structure and mentalities of French and English villages in the nineteenth century.

14. James Scott, *Weapons of the Weak: Everyday Forms of Peasant Resistance* (New Haven: Yale University Press, 1985); also his "Everyday Forms of Peasant Resistance," *Journal of Peasant Studies* (January 1986).

15. Although there are differences as to degree, it is generally agreed that the restrictions of the Penal Laws encouraged the persistence of traditional folk rituals in the practice of religion that lent Irish Catholicism an exotic quality in the eyes of outsiders. The most thorough discussion may be found in Sean Connolly, *Priests and People in Pre-Famine Ireland, 1780–1845* (Dublin: Gill & Macmillan, 1982). See also Patrick J. Corish, *The Irish Catholic Experience* (Dublin: Gill & Macmillan, 1985); Emmet Larkin, "The Devotional Revolution in Ireland, 1850–75," *American Historical Review* 73 (June 1972); Lynn Lees, *Exiles of Erin* (Ithaca: Cornell University Press, 1979), p. 173.

16. The *derbfine* included all adult males sharing a common great-grand-father. This system of land ownership conformed to the mainly pastoral economy of preconquest Ireland, in which the access to land for grazing cattle was more important than the permanent territorial divisions of Norman and English land law. Kerby Miller, *Emigrants and Exiles: Ireland and the Irish Exodus to North America* (New York: Oxford University Press, 1985), p. 12.

17. The stark contrast between the primacy of local community values in the English and the Irish countrysides is made abundantly clear in Carolyn A. Conley, *The Unwritten Law: Criminal Justice in Victorian Kent* (New York: Oxford University Press, 1991).

18. Evans, *Personality of Ireland*, p. 79, from Yan Goblet, *La Transformation de la Geographie politique de l'Irlande au XVIIe siecle*, 2 vols., (Paris, 1930), 1:355.

19. The "Plantation" or "Irish" acre was approximately 1.6 times the area of the newer "Statute" acre.

20. These measurements are described in detail in Edward Gibbon Wakefield, *An Account of Ireland Statistical and Political* (London, 1812), 1:309–16, and in the *First Report of Inquiry into the Condition of the Poorer Classes in Ireland*, *Parliamentary Papers*, 1836, App. F.

21. Lord George Hill, *Facts from Gweedore* (1845), cited in Evans, *Personality of Ireland*, p. 92.

22. Mary O'Dowd, *The Town in Ireland: Papers Read before the Irish Conference of Historians* (Belfast: Appletree Press, 1981).

23. "Notice of Eviction," 20 October 1836, Quit Rent Office Papers, Public Record Office, Dublin (hereafter cited as Q.R.O.).

24. Maria Edgeworth, *Ennui* (London: W. Glaisher, 1924), v.

Chapter 2

1. Daniel Corkery, *The Hidden Ireland: A Study of Gaelic Munster in the Eighteenth Century* (Dublin: M. H. Gill & Son, 1925), p. 5.

2. John Kelly to Commissioners of Woods and Forests, 2 December 1848, Q.R.O.

3. This version of the descent of the O'Conor estate in Roscommon was told in 1830 to Isaac Weld by Matthew O'Conor, Esq., a barrister and brother of the O'Conor Don, M.P. for Roscommon; Isaac Weld, *Statistical Survey of the County of Roscommon, Drawn up under the Direction of the Royal Dublin Society* (Dublin, 1832), pp. 5–6, 381–82.

4. Geoffrey Bolton, *The Passage of the Act of Union* (Oxford: Oxford University Press, 1966), pp. 146–47.

5. Returns to Orders of the House of Lords, 16 and 19 February 1847, p. 4, "Lands of Ballykilcline, County Roscommon" (hereafter cited as H. of L. Returns).

6. Revised valuation of 1821 survey of Brassington and Gale by James Weale, 1834, Q.R.O. The burning of dead stalks was used as a poor substitute for manuring, which, for the small farmers without cattle, was often an impossible expense. E. R. R. Green, "Agriculture," in R. Dudley Edwards and T. Desmond Williams, eds., *The Great Famine* (Dublin: Browne & Nolan, 1954), pp. 273–75.

7. The landlord's "demesne" usually referred to the lands immediately surrounding his residence, often walled parkland, pasture, and gardens. Some also

enclosed arable fields tilled by hired labor. In local usage the word referred to the whole physical entity: the mansion, the lands, and the enclosing wall. The word was also commonly abstracted into a symbol of local dominance and high social status.

8. Report of James Weale to the "Officer of Woods", 7 April 1834, on Lord Hartland's application to purchase Crown lands. Q.R.O.

9. See Kingwilliamstown, Irvillaughter, Boughill, and Pobble O'Keefe below.

10. H. of L. Returns, 16 and 19 February 1847.

11. H. of L. Returns, 1847, p. 4.

12. On the native technologies of distillation, see K. H. Connell, "Illicit Distillation," in *Irish Peasant Society: Four Historical Essays* (Oxford: Clarendon Press, 1968), pp. 1–51.

13. An introduction to the "rundale-clachan" of the 1830s and 1840s may be found in E. Estyn Evans, *The Personality of Ireland: Habitat, Heritage and History* (Cambridge: Cambridge University Press, 1973), pp. 55ff. It is also discussed at length in the Minutes of Evidence of the Devon Commission, which published its exhaustive investigation of land use in 1845, just months before the famine.

14. "To His Excellency the Lord Lieutenant of Ireland. The Memorial of Patrick M'Kye," dated 1837, in Lord George Hill, *Facts from Gweedore* (1845).

15. The 1841 census broke down the population into three classes: Class I, heads of families and professionals whose means allowed them to live without labor (2.6 percent of the whole population, 1.9 percent of the rural population, 6.6 percent of the urban population, and 1.6 percent of the rural population of Connaught); Class II, skilled artisans with fixed employment and farmers holding fewer than fifty acres (31.8 percent of the whole population, 28.3 percent of the rural population, 49.9 percent of the urban population, and 17.5 percent of the rural population of Connaught). The remainder, more than 80 percent in Connaught, made up the mass of townland tenants. The classifications are from Great Britain, "Reports of the Commissioners Appointed to Take the Census of Ireland for the Year 1841," *Parliamentary Papers, 1843*, vol. 24 (hereafter cited as 1841 Census). The percentage computations used above are from Joel Mokyr, *Why Ireland Starved: A Quantitative and Analytical History of the Irish Economy, 1800–1850* (London: Allen & Unwin, 1983), pp. 18–19.

16. The underlying changes producing such conflicts between farmer and cottier have been the subject of continuous debate among historians of this period. A succinct account may be found in Kerby Miller, *Emigrants and Exiles: Ireland and the Irish Exodus to North America* (New York: Oxford University Press, 1985), pp. 58–63.

17. Samuel Clark, *Social Origins of the Irish Land War* (Princeton: Princeton University Press, 1979), pp. 66–67; Miller, *Emigrants and Exiles*, pp. 60–63.

18. Miller, *Emigrants and Exiles*, p. 59; Joseph Lee, "Marriage and Population Growth in Ireland, 1750–1845," *Economic History Review*, v. 21 (1968), pp. 285–89.

19. Clark, *Social Origins*, pp. 66–67; Galen Broeker, *Rural Disorder and Police Reform in Ireland, 1812–36* (London: Routledge & Kegan Paul, 1970).

20. H. D. Inglis, *Tour throughout Ireland in 1834*, 1:109; Green, "Agriculture."

Chapter 3

1. Alexis de Tocqueville, *Journeys to England and Ireland* (New York: Anchor Books, 1968), p. 174.

2. Evans attributes the "noisy and prolonged disputes" over land to the old custom of periodically "reallocating" the scattered plots of land of varying quality among coheirs, a practice that survived in subdivision and joint-holding. E. Estyn Evans, *The Personality of Ireland: Habitat, Heritage and History* (Cambridge: Cambridge University Press, 1973), p. 60.

3. Stephen Campbell has written a soon-to-be published summary of the events surrounding Major Mahon's assassination from the Mahon family papers at Strokestown House and in the National Library, including contemporary published accounts: "The Strokestown Famine Papers: The Mahon Family and the Strokestown Estate, 1845–1848." I have drawn many of the local details surrounding the event from this account and am indebted to Mr. Campbell. A reasonable summary of the details elicited at the inquest and trials may be found in Billie Donlon, "The Mahon Murder Trials," *Roscommon Historical and Archaelogical Society Journal* 1 (1986). Particulars of the testimony and proceedings of the two trials may also be found in *Saunders News Letter* of July 1848 and March 1849, and the *Roscommon Journal and Western Reporter* of July 1848.

4. *Toronto Globe*, 4 August 1847; Cecil Woodham-Smith, *The Great Hunger*, p. 226, cited in Campbell, "Strokestown Famine Papers," pp. 35–36.

5. *Times*, 24 November 1847, cited in Campbell, "Strokestown Famine Papers," p. 42.

6. Campbell, "Strokestown Famine Papers," p. 39.

7. Great Britain, "Population," *Parliamentary Papers, 1852–1853, Census of Ireland* (1851), vol.13, pp. 410–11, 530 (hereafter cited as 1851 Census).

8. 1841 Census; Caoimhin ó Danachair, "Semi-Underground Habitations," *Journal of the Galway Archaeological and Historical Society* 26, nos. 3 and 4 (1955–1956): 75–82; Joel Mokyr, *Why Ireland Starved: A Quantitative and Analytical History of the Irish Economy, 1800–1850* (London: Allen & Unwin, 1983), p. 181.

9. 1851 Census, pp. 410–11. The figures for houses and occupations in these reports were taken from the data collected by the 1841 Census, but the Sessional Papers of 1852–1853, which were also concerned with presenting the differentials produced by the famine, offer a more valuable range of comparisons in these categories.

10. Daniel Corkery, *The Hidden Ireland: A Study of Gaelic Munster in the Eighteenth Century* (Dublin: M. H. Gill & Son, 1925), p. 10.

11. House of Lords, *Report of the Select Committee on Colonisation from Ireland*, vol. 6, p. 737 (1847), cited in Cecil Woodham-Smith, *The Great Hunger* (New York: Old Town Books, 1989), p. 325.

12. Friedrich Engels to Karl Marx, 23 May 1856, Karl Marx and Frederick Engels, *Ireland and the Irish Question* (New York: International Publishers, 1972), p. 85.

13. J. R. Bolton, *The Passage of the Act of Union* (Oxford: Oxford University Press, 1966), pp. 146–47, 168–69, 190–91, 204–5; Campbell, "Strokestown Famine Papers."

14. *Sanders' News Letter and Daily Advertiser*, 12 April 1836, cited in Campbell, "Strokestown Famine Papers," p. 8.

15. The reason for their leaving is uncertain, but rumors persisted that they

may have found some of the personal habits he had taken up, including his collection of erotica, to be unsavory. Mahon Pakenham Papers at Strokestown Park House, now the National Famine Museum of Ireland (hereafter cited as Strokestown Papers).

16. Skeffington Gibbon, *Recollections of Skeffington Gibbon, from 1796 to the present year, 1829; being an epitome of the lives and characters of the nobility and gentry of Roscommon, the geneology of those who are descended from the Kings of Connaught; and a memoir of the late Madame O'Conor Don* (Dublin, printed by Joseph Blundell, 187 Great Britain Street, 1829), p. 153; Hodges to Lady Hartland, 14 September 1830, Strokestown Papers.

17. Rent Book, May 1843, Strokestown Papers.

18. John Ross Mahon's survey of the estate in 1846 when he took up his job as agent counted sixteen hundred families, holding an average of three acres apiece. Pakenham-Mahon Papers, National Library of Ireland, MS 10,102.2 (hereafter cited as P-M Papers).

19. A cousin of Major Mahon and an aspiring beneficiary of the Hartland legacy, Charles McCausland, had made formal complaints before the dispute over the estate was resolved that "extravagant sums" were being employed by Mahon as executor for laying out "fashionable" improvements at Strokestown House. George Conry to Denis Mahon, 13 June 1845, P-M Papers, N.L.I. MS 10,101.5.

20. *Mayo Constitution*, 29 April 1843, and *Morning Chronicle*, 2 September 1843, cited in Campbell, "Strokestown Famine Papers."

21. Marquess of Westmeath to the Commissioners of Woods and Forests, 6 February 1849, file 2B.43.127, Q.R.O.

22. The ratio of Irish-born officers per capita to English-born in 1872 was about eleven to eight; among the rank and file it was an extraordinary two to one. David Haire, "The British Army in Ireland, 1868–1890" (M.Litt. thesis, Trinity College Dublin, 1977), pp. 280–307; Peter Karsten, "Irish Soldiers in the British Army, 1792–1922: Suborned or Subordinate?" (paper given at the Davis Center, Princeton University, 1986), p. 12.

23. P-M Papers, MS 10,106–10,108 (1802–1817).

24. 1851 Census, p. 414.

25. Denis Mahon's correspondence with John Ross Mahon in the spring of 1847, when the major was still in England, shows clearly that he was incensed about this practice and aware that his larger tenants were exploiting their relationship; e.g., Denis Mahon to J. R. Mahon, 7 June, P-M Papers, MS 10,102.2 and MS 10,102.3, cited in Campbell, "Strokestown Famine Papers," pp. 33–34.

26. Denis Mahon to John Ross Mahon, 4 March 1847, P-M Papers, MS 10,102.3.

27. "Thomas Conry Esq. Account, 1830" and "Yearly Rent Roll," 1 November 1823 and 1824, signed by Thomas Conry, Strokestown Papers.

28. The only other local Conry whose name survives in the record, Edward Conry of Strokestown, a shopkeeper, was a prominent Catholic of the town and testified publicly on behalf of Father Michael McDermott in his dispute with Mahon, P-M Papers, MS 10,098–099.8.

29. Denis Mahon to John Ross Mahon, 7 June 1847, P-M Papers, MS 10,102.3.

30. Reported in the *Times*, 17 December 1847, cited in Campbell, "Strokestown Famine Papers," p. 39.

31. This version was published in the *Freeman's Journal* on 29 April in the

spring following the murder and was the result of an investigation carried out by the Bishop of Elphin. See Campbell, "Strokestown Famine Papers," p. 40, for the full text.

32. *Times*, 17 December 1847.

33. *Evening Freeman*, 9 December 1847, cited in Campbell, "Strokestown Famine Papers," p. 46.

34. *Times*, 15 February 1848, cited in Campbell, "Strokestown Famine Papers," p. 52.

35. Strokestown Papers, 20 January 1848; cited in Campbell, "Strokestown Famine Papers," p. 54; Kerby Miller, *Emigrants and Exiles: Ireland and the Irish Exodus to North America* (New York: Oxford University Press, 1985), p. 68.

36. John Ross Mahon to Henry Sandford Pakenham Mahon, 1 January 1848, Strokestown Papers.

37. George Cornewall Lewis, *On Local Disturbances in Ireland* (Dublin, 1836), pp. 152–55, 196.

38. Miller, *Emigrants and Exiles*, pp. 63–65. Miller's observations on this relationship are helpful and accurate, particularly that "the most *immediate* source of grievances was the deteriorating relationship between the commercial and subsistence sectors of the agricultural population itself." See also J. S. Donnelly, *The Land and People of Nineteenth-Century Cork: The Rural Economy and the Land Question* (London: Routledge & Kegan Paul, 1975), pp. 18–19.

39. Read by Lord Farnham in the House of Lords, 7 December 1847, reported in the *Times*, 9 December 1847, cited in Campbell, "Strokestown Famine Papers," p. 45.

40. The high incidence of asylum commitments among the general population in Ireland has often been noted and was assumed to be related to alcoholism, but Mark Finnane, in *Insanity and the Insane in Post-Famine Ireland* (London: Croom Helm, 1981), suggests a much broader range of causes prevailing in the countryside before and after the famine.

41. "Yearly Rent Roll," 1 November 1824, Strokestown Papers, lists James and William Hogg, Esq., as sublessees of 238 acres of Ballykilcline, terminating in 1833.

42. Godfrey Hogg to Commissioners of Woods and Forests, 2 December 1842, Q.R.O.

43. Hogg to Brassington and Gale, 24 September 1836, Q.R.O.

44. A. R. Sandys to Commissioners of Woods and Forests, 23 February 1842, Q.R.O.

45. The firm of Shaw and Robinson and Son booked all the assisted passages both of the former Hartland Estate and of Ballykilcline. Ross Mahon was also in the process of arranging a similar assisted emigration from the Fitzgerald estates.

46. J. R. Mahon to Denis Mahon, 28 February 1847, P-M Papers, MS 10,102.2.

47. John Ross Mahon to Guinness, 28 November 1846, P-M Papers, MS 10,102.2.

48. John Ross Mahon to Denis Mahon, 28 February and 23 July 1847, P-M Papers, MSS 10,101.4, 10,102.2.

49. John Ross Mahon, "Memoir," 23 July 1847, P-M Papers, MS 10,101.4.

50. Denis Kelly to Henry Sandford Pakenham Mahon, 11 June 1848, P-M Papers, MS 10,103,1, cited in Campbell, "Strokestown Famine Papers," p. 70.

51. Great Britain, *Parliamentary Papers, 1876, Summary of Returns of Owners of Land in Ireland*, vol. 80, p. 59; J. Bateman, *The Great Landowners of Great*

Britain and Ireland (4th ed., 1883; reprint, Leicester, U.K.: Leicester University Press, 1971), pp. 87 *et seq.*; Mokyr, *Why Ireland Starved*, p. 100.

52. T. W. Freeman, *Pre-Famine Ireland* (Manchester, U.K.: Manchester University Press, 1957), pp. 71–73. Freeman's index estimates 685,309 holdings in 1841, 10 percent to 15 percent of them in the "medium" range of thirty to one hundred acres.

53. In a letter describing the trial of James Hasty for Mahon's murder, Kelly complained that "the Attorney General is a thorough Papist and will be privately influenced by the priests who through McDermott and the Bishops are all strong in favour of the assassins." Kelly to Henry Pakenham Mahon, 11 June 1848, P-M Papers, MS 10,103.1.

54. John Ross Mahon, "Memoir," 23 July 1847, P-M Papers, MS 10,101.4.

Chapter 4

1. Henry Glassie, *Passing the Time in Ballymenone: Culture and History in an Ulster Community* (Philadelphia: University of Pennsylvania Press, 1982), p. 503.

2. Knox to Burke, 24 May 1846, Q.R.O.

3. Knox to Commissioners, 17 August 1846, and "Board to Knox," 19 June 1846, Q.R.O.

4. Knox to Burke, 30 January 1846, Q.R.O.

5. Knox to Burke, 30 April 1846, Q.R.O.

6. *Ibid.*

7. As with absentee rents, the tithes were collected through an agent specializing in this business, in this case a Mr. Johnston of Carrick-on-Shannon. The Reverend Mr. Moorhead to Commissioners, and the Reverend Mr. Lloyd to Commissioners, undated [June–September 1846], Q.R.O.

8. Patsy Duignan of Strokestown Heritage Foundation, June 1986.

9. Knox to Burke, 18 February 1847, Q.R.O.

10. Interview with John Reynolds of Ballykilcline, June 1986.

11. Knox to Burke, n.d. [1848]; Burke, "First Emigration Grant," 13 June 1848, Q.R.O.

12. When the "tenants-at-law" are compared with the available surveys of lots of the same year, it is apparent that the list usually included the largest tenants but also some whose holdings were fewer than five acres. "Account of Occupants on the lands of Ballykilcline, 1846," Q.R.O.

13. The minimum claim the Defendants tried to make was that they had been "tenants from year to year" and were therefore entitled to six months' notice and appeal to law rather than mere "trespassers" who could be evicted summarily. "Report of the proceedings, Court of Exchequer, Easter Term, 1846: The Right Honourable, The Attorney General—Plaintiff," P.R.O., Four Courts, Dublin, ref. no. 223 (hereafter cited as Court of Exchequer.)

14. Knox to Burke, 18 February 1847, Q.R.O.

15. "Bartholomew Narry, Patrick Narry, Patrick Croghan, Richard Padian, Terence Connor, Patrick Colligan, Michael Connor, John Connor, Patrick Stewart, James Stewart, James Reynolds, Joseph Reynolds, Hugh McDermott and Bernard McDermott—Defendants." *Court of Exchequer.*

16. Knox to Burke, n.d. [1846], Q.R.O.

17. The lawyer's name is spelled "O'Ferrall" in local records, and usually "O'Farrell" in official correspondence.

18. Untitled affadavit of John Cox to James Burke, Clerk of the Quit Rents, n.d. [1846], Q.R.O.

19. Interview with John Reynolds, June 1988.

20. References to the size of holdings in the townland are taken from the Brassington and Gale survey of 1836. Since some holdings changed annually, they have been checked against the various rent lists maintained by Knox up to 1846. All are contained in file 2B.43.127, Q.R.O.

21. The name of Hugh McDermott disappears from the rent rosters in 1844. The only information regarding the family's emigration is based on the testimony of John Reynolds taken in 1988.

22. The age differentials at marriage in Ballykilcline were wider among the cottier-laborers and the larger farmers, who married later than those in the group between, corresponding roughly to the trend in peasant marriage elsewhere. Those marrying youngest in Ballykilcline were mostly of the middling group, with access as "tenants-at-will" to holdings between five and twelve acres. Laborers' wives, followed by large farmers' wives, were older at marriage than those of the small and middling tenants, in both cases corresponding approximately to marriage ages in this class generally. Kevin O'Neill, *Family and Farm in Pre-Famine Ireland: The Parish of Killashandra* (Madison: University of Wisconsin Press, 1984), p. 179; Michael Drake, "Marriage and Population Growth in Ireland, 1750–1845," *Economic History Review* 2 (December 1963): 301–13.

23. The Reverend Henry Brenan, of Kilglass, Rooskey, Dromed, to Viscount Morpeth, 12 April 1848, Q.R.O.

24. Terence Connor's household, his wife, Bridget, and a girl of fifteen and a boy of ten, also included his mother-in-law, Mary Maguire, eighty, the mother of Patrick Maguire, the "collaborator," who was the only tenant permitted to remain after the emigration.

25. Survey of Brassington and Gale, 1842, Q.R.O.

26. E. R. R. Green, "Agriculture," in R. Dudley Edwards and T. Desmond Williams, eds., *The Great Famine* (Dublin: Brown & Nolan, 1954), p. 111. See also E. Estyn Evans, *The Personality of Ireland: Habitat, Heritage and History* (Cambridge: Cambridge University Press, 1973), p. 60.

27. "Yearly Rent Roll," 1 November 1823–1824, *Strokestown Papers*. Conry also notes in this ledger that John Connor and Luke Narry had also kept joint tenancy on land in Farish Bottoms until this time.

28. The joint holdings of which the land agent had knowledge are found in "A List of Occupying Tenants on the Crown Lands of Ballykilcline in the Co. Roscommon Shewing the Respective acreage of each holding together with all Rent & Arrears due to 1st May, 1846," Q.R.O.

29. Burke to the Commissioners of Woods and Forests, 11 May 1848 and Connor to Burke, 24 March 1848, Q.R.O. The sheriff of Roscommon was to appear at noon on 15 May to eject all who had refused the bounty. These included Patrick Reilly, the "loyal" informer, John Stewart, John Connor, Jane and Bernard Magan, Patrick Connor, and Terence Moran.

Chapter 5

1. W. B. Yeats, ed., *Fairy and Folk Tales of the Irish Peasantry*, (London: W. Scott, 1888), p. 205.

2. "Lands of Ballykilcline, County Roscommon. Statement by the Commissioners of Her Majesty's Woods, Forests, Land Revenues, Works, and Build-

ings, in explanation of the Returns Nos. I. and II." H. of L. Returns, 16 and 19 February 1847.

3. "Rent-Day," in Yeats, *Fairy and Folk Tales*, p. 205.

4. John Ross Mahon to Denis Mahon, n.d. [1845], Strokestown Papers; cited in Stephen Campbell, "The Strokestown Famine Papers: The Mahon Family and the Strokestown Estate, 1845–1848" (unpublished paper), p. 9.

5. "Return of Crops and Cattle on the Lands of Ballykilcline in the County of Roscommon," 25 October 1841, Q.R.O.

6. Knox to Burke, 24 May 1846, Q.R.O.

7. "Return of Crops and Cattle on the Lands of Ballykilcline in the County of Roscommon," 25 October 1841, Q.R.O.

8. Monteagle's report to the House of Lords is contained in H. of L., Returns, 16 and 19 February, 1847, and was reported in the *Times*, 31 May 1848.

9. Cecil Woodham-Smith, *The Great Hunger* (New York: Old Town Books, 1989), p. 324.

10. Ibid.

11. Monteagle report.

12. Ibid.

13. Minutes of the Commissioners of Woods and Forests, 16 November 1847, *Crown Estate Papers*, 25/60, Public Record Office, Chancery Lane, London (hereafter cited as Crest).

14. New World opposition to assisted emigration was not directed solely against Irish emigrants but against paupers in general; H. J. M. Johnston, *British Emigration Policy, 1815–1830: "Shovelling out paupers"* (Oxford: Clarendon Press, 1972), pp. 86 *et seq.*

15. Crest 25/60, 26 March 1847.

16. Crest, 25/60, 3 December 1847.

17. *Times*, 15 February 1848, cited in Campbell, "The Strokestown Famine Papers," p. 52.

18. 12 May 1846, Q.R.O.

19. Knox to Burke, 24 May 1846, Q.R.O.

20. *Times*, 31 May 1848.

21. Ibid.

22. Campbell, "Strokestown Famine Papers," pp. 55–57, 75; Strokestown Papers, 5 February 1848.

23. Samuel Clark, *Social Origins of the Irish Land War* (Princeton: Princeton University Press, 1979), pp. 19–20; Salaman, *The History and Social Influence of the Potato* (Cambridge: Cambridge University Press, 1985), pp. 280, 296.

24. Billie Donlon, "The Mahon Murder Trials," *Roscommon Historical and Archaeological Society Journal* 1 (1986): 31.

25. Knox to Burke, 5 June 1844, H. of L. Returns, p. 56.

26. Chief Commissioner of Woods to Sir James Graham, Bart., H. of L. Returns, 29 June 1844.

27. Knox to Burke, 9 July 1844, H. of L. Returns, p. 62.

28. Ibid., p. 61.

29. Ibid.

30. Ibid., p. 62.

31. Ibid., p. 67.

32. Ibid., pp. 69–71.

33. Knox to Burke, n.d. [1846], Q.R.O.

34. Knox to Burke, n.d. [1847], Q.R.O.

35. Knox to Burke, 19 February 1847, Q.R.O.

36. Dublin Castle to C. W. F., 13 February 1846, Q.R.O.

37. Undersecretary for Ireland to Clerk of the Quit Rents, Dublin Castle, 12 May 1846, H. of L. Returns.

38. Ibid.

39. On two occasions during the evictions, John Stewart and Bernard Magan, protesting their innocence, blamed the disturbances in the townland on Molly Maguires; Stewart and Magan to Burke, 19 February and 7 September 1848, Q.R.O.; P-M Papers, MS 10,103.5, cited in Campbell, "Strokestown Famine Papers," p. 75.

40. George Knox Esq. to Clerk of the Quit Rents, 24 May 1846, H. of L. Returns, p. 76.

41. E. D. Steele, *Irish Land and British Politics* (Cambridge: Cambridge University Press, 1974), pp. 19, 34.

42. Knox to Commissioners, 23 December 1846, Q.R.O.

43. R. D. King-Harman, *The Kings, Earls of Kingston* (Cambridge: Cambridge University Press, 1959), pp. 94–95.

Chapter 6

1. "Account of Expenditures on Emigration," #2, Q.R.O.

2. Burke to Knox, and Riely [*sic*] to Burke, n.d. [1848], Q.R.O.

3. There is obviously a margin for error in accounting for the fate of individuals over the twelve-year period between 1836 and their departure. But comparisons of the rent books before the famine leaves a maximum of about twenty names in doubt, some of whom may be accounted for by death, marriage outside the townland, and movement within the neighborhood. With the coming of the famine, of course, a much higher attrition occurred, from about 496 individuals to about 347 at the time of departure.

4. The emigration of the McDermotts is remembered in Ballykilcline. When asked about those who had emigrated before the bulk of the townland left in 1848, Johnny Reynolds immediately recalled Hugh McDermott and his family, but no others. It is perhaps some indication that McDermott's departure had been something of an event in the townland.

5. See especially the petition of the spring of 1846 addressed to the Commissioners of Woods and Forests by "Richard Padian and the other persons in the occupation of the lands of Ballykilcline." "Appendix," Q.R.O.

6. The *Virginius* sailed from Liverpool on 27 May 1847, which would place the departure of the first batch from Strokestown in the third week of the month, about a week after Ballykilcline had received the proclamation. P-M Papers, 20 May 1847, MS 10,102.3.

7. *Times*, 31 May 1848.

8. Ibid.

9. The final count of those emigrated from the townland was given in the same report presented to Parliament by Lord Monteagle on 31 May 1848. It claimed that 173 of the occupants were sent off in September and October of 1847, and 236 the following spring, 409 in all. But in an account of the travel expenses paid to the first group, only 111 emigrants are named, eliminating the 62 individuals who had been evicted. *Times*, 31 May 1848; "List of the Tenants now holding Land . . . : Sum to pay their expenses to Dublin," 26 October 1847, Q.R.O.

10. There are reasons to suspect that many fewer than this number actually sailed from Liverpool; see Chapter 10.

11. Oliver MacDonagh, "Irish Emigration to the United States of America and the British Colonies during the Famine," in R. Dudley Edwards and T. Desmond Williams, eds., *The Great Famine* (Dublin: Brown & Nolan, 1954), p. 340.

12. Robert J. Scally, "Liverpool Ships and Irish Emigrants in the Age of Sail," *Journal of Social History* 17 (Summer 1984).

13. Strokestown Papers, MS, 5 February 1848, cited in Stephen Campbell, "The Strokestown Famine Papers: The Mahon Family and the Strokestown Estate, 1845–1848" (unpublished paper), p. 55.

14. *Times*, 2 February 1848, citing the *Ballinasloe Star*, cited in Campbell, "Strokestown Famine Papers," pp. 55–56.

15. *Evening Freeman*, 9 December 1847.

16. "A 'Spalpeen' at Dunmore" and "After the Eviction," reprinted from *Illustrated London News*, 16 and 22 December 1848, in Cecil Woodham-Smith, *The Great Hunger* (New York: Old Town Books, 1989), pp. 288–89.

17. *Times*, 24 December 1846.

18. Messrs. Hamilton and Co. to C. W. F., 22 February 1847, H. of L. Returns, p. 88.

19. Burke to Knox, 10 March 1848, Q.R.O.

20. "Petition of John Stewart and Bernard Magan," 19 February 1848, Q.R.O.

21. "Petition of John and Pat Connor," n.d. [1848], Q.R.O.

22. "Memorial," James Connor to Commissioners of Woods and Forests, February 1848; James Connor to C. W. F., 5 March 1848, Q.R.O.

23. James Connor to C. W. F., 24 March 1848, Q.R.O.

24. Bartly Connor to Burke, 22 February 1848, Q.R.O.

25. "Account of Emigration under the Treasury authorities," 18 September 1848, Q.R.O.

26. James Connor to Burke, 17 March 1848, and Knox to Burke, 23 March 1848, Q.R.O.

27. Patrick Reilly to Burke, 19 February 1848, Q.R.O. In passing, it is interesting to note that when writing in his own hand, "Reilly" chose the spelling "Riely," but may have been "corrected" by the scribe who took his dictation.

28. Patrick Riely to Burke, enclosed in Burke to Knox, n.d. [1848], Q.R.O.

29. "Account of Emigration under Treasury authorities," 12 August, 26 October 1847, 2 February, 18 September 1848, Q.R.O.

30. This choice was offered to the tenants of Irvillaughter and Boughill in Galway when the majority refused free emigration. T. F. Kennedy (Crown agent) to Commissioners of Woods and Forests, 10 March 1852, Q.R.O.

31. Thomas Geehan to Burke, 22 February 1848, Q.R.O.

32. "Account of Emigration under Treasury authorities," 10 March 1848, Q.R.O.

33. "Commissioners of Her Majesty's Woods and Forests to Treasury," 18 July 1848, Treasury #4691, Public Record Office, Kew Gardens.

34. Burke to Commissioners of Woods and Forests, 11 May 1848; "Account of Emigration under Treasury authorities," 18 September 1848, Q.R.O. The three families that returned as tenants in Ballykilcline after the clearance were those of Terence Reynolds, Patrick Coyle, and John Cox's brother, Michael Cox. Descendants of all three remain as residents today.

35. Joel Mokyr, *Why Ireland Starved: A Quantitative and Analytical History of the Irish Economy, 1800–1850* (London: Allen & Unwin, 1983), pp. 266–67.

36. "List of Tenants on the Crown lands of Ballykilcline," n.d. [1847], Q.R.O.

37. Ibid.

38. 1851 Census, p. 530; "List of Tenants on the Crown Lands of Ballykilcline . . . ," 1846, Q.R.O.

39. 1851 Census, p. 414.

40. Ibid., pp. 530 et seq.

41. Ibid., p. 414.

42. In the survey of literacy of the Barony of Balintobber in the 1841 census males who were able both to read and write outnumbered females by more than three to one (2,694 to 809). But among those who could read only, females were in the majority (1,837 to 1,647)! 1851 Census, pp. 410–11.

43. "The Widow Loughan of Boughill to Commissioners," Q.R.O.; Mrs. Maryellen Cooley, now of Roosevelt Island, New York.

44. 1851 Census, p. 530.

45. "Account of Expenditures on Emigration from the Crown lands of Ballykilcline," October 1847, Q.R.O.

Chapter 7

1. This is the finding of Eugen Weber in regard to the provincial communes of France, in *Peasants into Frenchmen: The Modernization of Rural France, 1870–1914* (Stanford: Stanford University Press, 1976).

2. Emmet Larkin, "The Devotional Revolution in Ireland, 1850–75," *American Historical Review* 27 (June 1972).

3. The case brought by the attorney general against the Defendants' claim for protection against the eviction was heard in the Court of Exchequer in the Easter Term of 1846 before Barons Pennefather and Lefroy, a Mr. Baker acting as barrister for the Defendants. The five Defendants appeared in Dublin to "negotiate" a settlement in the spring of 1846 but sat mute before the court and called no witnesses; "Court of Exchequer, Spring Term, 1846: 'Report'," Q.R.O.

4. William and Robert Chambers, *The Emigrant's Manual* (Edinburgh, 1851), cited in Terry Coleman, *Passage to America* (London: Hutchinson and Co., 1974), p. 64.

5. Conrad Arensberg, *The Irish Countryman: An Anthropological Study* (New York: Macmillan, 1937; Natural History Press, 1968), p. 53.

6. P. J. Dowling, *The Hedge Schools of Ireland* (London: Longmans Green, 1935), p. 42.

7. Isaac Weld, *Statistical Survey of the County of Roscommon, Drawn up under the Direction of the Royal Dublin Society* (Dublin, 1832), pp. 3a *et seq.*

8. Akenson, in *The Irish Education Experiment* (London: Routledge & Kegan Paul, 1970), (pp. 376–85), puts emphasis on the high level of illiteracy at this time, but given the depth of rural poverty the extent of literacy even in the West is at least as noteworthy: 28 percent in Connaught, 39 percent in Munster, 56 percent in Leinster, and 60 percent in Ulster. *Census of Ireland, 1901, Part II: General Report with Illustrative Maps, Diagrams and Appendix*, Cd. 1190. (1902), vol. 129, p. 59.

9. The teacher salaries estimated by the 1824 survey are uncertain, but they

were said to have ranged from £6 to £15, averaging between £8 to £12 nationally. Mary Daly, "The Development of the National School System, 1831–40," in A. Cosgrove and D. McCartney, eds., *Studies in Irish History Presented to R. Dudley Edwards* (University College, Dublin, 1979), p. 158.

10. "The master was paid by the parents, at so much per child per quarter, from about 1s. 6d. or 2/- for the small ones learning reading and writing to ten or twelve shillings for the young men learning the Classics. But with small classes and poor clients, the master was lucky if he made forty pounds a year—'passing rich' as Goldsmith says." Kevin Danaher, *In Ireland Long Ago* (Cork: Mercier Press, 1962), p. 166.

11. Daly, "Development of the National School System," p. 160.

12. Another factor that would diminish the status and standing of the teaching women is the predominance of girls among their pupils; about 70 percent in their schools compared to 45 percent overall and only 34 percent in the schools with male masters.

13. David J. O'Donoghue, *The Life of William Carleton* (London, 1896), p. 11; Daly, "Development of the National School System," pp. 151–52.

14. Dowling, *Hedge Schools*, pp. 82–83; W. S. Mason, *Parochial Survey*, (1824), 1:495.

15. William Carleton, "The Hedge School," in *Traits and Stories of the Irish Peasantry*, 6th ed. (London: William Tegg, 1865).

16. William Carleton may have had a axe to grind on the hedge-school masters, but he gives a plausible picture of their part in composing this category of letters. Ibid., pp. 240–41.

17. Dowling, *Hedge Schools*, p. 109.

18. Ibid., p. 63.

19. Hely Dutton, *Statistical Survey of the County of Clare* (1808), pp. 238–39, cited in Dowling, *Hedge Schools*, pp. 84–85.

20. See J. S. Donnelly, "Pastorini and Captain Rock," in S. Clark and J. S. Donnelly, *Irish Peasants: Violence and Political Unrest, 1780–1914* (Madison: University of Wisconsin Press, 1983), pp. 111–13.

21. Danaher, *In Ireland*, pp. 161–63.

22. Three records are used here in relation to the townland of Pobble O'Keefe: *Parliamentary Papers*, H.C. 1831–32, vol. 45, p. 207; Parliamentary Papers, H.C., 1834, vol. 51, p. 69.; file 2B.43.124 (#4), Q.R.O.

23. Of the population of 479, the commissioners emigrated approximately 238 in August and September of 1849. Boyan to Gore, 25 May 1850, "Kingwilliamstown Papers" Q.R.O., (hereafter cited as KWT).

24. The fee for children whose parents were not residents of the estate but worked on it was 3d., and for those neither resident nor employed on the estate, 6d. per month. KWT, pp. 11–13.

25. "Aid for Fitting-up of Schools," n.d. [1832], KWT.

26. Denahy's suspicions were apparently mutual. Weale described the brothers as "the most disorderly characters in Kingwilliamstown. . . ." "They are so connected with local factions that they are treated too mildly," he complained. Weale to Boylan, 20 October 1837, KWT.

27. Michael O'Connor to Weale, n.d. [1836], KWT. Weale was perhaps referring here to "Burton's Books," the sixpenny books published voluminously in cheap reprints in these years. Keating's *History* was most likely the Dermot O'Conor translation of 1720.

28. For the Munster poets, see Daniel Corkery's classic, *The Hidden Ireland: A Study of Gaelic Munster in the Eighteenth Century* (Dublin: M. H. Gill & Son, 1925).

29. John O'Reilly to James Weale, 11 August 1836, KWT.

30. The schedule of "Dues" was as follows: children from the Crown lands were to pay 1d. a month; children whose parents worked for the Crown lands but were not residents would pay 3d. a month; others could attend the school for 6d. KWT.

31. Akenson, *Irish Education Experiment*, pp. 161–87.

32. Boyan worked for thirty-one years (to 1854) as an engineer under Richard Griffith, the Crown surveyor after Weale, in charge of building roads in southern Ireland. He appears in Kingwilliamstown in 1832, and from that time was the principal employer of labor in the district.

33. *Fourth Book of Lessons for the Use of Schools* (Dublin, 1850), published by direction of the Commissioners of National Education in Ireland, p. 56.

34. Ibid., pp. v–vii.

35. See Coleman, *Passage to America*; Robert Scally, "Liverpool Ships and Irish Emigrants in the Age of Sail," *Journal of Social History* 17 (Summer 1984).

36. House of Commons, *Poor Inquiry*, Appendix D, "containing baronial examinations relative to earnings of labourers, cottier tenants, employment of women and children, expenditure, etc." 1836, vol. 1, pp. xxxi.

37. Jasper W. Rogers, *The Potato Truck System of Ireland* (London, 1847), p. 37; Samuel Clark, *Social Origins of the Irish Land War* (Princeton: Princeton University Press, 1979), p. 52.

38. By far the most important influence on the makeup of the National School's *Book of Lessons* was the Reverend James Carlile of Dublin, a Presbyterian, who was not only the sole full-time commissioner of national education but the author of most of the first of that series of textbooks in use from 1831 through 1865, as well as the books on geography, bookkeeping, scriptures, and sacred poetry. Akenson, *Irish Education Experiment*, pp. 231–32.

39. Lessons I and II, *Fourth Book of Lessons*, sec. II, pt. I, pp. 52–65.

40. Ibid.

41. Lesson III, *Fourth Book of Lessons*, sec. II, pt. I.

42. The inclusion of these sentiments need not have been accidental, since the author, the Reverend James Carlile, was part of a dissenting community in Dublin that included a strong abolitionist tendency in these years.

43. See, e.g., M. Alamgir, *Famine in South Asia: The Political Economy of Mass Starvation* (Cambridge, Mass.: Oelgeschlager, Gunn and Hain, 1980), and S. Ambirajan, *Classical Political Economy and British Policy in India* (New York: Cambridge University Press, 1978).

44. Akenson, *Irish Educaiton Experiment*, pp. 258–73; J. M. Goldstrom, "Richard Whately and Political Economy in School Books," *Irish Historical Studies* 15 (September 1966): 136–37.

45. *Fourth Book of Lessons*, pp. 200–204.

46. Ibid., p. 206.

47. Ibid., p. 224.

48. Ibid., p. 210.

49. Ibid., p. 211.

50. Ibid., p. 231.

51. Ibid., pp. 232–34.

52. Ibid., p. 238.
53. "Copy Book" of John Leahy, n.d., KWT.

Chapter 8

1. Letter from William Dermody of "Mile tree Birr King Co." to an un-named Dublin ticket agent, undated, *National Library of Ireland*, MS 15,784 (here-after cited as NLI).

2. The five batches from Ballykilcline arrived in Dublin from Strokestown on the following dates: 8 September, 22 September, and 13 October, 1847; 6 March and 17 April 1848. Departures from Strokestown are given on the as-sumption that from three to four days would be needed for the trip to Dublin. Burke to Knox, 22 May 1848, Q.R.O.

3. Isaac Weld, *Statistical Survey of the County of Roscommon, Drawn up under the Direction of the Royal Dublin Society* (Dublin, 1832), p. 581.

4. Kevin Danaher, *In Ireland Long Ago* (Cork: Mercier Press, 1962), p. 110; Weld, *Statistical Survey*, p. 581.

5. John Mitchel offers a lengthy note in detailing the quantities of food exported during the hunger, "good and ample provision for double her own popu-lation." *Jail Journal* (Kenthurst: Kangaroo Press, 1988), p. xlix, pp. 365–66 n.

6. Weld, *Statistical Survey*, pp. 627–28.

7. The Strokestown Dispensary had an annual endowment of £450; No other dispensary in the county received more than £93. Ibid., p. 628.

8. Walter Macken, *The Silent People* (New York: Macmillan, 1966), p. 83.

9. Ruth-Ann M. Harris, "The Nearest Place That Wasn't Ireland" (unpub-lished manuscript, 1990).

10. "Tradesmen's Bills," n.d., Q.R.O. Nothing is known of any purchases made by the tenants before leaving, but the prices paid by Burke for the emigrants' provisions were sharply inflated.

11. A change was made later, substituting the *Jane Glasson* for the *Progress* to carry one of the last two batches. See Chapter 10.

12. Burke to Commissioners of Woods and Forests, "Account of First Emi-grant Grant," 13 June 1848, Q.R.O.

13. The accounts of the Crown estates of Kingwilliamstown-Pobble O'Keefe in Cork, Irvillaughter and Boughill in Galway, and Kilconcause in Kings are found in the Quit Rent Office records 2B.43.121, 2B.43.126, and 2B.44.1.

14. According to Isaac Weld's survey, the price of brogues had declined between 1811 and 1831 from 6s.–7s. to 5s.–6s. a pair. *Statistical Survey*, p. 637.

15. No account of these miscellaneous expenses remains for those who emi-grated in the fall of 1847. For the 257 provisioned in this account, the cost of the clothing alone came to £181 2s. 10d. "Tradesmen's Bills," n.d. [1848], Q.R.O.

16. See Robert J. Scally, "Liverpool Ships and Irish Emigrants in the Age of Sail," *Journal of Social History* 17 (Summer 1984): 8.

17. Herman Melville, *Redburn: His First Voyage* (New York: Doubleday, Anchor, 1957), p. 192.

18. Burke to Commissioners, 13 June 1848, Q.R.O.

19. "Passenger Affidavit," Liverpool, 13 March 1848," Q.R.O.

20. Boyan to Gore, 24 September 1849, KWT.

21. Ibid.

22. Scally, "Liverpool Ships."

23. An account of the the the cross-channel ferries may be found in Frank Neal, "Liverpool, the Famine Irish and the Steamship Companies," *Immigrants and Minorities* 5 (March 1985): 28–61.

24. Elliot to Stephen, recommending that the Board of Trade take responsibility for the inland passenger trade, 9 March 1838, Colonial Office Papers, 384/46, #637.

25. *Freeman's Journal*, 21 January 1833.

26. John Mitchel, *Jail Journal*, p. xlix, p. 365, n. 12.

27. *Liverpool Custom Bills of Entry*, 1847–1848, Liverpool Public Record Office.

28. "Edward Morgan, Swansea, to Sec. of State for the Home Department," Home Office Papers, 45/2545, 9 June 1849; Cecil Woodham-Smith, *The Great Hunger* (New York: Old Town Books, 1989), p. 270.

29. Posters signed by T. Watkins, clerk to the Cardiff Union and the "Sanitary Committee," and printed in June of 1849 during a minor outbreak of cholera in the town, which produced a total of 143 cases, resulting in ten deaths. Home Office Papers, 45/2545, #14940, n.d.

30. *Liverpool Custom Bills of Entry*: "Pride of Erin," 1 May 1848; "Erin," 1 May 1848; "Forget Me Not," 3 July 1848.

31. J. Buck, "The Forget-Me-Not; Last Hours on the Mersey," *Mission Society and Bethel Union Evangelist*, no.11, 1848.

32. "Irish Packets," *Picturesque Handbook to Liverpool* (1842), p. 40.

33. For Lloyd's classification of cargo insurance rates, see Scally, "Liverpool Ships," p. 16.

34. Cited in Thomas Gallagher, *Paddy's Lament: Ireland, 1846–1847* (New York: Harcourt Brace Jovanovich, 1982), p. 150, from the Minutes of the Select Committee of the House of Lords on Colonization from Ireland, 1847, pp. 712–14.

35. "Annual Report from Major-General Sir William Warre: 'Disturbances: North and Midland Districts,'" Home Office Papers, 45/2793.

36. "Riot on board Irish Passenger Vessel," *Londonderry Journal*, 6 December 1849; Report to the Home Office from Londonderry, Home Office Papers, 45/2428.

37. Home Office Papers, 45/2793, n.d. [1848].

Chapter 9

1. It is not possible to tell whether Buck's use of the "*Forget-Me-Not*," the vessel that carried the hair and rags of famine victims to Liverpool, was merely an apt title for his sermon or was based on a personal knowledge of that sinister boat.

2. Arthur Redford, *Labour Migration in England, 1800–1850* (Manchester: Manchester University Press, 1964), pp. 23–25.

3. S. Mountfield, *Western Gateway: A History of the Mersey Docks and Harbour Board* (Liverpool: Mersey Docks and Harbour Board, 1965).

4. Herman Melville, *Redburn: His First Voyage* (New York: Doubleday, Anchor, 1957), p. 184.

5. Nancy Ritchie-Noakes, *Liverpool's Historic Waterfront: The World's First Mercantile Dock System* (London: H.M.S.O., 1984), pp. 5–7.

6. Lt. Low to Hay, 16 May 1833, Colonial Office Papers, 384/32/149, 2571 Emigration; Robert J. Scally, "Liverpool Ships and Irish Emigrants in the Age of Sail," *Journal of Social History* 17 (Summer 1984): 17.

7. J. Buck, "The Forget-Me-Not; Last Hours on the Mersey," *Mission Society and Bethel Union Evangelist*, no. 11, 1848, p. 1.

8. Ibid.

9. The testimony of Lieutenant Robert Low, the first government emigrant agent for Liverpool, provides a richly detailed and vivid description of the trade based on daily observation. See Scally, "Liverpool Ships."

10. Ritchie-Noakes, *Liverpool's Historic Waterfront*, p. 6.

11. Melville, *Redburn*, p. 195.

12. While it is an obvious hyperbole, the growth of Liverpool ship registrations in the first half of the century was unprecedented. Frank Neal, "Liverpool Shipping in the Early Nineteenth Century," in J. R. Harris, ed., *Liverpool and the Merseyside: Essays in the Economic and Social History of the Port and its Hinterland* (London: Frank Cass, 1969), p. 158.

13. Oliver MacDonagh, "Emigration and the State, 1833–55: An Essay in Administrative History," *Transactions of the Royal Historical Society*, 5th ser., 5 (1956), pp. 133–61; Frank Neal, "Liverpool, the Irish Steamship Companies and the Famine Irish," *Immigrants and Minorities* 5 (March 1986): 34–35; evidence of Dr. Duncan of Liverpool, "On the Physical Causes of the High Rate of Mortality in Liverpool," *Commissioners of Enquiry into the State of Large Towns and Populous Districts*, MS 4182, NLI, appendix, p. 16; Iain.C. Taylor, "Black Spot on the Mersey" (unpublished manuscript, Department of Geography, University of Liverpool); *Times*, 2 April 1847.

14. Although the 1851 census speaks with authority on the increase in Liverpool's population in the preceding decade and the overall emigration from the country, no firm estimate can be made of the number of Irish merely passing through the town each year, since many entered and left by road and no coherent count was made of the incoming ferry passengers. Neal, "Liverpool, the Famine Irish and the Steamship Companies," *Immigrants and Minorities*, 5 (March 1985): 28–61, p. 33; W. H. Duncan, M.D., *Report of the Health Committee of the Borough of Liverpool on the Health of the Town*, 1847–50 (Liverpool, 1851).

15. *Gore's Directory of Liverpool and its Environs* (Liverpool, 1847). The most replete testimony on the quantities of water-borne traffic on the Mersey is contained in the reports to the Colonial Office of the migrant agents, whose duty it was (among other things) to keep track of vessels carrying passengers. See also the Liverpool *Customs Bills of Entry*, which contain verified manifests of all vessels carrying goods into the port.

16. Karl Marx and Frederick Engels, *Ireland and the Irish Question: A Collection of Writings* (New York: International Publishers, 1972), p. 191; Joel Mokyr, *Why Ireland Starved: A Quantitative and Analytical History of the Irish Economy, 1800–1850* (London: Allen & Unwin, 1983), p. 288.

17. Stephen Campbell, "The Strokestown Famine Papers: The Mahon Family and the Strokestown Estate, 1845–1848" (unpublished paper), pp. 31–32; P-M Papers, 10,102.3, 13 May 1847; "Kennelly to Harnden, 1 September 1849, KWT. Both Ross Mahon and George Knox also employed Robinson and Son of Dublin, who were general shippers' agents, to book steerages in Liverpool. Terry Coleman, *Passage to America* (London: Hutchinson & Co., 1974), pp. 82–83.

18. *The Picturesque Hand-Book to Liverpool; A Manual for the Resident and Visitor, being a new and Greatly Improved Edition of the Stranger's Pocket Guide* (Liverpool: Waring Webb, Castle St.); also printed in the *Lancashire Parochial Topography*, vol. 13 (1842).

19. *Limerick Chronicle*, 10 March 1846; 3 March 1847; 13 May 1848; *Nation*, 21 February 1846; cited in Oliver MacDonagh, "Irish Emigration to the United States America and the British Colonies during the Famine," in R. D. Edwards and J. D. Williams, eds., *The Great Famine* (Dublin: Browne and Nolan, 1954).

20. "Journal of Thomas Edwards, Carlow, sometimes emigrant agent, 1840–47," NLI, MS 16,136, cited in MacDonagh, "Irish Emigration."

21. Evidence of C. W. Williams given before "an inquiry as to the Condition and Behaviour of the Irish in Britain," NLI, MS 4182.

22. Redford, *Labour Migration*, pp. 165–71; Mountfield, *Western Gateway*, pp. 93–95.

23. R. Lawton, "Irish Immigration to England and Wales in the Mid-Nineteenth Century," *Irish Geography* 4, no. 1 (1959); Redford, *Labour Migration*, pp. 62–67.

24. Melville, *Redburn*, p. 154.

25. E. P. Thompson's elegant application of the "reserve army of labor" theory to the "character" of Irish manual laborers pouring into England probably says more about the persistence of ethnic stereotyping than the realities of their experience, but it is founded on a highly instructive grain of truth. See *The Making of the English Working Class* (London: Pantheon, 1963), pp. 432–33.

26. Crest 25/60, 24 September 1847.

27. John Denvir, *The Irish in Britain* (1892), p. 9; P. J. Waller, *Democracy and Sectarianism; A Political and Social History of Liverpool, 1868–1939* (Liverpool: Liverpool University Press, 1981), p. 8.

28. *Picturesque Hand-Book*, p. 37.

29. Waller, *Democracy and Sectarianism*, p. 4; Melville, *Redburn*, p. 130.

30. Melville, *Redburn*, p. 171.

31. Ibid., pp. 157, 171.

32. Ibid., p. 154.

33. Ritchie-Noakes, *Liverpool's Historic Waterfront*, pp. 17–79. A graphic correlation between the growth of the Liverpool docks and the reorientation of English trade to the Mediterranean, South America, and the colonial empire is found in François Vigier, *Change and Apathy: Liverpool and Manchester during the Industrial Revolution* (Cambridge: MIT Press, 1970), fig. 7, p. 39.

34. Minutes of Evidence, M. M. G. Dowling, Chief Constable of Liverpool, *Select Committee on Railway Labourers* (1846), q.3056–57, cited in Neal, "Liverpool Shipping," p. 143; Ramsay Muir, *A History of Liverpool* (Liverpool: Liverpool University Press, 1907), pp. 304–5.

35. Nathaniel Hawthorne, *The English Notebooks*, ed. Randall Stewart (New York: MLSA, 1941), p. 18.

36. Scally, "Liverpool Ships," p. 12; Colonial Office Papers, MS #4182.

37. Lt. Low, "An Exposition of Frauds upon Emigrants," Colonial Office Papers, 384/32, 5972 Emigration; Scally, "Liverpool Ships," p. 15.

38. Melville, *Redburn*, p. 194.

39. The Culkin case was reported in the *Liverpool Albion* during August of 1849; cited in Neal, *Sectarian Violence: The Liverpool Experience, 1819–1914* (Manchester: Manchester University Press, 1988), pp. 92–100.

40. Melville, *Redburn*, p. 194.

41. Ibid., cited in Lynn Hollen Lees, *Exiles of Erin* (Ithaca: Cornell University Press, 1979), p. 173.

42. Melville, *Redburn*, pp. 172–73. See report of Dr. Duncan to the Health Committee, Medical Officer's Health Reports, *Minutes of Health Committee*, 1847–1848, Liverpool Record Office.

43. Melville, *Redburn*, pp. 179–80.

44. *Case Books of the Rainhill Lunatic Asylum*, cited in Linda Merrill, "The Rainhill Asylum of Liverpool" (doctoral dissertation in progress, New York University, 1987); John K. Walton, "Lunacy in the Industrial Revolution: A Study of Asylum Admissions in Lancashire, 1848–50," *Journal of Social History* 13 (1979): 1–18.

45. "Minutes of Evidence, Rev. A. Campbell," *Select Committee of Poor Removal* (1854), cited in Neal, *Sectarian Violence*, p. 81.

46. Neal extrapolates this estimate from reports of Irish steamer arrivals printed in the *Manchester Guardian* for the year 1848. Since these were also based on the police counts, even this large figure must be taken as a reasonable minimum estimate of the flow. Ibid., pp. 81–82.

47. "Evidence of Dr. Duncan, given at an enquiry as to the Condition and Behaviour of the Irish in Britain," MS 4182, NLI.

48. M. A. G. O'Thuathaigh, "The Irish in 19th-Century Britain: Problems of Integration," in Roger Swift and Sheridan Gilley, eds., *The Irish in the Victorian City* (London: Croom Helm, 1985), p. 22; J. H. Treble, "Liverpool Working Class Housing, 1801–1851," in S. D. Chapman, ed., *The History of Working Class Housing* (Totowa, N.J.: Rowman and Littlefield, 1971); Neal, *Sectarian Violence*, pp. 90–91.

49. *Liverpool Herald*, 17 November 1855, cited in Neal, *Sectarian Violence*, pp. 113–15. Sander Gilman, in *Difference and Pathology: Stereotypes of Sexuality, Race and Madness* (Ithaca: Cornell University Press, 1985), assigns some responsibility for the development of the pathological features of these stereotypes to medical speculation earlier in the century. Only Neal attributes a special place to Liverpool in Victorian bigotry. The subject is treated more generally in L. P. Curtis, *Anglo-Saxons and Celts: A Study of Anti-Irish Prejudice in Victorian England* (Bridgeport, Conn., Conference on British Studies, 1968).

50. William McNeill, *Plagues and Peoples* (Oxford: Basil Blackwood, 1977), pp. 258–60.

51. "Annual Report, January, 1849, of Sir William Waere to Home Office," Home Office Papers, 45/2793.

52. R. J. Morris, *Cholera 1832: The Social Response to an Epidemic* (New York: Holmes & Meier, 1976), p. 7. According to the census of 1851, the number of Irish-born and their proportion of the total population of these cities in that year were as follows: Liverpool, 83,813 (22.3 percent); Glasgow, 59,801 (18.1 percent); Manchester and Salford, 52,504 (13.1 percent); London, 108,548 (4.6 percent).

53. Thomas Carlyle, *Chartism* (1839), pp. 28–31; Frederick Engels, "The Condition of the Working-Class in England," in *Karl Marx and Frederick Engels: Collected Works*, vol. 4 (New York: International Publishers, 1975), p. 390.

54. Engels, *"Condition of the Working-Class."*

55. Ibid., p. 361.

56. *M'Corquodale's Annual Liverpool Directory* (1848); W. H. Duncan, M.D., pp. 17 et passim.

57. "Evidence of Dr. Duncan."

58. Engels, "Condition of the Working-Class," p. 368.

59. According to Roger Swift, local studies suggest that the extent of the Irish burden on the poor rates seems to have been generally exaggerated. "Outcast Irish," in R. Swift and S. Gilley, eds., *The Irish in the Victorian City* (London: Croom Helm, 1985), p. 267.

60. Melville describes the Lascar seamen he met in Liverpool as being a mixture of Malays, Mahrattas, Burmese, Siamese, and "Cingalese". *Redburn*, p. 164.

61. Ibid., p. 165.

62. Ibid., pp. 173–74.

63. The Poor Law Removal Act of 1847 (10 & 11 Vic., cap. 33) allowed parish relieving officers to apply to two magistrates for a warrant of removal if they could show that the pauper had been born in Ireland and received relief without a settlement in the parish.

64. This term was used more than any other in the *Casebooks* of the Rainhill Asylum to describe the most common condition of the female Irish inmates during the 1840s and 1850s. Cited in Merrill, *Rainhill Asylum*. The relationship of migration and mental health among Irish migrants in Lancashire in these years is now the subject of a two-year study at the Institute of Irish Studies at the University of Liverpool funded by the Wellcome Trust. See also Elizabeth Malcolm, *Swift's Hospital: A History of St. Patrick's Hospital, Dublin, 1746–1989* (Dublin: Gill & Macmillan, 1989).

65. On the defrauding of emigrants in Liverpool, the most detailed treatment is found in Coleman, *Passage to America*, esp. chap. 5, "Liverpool and the Last of England," pp. 73–101. See also Scally, "Liverpool Ships."

66. Among Irish prisoners at Spike Island in Cork Harbor awaiting transportation to New South Wales, men under forty were frequently rejected by the medical officer for reasons of "old age and debility." *Spike Island Register*, NLI.

67. The act was passed after a campaign by the authorities of Liverpool, Manchester, Glasgow, and the other cities that had experienced large-scale Irish immigration and wanted to reduce rising poor rates. Rushton estimated that some forty thousand might be removed from parish relief in Liverpool alone, but the act proved too difficult to enforce on this scale. Neal, *Sectarian Violence*, pp. 96–97.

68. Liverpool's cellars appear in virtually all accounts of the city and emigration in the 1840s. By far the most complete and moving description of these, based on rich original sources, is in Coleman, *Passage to America*; see especially chaps. 5 and 6.

69. Burke to C. W. F., 12 May 1848, Q.R.O.

Chapter 10

1. Herman Melville, *Redburn: His First Voyage* (New York: Doubleday, Anchor, 1957), p. 250.

2. Ibid., pp. 251, 271, 278.

3. The accounts of Stephen de Vere and Vere Foster, unrelated philanthropists, are generally regarded as moderate depictions of the common abuses aboard the emigrant ships of this time, and they describe conditions that correspond closely with Melville's. See also Terry Coleman, *Passage to America* (London: Hutchinson & Co., 1974), pp. 120–29. See Robert J. Scally, "Liverpool Ships and Irish Emigrants in the Age of Sail," *Journal of Social History* 17 (Summer 1984), for an account of the Liverpool ships of the prefamine and famine era.

4. There have been numerous accounts of the emigrant voyage, both first-

hand and retrospective. Both Cecil Woodham-Smith's foundation work, *The Great Hunger* (New York: Old Town Books, 1989), and Coleman's *Passage to America* offer more details of the emigrant crossing and references to the firsthand sources than is needed to envision the worst conditions of the voyage.

5. Scally, "Liverpool Ships"; Coleman, *Passage to America*, "The Voyage," pp. 120–46. For the cholera epidemics in North America, see Charles Rosenberg, *The Cholera Years* (Chicago: University of Chicago Press, 1987). For the Grosse Ile tragedy, see *The Ocean Plague: or, a voyage to Quebec in an Irish emigrant vessel embracing a quarantine at Grosse Isle in 1847 . . . By a cabin passenger* (Boston, 1848).

6. Mortality figures derived from official reports arrive at an estimate of mortality of 5 percent of total overseas migration during the period 1846–1851. Estimates for the year 1847 are much higher; the Emigration Office in Quebec reported 98,125 predominantly Irish passengers embarked or were born aboard Canada-bound ships, of whom 5,282 died at sea, 3,389 died in quarantine at Grosse Isle, and 8,154 died later in hospitals, amounting to about 17 percent of the year's emigrants to Canada. Oliver MacDonagh, "Irish Emigration to the United States of America and the British Colonies during the Famine," in R. Dudley Edwards and T. Desmond Williams, eds., *The Great Famine* (Dublin: Browne & Nolan, 1954), pp. 319–88; Joel Mokyr, *Why Ireland Starved: A Quantitative and Analytical History of the Irish Economy, 1800–1850* (London: Allen & Unwin, 1983), pp. 267–68.

7. Woodham-Smith, *Great Hunger*, pp. 229, 254; U.S. Senate, *Report of the Select Committee on . . . sickness and mortality on board emigrant ships, etc.*, 33d Cong., 1st sess. (1849), p. 49; William P. McArthur, "The Medical History of the Famine," in R. Dudley Edwards and T. Desmond Williams, eds., *The Great Famine* (Dublin: Browne & Nolan, 1954), pp. 263–315.

8. Woodham-Smith, *Great Hunger*, p. 230.

9. Melville, *Redburn*, p. 275.

10. Lists of passengers arriving during 1847–48 were compiled by the emigration commissioners of the State of New York and later published in *The Famine Immigrants: Lists of Irish Immigrants Arriving at the Port of New York, 1846–51, vol. 2, July, 1847–June, 1848*, ed. Ira A. Glazier, (Baltimore: Genealogical Publishing Co., 1983). The *Roscius* arrived on 22 October 1847, and the remaining ships bearing the Ballykilcline emigrants followed during the next six months. Unfortunately, the New York lists are sometimes incomplete and cannot be compared with the embarkation lists taken by the government emigrant agents in Liverpool for the Colonial Office, which are only fragmentary for these years; see Scally, "Liverpool Ships." Some, but not all, of the missing Ballykilcline emigrants might be accounted for by these gaps in the record.

11. "Officers of Woods and Forests to Burke, 27 March 1848, and Hodder to Commissioners, 14 March 1848, Q.R.O.; Passenger lists for the *Channing*, 18 April 1848, from Liverpool, in Glazier, *Famine Immigrants*.

12. "Scott to Burke," 4 May and 4 July 1848, Q.R.O. The report of Stewart's death in New York did not come till the following year, so it is not clear that it was directly related to the voyage.

13. "Emigrants' Receipts: 3," n.d., Q.R.O.

14. Mokyr estimates the excess mortality of Roscommon for the years 1846–51 at between 49.5 and 57.4 per 1,000, about the level of Galway and slightly lower than that of Sligo. *Why Ireland Starved*, p. 267.

15. The effectiveness of storytelling in preserving the identity and history of family and community is explained most insightfully in Dennis Clark, *Erin's Heirs: Irish Bonds of Community* (Lexington, Ky.: University Press of Kentucky, 1991), pp. 7–49.

16. In the period 1848–1859, 85 percent of all foreign-born admissions to Bellevue hospital were Irish; in the same period, 75 percent of admissions to the lunatic asylum on Blackwell's Island were foreign-born, two-thirds of them Irish. Robert Ernst, *Immigrant Life in New York City, 1825–63* (New York: King's Crown Press, 1979), pp. 53–62.

17. Mrs. Maria Murray to Mr. Roberts, 7 September 1864, Strokestown Papers.

18. Margaret McCarthy to Michael Boyan Esqre., New York, 22 September 1850, reprinted in Eilish Ellis, *Emigrants from Ireland, 1847–1852: State-Aided Emigration Schemes from Crown Estates in Ireland, ca. 1850* (Baltimore: Genealogical Publishing, 1978), pp. 64–67.

19. Michael Byrne to Golding Bird Esquire, Collector of Excise, Galway, in Ellis, *Emigrants*, p. 68.

20. Ibid., p. 61.

Epilogue

1. Frederick Law Olmsted, *The Cotton Kingdom, a Traveller's Observations on Cotton and Slavery in the American Slave States* (New York: Knopf, 1953), p. 223.

2. There was no question of the emigrants' fidelity to the faith, but some Catholic clerics complained of their ignorance of doctrine and ritual, describing them as "Catholic by instinct." Lynn Hollen Lees, *Exiles of Erin* (Ithaca: Cornell University Press, 1979), pp. 183–84.

3. Jarlath Waldron, *Maamtrasna: The Murders and the Mystery* (Dublin: Edmund Burke, 1992), p. 19.

4. E. P. Thompson, *The Making of the English Working Class* (London: Pantheon, 1963), pp. 432–33.

5. David Landes, *The Unbound Prometheus: Technological Change and Industrial Development* (London: Cambridge University Press, 1969).

6. Edward Banfield, *The Moral Basis of a Backward Society* (Glencoe, Ill.: Free Press, 1958).

7. Brinley Thomas, *Migration and Economic Growth: A Study of Great Britain and the Atlantic Economy* (Cambridge: Cambridge University Press, 1973), pp. 83–89.

8. James C. Scott, *Weapons of the Weak: Everyday Forms of Peasant Resistance* (New Haven: Yale University Press, 1985); Albert Memmi, *The Colonizer and the Colonized*, translated by Howard Greenfield (London: Souvenir Press, 1974).

9. David Doyle, "The Irish and Urban Pioneers in the United States, 1850–1870," *Journal of American Ethnic History* 10 (Fall 1990/Winter 1991): 36–59.

10. Eric Leed, *The Mind of the Traveller: From Gilgamesh to Gloval Tourism* (New York: Basic Books, 1991), p. 45.

11. Frederick Barth, *Ritual and Knowledge: Among the Baktaman of New Guinea* (New Haven: Yale University Press, 1975); Leed, *Mind of the Traveller*, pp. 20, 45.

Index